W0232957

VINTAGE

COURTESY OF CRITICISM

Kirtinath Kurtkoti (1928–2003) was a renowned scholar, critic, playwright and translator who wrote in both English and Kannada. Born in Gadag, Karnataka, he pursued his education in Gadag and Dharwad. Kurtkoti began his career as an English lecturer, initially teaching in Belgaum and Pune before joining Vithalbhai Patel College, Vallabh Vidyanagar in Gujarat, and later Sardar Patel University, Anand, Gujarat. Although he began his writing career with poetry and drama, his shift to critical writing was decisive. He wrote extensively in Kannada and occasionally in English. Kurtkoti served on several prestigious literary organizations, including the Language Advisory Committee of the Jnanapith Award, Sahitya Akademi, New Delhi, and the Karnataka Sahitya Akademi, Bangalore. He was also an adviser to the renowned Kannada language publishing house Manohar Grantha Male. After retiring in 1988, Kurtkoti lived in Dharwad until his death in 2003.

Kamalakar Bhat is a professor and head of the Postgraduate Department of English of Ahmednagar College, Ahmednagar, Maharashtra. He is an award-winning bilingual writer, a columnist and a translator between English, Hindi, Marathi and Kannada. He has three collections of poems and three collections of translated verse in Kannada. He has edited three books in English. His essays and translations have appeared in *Outlook* magazine, Scroll.in, Wire.in, Muse India, Indian Literature, Kitaab.org, Indianculturalforum.com, The Bombay Literary Magazine and The Bangalore Review.

Courtesy of Criticism

Selected Essays of
Kirtinath Kurtkoti

Edited and Translated from the Kannada by
Kamalakar Bhat

VINTAGE

An imprint of Penguin Random House

VINTAGE

Vintage is an imprint of the Penguin Random House group of companies
whose addresses can be found at global.penguinrandomhouse.com

Published by Penguin Random House India Pvt. Ltd
4th Floor, Capital Tower 1, MG Road,
Gurugram 122 002, Haryana, India

First published in Vintage by Penguin Random House India 2024

ISBN 9780143473480

Typeset in Garamond by MAP Systems, Bengaluru, India
Printed at Replika Press Pvt. Ltd, India

www.penguin.co.in

Contents

Section 3: Literary Criticism

About the Chronicles Series

The Ashoka Centre for Translation, through its initiatives, is committed to thinking about translation from a many-to-many perspective to foster India's multilingual ethos. Chronicles is a groundbreaking non-fiction translation series aimed at bringing creative–critical textual narratives from various Indian languages into English. In the inaugural list supported by the Manju Deshbandhu Gupta Fellowship, ten books are being published in partnership with Penguin Random House India.

translation.ashoka.edu.in

Introduction

The Critical Genius of
Kirtinath Kurtkoti

Kirtinath Kurtkoti (1928–2003) stands as a towering figure in Kannada, indeed Indian, literary criticism, notable for his erudition, distinctive methodology and ability to harmonize a wide spectrum of literary and philosophical traditions. His unique multilingual and pluralistic approach blends close reading, cultural analysis and a commitment to integrating the ancient with the modern, the text with the context, the word with the meaning. As a scholar with a vast command of multiple languages and literary traditions, Kurtkoti in his body of work reflects a deep, integrative literary consciousness rooted in both Kannada heritage and national and international intellectual currents.

Kirtinath Kurtkoti was born on 13 October 1928, in Kurtkoti near Gadag in Dharwad district, into a scholarly family. Named Kirtinath Dattappa Gowda Kurtkoti, he carried the legacy of his grandfather, revered as 'Kurtkoti's Gowda'. After completing his education in Gadag and graduating from Karnataka College, Dharwad, in 1950, he began teaching at Vidyadana Samiti High School, Gadag, and later held brief teaching posts, including at RPD College, Belgaum. Earning his master's in English literature in 1958, he went on to teach at Sardar Patel University, Anand, Gujarat, ultimately becoming a professor. After retiring in 1989, he returned to Dharwad, remaining active in literary circles and contributing to various advisory committees. He was the literary adviser of Manohara Granth Male, Dharwad, throughout his career. He was also a member of the Regional (Kannada) Committee of Bharatiya Jnanpith Award. Over his career, he received honours like the Karnataka Sahitya Akademi Honorary Award (1972), Karnataka Rajyotsava Award (1991), Central Sahitya Akademi Translation Award (1993) and the Central Sahitya Akademi Award (1995) for literary criticism.

Growing up in a rich literary environment, Kurtkoti acquired an intimate familiarity with the literary cultures of Kannada, Sanskrit, English, Marathi and Gujarati. His knowledge extended beyond these languages, encompassing European and Indian philosophies, as well as literatures in various other languages accessed through translations. Kurtkoti's literary journey began in his twenties with his debut work, a poetry collection titled *Ganakeli*, which featured six of his poems published alongside poems by Shankar Mokashi Punekar and Govinda Kanekalla. Subsequently, in 1956, he authored his first independent book, *Aa Mani*, a play. Kurtkoti's oeuvre spans various genres, including drama, poetry, essays, column writing and criticism. Additionally, he translated literary and scholarly works from languages like Sanskrit, Marathi and English. However, it is undeniable that his greatest achievements are in criticism.

Yugadharma and Other Early Critical Frameworks

One of Kurtkoti's earliest contributions to Kannada literary criticism is his use of the concept of 'Yugadharma', as a lens through which he assesses modern Kannada literature. In his inaugural critical work, *Yugadharma Mattu Sahitya Darshana* (1962), Kurtkoti contrasts the Yugadharma—the prevailing cultural and intellectual ethos of a given period—with the literary traditions that preceded it. He highlights how the modern Kannada literature of the late nineteenth and early twentieth centuries marked a significant departure from its past, particularly in terms of genre, style and content. This new literature, shaped by the colonial encounter, both embraced and resisted Western influences, a duality that Kurtkoti meticulously examines.

Kurtkoti's concept of Yugadharma, reflecting faintly T.S. Eliot's idea of tradition adapted to suit the Kannada context, is used as a 'touchstone' to evaluate the extent to which modern Kannada authors are able to reflect the spirit of their time. He believes that a successful literary work is one that embodies the Yugadharma, while still maintaining a connection to its cultural and literary heritage. This balance between tradition and the modern is central to Kurtkoti's early critical methodology, and his evaluation of literature is grounded in the degree to which it achieves this harmony.

Kurtkoti also sees literary innovation in terms of a creative reordering of tradition. In his analysis of Pampa's retelling of the Mahabharata, Kurtkoti highlights how the deviation from established narrative forms (like making Arjuna the hero instead of Dharmaraja) reflects a deeper transformation. He extends this framework to Kumaravyasa turning the Mahabharata into a Krishna story and to Bendre's poetry, noting how the poet's use of 'bhava' integrates classical, folk and modern elements, disrupting and remaking the order of Kannada poetry. This idea of breaking tradition to create a new order demonstrates Kurtkoti's nuanced understanding of literary evolution. He doesn't simply valorize the past but recognizes the dynamic nature of tradition, which allows new interpretations and forms to emerge. His essays on Pampa, Kumaravyasa and Bendre reflect this innovative approach, showing how reimagining canonical texts leads to the creation of new literary meaning.

S.R. Vijayashankar observes that for Kurtkoti, literary criticism primarily involves discerning the form, intellectual and emotional details, and savouring the rasa.[1] Another central element of Kurtkoti's critical framework is his integrative vision, due to which he looks for harmony across the spectrum of literary traditions. He seeks out ways in which different literary eras—ancient, medieval and modern—are in harmony with one another. This integrative imagination is most clearly seen in his evaluation of three key figures: Kalidasa, Kumaravyasa and D.R. Bendre. Kurtkoti views these poets as epitomes of literary excellence, and he formulates his critical framework based on the qualities of their poetry.

Kurtkoti is deeply engaged with the cultural and philosophical challenges facing Kannada literature. In his essays, Kurtkoti consistently emphasizes the need for Kannada literature to maintain its connection with ancient and medieval traditions of Kannada literary practices, even as it evolves under the influence of modernity. He warns against the dangers of neglecting this heritage, particularly in the face of colonial and post-colonial pressures to conform to Western literary models.

Kurtkoti's work is thus characterized by a tension between his appreciation for the new and his deep reverence for the past. He acknowledges the benefits of English education in fostering new forms of Kannada literature, but he remains critical of the uncritical adoption of Western literary and aesthetic standards in a monochromatic manner. He asserts that symbols and literary forms are culture-specific and must be analysed using tools that are appropriate to their cultural context. As pointed out by M.G. Hegde,[2] Kurtkoti's key argument in this respect is that a society's poetics reflect its intellectual traditions; and hence he highlights, for instance, how simile is central in Indian aesthetics, while European aesthetics often prioritize contrast and opposition.

---

[1] In *Kirtinath Kurtkoti* (New Delhi: Sahitya Akademi, 2019).

[2] 'Kirtinath Kurtkoti' in *Sahitya Sanvada*, April–June 2005.

Kurtkoti's later works move beyond pure literary analysis to engage with broader cultural questions. His essays, especially in works such as *Bhashe Mattu Sanskriti* (2006) and *Uriya Nalage* (1993), explore the ways in which literature mediates cultural conflict, particularly the tension between tradition and modernity. This shift towards cultural critique marks a significant development in Kurtkoti's intellectual trajectory, as he increasingly seeks to understand how literature reflects and shapes the cultural heritage of Karnataka. At a time when Kannada literary criticism was increasingly influenced by Raymond Williams-inspired Cultural Studies, which emphasized analysing societal power dynamics in literary and cultural texts, Kurtkoti pursued a cultural study focused on the subtle markers of formation, reformation, and transformation within societal structures reflected in cultural texts and practices.

In works such as *Kannada Sahitya Sangathi* (1995) and *Nooru Mara Nooru Swara* (1998), Kurtkoti considers the relationship between the Puranas and history, and the evolution of modern literary genres under colonial influence. The essays are marked by objective analysis, close reading and exploration of the deeper cultural implications of literary works. There is a historiographical leap in these books as Kurtkoti goes beyond chronological narration, picking up evolving strands of ideas, themes and techniques across the centuries of Kannada literature.

Pratyabhijnana and Other Cultural Concepts

Kirtinath Kurtkoti gives us an important insight in his essay 'Pratyabhijnana', when he says that the severance of the link between experience and understanding constitutes 'a tragedy of human consciousness'. For Kurtkoti, narratives, poetry and drama are not only foundational to societal cohesion but also retain their relevance in contemporary discourses as 'sources of meanings'. He emphasizes the significance of pursuing *artha* (meaning), advocating for an attentive exploration that transcends the surface to encompass *arthantar* (alternative meanings). His analytical endeavours reveal a commitment to teasing out the intricacies of meaning.

In examining the concept of artha, Kurtkoti also explores its absence and the implications that arise from this void. His interpretation of Bhavabhuti's *Uttararamacharita* illustrates this point, where the disunity of Rama and Sita symbolizes the disconnect between speech and meaning. He posits that Bhavabhuti's work articulates the decline of Sanskrit as a communicative medium, with the separation of the iconic couple reflecting the fragmentation of utterance and meaning. This analysis not only highlights the challenges of effective communication but also serves as a commentary on the broader existential dilemmas faced in the pursuit of understanding.

Furthermore, Kurtkoti connects the notion of Pratyabhijnana to the recreation and production of new meanings. He views Pratyabhijnana as a new recognition or rediscovery of knowledge that facilitates the emergence of fresh interpretations and significations. This process of rediscovery is necessary for revitalizing understanding within both the literary and cultural domains, fostering an environment in which meanings can be continuously generated and redefined.

Kurtkoti draws comparisons between Pratyabhijnana and anagnorisis, acknowledging their similarities while also emphasizing the differences between them. This nuanced approach allows him to reject simplistic models of cultural conflict or primacy, instead promoting a recognition of the complex interplay between similarities and differences across cultural narratives. His examination of *krama, kramabhanga* and *vikrama* further illustrates this point, highlighting a divergence between his perspective and that of other critics, such as D.R. Nagaraj, who view kramabhanga as a democratic movement against feudal structures. This contrast in approaches to the past underscores Kurtkoti's belief in the importance of continuity and order within literary traditions.

In Kurtkoti's view, literature is fundamentally aimed at the production of new meanings. He pays particular attention to *dhvani* (suggestiveness), as it points to meanings that transcend the literal interpretation. For him, the richness of meaning becomes a crucial measure of a literary work's success and merit.

Kurtkoti's concepts of *satatya* (continuity) and krama (order) extend beyond aesthetic considerations; they are inherently political. He employs these concepts as frameworks for resisting colonial influences that pervade Indian society and culture. By interpreting both ancient and contemporary literature, Kurtkoti asserts the vitality of Indian culture and its enduring ties to its past, thereby maintaining a sense of continuity (satatya) without disruption (kramabhanga). Yet, it is clear that he is not merely advocating blind adherence to the past or tradition, as evidenced by his concept of vikrama or the reformulation of order. Kurtkoti explores how Indians, in response to colonial influences, enact this reformulation of order through translation and rewriting. Thus, Kurtkoti formulates a complex notion of continuity and change, one that does not find it necessary to reject the old in order to embrace the new. His critical framework is thus deeply invested in decolonization, striving for a nuanced understanding that acknowledges both continuity and change without entirely rejecting 'outside' or 'other' influences.

Kurtkoti posits that *bhashantar* (translation) must be accompanied by arthantar (interpretation), thus framing translation as a form of recreation. He contends that a translated text becomes a new creation for monolingual readers, necessitating a comparative framework that allows readers to engage with the original text. This comparative reading extends beyond individual translations; Kurtkoti examines Kannada literature, such as the works of Pampa, alongside classical texts like the Mahabharata and Ramayana, illustrating a broader intertextuality that enriches understanding.

Kurtkoti's own plays, especially the ones in the collections *Swapnadarshi Mattu Itara Geetanatakagalu* (1956), are often reimaginings of myths or works by other writers, embodying the process of rewriting that he advocates. This rewriting involves reframing characters and narratives to humanize mythological figures, thereby breeding new interpretations. He also engages with discursive texts, further illustrating his commitment to a comparative literary sensibility.

Despite not explicitly pursuing literary history, Kurtkoti's essays, particularly the prefaces to his volumes, frequently adopt a novel historical approach. He frames literary criticism as a means of capturing the resonances within a text and situating them within a broader historical context. For him, criticism is not merely an ancillary activity but rather a creative engagement that transcends the hierarchical divides between literature and criticism. Even when engaged in tracing the chronology of Kannada literature in works like *Kannada Sahitya Sangati* and *Nooru Mara Nooru Swara*, Kurtkoti develops a subtle form of narrative that manages to avoid 'historicity', and yet attends to the flow of continuity and rupture in literary traditions.

Kurtkoti conceptualizes modernity as a mindset informed by historical consciousness, distinguishing the present in relation to the past. He critiques a view of modernity that sees it as a rupture from tradition, favouring instead a perspective that emphasizes continuity and integration. This understanding aligns with his notions of arthantar and *punarlekhana* (rewriting), illustrating his preference for revisiting the past to derive new meanings rather than advocating for a complete severance from it. This perspective has led some critics to observe that while Kurtkoti excels in interpreting the past, his engagement with contemporary issues may occasionally lack the same vigour.

In contrast to other critics like D.R. Nagaraj, Kurtkoti approached literary criticism not primarily as a vehicle for societal critique. In the sphere of Kannada literary criticism, the main objection to Kurtkoti is related to the perceived lack in him of social consciousness along with modern and contemporary consciousness. While he acknowledged the interconnectedness of art and society, and while he did not subscribe to the notion of art for art's sake, he framed his critical practice rather as being intrinsically related to the art itself. For him, literary criticism had the potential to impact society through the advancement of literary interpretation, fostering a deeper understanding of texts and their meanings rather than fashioning itself as social commentary.

Kurtkoti's literary criticism reflects an enthusiastic engagement with literature, characterized by intellectual rigour. His critical framework is primarily informed by Sanskrit poetics and poetry, yet he demonstrates a familiarity with Western poetics as well. This is particularly evident in his conceptualization of zeitgeist in his work *Yugadharma*, as well as his discussions on tradition in 'Literature and Literary Consciousness'. His ability to bridge Indian and Western literary theories enriches his critique, allowing for a more nuanced understanding of the complexities within Kannada literature and beyond.

Multilingual Literary Consciousness

In discussing the literary contributions of Kurtkoti, it is crucial to understand how his multilingual imagination reshaped Kannada literary history by countering singular frameworks of literary study, expanding the meaning of texts and revising traditional literary concepts through comparative perspectives. Kurtkoti's scholarly approach highlights how a deep engagement with literatures of various languages and nations allows for a reconstitution of literary history that is both culturally rooted and intellectually expansive.

A significant aspect of Kurtkoti's methodology lies in his expansion of meaning within texts. Through his comparative studies, which draw on diverse writers, including European thinkers such as Rousseau and St Augustine, and by placing Kannada literary works alongside those of Sanskrit luminaries like Bhasa, Kalidasa, Bana and Bhavabhuti, as well as Marathi figures like Harinarayan Apte, Gujarati writer K.M. Munshi and Bengali novelist Bankimchandra Chatterjee, Kurtkoti broadens the interpretive possibilities of Kannada literature. He not only brings out the inherent connections between these literary traditions but also reveals how Kannada literature contributes to a richer, more nuanced understanding of broader literary themes.

Kurtkoti's comparative literary criticism exemplifies how multilingual competence can revise and reconstitute long-standing literary concepts. His cross-linguistic analysis draws on key figures from different traditions, creating a dynamic dialogue between Kannada literature and its counterparts. By doing so, he rethinks canonical ideas, challenging conventional interpretations while remaining rooted in Kannada culture. His engagement with texts across languages demonstrates that literary criticism is not a static response but an evolving narrative shaped by intercultural exchanges.

In essence, Kurtkoti's scholarship represents a template of multilingual literary consciousness. It is no wonder therefore that D.R. Nagaraj places him in a line of rare scholars such as Namvar Singh, Vidyanivas Mishra, G.C. Pandey, and Gopinath Kaviraj.[3] His ability to navigate and integrate various linguistic, aesthetic and philosophical traditions demonstrates that Kannada literary tradition cannot be understood in isolation but

---

[3] In 'Kannadada Kirtige Abhinandane', *Sahitya Kathana* (Heggodu: Akshara Prakashana, p. 312).

must be viewed as part of a larger, interconnected multilingual literary heritage. Through his comparative, culturally rooted perspective, Kurtkoti redefines Kannada literature's place within broader literary traditions, underscoring the importance of a multilingual imagination in the creation of a truly inclusive literary consciousness.

Criticism as Passion and Cultural Responsibility

For Kurtkoti, literary criticism was both a cultural responsibility and a deeply personal passion. His approach to criticism was driven by an unwavering commitment to nurturing literary conversations across various platforms and audiences. This duality—of responsibility and personal engagement—shaped his unique approach to the field, where intellectual curiosity and cultural stewardship intersected. Kurtkoti's sense of cultural responsibility as a literary critic stemmed from his recognition of the vital role literature plays in shaping and reflecting cultural ethos in a society. He viewed literary criticism not merely as an academic exercise but as a crucial element in the broader cultural discourse. To this end, Kurtkoti did not confine his critical work to academic circles or specialized audiences. Instead, he actively sought to engage with people from all walks of life, whether addressing students, colleagues, literary enthusiasts, the general public, newspaper readers or researchers, Kurtkoti consistently shared his literary insights with an infectious enthusiasm, making complex literary concepts accessible and engaging for everyone.

This inclusive approach to literary discourse reflects Kurtkoti's personal passion for the subject. For him, literary criticism was not a detached, intellectual endeavour but a living, dynamic practice. His literary conversations, 'harate' as he calls it, are legendary. Several litterateurs recall the lively conversations about diverse literary topics with Kurtkoti on the 'atta' (attic) of Manohar Granth Male office in Dharwad. He took every opportunity to engage with literature on multiple levels, treating it as an ongoing conversation rather than a static object of analysis. His personal investment in the field meant that he was always eager to discuss, debate and reinterpret literary works, and he believed that literature had the power to inspire and enrich lives. What set Kurtkoti apart was his insistence on approaching literary criticism through a pluralistic lens. For him, no text existed in isolation; every text was illuminated by its relationship to other texts. Kurtkoti believed that the meaning of a single work could only be fully understood in the context of its connections to other works, both within its own tradition and across cultural and linguistic boundaries. By reading texts alongside each other, Kurtkoti uncovered the layers of meaning that emerge from their interactions, whether they were works from Kannada literature, Sanskrit classics or European philosophical writings.

Kurtkoti's pluralistic reading practice also reflects his broader understanding of literature as a community and comparative activity. He encouraged readers to consider how texts resonate with one another, how they respond to and reinterpret each other across time, space and language. In doing so, he championed a more expansive and interconnected vision of literary criticism, one that transcended narrow disciplinary boundaries. By treating literature as an ongoing conversation, Kurtkoti invited readers to see themselves as active participants in this dialogue, capable of contributing their own interpretations and insights. Ultimately, Kurtkoti's work as a literary critic demonstrates that literary criticism is not a solitary pursuit, nor is it the domain of a select few. For him, it was a shared cultural responsibility, a means of engaging with the world, and a deeply personal passion that enriched his life and the lives of those around him. His ability to communicate literary ideas to diverse audiences, combined with his pluralistic, intertextual approach to criticism, underscores his belief in the transformative power of literature to connect people, ideas and cultures.

In this way, Kurtkoti's legacy as a critic is one of inclusion, enthusiasm and intellectual generosity. His unwavering dedication to literary conversation at all levels ensures that his work continues to inspire and challenge readers, reminding us that the richness of literature lies not in any single text, but in the vast, interconnected web of stories and ideas that make up our shared literary heritage.

Kirtinath Kurtkoti's literary criticism stands as a testament to his belief in the importance of continuity in literary evolution. His commitment to a multilingual and comparative framework, coupled with his enthusiasm for intertextuality, positions him as a pivotal figure in the discourse of Kannada literature. By asserting the relevance of both indigenous and Western influences, Kurtkoti navigates the intricate landscape of literary criticism, ultimately contributing to a deeper understanding of the dynamic interplay between literature and society.

Kurtkoti's conception of the critic's responsibility is clearly articulated in his essay 'Courtesy of Criticism', where he asserts, 'Old cultural structures must be reconstructed before they crumble. This task becomes imperative if the critic genuinely regards criticism seriously.' He believed that this effort 'embodies the courtesy of criticism'.

The Selection

Courtesy of Criticism: Selected Essays of Kirtinath Kurtkoti introduces some of his most important essays on Kannada literature to non-Kannada readers. Even though these essays focus on Kannada literature as their immediate subject, discerning readers will detect a theoretical dimension in Kurtkoti's writings that makes his essays not only relevant but also compelling to a broader audience interested in literatures of India. Divided into three sections—'Literary History', 'Literary Theory' and 'Literary Criticism'—the book presents thirty-one short and long essays that comprise Kurtkoti's essential writings. The book serves a twofold purpose: to introduce to the reader Kurtkoti's significant body of work and, through these essays, to illuminate key strands of the Kannada literary tradition. *Courtesy of Criticism* exemplifies the subtle ways in which a mind, enriched by its own traditions and eclectic literacy, can transcend conventional structures of knowledge.

The 'Literary History' section contains six essays drawn from five separate publications. The first four are extended prefaces that Kurtkoti wrote for his own books. His other works, such as *Navya Kavya Prayaoga* (The Experimental Modernist Poetry), *Pratyabhijnana* and *Shravana Pratibhe*, include similar historiographical essays that could not be included in this section. These essays provide a broad perspective on Kannada literature, from its earliest extant writings to the literary movements of the late twentieth century. Each essay combines data, analysis and reinterpretations to shed light on the significance of Kannada literature's heritage. What stands out in these essays is Kurtkoti's ability to blend dense description with close analysis, while tracing patterns across periods. Through this novel approach, he not only historicizes literature but also highlights the significance of the periods, genres, authors and movements he discusses. In fact, because of his reservations about the 'historical method', Kurtkoti instead offers an analytical approach to temporality that addresses patterns of continuity and change, which he frames within the broader notion of *parampare*. By presenting such subtle alternatives, Kurtkoti demonstrates his significance as a scholar of decolonization.

The second section, 'Literary Theory', contains twelve essays from six different publications: *Sanskruti Spandana* (1986), *Uriya Nalige* (1993), *Kannada Sahitya Sangati* (1995), *Rajasparsha* (1996), *Nooru Mara Nooru Swara* (1998) and *Panditara Tappu* (2001). Kurtkoti wrote these books on various occasions and for different purposes. Some are collections of his columns, while others were written as independent volumes. These books mark a period in his career when he refined and developed a

Kannada prose style that brought the charm of literature to literary criticism without losing academic precision. The essays reveal the passion and enthusiasm that marked Kurtkoti's literary conversations in private gatherings. However, the selected essays focus primarily on concepts in literary theory. Kurtkoti in several essays engages in an implicit dialogue with contemporary literary theories of Western origin, while elaborating theoretical concepts from either Sanskrit or Kannada sources. Notably, Kurtkoti's calm, reflective voice, aware of international, particularly Euro–American, literary theories, encourages readers to explore literary ideas drawn from Indian, largely Sanskrit, sources. Therefore, the selection here is dictated by the comparative significance of the concepts Kurtkoti chooses to discuss. While his preference for Sanskrit literature and aesthetic theory likely stems from his first-hand familiarity with them, this focus has attracted some criticism for being overly exclusive.

The third section, 'Literary Criticism', presents essays that showcase Kurtkoti's approach to textual criticism. Throughout his many books, Kurtkoti wrote numerous essays focusing on individual authors or texts. In each of these, he manages to engage readers with the specific significance of the author or text by highlighting its literary merit and placing it in the broader context of Kannada and world literature. His comparative lens draws connections between literary texts, folk traditions, drama, cinema and even allied fine arts such as sculpture and painting. The essays in this section focus on major Kannada authors who are easily recognized by readers beyond the borders of Karnataka and India, and their texts that are often studied in colleges and universities.

Courtesy of Criticism is a significant work that not only introduces Kurtkoti's literary contributions but also deepens readers' understanding of the Kannada literary tradition through history, theory and criticism. The essays collected here represent exemplary instances of a method of literary and cultural criticism that is keenly aware of international critical discourses, yet refuses to abandon the resources of local literary and philosophical traditions that span centuries and millennia. It is a method capable of infusing readers with enthusiasm for literary texts and expanding their intellectual horizons, built on extensive familiarity with diverse linguistic, literary, cultural and philosophical traditions and texts.

                                                    Kamalakar Bhat

Section 1

Literary History

SECTION I

(Literary History)

Yugadharma and
Literary Evolution

In 1958, Kirtinath Kurtkoti authored an insightful essay serving as an introduction to the three volumes of selections of Kannada literature, published by the Manohara Grantha Male under the title, Nadedu Banda Dari *('The Road So Far') that were collected together under the title 'Yugadharma haagoo Sahitya Darshana' in 1962. The anthologies carried Kurtkoti's comprehensive survey of Kannada literature during the modern era, spanning from the late nineteenth century to the mid-twentieth century—works that came to be celebrated as landmarks in the modern Kannada critical tradition. Within this literary period, two distinct phases emerge: Navodaya (Romantic) and Navya (Modernist), collectively constituting modern Kannada literature and distinguishing it from ancient and medieval literary traditions. The essays adhered to fundamental principles of criticism, aiming to foster intellectual growth and deeper understanding. As Kurtkoti explored the rich heritage of modern Kannada literature, he undertook meticulous scrutiny of the various genres, tailoring each critique to the specific context of the works. By adopting a historical lens, he traced the evolution of literary forms, considering the socio-cultural backdrop against which authors penned their masterpieces. Rather than relying on rigid, universal assessment criteria, Kurtkoti's focus lay in discerning whether a work's essence was fully articulated. Collectively, these articles embarked on an investigative journey, acknowledging the inevitability of diverse critical perspectives that extend beyond immediate boundaries. Kurtkoti's survey not only examined the impact of colonialism on modern Kannada literature but also investigated the democratization processes and their influence on literary expression. Notably, he attributed certain literary tendencies to the discerning taste cultivated by newspapers among readers. Furthermore, Kurtkoti grappled with the intricate relationship between literary tradition and modernity, emphasizing the value of the former without belittling the latter. He unequivocally opined that modern Kannada literature must not be studied in relation to the English literary tradition; despite the inspiration drawn from it, he asserts that modern Kannada literature should be seen as a continuation of the centuries-old Kannada literary tradition. This essay invites readers to explore the dynamic landscape of modern Kannada literature, where tradition and innovation intersect, and critical perspectives flourish.*

1

It is necessary to write a few words as an introduction to the historical essays collected in this volume. The essays collected here are imbued with a historical perspective on the literature of modern Kannada rather than strictly historiographical writings. The discussion here is limited to the examination of the developmental trajectory of diverse literary genres in Kannada. A palpable sense of being in the nascent stages of historical inquiry pervades, owing to the relatively brief existence of the modern Kannada literary epoch, making comprehensive historical coverage challenging. It is imperative to underscore that the principal objective of these essays is not to separate modern Kannada literature from its ancient counterpart. The modern phase is conceived as merely one stage in the ongoing developmental continuum of Kannada literature. The impact of numerous theories and philosophies on Kannada literature during this epoch appears more as a manifestation of emulation than a historical imperative. Despite distinctions between modern and ancient Kannada literature, the former has organically assimilated the quintessence of the latter. A noteworthy reinvigoration transpired in Kannada in the latter part of the nineteenth century, concomitant with the broader Indian Renaissance. Consequently, a novel literary corpus emerged, characterized by varied forms and distinctive innovations. It is imperative to acknowledge that the linguistic idiom employed by contemporary authors has a lineage extending over millennia. Although the terrain has shifted, the continuity of Kannada literature persists, like the unbroken flow of intellectual currents.

Literature that has thus developed is discussed in these articles for the purposes of gaining an intimate understanding of the texts and offering a discussion of the several literary genres that have developed in modern Kannada during this period. It is not an evaluation of authors. No definitive evaluation can be offered on the literature I have discussed here as they are contemporary. The challenge of definitive evaluation arises primarily due to the contemporaneity of the literature under consideration. The majority of the authors discussed herein are living, actively contributing to the literary landscape, thereby precluding a comprehensive historical backdrop essential for a nuanced evaluation. While some insights into the historical context of our literature can be gleaned, a comprehensive comparison with the Old Kannada is not always feasible. Attempting a comparison between Kannada literature and English literature is inappropriate, notwithstanding the discernible influence of the latter on the former. While acknowledging the inspiration drawn from English literature and its pivotal role in shaping new literary genres, it is essential to underscore the distinct trajectory of modern Kannada literature. Despite the undeniable debt to foreign literary traditions, the resilience and longevity of Kannada literature are inherently tied to its indigenous roots. The assimilation of modes of expression from English literature should not overshadow the fact that the vitality of Kannada literature resonates with the essence of the Kannada language. Consequently, a more apt approach involves situating literature in modern Kannada within the contextual framework of its ancient counterpart, recognizing the symbiotic relationship that defines its literary continuum.

The genesis and development of literature in modern Kannada was initially propelled by a fervent aspiration for innovation and a patriotic spirit. The literary landscape then burgeoned in accordance with the organic principle that governs the growth of all things born. The germination of this literary movement found fertile ground in the works of accomplished writers, whose contributions became the seminal seeds of strength for literature in modern Kannada. These literary luminaries played a pivotal role in assimilating the distinctive milieu of the Kannada environment into the fabric of the burgeoning literary tradition. By the latter part of the nineteenth century, the antiquated Kannada literary tradition had declined in vitality. It was a period in which the people of India were in awe of the new era unfolding in front of them. It is noteworthy that the poets of the eighteenth century seemed oblivious to the fact that the Old Kannada language had become obsolete during the period of Raghavanka and Harihara, and a linguistic paradigm shift had taken shape. The literary productions of the eighteenth-century poets, including Tirumalarya and Singararya, primarily served to perpetuate past glories as stereotypes, lacking the vivacity and dynamism indicative of a thriving literary tradition. Hence, modern Kannada literature did not draw inspiration from its predecessors; rather, it exhibited a vigorous response to this perceived stagnation. However, in this context, two poets stood out for their vitality and unwavering connection to tradition: Muddana and Kempunarayana. A comprehensive examination of these poets and their contributions will be undertaken subsequently.

The reaction against the perceived stagnation in ancient Kannada literature propagated a regrettable notion among Kannada literary critics. Some critics contended that ancient Kannada literature was merely an artificial concoction of poeticisms. However, a literary tradition could not have evolved for a millennium at the same pace. Despite the pervasive influence of Sanskrit and the reverence accorded to Sanskrit literary luminaries such as Kalidasa and Bana, the literary tradition of Old Kannada continued to witness the emergence of newer literary genres. Abundant examples within Old Kannada literature attest to the continual evolution of literary forms, necessitating a nuanced study of the ancient canon. The configuration of a literary work is contingent not only upon its material substance but also on the linguistic genius, the suggestive power, the audience's discernment and the poet's vision.

The evolution of certain literary conventions in Kannada predates the era of Pampa. The poetic license pertaining to 'yatibhanga' or line-pause, as articulated by Keshiraja, was a characteristic feature of Kannada even before the Pampa period. Consequently, Kannada poets, while employing Sanskrit syllabic metres, maintained semantic line-pauses for rhythmic coherence in their compositions. This distinctive feature of Kannada poetry has played a pivotal role in the development of poetic forms such as Shatpadi (six-line stanza), Sangatya (a ballad-like composition in quatrain), Kandapadya (quatrain), and the contemporary Saralaragale (a blank verse-like composition) and Ashta Shatpadis (a fourteen-line poem). Additionally, the structural blueprint of epics seems to have been delineated during this period, with Sanskrit genres like prose, verse, Champu (a composition that combines prose and verse), and drama, serving as foundational models. Drama had assumed a significant and distinct role, characterized by its performative attributes. This demarcation is observed in the composition patterns, wherein epics are crafted in poetic form, legends find expression in prose, and Puranas and histories were written in the prose-mixed verse known as Champu. Notable poets such as Kalidasa, Bharavi, Magha, Dandi and Bana exemplify the composition of epics and narratives in Sanskrit. In addition to the Mahabharata, certain other Puranas exhibit the use of Champu as a literary form. An exemplar of historical composition in Champu may be seen in the essay by Harishena, as evidenced in the inscriptions at Allahabad. The adoption of Champu as a medium for epic composition in Kannada is exemplified in early works like *Vikramarjunavijaya* and *Adipurana* by Pampa.

Pampa's choice of Champu form for his poetic expression is significant. Credited with transforming a previously disorderly structure found in Puranas and historical compositions, Pampa infused this literary form with a distinctive voice, drawing material from the Mahabharata and Jain Puranas. His poetic endeavours were notably shaped by considerations for his patron, King Arikesari, and the erudite scholars in the royal court. Pampa's literary works were influenced by the piety and heroic ethos encapsulated in both Jain and Vedic Puranas, reflective of the societal milieu contemporaneous to him. Additionally, Pampa likely drew upon extant literature predating his era, a conjecture supported by inscriptions and the characteristics elucidated in the *Kavirajamarga*. Pampa's innovative use of Champu, previously employed in Sanskrit Puranas, histories and Kannada inscriptions, elevated it to a timeless medium of poetry, an accomplishment unparalleled before his time. His mastery of this genre surpassed his predecessors, even influencing later Sanskrit compositions such as Champu Ramayana and *Vishwagunadarsa*.

The significance of Pampa's use of this poetic form is better understood if we look at the differences between verse epics and Champu poetry. The extensive use of prose not only introduced variety but also facilitated a nuanced depiction of complex situations. Champu poetry combines the comprehensiveness of epics with a dramatic quality. Pampa's adherence to the Sanskrit Mahabharata tradition in terms of characterization, plot and style aligns him with the literary conventions established by Vyasa. Possibly influenced by the classification of Vyasa's Mahabharata as 'history' by literary scholars, Sanskrit poets including Kalidasa, were instead inspired by Valmiki's Ramayana. The amalgamation of historical elements with mythology, and secular with the spiritual, constitutes the distinctive poetic form characteristic of Pampa's works. His ambition extended beyond poetic ends; Pampa sought to popularize and uphold Jain religion, leveraging the rich religious and sublime experiences observable in the societal milieu surrounding him. Aligned with the dignity and ideals pervasive in his surroundings, Pampa was uniquely positioned to comprehensively articulate and holistically express these experiences in his poetry.

While some alterations to the narrative may be deemed errors, particularly the ones necessitated by the elevation of Arikesari to the heroic role, they do not significantly detract from the overarching purpose of Pampa's poetry. One may contend that the marginalization of Krishna in *Vikramarjunavijaya* can be attributed to Pampa's adherence to Jainism. Conversely, an alternative perspective is that Pampa, from a political standpoint, has strategically elevated Arikesari as the protagonist, employing a historical metaphor. Nevertheless, the robustness of his persona appears to mitigate any perceived hindrances in Pampa's creative expression. Pampa's tolerance towards diverse religious beliefs is evident in his reconstruction of Vyasa's Mahabharata, where Krishna's centrality is nuanced and multifaceted. The underlying purpose of Pampa's poetry, to propagate his religion, is not undermined by the nuanced treatment of Krishna. Pampa, like Vyasa, aspires to illuminate the complex depths of human nature, and his poetry, exemplified by verses like the one that opens with 'Chaladol Duryodhanam' ('Duryodhana in determination'), seeks to shape the inherent philosophies within individuals. From the point of view of Bhagavata (this is the view of Kumaravyasa) Krishna is the Supreme Being, so Pampa's poetic purpose (that of propagating his religion) has nothing to do with it. In the depiction of the conflict between Bharata–Bahubali, the victorious

campaigns of Bharata, the martial prowess of Arikesari, the
steadfast determination of Duryodhana, the arguments between
Karna and Bhishma, and Karna's internal conflict, Pampa's poetic
objectives manifest prominently. The crux of Pampa's poetic
endeavour lies in reconciling the inherent opposition between
human nature and religious tenets, a balance that becomes
the thematic core of his poetry. Therefore, he doesn't see any
contradiction between the spiritual and the secular. He describes
the heroes who with unwavering resolve, extract arrows lodged in
their heads and the idyllic beauty of the place Banavasi, equally
poetically because of this spiritual experience.

Through the production of such poetry, Pampa established
an enduring and influential poetic tradition, earning the epithet of
the 'premier poet' for his capacity to elevate the poetic sensibility
of contemporary connoisseurs. His departure from the prevailing
forms of Sanskrit poetry showcased his individual talent,
underscoring his claim that his compositions surpassed earlier
poetic works, a declaration that has since become a historical
truth. Pampa's linguistic prowess is noteworthy, employing the
'sweet Kannada of the Puligere region lorded over by a radiant
king' ('Sajada Puligereya Tirul Kannada'), characterized by
literary sophistication yet flavoured with idiomatic expressions.
The seamless harmonization of 'desi' (native) and 'marga' (elite)
linguistic elements in Pampa's works rendered him an exemplar
for subsequent poets.

For approximately two-and-a-half centuries until the advent
of the twelfth-century Vachana poets, Pampa's poetic tradition
persisted. This continuity is attributable in part to Pampa's
enduring influence and the preservation of the spirit of his
age. Despite the emergence of many eminent poets during this
period, none succeeded in creating a poetic tradition as distinct as
Pampa's. Although some of them had the abilities and skills to do
so, the milieu was not favourable. Ranna, titled the poet-emperor,

followed in Pampa's footsteps, albeit with a dramatic emphasis and a vision less comprehensive than Pampa's. In terms of stylistic merit, the title of Mahakavi (grand poet) is aptly bestowed upon Ranna as he showed greater mastery over style than Pampa. Ponna, recognized for his religious devoutness, mirrored Pampa in illuminating Jainism but displayed little inclination towards secular themes. A conclusive assessment of Ponna's contributions awaits the rediscovery of his lost work, *Bhuvanaikaramabhyudaya*. Nagachandra, known as 'Abhinavapampa' ('modern Pampa') in the twelfth century, is significant for his distinctive poetic form, evident in works deviating slightly from Pampa's compositions. In his *Mallinath Purana*, the verse exhibits simplicity, free of excessive embellishments. Although the *Ramachandracharita Purana* shares a secular plot with Pampa's *Vikramarjunavijaya*, notable distinctions arise in terms of characterization and narrative technique. This difference is attributed to this work relying on Vimalasuri's Prakrit Ramayana. Unlike Pampa's adherence to the popular Vyasa Bharata, the poetry of Nagachandra displays a marked inclination towards extreme piety and bias in favour of Jainism. Importantly, these attributes are not idiosyncratic to the poet but emanate from the origin from which it derives. This phenomenon signifies the introduction of religious discord within the Kannada literary landscape, even during Nagachandra's era.

With changing times, a transformation in poetic manners became imperative. Notwithstanding the continued presence of Champu compositions, subsequent works lacked Pampa's poetic strength. Exceptions to this trend are found in Janna's oeuvre, particularly his *Yashodharacharite*, which addresses fundamental human dilemmas, transcending religious constraints. While the *Ananthanath Purana* adheres to Jain poetic traditions, its religious vigour is comparatively subdued. Janna's timeless poetry, exemplified in *Yashodharacharite*, explores the enduring human struggle between religious fervour and sensual desires.

Janna posits poetry not merely as entertainment but as a path to transcendence, as encapsulated in the phrase 'Balabatte Paramagama' ('holistic philosophy of life'). Despite narrating a tale of adultery, *Yashodharacharite* serves a purpose beyond mere romantic storytelling.

The Vira Saiva religious movement, originating gradually in the early twelfth century, significantly altered the prevailing ethos in its later phase and induced transformative social changes through Vira Saivism. As empires waned, the traditional patronage extended to poets dwindled, leaving them without the customary refuge. Concurrently, the advent of the new religious fervour propagated by Vira Saivism swiftly spread, engendering a new awareness. Importantly, it should be underscored that even amid such transformative circumstances, the fundamental values of life remained uncompromised. The era of the Vachana poets assumes significance from another standpoint. The valour that served as the focal point of inspiration during Pampa's era dissipated, giving way to a group of philosophically conscious adherents fostered by the emergent Vira Saivism. This religious awakening precipitated a shift in the mode of poetic expression, imbuing it with novel vigour and sentiment.

Given this context, it is not surprising that Vachanas mark a rebellion against the literary heritage of the past. The Vachana poets crafted their verses with a dual focus: on the one hand, addressing the Saivite devotees inspired by the tenets of Vira Saivism, and on the other hand, reaching out to the dispirited common populace still adhering to mythological paths. In contrast to Jainism, which held sway as an elite religion during Pampa's era, Vira Saivism, the inspiration for contemporary literature, was still in the process of taking root, a development significantly facilitated by Vachana literature. Literary language became accessible to facilitate the communication of religious principles to the commoners.

However, this does not imply that literature was subordinated to a proselytizing agenda. The Vachana compositions suggest that the Vachana poets brought an intense cultural refinement to the Kannada language. The Vachana poets, including Saivite luminaries such as Allama Prabhu, Basavanna, Siddharama, Channabasavanna and Muktayakka, enriched the language with the essence of mystic experiences, elevating its expressive potency manifold. Some contend that Vachanas should not be categorized as literature, emphasizing literature's concern with worldly rather than spiritual or mystic experiences. Such an argument would be moot when poetry is reduced to the realm of didacticism and moralizing, but when it becomes the living voice of profound experiences, as did the works of the Saivite devotees, no such arguments hold up. The Saivite devotees, having perceived a novel dimension of philosophical truth, articulated their insights through inspired compositions. Their expressions resonate as potent manifestations of inevitable experiences. Consequently, Vachana poets have achieved a distinctive articulation, wherein words transcend their conventional role merely signifying meanings, as observed in the Vedas and Upanishads. In this context, the language becomes pervasive enough to evoke the nuances of the mind's meaning. These characteristics find exemplification in the verses of notable figures such as Allama Prabhu and Akkamahadevi.

Regrettably, the vibrancy of this religious reawakening proved transient, and subsequently, literature began to lose its authentic character. Once the purpose and milieu of a literary form are compromised, its misuse poses a serious threat to the integrity of literature. During this period, literature regrettably devolved into a form of low-class pamphleteering, marked by the intrusion of obscenity masquerading as derision of other religions. When the simplicity of the Vachanas lost its integrity, it led to a degradation of language, diminishing its vitality. Harihara and Raghavanka should be acknowledged for their role in reinstating literature to its original state amidst this transitional phase.

Harihara, often derided as a 'Ragale Kavi' due to his predilection for composing exclusively in the 'ragale' metre of Kannada, emerges as a distinguished poet comparable to Pampa, having pioneered a novel literary genre. Unlike Pampa, Harihara eschewed the attempt to reconcile spiritual and secular realms, focusing exclusively on the motif of heroic, selfless devotion. An intense devotion to his religion pervades all of Harihara's poetic compositions. The Vachana poets are essentially poets imbued with mysticism. Harihara composed poetic works that drew inspiration from mystic experiences and the historical narratives of Saivite devotees (Sivasharanas). Harihara's extensive works, such as *Basavarajadevara Ragale* and *Nambiyannana Ragale*, exhibit a literary quality on par with traditional epics. However, Harihara's unwavering religiosity and aversion to eulogizing human attributes precluded him from engaging with themes such as heroism and beauty, which, while present in his poetry, were subordinate to the overarching theme of bhakti. Despite this thematic dominance, Harihara's poetic breadth is remarkable, producing numerous works marked by profound and powerful devotion. The structural expanse of these works is noteworthy, as Harihara skilfully combines metrical verse with elegant prose. While the mechanical aspects and repetitiveness in his 'ragale' verse may be perceived as monotonous, the rapidity of Harihara's poetic prowess adeptly absorbs such potential flaws. The mechanical rhythm aids in vividly visualizing scenes, as exemplified in the episode of 'Kumbara Gundayya' ('Gundayya, the Potter'). Harihara's adept utilization of repetition stands out, captivating the common populace through eloquent simplicity in his poetic form.

In comparison, Raghavanka's scope is relatively limited. While sharing common poetic qualities, emotions and purpose with Harihara, Raghavanka lacks Harihara's bold imagination. In fact, Raghavanka's prose work does not match Harihara's. It is Harihara's name that needs to be mentioned after *Vaddaradhane* when it comes to competent prose composition. However, Raghavanka relinquished prose altogether, not attempting to transform pure philosophical experience into poetry as Harihara did, focusing more on storytelling and technique. As the pioneer of Shatpadi, Raghavanka introduced a new poetic form in Kannada. Despite *Harishchandrakavya* being his singular complete composition in terms of poetry, Raghavanka's enduring legacy lies in introducing the Shatpadi, a verse form considered as a major genre in Kannada, which became a prominent medium for Varnaka (a desi form of songs) poetry by the seventeenth century.

This historical transformation is significant because Harihara's prose-mixed verse style was not emulated by subsequent poets, whereas Raghavanka's narrative verse in Shatpadi survived. The shift can be attributed to changing reader preferences. From Pampa to Harihara, Kannada poets employed distinctive approaches to prose-verses in their literary endeavours. It is conjectured that the discontinuation of this tradition can be attributed to the advent of the Vaggeykara, the poet of musical compositions. In the preceding era, poetry reached the general populace subsequent to receiving approval from scholarly circles within the court. This paradigm underwent a transformation, as poetry became common people's property. During the Vijayanagara Empire, Gamaka kale (musical recitation of poetry), emerged as a popular artistic form. Poetic expression assumed the responsibility of inculcating piety in the populace through the dissemination of local myths and narratives surrounding venerable figures. This era saw poets collaborating with ascetics and sharanas (Saivites) to foster a vibrant, sustainable religious environment. In ancient times too, both Jainism and Buddhism employed the Prakrit language and local mythological elements as vehicles for propagating their respective religious doctrines. During this era, poets harnessed the linguistic vitality of Kannada and embraced natural melodic forms to craft poetry tailored to the sensibilities of the general populace. Additionally, it is noteworthy that during this period, readers grappled with religious perplexities. The emergence of sectarian discord and religious conflicts, commencing in the twelfth century, may reasonably account for a prevailing apathy towards matters of religious conviction. The establishment of the Vijayanagara Empire brought political stability, reducing religious conflicts, as attested by Bukkaraya's inscription. In response to the need for a coherent understanding of religious principles, poets from different religious traditions began presenting their beliefs through poetry. Jain, Vaishnava, and Vira Saiva poets composed poetry keeping their readers in mind. The way 'Shunya Sampadane' became 'Prabhulingalile' is an example of how the religious dons the poetic avatar. It was necessary in those times for the transcendental religious truths to be presented through the refreshing expressive forms of poetry. Chamarasa, Ratnakaravarni, Kumaravyasa are three poets who need to be studied from this perspective.

The transformation in religious perspectives is discernible through the prism of these forms of poetry, marking a departure from the principles upheld in Pampa's era. In Pampa's time, religion encompassed the veneration of the Nirguna principles and the regulation of life in accordance with them. The religious ideal was like the pursuit of heroic prowess, constituting a fundamental goal (*purushartha*) of life. In the absence of explicit scriptural commandments, personal intuition served as the standard for ethical conduct. The pursuit of liberation aligned with one's life path. An individual who obtained all he could through the conscientious shaping of the life bestowed upon him either by divine providence or circumstantial factors sought liberation in accordance with his life trajectory, mirroring the endeavours of

Tirthankaras and Mahabharata heroes ascending the steps of repeated births before achieving liberation. Bharata, Baahubali, Arjuna, Karna, Duryodhana and others adhered to their inherent nature even when following the religious path. For them, salvation was not perceived as a divine gift but as a consequence of their life choices, comparable to victory. The attainment of religious goals, or Dharmasadhana, was construed as a human endeavour, integral to the unfolding process of life. The enduring belief was in the eternal nature of religious and ethical principles, with virtues and sins appraised in relation to their alignment with these principles. This framework served as the foundation for both worldly and religious accomplishments, guiding individuals on the path towards the ultimate goal, Paramartha. Religiosity, viewed as the moral responsibility of every individual, entailed moral freedom.

However, a profound shift in the nature of religion became evident during this period. While the ultimate goal remained consistent, the chosen path diverged significantly. Saguna principles supplanted Nirguna, and narratives of divine incarnations in human form and their miraculous exploits became central to the transcendental mystery of religion. The pursuit of knowledge involved recognizing one's place, diligent adherence constituted karma and devotion took precedence over both. Figures such as Allama Prabhu and Krishna exemplified these divine incarnations, manifesting sublime divinity and unmanifest energies. What they say is the Veda, where they walk is the way, what they stand for is the abode. Although Ratnakaravarni's Bharatesh is not an incarnation, he was born in the crucible of such a mentality.

This metamorphosis in the nature of religion exerted considerable impact on poetry. Pampa's Arikesari is a heroic character for historical reasons, though other characters are not subordinate to him. Pampa, adept at reconciling religious doctrine and poetic requisites, maintained a harmonious creative balance. He achieves the reconciliation of the spiritual and the material but sees them as separate entities in one mode of existence. In contrast, Chamarasa and Kumaravyasa, seamlessly blend the spiritual and the secular, the way word and meaning naturally coalesce. The poetic quality wavers when this balance slackens. Intensity of emotions in these poets is also greater. Ratnakaravarni's exploration of Shringar Rasa surpasses Pampa's intensity, while Kumaravyasa's depiction of Vira Rasa exhibits heightened passion. Pampa's approach to emotion is characterized by temperance, whereas Chamarasa and Kumaravyasa express a more passionate demeanour, with the latter focusing intensely on the presentation of Rasa. A distinctive difference is also discernible in characterization. In Pampa, Ranna and Nagachandra, despite the elevated stature of the characters, who may be monumental, yet they remain human in essence. Excessive spiritual elements are present but not supernatural ones. This balance tilts in Chamarasa and Kumaravyasa's works, where protagonists like Allama Prabhu and Sri Krishna, even when assuming human forms, exhibit supernatural attributes. Allama Prabhu embodies the inaccessible void, while Sri Krishna personifies the principle of undefinable divinity in a visually appealing human form—essentially, a god in tangible guise.

Such an emphasis on Rasa tends to disrupt the inherent balance of poetry. When the narrative focal point narrows down to the actions of the protagonist, other characters are deprived of independent agency. Consequently, the anxieties inherent in life fail to find a place within the Rasa framework. Such shortcomings are evident in *Bharateshavaibhava* by Ratnakaravarni. However, given that all three poets were epic poets, they were adept at rendering these errors inconsequential and upholding the poetic requirements (*kavyadharma*). Subsequent poets following in their footsteps manifest these faults more prominently. The tradition of Varnaka Kavya, which began with Raghavanka, reached its zenith in Kumaravyasa, who not only unveils the essential spirit and poetic style of his era but also encapsulates the essence of the poetic tradition originating with Pampa. In *Bharateshavaibhava*, aside from Bharata, all other characters are ensnared in the web of his yogic pleasures. In contrast, Krishna in Kumaravyasa's work is entirely independent, allowing all other characters to retain their individuality. Kumaravyasa infuses Kshatra (the heroic rasa) with Bhakti (devotional rasa), providing a solid foundation to the thematic substance of his poetry. Moreover, with a highly imaginative language and mastery of prosody, he seamlessly incorporates the essence of various poetic genres. Each chapter of his *Bharata* (*Karnata Bharata Kathamanjari* or also called *Gadugina Bharata* and *Kumaravyasa Bharata*, composed in 1430) is cast in a distinct form, showcasing Kumaravyasa's capability, comparable to Shakespeare, in presenting the astonishing diversity of life. Kumaravyasa's *Gadugina Bharata* stands unparalleled in its all-encompassing nature within Kannada poetry.

Subsequently, Old Kannada literature predominantly assumed imitative traits, though individual talent was not entirely absent. Lakshmisha aimed to present the grandeur of Rasa through his poetry. The Dasa songs, beyond being exemplary lyrical poetry, serve as classic instances of argumentative lyric. Sarvajna's vachanas embody the sincerity of folk poetry and persist in popular memory. However, a form of poetry capable of capturing the lifestyle, philosophy and 'yugadharma' of the period did not emerge. The Kannada populace remained dispersed, with repeated attempts at religious mobilization failing to unify Kannada life politically. Neither the empire nor the reigning religion achieved unity in the Kannada land. In the absence of a coherent lifestyle that could be presented through epic, personal lyrics such as the songs of Dasa poets, Sarvajna's tercets and the mystic verses became prevalent.

Until the era of Kempunarayana (1794–1868) and Muddana (1870–1901), no new literary genre surfaced. Kempunarayana endeavoured to combine the form of novel with the Sanskrit narrative form, introducing historical materials into his works. Transforming 'Mudra Rakshasa' into a novel, Kempunarayana applied imaginative changes, considering modern readership. His language, gradually liberated from the constraints of Old Kannada, reflects a new approach, and after Harihara, Kempunarayana is the first to showcase equally adept prose composition. Noteworthy is the fact that while introducing a fresh approach, he did not disrupt the established tradition of Kannada literature.

Muddana's literary contributions hold paramount significance, especially within the context of the emergence of modern literature. His poetry, representing the inaugural efforts of modern writers, continues to captivate critics, warranting a thoughtful examination. In contrast, Kempunarayana sincerely echoes the old and new sensibilities, with a focus on new developments that limit extensive debate on form. Muddana, however, piques our curiosity in various aspects. The core of his Old Kannada remains inherently authentic, exemplified by the seemingly archaic tale of *Ramashwamedha* and the nuanced dialogues between Muddana and Manorame. Despite misconceptions characterizing it as a 'golden frame for the image of the ordinary', it is crucial to recognize that Muddana was at the cusp of forging a new literary genre. The dynamic interplay between Muddana and Manorame in the narrative of *Ramashwamedha* signifies their integration as characters within the story. The metaphor of incessant rain in the line 'Pagalumirulum Suriva Bansone' ('heavy rain pouring day and night') enables them to seamlessly traverse temporal gaps. Additionally, it is pertinent to note that Muddana not only wrote Yakshagana (a performative genre of dance drama) episodes like Kumaravijaya but actively participated in Talamaddale (a performative genre of verbal narrative interpretations) performances, interpreting these episodes. Muddana's *Ramashwamedha* may have been crafted for a Yakshagana audience, where Talamaddale's strategy of building drama through the individuals playing the characters themselves providing interpretations is evident, especially in the nuanced examination of Rama's character by both Muddana and

Manorame. There are many digressions in this poem, like the multiple trajectories of Rama's Yajna Horse, the narrative unfolds in multiple directions. Yet the vigilant Manorame, notwithstanding her drowsy state, ensures judicious restraint in the exploration of these tangential paths. This discernment in the narrative approach aligns seamlessly with the strategic choices made by Muddana.

Through this composition, Muddana embodies certain essential principles of literary criticism. First, his unwavering honesty towards readers and language is notable, with his archaic, yet naturally flowing Kannada. Using the material available to him and with a keen awareness of contemporary life, Muddana has created a work that will retain its novelty over time. No matter what period the great works belong to, they recreate the spirit of their time, so the rasa experience they provide remains fresh. The interplay between Muddana and Manorame within the narrative reflects literary discussions, exemplifying the birth pangs of a new literary genre.

Muddana emerges as a trailblazer among modern writers, not only due to his temporal positioning but also for his assimilation of ancient literature from the time of Pampa till his own time. His era marked a transitional period where the old epic form no longer aligned with the prevailing way of life. Mentally unprepared to fully embrace the new age, Muddana found a middle ground by incorporating elements of the old fabric to weave a new literary narrative. Despite initial appearances of detachment from modernity, Muddana's homage to ancient literature was, in fact, a final salute on behalf of all of us.

This comprehensive exploration has encompassed the spectrum of ancient Kannada literature, spanning from the seminal works of Pampa to the innovative contributions of Muddana. The inherent vitality of the Kannada language has manifested in diverse expressions, resonating with the native predilections of Kannada readership. Nripatunga's assertion that the Kannada populace exhibits a natural inclination towards poetry, even without specific training, finds validation in the fluidity of folk poetry that has coursed through the cultural landscape like a perennial river. Eminent poets such as Pampa, Harihara, Kumaravyasa, and Muddana have channelled their artistic prowess into enriching the expressive potential of the Kannada language. While Kannada literature is rooted in the foundational principles articulated by Sanskrit poets, the majority of Kannada poets, with a few exceptions, have upheld the tradition of euphonic poetry, eschewing idiosyncratic forms like Chitrakavya (in which verbal literary meaning is more important over figurative meanings). Pampa's poetry displays an unbroken tradition of euphony that is rarely found even in Sanskrit poetry. Nagachandra, Janna, Ranna, Nemichandra and Rudrabhatta, among others, have contributed significantly to sustaining this poetic vision. The exploration of Vachana poets, Harihara and Kumaravyasa, necessitates the development of a distinctive poetics. Vachana poets, in their pursuit, transcend mere resonant meaning, endeavouring to delve into the ineffable realms behind word. Harihara, meanwhile, harnesses the full spectrum of linguistic capabilities, while Kumaravyasa's verses resonate with discernible rhythmic patterns, like the countable beats of a heartbeat. Although Old Kannada literature derived inspiration from Sanskrit, it gradually evolved into an independent literary tradition through meticulous cultivation while preserving its distinctive character. Even in contemporary times, the practice and appreciation of this literature require a nuanced perspective. Recognizing the pivotal role of inheritance in literary development, the new Kannada literature must draw upon the essence and vitality embedded in the Old Kannada literary corpus.

2

Muddana stands as a tranquil island amid the turbulence of modernity; however, the Kannada literary landscape could not remain impervious to the currents of contemporary changes. Western education and the study of English literature were instrumental in reshaping the mental disposition of the Kannada-speaking populace. Concurrently, scientific discoveries and political upheavals heralded the advent of a new era that left an indelible mark on both the literate and illiterate. The palpable scent of novelty pervaded the air, instigating a fervent desire for innovation that, in turn, catalysed a formidable shift in the literary milieu. Authors born into this era directed their gaze towards Western literature, facilitated by the preceding wave of modernity in Bengal, rendering the assimilation of this external influence relatively seamless. Hence, the currents of innovation permeated the Kannada language from both extrinsic and intrinsic sources. As it was not a time of studied reflection, a nascent literary epoch emerged, characterized by a pronounced reaction to the ancient literary canon.

This transformative phase in Kannada literature was unprecedented, and witnessed not only the emergence of new literary genres but also a radical metamorphosis of traditional genres beyond recognition. Poetry underwent a paradigm shift towards lyricism, while drama relinquished its antiquated techniques and themes. Concurrently, new forms such as essays, diaries, short stories, travelogues and autobiographies made their debut. The press, conceived to articulate the sentiments of the freedom struggle, not only facilitated the development of a new linguistic idiom but also provided a platform for the dissemination of diverse literary genres. The literary contributions of figures like Panje Mangesharaya, M.N. Kamat, Kerur Vasudevacharya, Krishnarao Muduvidkar and Shantakavi (Sakkari Balacharya) often found expression in journalistic writings, underscoring the symbiotic relationship between literature and the socio-political context. The impact of English education, coupled with the study of English literature and the literatures of other European nations, guided our authors, according to their respective sensibilities.

While some were influenced through translations, a pervasive engagement with English literature fundamentally altered the literary temperament of our writers. Those closely aligned with Western lifestyles and literature became pioneers in shaping modern Kannada literature, even as some authors, motivated by a sense of patriotism, retained a connection to ancient Kannada literature, as exemplified by B.M. Srikantaiah's dual expertise in English and ancient Kannada literature, as demonstrated in his publication *English Gitegalu* (English Songs) in Kannada.

This dynamic interplay proved advantageous for literature, as the extant forms of literary expression, having grown antiquated and blunted, failed to accommodate the innovative impulses of the authors. The expressive forms found in English literature exerted a magnetic pull on these writers, leading to a rapid surge in literary production. The lifting of earlier constraints afforded authors newfound freedom, enabling them to transmute any facet of life into literature. Poets like Panje and Govinda Pai, whose initial works adhered to traditional 'kandapadya' and 'vritta' (a metrical arrangement based on alphabets), eventually transitioned to new rhyme schemes, indicative of a paradigm shift spurred by the influx of innovation. The spirit of adventurous exploration and the advantages of a novel language facilitated swift mastery of writing techniques among these authors. Poets like D.R. Bendre not only cultivated distinctive artistic styles but also pioneered numerous avenues for literary experimentation. The new living conditions of the time, like a field, long uncultivated, yielded literary fruits at a remarkable pace, resulting in a robust and affluent literary landscape.

Beneficial though they may be, it is imperative not to overlook the inherent demerits accompanying these transformations. The intrinsic and extrinsic facets, namely semantic and structural aspects, of a literary work are intricately interconnected. The symbiosis of words and meanings constitutes the vitality of literature, and it is only natural that the literary form evolves in tandem with the emerging consciousness. Consequently, the external form should seamlessly align with the internal essence of the work to engender an expression rich in innovation. Without such harmony, merely embracing the novel forms, may lead to rupture. In such circumstances, only the fundamental sentiments retain their unaltered state.

In certain areas of modern Kannada literature, the revolution exhibits an extremity of transformation. New literary forms swiftly permeated the works of authors, inducing a corresponding shift in their perspectives. This phenomenon is apparent in many instances, save for some individualistic writers. Notably, the proliferation of new nature songs serves as an illustrative example. As poets endeavoured to emulate nature songs similar to those in English literature, their attitude towards nature underwent a discernible change. In contrast to the sincere nature songs of ancient Kannada poets that emanated as expressions of love for life, tinged with intense desire, as in Pampa's verses about Banavasi, modern counterparts seemed to adopt a more subjective approach influenced by Western literature. The poets' failure to temper the language in accordance with such contexts inevitably led to contradictions. Such a predicament may be an unavoidable consequence during revolutionary transitions, extending its implications to other literary genres as well. Dramas and novels, despite addressing native issues, underwent shifts in authors' perspectives, with solutions to problems being gleaned from the authors' readings. A single author's works often exhibit a range of changes over time, as exemplified by Sriranga's career. In essence, Sriranga's dramatic oeuvre represents a quest for originality. Initially, he looked to the novelty offered by the West for solutions, even considering improbable ones. However, in his later works, he shifted focus to delineating problems and sought answers in the wisdom of his native soil.

While change is not inherently unwelcome, it is essential to examine the consequences of this ideological upheaval, considering both its merits and demerits, particularly within the literary realm. This holds particular significance concerning life values, as literature, being a potent medium, possesses the capacity to distort truth by propagating bogus values. A literary revolution should ideally lead to an elevated state rather than stagnancy. Although Kannada literature is rooted in a rich tradition, it has recently embarked on explorations of new terrains, necessitating a nuanced approach that does not entirely forsake its heritage. If the revolutionary spirit becomes an intrinsic consciousness, literature may continually be unstable. Western influence, still coursing through Kannada literary veins, often shapes the authors' perceptions, resulting in a misrepresentation of the local situation. Furthermore, the rapid pace of literary evolution can contribute to a loss of stability, as the forces influencing, shaping, controlling and informing the literary experience contend with contradictions. The nature, purpose and benefits of literature hinge not solely on the author's talent but also on the culture and ideologies of a society. Literature must align with the moral and emotional fluctuations of the people it represents, making it challenging for individuals from one society to fully comprehend the subtle nuances and limitations of another society's literature. The intricacies of literature have evolved in tandem with the structure of thoughts and emotions within a society, contributing to a diverse array of literary expressions. However, contemporary misunderstandings about these fundamental principles are often attributed to the influence of Western culture, even as literature advances beyond a point of return. Consequently, our responsibility now is to dispel this confusion and, at the very least, foster an awareness of the prevailing status quo.

Since 1920, spanning approximately forty years (up to the time of this essay's composition in 1958), modern Kannada literature has grappled with a diverse array of ideologies and debates. These intellectual currents, however, are not indigenous but rather reverberations of movements in English literature. The seeds of revolutionary impulses in modern Kannada literature can be traced back to the deteriorating status of ancient Kannada literature. Consequently, poets such as Panje Mangesh Rao, B.M. Srikantaiah, and D.R. Bendre drew inspiration from English poetry, infusing it with fresh perspectives. The transition towards this form of poetry necessitated the gradual cultivation of a readership with a newfound sensibility to appreciate such verse. Before this poetic lineage could firmly establish itself, other poetic conventions emerged, introducing an element of uncertainty that was absent in the literature of ancient Kannada. Poetic conventions did not undergo drastic transformation without strong reasons. The historical evolution of Kannada poetry, extending from Pampa to Harihara, witnessed a shift in direction catalysed by religious revolution. This medieval literary revolution, a historical imperative, succeeded in instilling a novel cultural sensibility among the masses, thereby achieving its true purpose. In contrast, modern Kannada literature aspires to effect radical changes swiftly, championing personal causes. Unfortunately, this fervour has engendered a detrimental confusion in the sensibilities of readers, extending beyond Karnataka to neighbouring Indian states.

In a sense, the issue is pervasive, necessitating an examination of our prevailing lifestyle as a determinant of the current circumstances. Following Independence, the adoption of democracy, whether advantageous or otherwise, constituted a significant paradigm shift. Anticipating this transition, democratic ideals were instilled in the collective consciousness from the nascent stages of the political movement. The notion of democracy prevalent internationally became our ideal too, echoing similar aspirations across the world. However, like numerous human-conceived utopias, the global community has recognized democracy as a flawed construct. Later, democracy went beyond its role as a mere state system, permeating various facets of our societal existence. Fundamental to democracy is an elevated social consciousness, a prerequisite that is cultivated through mechanisms such as newspapers, pivotal components within a democratic framework. Through this medium, the intellectual purview of the common citizens expanded, fostering mental connections with other nations. Moreover, the democratization of university education has furthered this trend. However, the dissemination of knowledge through newspapers resulted in a society that was, at best, half-educated. Kannada was no exception to this. While a few possessed genuine knowledge, others merely assumed an air of knowledge, contributing to the proliferation of opinions rather than genuine understanding and experience. The lay public, forming opinions based on newspaper gossip, often imposes these preconceived notions on literature, expecting ideas and emotions that align with their views. Motivated by a desire for progress, readers frequently demand new ways and fresh feelings. In an era characterized by speed, ideas become stale rapidly. Given that these opinionated readers constitute the contemporary readership, literature often succumbs to the violence of their opinions. While the situation in India may not be as extreme as it is in Western countries, such a scenario is rapidly emerging.

Consequently, a new issue has emerged, significantly contributing to the uncertainty in literary forms. 'Modernity' has become a contemporary life value, not only in literature but across various domains. In the past, assimilating with tradition signalled excellence in literature, music and dance. Artists risked their personalities to preserve the integrity of tradition. However, breaking away from tradition is now considered an accomplishment, and individualism has taken root. The fear of surrendering to tradition is deeply ingrained, marking a contemporary sensibility that quickly experiences and forgets *rasanubhava* (experience of rasa). While this tendency has not reached excessive levels in Kannada literature, it is nonetheless noteworthy. Novelists, in particular, grapple with the weight of this situation as novel publishing has surged in recent years. A significant portion of these novels focuses on 'new technique' and 'new style', reflecting a longing for innovation. In poetry, new trends emerge before readers fully comprehend existing poetic trends, leading to accusations that modern poetry is obscure. Certain duration is essential for priming the cognitive receptivity of readers to apprehend emotive nuances rather than semantic content. The disposition to cultivate such sensibility resists frequent alteration by bringing in another sensibility. The attempt to experiment with literature solely for the sake of experimentation fosters concerns about a gap between readers' tastes and literary creations. Amid this modern frenzy, traditional values risk being overlooked. New virtues such as neatness and regularity have emerged, while some values are mere opinions detached from the experience of life. In contemporary times, urban life has limited every individual's experience of life, and the flow of life from one person to another has been replaced by the expression and reception of feelings through newspapers. If the situation of the well-educated sections of society is like this, the fate of an illiterate is different. Even though the world is changing every instant, their problems have not disappeared. All the fundamental policies and principles that they reposed their faith in traditionally are being trampled upon in the middle of all these troubles. Literature, today, must navigate this atmosphere or confront it. Writers, rather than building their works on their exclusive experiences, often seek material in newspapers, echoing similar practices in English literature, as seen in authors like Somerset Maugham, who base their stories on news reports. Authors must have the stubborn will to write out of real experiences. In such a context, the responsibility to ensure that the author's personality remains intact becomes particularly weighty.

An additional peril arises from the prevailing literary atmosphere, characterized by an excess of production. As plots can be readily gleaned from newspapers and cinema, authors often engage in prolific production, facilitated by the ease of publishing. While the volume of published books in our country may still lag behind their Western counterparts, there has been an exponential surge in the last decade. Some writers demonstrate an ability to produce a novel each month. Since novels encompass entire experiential worlds, how can a single author find material for so many novels? This raises questions about the literary value of such hastily produced works, with concerns extending beyond diminishing quality, to the alarming growth of competitiveness among writers. The pressure to present 'new material', 'new style', and 'new technique' in order to distinguish one from peers may lead to a lack of comprehensive expression for individual experiences. The competitive drive fosters a tendency to consider any novel already in circulation as antiquated, prompting authors to focus on depicting life's perversities. Distorted narratives, being inherently provocative, easily capture readers' interest, whereas the delicate portrayal of ordinary experiences demands patience and talent. Despite these efforts, there is no guarantee of reader appreciation, compelling authors to rely on the vicissitudes of life and draw inspiration from Western literature.

The contemporary problem of literary perversion, particularly noticeable in the novel genre, stems from multiple factors. It is not solely a result of obscenity infiltrating public taste or authors harbouring a heightened sense of guilt. It is tough to find materials for the increasing number of novels published daily. Our novels earlier aimed at presenting a realistic depiction of ordinary experiences, catering to emotional needs. Over time, even emotional necessities evolved into portrayals of passion and violence. Present-day authors seem inclined towards perversions, filling novels with distorted images of sexuality, often without clear authorial intent. These are passed on as true depictions of reality. The question of what constitutes reality in literature becomes pertinent in such turbulent times. The tradition of realism in literature, with foundations more substantial than contemporary writers may realize, has a healthy curiosity about life's mysteries, an artistic urge to reconsider them, and a broad enthusiasm for life as the driving force. It is not necessary for literature to include every moment and every experience, since the pattern of the literary work decides what aspects of life find place in literary depiction. Realism, therefore, seeks to express in literature the life experiences that can and should be articulated, thereby enhancing an understanding of life. When an author's aim diverges from this pursuit of knowledge, the portrayal of perversion assumes a more dangerous dimension. Experiences that could fade into the background of life's details can be vividly and passionately presented through the stages of literary creation, leaving a lasting impact on the reader's psyche. At this juncture, the author cannot evade moral responsibility, emphasizing the need for a thoughtful and ethical approach to literary creation. It is also imperative to dispel the unexamined and charming notion that literature is an end in itself. This formula pertains to imaginary literature rather than realistic literature. In Western countries, arguments such as 'art for art's sake' arose out of context, giving undue importance to techniques and styles in literature and establishing a new critical standard that attributes a work's greatness to its form. The literature of our country must grapple with and address this problem in order to progress.

Consciously or unconsciously, certain scholars adhere to the belief that the personal ethics of authors are unrelated to their literary works. This misunderstanding of critical principles has given rise to confusion. Whether an author should be righteous or not, remains within the purview of the author alone. To that extent, it may be argued that authors' ethics and their literary works are not interrelated. However, if an author produces unethical literature, such a matter warrants serious consideration. It is incorrect to posit that art and ethics bear no connection, especially when literature serves as a mirror reflecting the culture and customs surrounding it. This does not imply that the elements of an author's life are obligatory in their work or that literature becomes a medium of propaganda. A nuanced understanding of ethics, considering morality as a life experience, would offer a different perspective. The extreme implications of the argument could have been averted had literary morality been perceived as an aspect of life experience. In Western countries, morality remained aloof from the developments in life and remained entrenched as a blind faith. While India is not devoid of blind beliefs, religion has not exerted the same authoritative control as the church did in the West. India boasts unparalleled freedom of religion, and religious life is not an experiment or an externally imposed compulsion. Neglecting morality by treating it as an outmoded tradition would distance literature from a crucial aspect of life.

The source of this confusion lies in the direct adoption of critical methods from the West. Notions such as 'art for art's sake', the emphasis on technique and symbolism in writing emerged in the West as a response to the oppression felt by authors on their individuality by the religious and social tendencies of their societies. In such a context, these arguments find justification. Continuous turmoil caused by religion and political forces has been prevalent in Western societies, resulting in the frequent absence of individual freedom for various reasons. Consequently, the emergence of the cult of personality on one side and 'pure art' on the other became inevitable. These opposing forces stemmed from the imperative of safeguarding personal freedom and the freedom of art against oppressive trends. Numerous movements in European history, from the Middle Ages to the present, bear witness to artists breaking away from oppressive religious, ethical and political constraints, and becoming 'aestheticists'. When the scientific age took its roots, it too invited reactions. The history of English literature, from its inception onwards, appears as a chain of reactions to such oppressive forces. While a reaction may serve as a driving force for a certain period, it invariably invites other reactions. Writers of considerable talent transcend these reactions to create literature, whereas second-rate writers may rely on a singular point of view or argument to survive. Such instances often trigger strong responses in English literature. The application of arguments originating from this specific historical context to our literature requires scrutiny, questioning the extent to which it is reasonable to defend what is not literature. It is essential to contemplate whether literature's origin lies in such reactions. Literary interpretations claiming that mental illness is a prerequisite for being a poet or that all literature is a form of psychosis, arise from a similar milieu.

Old Kannada literature, too, saw many transformations. Changes in the ideas of poetry, writing styles, rhyme and language have been observed. However, the literature of one period did not react to its predecessor; rather, it flowed as a continuous stream, adjusting its tempo with changing circumstances. Poets from Old Kannada did not share the same caste, creed or religion. Their poems reflected intense conflicts between religions. The inclusion of religious animosity in poetry arose as a facet of life rather than as a poet's reaction to their past or the poetry of a different religion. Faith in religion, devoid of the complexities of caste, creed and sects, perhaps aided poets in embracing myriad reactions while maintaining equilibrium. Religion, viewed as a pure way of life, allowed poets like Pampa, Ranna, Harihara, Chamarasa, Kumaravyasa and Janna to transcend these religious experiences and write their poems without opposing one another. Their unwavering devotion to literature is remarkable, as literature served as one of the indispensable means of life for them.

The predicament of contemporary literature prompts a serious examination of whether present-day literary endeavours should be positioned in opposition to their antecedents. The prevailing climate is marked by pervasive disagreement, and it becomes a mark of decorum to navigate these differences with a disposition not to dismiss others' opinions. Furthermore, given the diminished influence of religion as a primary motivator and life experience in contemporary contexts, authors turn to a diverse array of arguments and perspectives to draw inspiration and convey experiences. Lacking a cohesive impetus derived from life experience, literature often seeks inspiration and encounters from a multitude of arguments and perspectives, necessitating the reliance on political ideologies or psychology in lieu of religious or folk sentiments as observed in earlier epochs. However, even after adopting these alternatives, issues persist. The intellectual dismissal of religious viewpoints, coupled with the critique and dismissal of various arguments as partial truths, invariably spawns new perspectives and counterarguments.

A historical perspective, particularly in the context of English literary criticism, elucidates the evolution of two major traditions: the 'classical' and the 'romantic'. The 'classical' tradition, rooted in the Elizabethan era and championed by figures like Ben Jonson, underwent transformations into the 'neoclassical' tradition during the eighteenth century, exercising a profound influence on literature. Deviation from the standards set by this tradition led to the condemnation of authors as non-literate. In the eighteenth century, there were poets who rewrote Shakespeare to suit this taste. Subsequently, in response to the perceived inertness of the 'classical' tradition, the 'romantic' tradition emerged, emphasizing imagination as its driving force. Like Shakespeare, Ben Jonson is an important dramatist; similarly, like Pope, Wordsworth is a great poet. Both traditions produced literature that remains intact, comprehensive and exemplary; yet authors who rigidly adhered to either tradition produced incomplete works due to the limitations of their chosen critical principles. And the significance of these traditions is measured by considering the literature of such authors. The incompleteness of literature generated through reactionary stances is evident in this historical trajectory.

In the 'romantic' literary tradition, which stood in opposition to the 'neoclassical' tradition, the Gothic novel also emerged along with the works of great poets such as Wordsworth, Shelley and Keats. These literary productions not only encapsulated the ethos of the 'romantic' tradition but also precipitated a subsequent reaction. Some scholars sought to reconcile the perceived inadequacies inherent in both traditions, yet this endeavour gave rise to alternative arguments that espoused reconciliation in name only. In the same way, the naturalist and realist traditions were established. However, these arguments prove futile for literary geniuses grounded in unadulterated experiential expression, while lesser writers succumb to them unnecessarily. The blame goes to the nature of criticism, wherein many critics assess an author by scrutinizing their adherence to a particular literary tradition, illustrating the imperfections of the said tradition through the examination of their poems. Journalists and professors contribute to the propagation of such evaluative frameworks. Originally employed as commendations, terms like 'neoclassical', 'romantic' and 'Victorian' have undergone a semantic evolution to become pejorative terms. Caution is warranted when accepting such critical methods and a discerning use of our ancient critical wisdom becomes imperative. Notably, critics such as Abhinavagupta and Mallinatha eschewed standards beyond the purview of fundamental principles of criticism in their assessments of literary works. Failure to exercise such discretion may expose us to the risk of adopting Western critical practices that could compromise our own critical integrity.

This mode of thinking may appear conservative, yet it needs to be emphasized that unexamined acceptance of any system is not prudent. Should such arguments contribute to fissures in the social fabric, how is a comprehensive understanding of truth attainable? Political contentions, societal disintegration, the rapid advancement of scientific endeavours, the uncertainty inherent in reality, and notably, the proliferation of half-truths within modern humanities have disrupted the intellectual landscape of the Western world. The civilization of the West, unbeknownst to itself, treads upon a metaphorical volcano containing a myriad of emotions—such as anger, reaction, mistrust, bloodlust and greed—suppressed for the sake of societal decorum. The artist's freedom is forever under threat. Understandably, such societal dynamics exert a profound influence on literature, prompting a continual evolution in style and technique. In response to the exigencies of a fast-paced age, literature has witnessed the emergence of concise narratives, readable within a brief time frame. There have been advancements in mechanical equipment as well. We have embraced such modified literary forms as a catalyst for innovation. No amount of caution is enough while using them. This is particularly relevant when examining genres such as lyric, short story and essay—each representing brief literary experiments centred on a singular emotion, idea, moment or situation. Consequently, the resultant literary output offers only fragmentary glimpses of experience, affording the reader a vision of an isolated experience rather than a comprehensive perspective on life. Moreover, the constraints of these genres strip away the context's formulaic underpinnings, leaving the reader's sense of taste unfulfilled. Moreover, the strands connecting such a vision to its context are also severed, leaving the reader's sense of taste also empty. It is necessary to acknowledge that literature, in these instances, serves as a constrained expression of emotion rather than an authentic representation of the author's life. A further concern pertains to the potential for a single author to harbour conflicting passions, leaving the reader perplexed in the absence of a unifying vision that integrates these disparate elements. This dilemma extends to the evaluation of poets who produce a series of lacklustre poems interspersed with an occasional exceptional work, thereby prompting apprehension in the discerning common reader. The same concern extends to the short story genre as well. Contrastingly, such reservations do not extend to major literary genres such as the novel, drama and narrative verse. In these forms, there is no latitude for absurdity, as the author presents an unadulterated life experience, facilitating a more straightforward appreciation of their literary merits. While the advent of genres such as poetry and short story is certainly welcome, it is imperative to recognize the consequent shift in critical principles. This transformation has engendered a misconception that poetry, as an art form, exclusively thrives in moments of impassioned inspiration, culminating in the dismissal of long narrative poems and epics as non-poetic endeavours. It is not that the lyric has no place in the poetic genres. But if it tramples other genres, its own limitations would be brought into focus.

Contemporary poetry predominantly gravitates towards the lyric and it would be absurd to demand that our poets abstain from writing lyrics or fiction authors from writing short stories. However, it is imperative to recognize and address the deficiencies inherent in these genres. Poets and fiction writers should strive to maintain the integrity of their personalities. The original melodic nature of lyric, rooted in song, gradually dissipated over time, complicating the transformation of sentiment into general feelings. This issue becomes more intricate in the present. Whether a poet is immersed in a vibrant religious tradition or devoted to the diligence of their cultural milieu, he is obligated to uphold the integrity and coherence of their personality. Poets must learn from our ancient Marga (classical) and Desi (folk) poetry, to arrive at the realization that each poem might resonate with an ironically throbbing vision of life. While poets possess the freedom to express themselves through complexity of experience, symbolism or linguistic style, they also bear the responsibility of facilitating an experience of rasa (rasanubhava) for the readers through their poetry. The means to achieve this depend on the poet's materials, and while lyricism may have been instrumental in the past, alternative methods must now be explored to evoke the experience of rasa, establishing a common ground between reader and writer.

Some of the specific challenges within our literary sphere have been addressed in this essay, refraining from an evaluation of the qualities of individual authors or works. Instead, it endeavours to engage with the confusions in literary consciousness. This discussion is limited to the complexities manifested solely within literary awareness and does not purport to encompass every literary genre. Subsequent articles will explore the nuances of specific genres, focusing on the apparent confusion within literary consciousness. These problems, upon closer scrutiny, are less intricate in nature and tend to dissipate upon proper comprehension. While acknowledging the positive impact of English education contributing to the creation of literature attuned to contemporary culture, the central tenet of this article posits the importance of not neglecting the rich legacy of ancient literature in this fervour for innovation. The literary heritage of Old Kannada stands as a testament to the yugadharma of bygone eras, and it is incumbent upon the new literature to draw inspiration from this poetic legacy. Literature holds the potential to serve various purposes, functioning as a historical account, a portrayal of contemporary life or a vision of the future. The notion that only literature adhering to specific criteria is commendable, while others deserve to be disparaged, is untenable. Honest literary expression, emerging from sincere experiences, should not be kept out of the literary sphere.

The imperative, therefore, lies in the development of a robust science of criticism. While modern Kannada literature is diverse, genuine criticism remains in its infancy. Upon the publication of a literary work, various opinions swiftly circulate regarding its merits or demerits. Individuals engage in discussions, albeit transient, before the work fades from collective memory. However, a comprehensive system of genuine criticism has yet to evolve. The prevailing assessments often echo Western critical paradigms and a critical framework aligned with the unique attributes of Kannada literature is yet to be established. An appraisal of a literary work, analogous to the shadow cast by an object, is contingent upon the nature and form of the work itself. To undertake such assessments, our critics should be well-versed in Sanskrit aesthetics and possess a comprehensive understanding of the historical trajectory of English literary criticism. Beyond scholarly rigor, critics should cultivate empathy, an ability to discern the nuances of literary works akin to a jeweller examining gems. This discernment is nurtured through experience, interest and a genuine affinity for the subject matter. In bygone eras, the 'sahrudaya' (connoisseur) held a position of esteem, influencing the norms of literary discourse. Contemporary critics need to earn a similar standing through diligence and scholarly contributions. The misconception that criticism is primarily a fault-finding mechanism needs to be dispelled, paving the way for a renewed appreciation of the critic's role as a constructive force.

The literary essays collected in this volume are written with the healthy principles of criticism in mind, aiming to foster growth and understanding. Various genres in modern Kannada literature undergo scrutiny, with critiques tailored to the respective positions of each work. The essays adopt a historical perspective, considering the evolution of literary genres and accounting for the historical context of authors. The absence of fixed, transcendental assessment formulas is acknowledged, with the focus on evaluating whether a work's essence is fully expressed. This necessitates an exploration of the internal instincts and rational sensibilities of the 'sahrudaya'. These articles constitute an exploratory endeavour in that direction, recognizing the inevitability of diverse critical perspectives beyond their scope.

This article constitutes a preliminary endeavour in the direction of literary criticism. It is acknowledged that the scope of criticism extends beyond the confines delineated herein. A seminal work invariably begets novel ideas, a testament, perhaps, to its intrinsic greatness. The realm of modern Kannada literature is replete with such exceptional works. It must be noted that the assessment of these works cannot be undertaken by a single critic or using a singular methodology. The articles herein are not intended as exhaustive appraisals of the entire literary corpus; rather, they endeavour to trace the evolutionary trajectory of modern Kannada literature, recognizing the ongoing potential for the emergence of distinctive texts within respective genres. A profound examination of literature, delving into its vital currents, allows criticism to unfold in an organic manner. As established orders stagnate, new literary endeavours burgeon like saplings nurtured by rich soil. In tandem, a fresh evaluative framework takes root. It is essential for this intellectual pursuit to persist in this dynamic and evolving fashion.

In the symbiotic relationship between literature and its connoisseurs, a deleterious atmosphere often emerges due to preconceived notions, greed, illiteracy and misunderstandings. The problems discussed here are emblematic of this context. In an era dominated by revolutionary norms, characterized by uncertainty in both literature and life values, a pervasive sense of dissatisfaction pervades all fields, despite varying degrees of success. Literature, therefore, finds itself at a critical juncture, necessitating the contemplation of these issues to uphold its standing. Fortuitously, modern Kannada literature has not yet confronted an extreme situation and viable solutions exist for the identified challenges.

The reliance of our literature on belief in our people remains unparalleled. The debt owed to contemporary literature is justified, given the honest portrayal of Kannada life by modern

Kannada writers, effectively amalgamating its aspirations and emotions. They have encapsulated elements of a comprehensive life, ranging from the inherent natural beauty of the Kannada region to the nuances of romantic expression within the cultural milieu. Beyond the reconstruction of life, literary satisfaction should encompass an understanding of the wisdom inherent in the generational order of existence among our people. Except a few of our front-ranking writers, it is doubtful if the others have any understanding of our people and their life. All they need to do is to authentically depict the challenges of our life without the distortion of arguments or debates. Literature thrives when writers engage in this experience free from the encumbrances of conflicting arguments. For literature to flourish, the author must become an integral part of the joys, sorrows, passions, hatreds, religious beliefs, dreams and hearts of their people. This necessitates a unity between the poet and the people, representing a foundational aspect of literature, rather than an ideal. Literature should not be an isolated organism but a dynamic entity immersed in the ebb and flow of a people's life, capturing the nuances of their virtues, sins, faith, disbelief, attraction and repulsion. While imagination and artistry are an author's personal accomplishments, and their creation is entirely in his control, the language and experiences belong to the collective world. Language is not merely an expression of the lifestyle of its speakers but also a repository of their culture, history and heartfelt poetry. Its form is non-individualistic as it contains the foundational experiences and emotions of people.

The poet must derive such language from the people, transforming it into raw material to express genuine experiences visible to the hearts of the people. A talented poet possesses the ability to interconnect novel experiences with pre-existing ones. Conversely, a less talented poet whose sphere of perception is constrained may enhance the experience through a process of

heightened radiance. The production of literature of exceptional
quality is contingent on various factors, including time, situation,
dignity of experience, values, talent and the aesthetics of the
readers. While golden ages in literature may occur sporadically in
history, the sense of literature should not be compromised, and the
misattribution of non-literary works as literature is indicative of
unfavourable times. Both writers and critics bear the responsibility
to prevent such mischaracterizations. Literature, like other
significant works, incurs a debt, and it is the duty of literature to
preserve and accord it due credit. The ultimate goal is to recognize
talent. But since the source of genius is at the root of life, there
is an inextricable symbiotic relationship between them, and since
language is the common medium for the expression of both genius
and life, it may be said that literature, poet and people are the
common property of the two. Therefore, literature is a powerful
medium and is a potential source of knowledge to even the non-
literate. Consequently, literature should be produced without doing
injustice to the experiences, people and language it represents.
Literature should not become what the Vedic verse states: 'Deveem
Vacham Ajanyanta Devah Tam Vishwarupam Pashao Vadanti'.
(*Rigveda*—8.100.11: The gods have given speech to beings; the
herds [animals] utter it in all the forms that being has taken).

A brief discussion on the merits of literature is warranted.
Over time, numerous arguments have surfaced and subsided on
this matter. Some individuals seek to discern the significance
of opposing viewpoints and endeavour to reconcile them.
Furthermore, literature has been created with diverse objectives,
with assertions positing its indifference. Conversely, arguments
posit that purpose-driven writing can yield beneficial outcomes.
In philosophical terms, the former aligns with Nirguna worship
in literature, while the latter can be analogously construed as
Saguna worship. The utility of literature, whether construed as
instructional, entertaining, rule-based, facilitating comprehension,

experiential or motivational, is contingent upon the cultural proclivities of its connoisseurs. These consumers engage with literature based on their temperaments and preferences, forming a reciprocal exchange. However, authors should not debase the quality of literature. A clandestine undercurrent of low taste persists in life, and if the author fosters and satisfies such inclinations in literature, it would be a disservice to the audience, constituting an affront to their discernment. A mark of cultural refinement is the author's adherence to showing respect towards their readership. Examining historical instances, not all enthusiasts during the Elizabethan era were drawn to Shakespeare's poetry and artistic prowess; the spectrum of admirers ranged from those appreciating the unique character of Hamlet to those drawn to the play's scenes of combat and revelry. However, Shakespeare consistently upheld the dignity of his plays, never compromising his respect for the audience. Similarly, poets like Kalidasa and Pampa in our own cultural heritage have exhibited a similar reverence towards their followers. It is asserted that an era begets literature reflective of its unique yugadharma—an adage that resonates with a profound veracity.

Literature and Literary Consciousness

*In 1986 and 1987, Kirtinath Kurtkoti curated a series of anthologies
of Kannada literature titled Puta Bangara, comprising four volumes,
to commemorate the fiftieth anniversary of Manohara Grantha Male,
a publishing house for which he served as an adviser. Kurtkoti crafted
scholarly prefaces for these anthologies, delving into broader literary
concerns rather than simply introducing the selected texts. He aimed to
present a historical overview of evolving literary paradigms in Kannada,
with the goal of establishing a systematic framework for Kannada poetics.
Kurtkoti contended that the uncritical embrace of Western poetics had
resulted in intellectual confusion, advocating instead for the exploration
of Sanskrit poetics and classical poetry in both Sanskrit and Kannada
as reservoirs of valuable insights comparable to modern Western literary
theories. He even offered analytical models derived from Sanskrit poetics
that mirrored the emerging structuralist framework of literary analysis.
This excerpt exclusively focuses on sections of Kurtkoti's prefaces related
to poetics, omitting discussions regarding the circumstances surrounding
the publication of the anthologies. In his comprehensive historical review,
Kurtkoti asserted that colonial influence had precipitated cultural
confusion, as Kannada poetics had adopted Western concepts divorced from
their original intellectual context. To support his argument, he specifically
highlighted the distinctions between 'history' and 'Purana', observing that
English education had endowed us with historical consciousness while
reshaping our intellectual trajectory. This essay serves as an introduction
to Kurtkoti's exploration of intertwined issues such as literary history,
colonial influence, the use of ancient Indian poetics in the analysis of*

contemporary literature, and areas of convergence between Western and
ancient Indian poetics.

I

In the past, we had texts but not writing and so, with our
newfound education, writing has become crucial. I feel we haven't
fully grasped the overall impact of this situation on our cultural
life. Writing has influenced us so much that we might question
whether what is not written is art at all. The inclusion of literature,
music, dance, film, sculpture and, more recently, cinema, within
our concept of art is a result of our new education. If the West
didn't recognize these as arts, we likely would have shared the
same view.

This isn't just my idea. A recent symposium on
'Contemporaneity in Drama' delved into this issue. During an
informal discussion following the seminar, Girish Karnad praised
the brilliant performance in a Manipuri play titled *Chakravyuha*.
However, others argued that, despite the skilful performance,
the play's material isn't contemporary; it was likened to the
craftsmanship of a Banarasi saree. The discussion then turned
to the difference between the artistic experience afforded by a
saree's design and that by Girish Karnad's play *Tughlaq*. Girish
Karnad himself refuted this opinion. Girish Karnad emphasized
that, regardless of a saree's market price or its mundane use, it is
a work of art and carries artistic significance.

Interestingly, no one has asked why a saree or household
utensils aren't considered works of art. Answering such a question
might be difficult. This is a situation which has a very narrow
view of literature and music. Each art form has its own class of
experts. Their opinion carry weight: what these experts consider
to be art is accepted as such, and what they do not deem as art
may be something other than art. Such opinions are gathering

wide acceptance these days. An unfortunate consequence of this is that the art appreciated by experts evolves independently, while popular art follows its own worldly codes. An example is the divergence between film music and classical music. If art is Prakrit at one end and Sanskrit at the other, yet continuing to symbolize a harmonious growth, there is nothing to worry about. However, today, both have developed with distinct prejudices between them. I have no expertise to discuss other arts, but this issue can be explored further with illustrations from literature.

It appears that a play being recognized primarily as a literary text is a situation comparatively more widespread in Kannada. In Marathi and Bengali, more performances of plays might take place, but the writers in those languages haven't written as many plays as our new writers have. In Kannada, the plays written for professional theatre and literary plays have evolved differently. Our literary dramas are highly commendable, with some being masterpieces. Amateur theatre groups have also staged these plays, but the habit of watching drama hasn't developed among our people. Professional theatre has limited itself to staging mythological plays like *Usha Swayamvara*, *Shakunthala*, *Echhammanayaka*, *Paduka Pattabhisheka* and *Kurukshetra*, which were initially successful but didn't endure as literary works. Why has theatre in Kannada been split into so many divisions as folk theatre, professional theatre and amateur theatre?

Drama critics attribute this to factors like a lack of taste, the impact of cinema and societal norms. While these are valid reasons, the fundamental reason is that in our contemporary lifestyle there is no room for the rhythm of drama, especially within the well-educated middle class. We need to find out the origins of the notion prevalent in our society that drama and acting are false and illusory, and how it came to be ingrained in us. In Europe, scepticism about drama dates back to Plato and Socrates, with the influence of Christianity's debunking of pretentious social attitudes in later periods. These factors have left an intriguing imprint on the nature and expression of drama, forming an interesting historical trajectory.

The importance that our Alankara system has given to simile and analogy surpasses the importance that Europe gives to opposition or conflict. The principle of opposition drawn from the history of philosophy has also found its place in the philosophy of literature. While dualism is inherent in philosophy itself, duality in the substance and expression of literature is inevitable. Although it was not Aristotle who stated the idea 'there is no drama without conflict', it holds as much authority as his *Poetics*. For conflict to arise and be potent, opposition in the plot and characters of the play is essential. Numerous dichotomies like darkness–light, good–bad, true–false, past–present manifest in the plot. This contrast should also be evident in the characters. One scholar suggests that the contrast between Achilles and Ulysses symbolizes the diversity found in all the characters in Europe. Furthermore, some eminent dramatists have centred their plays on the dilemma of truth. Shakespeare, in particular, dramatically explored this theme in many of his works. In his historical dramas, even kingly characters, in their weakest moments, assert themselves as the 'Kings of the Drama'. Shakespeare effectively exploits the rift that emerges in the individuality of the actor and the character.

This practice did not exist in the tradition of our ancient drama. While contrast was used in Sanskrit dramas, there was no outright opposition or conflict. The interplay of urban and forest life in the play *Shakuntala* unifies the entire narrative, like the harmonious blending of colours in images. In *Mrcchakatika*, a seeming contrast unfolds between the destitute Charudatta and the affluent courtesan Vasantasena. The absence of conflict in Sanskrit dramas is so pronounced that they may not appear as dramas to the eyes of modern observers. Times have changed, yet the structural intricacies of Sanskrit dramas remain elusive to

our understanding. In European dramas, adhering to Aristotle's
dictum, the story is enacted, not narrated. However, Sanskrit
drama does not outright forbid narration; what is audible
seamlessly transitions into the visual realm. The advantage of this
approach lies in endowing the actions of the characters with a
history within the narrative. The memory of these actions imbues
the character's deeds with a profound essence, ensuring that no
action appears arbitrary. In *Urubhanga*, Durjaya's yearning to enter
the lap of Duryodhana elicits compassion, with the character's
actions steeped in a vividly portrayed history of misfortune.
What is heard transforms into a visual spectacle before our eyes.
In *Pancharatra*, when Abhimanyu falls captive in Bhima's arms,
Bhima's words, 'Suyodhana, vardhate te shatrupaksha ('See how
your enemy camp is growing, Suyodhana'), encapsulate the saga
of the Kaurava–Pandava enmity.

The notion that everything passionate is inherently dramatic
has been ingrained in us through Western influence. Shelley, in
the preface to one of his verse plays, contends that evil possesses
a greater dramatic quality than virtue. The influence of such a
perspective has led our contemporary dramas to recast the
villains of our mythology as noble heroes. The characters that
exude passion yet remain incomplete, such as Karna, Bhima and
Duryodhana, hold a more dramatic allure than the 'complete
characters' like Yudhishthira, Savitri and Harishchandra. Pairs like
Karna–Arjuna, Bhima–Duryodhana and Vali–Sugriva appear as
mirror images, relying on external factors for the evolution of
their personalities, because of which they are termed incomplete
characters. Significantly, these characters are the 'colourful roles' in
performance genres like Yakshagana and Doddata (a folk theatre
of Karnataka). In 'complete characters', all facets of human
personality are fully developed. However, incomplete characters
hold a greater appeal to the modern sensibility.

Here, we can explore the tendencies of our new theatre.
We have discarded the formalities of the prologue from old

dramas, where the sutradhara or narrator played a vital role in initiating the drama. Those traditions are now obsolete. The proscenium theatre, a legacy from the West, has reshaped the norms of our drama. This theatre, which facilitates a view into the interiors, selectively illuminates elements crucial to the play. As acknowledged by Western critics, the essence of drama, dating back to its origin in Italian theatre, lies in exposing innermost secrets while concealing external associations. From the make-up equipment to the arrangement of electric lights, everything is veiled in darkness. Only the most intimate aspects of individuals are brought into focus. Even the audience watching the drama remains in the shadows. In this strange stage set-up, the interior is laid bare, transforming reality into a dream and, for the well-educated middle class, even into a myth.

> Consider the western theatre of the last few centuries. Its function is essentially to reveal what is reputed to be secret ('feelings', 'situations', 'conflicts') while concealing the very artifice of the process of revelation (machinery, painting, makeup, source of light). The Italian stage is the space of this deceit, everything there taking place in a room surreptitiously thrown open, surprised, spied on and relished by a hidden spectator; a theological space, that of the moral failing: on the one side, under a light of which he pretends to be unaware, the actor, that is to say, gesture and speech; on the other, in the darkness, the public, that is to say, consciousness and conscience.

> —Roland Barthes, 'Lesson in Writing',
> *Image, Music, Text*[1]

If the stage scenery is depicted in such a manner, the case for performance becomes even more peculiar. When we envision

---

[1] Translation by Stephen Heath (London: Fontana Press, 1977), pp. 172–73.

primitive performances derived from our dances, they starkly differ from actual behaviour. Remnants of ancient performance techniques can still be seen in our puppetry, characterized by a structured choreography of puppet limbs—a visual language of symbols. In antiquity, actors utilized this language, treating their bodies as machines, employing hundreds of distinct postures to convey emotions directly rather than through imitation. In works like *Uttararamacharita*, where Rama faints multiple times in a single episode, a mere imitation of fainting by the actor would appear ludicrous and risk boring the audience. Instead, the artistic expression of these emotions in various ways allows the actor to be appreciated. In contrast to ancient practices, contemporary actors tend to imitate, portraying lively characters with a seamless mind–body connection on stage. Their performances thrive on natural speech and corresponding gestures, constituting the lifeblood of their craft. However, their identity as actors is often confined to this ability. Constructing meaning for the character or the drama solely through acting is a challenge. At best, an actor can immerse themselves in a character, wearing its mask while momentarily forgetting their own identity.

The history of masks in our country, whether tangible or symbolic, diverges from the European mask tradition. In Europe, masks serve as a means to conceal the truth, giving rise to an inherent dichotomy between authenticity and falsehood. Various theories have emerged, grappling with the dilemma surrounding the meaning of masks. Conversely, in our performance traditions, masks reveal the true colours of one's genuine personality. In Yakshagana, costumes don't obscure the beauty or ugliness of the body, nor do they hide the virtues or vices of character. Instead, these masks amplify the personality, akin to how applying mascara enhances the size and brightness of the eyes.

The difference between ancient and modern approaches to acting appears to lie in how they are managed and in the advantages each offers. Ancient techniques of acting had the ability to interpret one object in multiple ways, portraying emotions like affection and kindness through diverse acting techniques. At times the gesture, at other times the movement of the fingers and, again, the hand posture—thus, the original Bhava is reiterated, and through this repetition, the Bhava is elevated to rasa. This process continues to unfold in dance and music, deeply entrenched in traditions passed down through centuries. Similar principles used to be perhaps applied to acting. The advantage of such a performance lies in its ability to transform raw experiences, bringing them to a state of rasa without compromising their vitality. While theorists and critics may have disagreements about the nature and usefulness of the experience of rasa, it remains an undeniable collective and generalized phenomenon. Unlike life experiences, the experience of rasa lacks a clear cause-and-effect structure; it must be born from the work of art and find completion there. This is why earlier plays used to incorporate Naandi (invocation verse) and Bharatavakya (valedictory statement), invoking and discharging elements to create an experience similar to a religious ritual. Various forms of Alankara in poetry, rhythm and tune in music, along with dance and drama performance, contribute to embodying the experience of rasa.

The acting style that has become now prevalent with us is quite the opposite. An essential tenet of acting is the imitation of life experiences. We are turning to a new interpretation of the idea of drama as a 'Kritanukaran' (imitation of action), where the more realistic the imitation of life, the more effectively it facilitates communication of experiences. Use of realism brings us closer to the essence of life experiences. The adoption of realism initially surfaced in our company plays (plays performed by professional troupes called 'natak company'), notably evident in the contrast between Yakshagana costumes and those of company plays. The impracticality of incorporating Yakshagana costumes into daily life is worth noting. The costumes in mythological dramas performed by our companies adhere to the visual aesthetics of Ravi Varma. For instance, the visual representation of the Krishna Sandhana (Krishna's negotiation with Kauravas prior to the Kurukshetra war) scene in the drama *Kurukshetra* literally mirrors Ravi Varma's imagery. Incidents with similar dramatic effects, even if they are fantastic, retain an underlying sense of reality. In company dramas, experiences are not merely symbolic. A notable scene in the play *Sangeetha Saubhadra* by the Gandharva Natak Company of Maharashtra took place in front of the tulsi (basil) plant. The scene had a large silver tulsi plant. Although the silver plant itself wasn't real, serving as a symbolic representation, the scene's impact went beyond symbolism. The silver gleam of the plant effectively conveyed the splendour of Krishna's palace. Reality maintains its authenticity even when it takes on symbolic dimensions. The audience, enthralled by the revelation that the tulsi plant was made of pure silver, sought the thrill of this knowledge. It is true that Balgandharva (a popular actor–singer from the Marathi musical dramas of the mid-twentieth century) was a great actor of his time. However, it wasn't solely his art that captivated the audience but also his feminine charms and the luxurious gold-bordered sarees he adorned. The silver maces and golden robes served as tangible proof of the authenticity of his art. Nowhere else could a more misconstrued realism be found.

Certainly, the audience of such grand company plays comprised the well-educated middle class of that era. Individuals in this category find little value in the experience of rasa because it doesn't make sense to them. Rasanubhava with its limited worldly benefits, appears false in their eyes. What they crave is genuine experiences, even through art. This longing stems from the fact that they are often deprived of real experiences due to various social constraints. Reflecting real-life experiences in art allows them to savour these experiences freely, without bearing responsibility for the consequences. Abhinavagupta explicitly stated that a debauchee cannot have Rasanubhava. Such individuals find pleasure in translating Rasanubhava into inexpensive life experiences. For instance, an audience captivated by the beauty and sensual charms of female characters played by Balgandharva, may immerse themselves without having to be responsible for the character's ensuing journey of love. For such spectators, the joy of experiencing sensory pleasures indirectly, without direct sensory contact, is profound. There exist serious differences between desiring sensual pleasure and seeking it through art without the courage to pursue it in real life—enjoying it in solitude and to obtain Rasanubhava collectively. It is evident that those who directly experience life are considered more righteous than those who indulge in such pleasures through art.

The difference between the reality depicted in company plays and our new plays is noteworthy. Literary text in company plays, much like the lyrics in our classical music, is a pretext. However, in the new plays, the literary text takes centre stage. The dramas unfold the events of contemporary life, departing from the mythological realm. Similar to the enthusiasts of company dramas, fans of these plays belong to the well-educated middle class. Embracing the philosophy of progress, they transitioned from company plays to this new form, finding fulfilment in the latter. Notably, one of the most creative aspects of company plays is their music, whereas in the new plays it is the literary text that claims a prominent role, thus transforming drama into primarily a literary endeavour.

Emerging from the consciousness of the well-educated middle class, these plays are infused with acute social awareness. Logical intelligence plays a vital role in this context, exploring societal issues such as superstitions, ignorance, poverty and problems in male–female relationships. To address these issues, our new plays wield satire as a potent weapon. Like Western dramas, conflict becomes a fundamental principle in these plays, predominantly involving clashes between old and new, and society and individual. The selection of these conflicts is deliberate, suggesting the inevitability of conflict rather than focusing on victories and defeats resulting from conflicts.

Conflict inherently involves two parties, with the aim of proving one wrong. As previously mentioned, the choice between the two parties is apparent. Drama consistently endeavours to validate the reality and relevance of one of these entities. In Sriranga's early plays, the old generation is portrayed as half-dead, juxtaposed with the new generation that brims with vitality. The intellectual maturity and lack of experience in the new generation serve to mask their vitality. If this were the sole consideration, the narrative could uplift the youth, asserting that the future belongs to them. However, individual consciousness of youth transforms all individuals from the older generation into a backdrop. As the personality of the older generation wanes, only the intrigue of their environment remains. The individual persists as a person, while the living aspect of the environment is reduced to a concept. Since the audience's sympathy lies with the person, even if the hero succumbs in the story, they emerge victorious in the eyes of the audience. Although the conflict between god and man in Greek plays might seem similar, there exists a considerable difference between the two. It cannot be definitively stated that one of these entities is just, while the other is not. Only in the new plays is there a notion that anything which opposes the individual is unjust. From the perspective of the art of drama, this singular focus of the play proves to be exasperating.

Although it might appear somewhat abrupt, it seems that writing is a factor in bringing about this shift. In the past, Sanskrit dramas had written scripts, while folk theatre didn't. The Sanskrit dramas, characterized by their poetic structure, didn't separate sentiment and ideas. In contrast, folk drama, emerging spontaneously on stage through the actors' improvisation, had a free-form structure. While Sanskrit drama had a 'form', folk drama was free and open. In open drama, the foundation isn't the script; the actor is—proficient in all four forms of acting, capable of bringing the drama to life on stage. Whenever the need for openness arose, Sanskrit drama also adopted the folk style. However, our new plays are entirely scripted. The main purpose of writing is creating meaning, and the emphasis on the process of Bhava becoming rasa is less pronounced here. Since meaning is a product of our understanding, its nature is logical, and it manifests as a force inherent in language. Harnessing the power of language, new drama is flourishing—a drama that evolves in tandem with our well-educated consciousness.

Company drama rendered all miracles realistic, reducing them to the literal, and eroded symbolic consciousness. What is visible is also directly understood and hence, the indescribable and the invisible are deemed irrelevant. This truth becomes evident when comparing company drama with Yakshagana. In Yakshagana, only the costumes exude visual splendour; the rest demands interpretation, fuelled by imagination. Conversely, company drama leaves little room for imaginative engagement. The new play lacks the 'directness' of company plays. Exaggeration, in any form, proves detrimental to a well-educated consciousness, and the use of hyperbole in modern literature is typically reserved for humour. The distinct feature of new drama appears to be the emphasis on 'Vachikabhinaya' or verbal expression. While this holds true for our 'Talamaddale' genre also, there exists a difference between the two. The performance of 'Talamaddale' serves as a substitute for the other three performances without negating their significance. However, new drama employs the remaining three forms of acting (i.e. Angikabhinaya or gestures, Aharyabhinaya or costumes and Satvikabhinaya or physical expression of mental state) but downplays their importance. The strength of language is the driving force here. The remaining three forms of acting in the play contribute to Rasanirmana—the production of rasa. Rasa can be expressed through language, just as logic and reasoning can. New drama fully harnesses this power of language, given its intense urge to speak of something or to make a statement. Hence, the exchange through language becomes an intellectual transaction. Even though our absurd plays may appear, on the surface, to sidestep this process, they, too, involve an intellectual dimension. To dismiss a play by claiming not to understand it, is an insult to the play. And it is true that there are some who attribute this lack of understanding to the audience's intelligence.

Drama, as an art form, has evolved through various mediums such as music, dance, poetry and more. Each contributed its essence, shaping the development of drama. However, at present, all three—music, dance and poetry—have been excluded from the realm of drama. They visit briefly, receive hospitality and depart. What remains for drama is solely argumentative language.

II

'The notion that Indians lack a sense of history is so antiquated that we often overlook it. Following the arrival of the British in our country, we gained significant historical knowledge through their influence. Our people made little distinction between history and Purana. We have treated Kalidasa, Bhavabhuti, Dandi, Bharavi and Magha as contemporaries, placing them in the court of Raja Bhoja. We don't count the number of Vikramadityas, King Bhojas and Shudrakas who ruled Ujjain in the Malava region. Even a ruler of two or three villages would be elevated to the status of the ruler of the entire land encompassed within the four seas. It is perhaps not possible to write a history book in Sanskrit. The people who called the Mahabharata as history, and the Ramayana as poetry, later went on to create several myths and did not attempt to write a coherent history. Accounts of kings such as Chandragupta and Harshvardhana are found only in poetry and dramas, not in history. Determining whether *Buddha Charita*, *Sahasankaracharita*, *Rajatarangini*, and *Kampanarayacharita* are historical texts or poems is tough.'

These are the objections that can be raised and our response to them has been to be ashamed. We are perceived as having Purana but no history. However, should we conform to the established principles of history when examining the Puranas, or should we be embarrassed that we lack reverence for reality and worldly knowledge? Once again, we find ourselves seeking validation from the West to acknowledge that Purana and histories are distinct tools for understanding. Scholars familiar with the works of Roland Barthes, Claude Levi-Straus, James George Frazer and others are gradually recognizing that myths must hold some meaning. While Purana posits that the power that creates and sustains this world resides in another realm, history is solely concerned with the occurrences of this world. Yet, god-centric Purana, in its own way, parallels the pursuits of human-centric history. Secular history doesn't have the same concerns as Purana. It examines the reality of human existence, unveiling the secrets of political strategy. History can analyse and reveal how individuals behave in various situations, exposing their strengths, weaknesses, and the intricate connections between their nature, actions and life circumstances. In essence, the life of this world becomes the subject of history. However, in fulfilling this role, history transforms into a force, asserting control over the course of worldly affairs. It becomes the 'destiny' for the lifestyles of humans.

It has been mentioned that the sense of history emerged in our country with the arrival of the British. We may say that by studying the extensive history of our nation, we have now entered history. However, the threads of our history are still dispersed.

We remain unaware, for example, of all the factors leading to the spread of Buddhism from our country to foreign lands, indicating that we have not yet unearthed all the remains of our past. It is undeniable that we are presently situated within the realm of history. This shift is linked to the nation gaining Independence, bringing forth a series of challenges and issues. We are no longer exempt from the influences of such historical developments. Our joy and sorrow can no longer rely solely on nature's benevolence or wrath. Human happiness, sorrow, gains, losses, and good or ill fate have all become the responsibility of humanity. Consequently, it has become imperative to analyse every aspect of life within the context of history. We too now speak of progress, which serves as the driving force behind historical imagination.

There is a considerable difference between the era of history and that of the Purana. Human chronology holds more significance in this context than solar or lunar calendars. The progression of time in history is mechanical. In contrast, the Purana is beyond time, as it depends on eternal time. Legendary figures within it can rule or engage in acts of penance for 10,000 or 16,000 years. Despite the seemingly dictatorial nature of Time, it behaves submissively in mythological narratives. Time, in these stories, can be stretched infinitely or reduced to insignificance. While history is centred on detailing what happened, how it occurred and why, Purana, articulates cultural potential rather than depicting concrete realities.

What exists in history is not necessarily absent in Purana. This is especially true for our country. In our great poems and the Purana, history and poetry are intricately woven together. One cannot confidently make assertions about the absence of history in the genealogical story of the Mahabharata. However, each king of that dynasty, up to the Pandavas, sought immortality in various ways—whether by marrying Apsaras, aiding Indra in the war against Asuras, borrowing youth from children or securing the title of Indra during a celestial supremacy crisis. This desire for immortality was manifested and, to some extent, fulfilled. Similar to Yajna, this interaction between men and gods represents a crucial facet of worldly transactions. The struggles these kings faced, the challenges encountered in their pursuits, did not appear solely as spiritual dilemmas. Puranic symbols differ from poetic symbols, which often veil the truth. The significance of Purana is not that it is a symbol of the truism of reality; it is true because it is a Purana. While this truth may deviate from factual reality, it is not inherently untrue.

For this reason, the interpretation of mythological symbols can be precarious. Take, for instance, the symbolism of light and darkness representing good–evil or truth–untruth. If we simplify light and darkness to serve as direct representations of these concepts, we risk overlooking their nuanced truths. Humanism, both in Europe and in our own country, has translated mythology into simpler terms. Humanism tends to humanize mythical figures, a task that Jainism and Buddhism also undertook at one point. When Ravana transforms into a man defaulting his vows, the need for ten faces dissipates. Nine faces may now be explained away as reflections in the gem he held, leaving only one flesh-and-blood face. Similarly, the 'mukhabhanga' or breaking of the face of mythological figures is evident in contemporary literature. However, the Ravana with one head cannot be equated to the Ravana with ten heads. Whether it is a person, a situation or an inanimate object, their uniqueness encapsulates their meaning. This notion is underscored in the story 'Masumatti', by the Kannada writer Masti Venkatesh Iyengar, where Emily conveys the same message to her elder brother.

The crucial point to note is that, like history, the Purana also adheres to its own science, its own rules. Approaching Purana from a historical perspective, dismissing it entirely as lies and illusions is not advisable. The vitality of both the individual and

the race holds significant value. However, humanity soon grapples
with the realization that life is burdened by the impermanence
of mortality. The enduring question of how to transcend the
individuality of personality and perceive a greater truth has
haunted humanity through the ages. While religion once served
this purpose, science has taken on the role in contemporary
times. Despite differences in expression and media, there doesn't
seem to be any other difference. That is why Claude Lévi-Strauss
referred to mythology as the 'science of the concrete' (*The Savage
Mind*, ch. 1). In today's context, Purana and literature no longer
share the same hostility as science and literature do. Many of our
traditional poetic dramas drew inspiration and vitality from the
Puranas. However, modern authors who embrace a scientific
outlook often find limited influence from science. An exception to
this is Poornachandra Tejaswi's novel *Carvalho*. Understanding the
intricacies of the relationship between the characters, Carvalho
and Mandanna in the novel, is essential. The unique structure of
these two characters challenges the principles of character design
in our novels.

There exists a connection between Purana and antiquity.
As the term 'Purana' was in use during the Upanishad period, it
hints at their ancient origins. These works were labelled 'Puranas'
because they dealt with matters preceding the commencement of
human history. From this perspective, our history is very recent.
However, the Puranic imagination didn't decline too soon; new
mythological concepts about the world's creation, its conditions,
and the relationship between god and man have emerged over
time. Consequently, our social and cultural frameworks, as well
as the boundaries of our knowledge, are perceptible in Puranas.
In essence, the roots of the universal human race are found
in the Puranas. Legends, ghost stories, fantasy tales and folk
beliefs all form part of our Purana. Even our present scientific
comprehension of solar and lunar eclipses, in the context of

our country, is ancient. However, the story of Rahu and Ketu capturing the moon and sun, and the story of the churning of the sea as its background, continue to persist. It is a significant misunderstanding to say that these stories were fabricated solely to elucidate the mystery of solar or lunar eclipses. The celestial arrangement is the essence of these tales, not an explanation for eclipses. One may have to write a thesis to explicate the meaning of the story of the war between Devas and Asuras. On initial inspection, the symbols in this narrative possess a captivating brilliance, prompting a careful unravelling of its secrets.

As Puranas represent the cultural treasures of our country, it is fitting to approach them differently concerning the scheme of symbols and its meaning. The Puranas persist as ongoing narratives, and there is still much to uncover about the narrative order of these stories. The extent to which our literary works, such as Bana's *Kadambari* and Dandi's *Dashakumaracharite*, owe their inspiration to these Puranas remains to be determined. The narrative style of epics differs from this. To express the vastness of our knowledge, the nuances of rasa and bhava, the modes of our conduct and perspectives, the concepts of virtues and sins, the concealed facets of life unknown to us, the dim light within the human mind, and the aspects that both amaze and displease us—we required the medium of story, the language of narrative. In Greek mythologies, gods are denuded, whereas in Christian mythology, Adam and Eve are denuded; the meaning of nudity hinges on the cultural understanding in the respective race. Similarly, in our context, Pururava stands exposed in the lightning created by the gods. Examples range from Shiva and right up to Akka Mahadevi. To comprehend the significance of the nudity of a person or a deity, we must seek reasons within our cultural context or the language of our objects. This process requires delving into the innermost aspects of culture. Every culture possesses its Abhidhartha or literal meaning,

Lakshanartha or contextual meaning, Vyanjanartha or implied meaning, and, importantly, its Antarartha or inherent meaning. Without illuminating the inner context, the external language loses its meaning. This understanding transcends material knowledge and philosophy, embodying an awareness that renders both meaningful—a fundamental understanding that underlies all our interpretations.

Literature is an art that is formed of language. Language, as a system, captures both the living and non-living realms. The unbearable nature of being in a world one doesn't understand led humans to create and organize language. Language holds such sway over us that we can, at times, forget the world and live solely through what is expressed in language. There is in the Purva Mimamsa (the first two parts of the Vedas dealing with sacrificial rites) a suggestion that the oblation we offer is to words rather than to deities. Language plays a role in the numerous joys and sorrows in the world, embodying both meaning and that which is devoid of meaning, dangerous or worthless. We rely on language to convey the truth, to deceive, to express love and to even quarrel. Through this duality of language, stories and poetry have emerged. Our country could be credited to be a global leader in the telling of and listening to of stories! A rigorous study of the variety of our narrative techniques and their significance is yet to take place. Even within the Mahabharata alone, there exists a remarkable diversity of stories. This epic encompasses storytellers who relay what they have witnessed, those recounting what they have heard, those transmitting inherited tales and those who narrate stories based on their own speculation of what may have happened. Various types of storytellers coexist within this epic, showcasing the richness of our narrative tradition. One story serves as an allegory for another, as an illustration; stories are essential to accept what has happened, to justify actions, to comprehend the meaning of principles and to foster a sense of rebirth. Stories are born of diverse life experiences: when life's secrets are unravelled through the guise of death; when the exuberance of bravery is subjected to divine regulation; when separated lovers find simultaneous demise; when a king on a hunt is infatuated by a woman. When an experience transforms into a story, it adheres to the rules of storytelling, not those of the original experience. The question as to whether Chandrapeeda pursued the Kinnara Mithunas (mythic hybrid creatures—part human and part bird) in reality, should not arise. We should be satisfied that at least in the story, Kinnara Mithunas reveal the secret of life. Reading just one story by the parrot in Bana's *Kadambari* reveals the unviability of the notion that 'man is the proper study of mankind'. If everything experienced is life, then everything narrated is a story. How can we maintain that what is experienced only is true and not what is merely narrated!

We lack an equivalent term for the English word 'fiction' in Kannada. While it can be termed 'kalpaka sahitya' (imaginative literature), this phrase doesn't fully encompass all the nuances of the word 'fiction'; the reason is the absence of an indigenous concept of fiction. Fiction is quite distinct from history and Purana. This genre, evolving since the eighteenth century, has now become pervasive. Initially, the characteristics of this literature were unclear, and features of the ancient epics and dramas were attributed to it. Only recently have the distinct outlines and characteristics of this form of literature been delineated. Liberated from the influences of epic poetry and drama, it has now flourished independently, paving the way for the emergence of a new poetics. In Europe, there is ongoing work to reassess old narrative formulas and derive serious poetics from them. The principles obtained by applying the rules of linguistics to narrative literature can be taken as an example. One such principle points to categories such as subject and predicate in a sentence, and claims that such categories may also be analogously found in stories. As the intentions and actions of the subject are indicated by the rest of the sentence, similarly the entire plot describes the protagonist's sphere of action. Therefore, the two should be coherent. This echoes Mammata's perspective that the success in a sentence's meaning involves not only grammatical rules but also three other principles: 'akanksha' (mutual requirement or intent), 'yogyata' (congruity) and 'sannidhi' (mutual proximity or setting), which can be understood as principles of narratives, from the viewpoint of the study of fiction. It is crucial that the story's requirement is present at the beginning of the story; and equally vital is the characters' congruity to carry the kind of life that the story intends to portray. Setting serves as the story's lifeblood. The meaning of a sentence emerges when words within it come together, each finding its place through a fitting connection to the preceding word.

This principle can also be applied to stories. Much like a sentence that gains meaning through the arrangements of words following grammatical and other rules, a story derives meaning by organizing characters and situations in a sequence. The debate on whether meaning resides in words or sentences is age-old. However, until words evolve beyond mere words, they do not possess the intent to produce meaning. Words, in themselves, convey meaning; for instance, the word 'gold' is merely the name of a metal among many in that category. The true value emerges in the space between these words. Transforming words into sentences requires a creative effort where the speaker's intent to express and the urge to communicate converge to craft a sentence. Meaning is then derived from this creative process. For a sentence to carry meaning, the intent must align, accompanied by two additional prerequisites. Congruity, the rational of the sentence, is essential as meaning thrives on harmony. As the meaning of 'setting' is clear enough, no further elaboration is required.

How does meaning manifest within a sentence? This question led to the development of two theories: 'Abhihitanvaya Vada'

and 'Anvitabhidhana Vada', with Anvitabhidhana being the more
widely accepted. Abhihitanvaya theory relies on a mechanical
approach, assigning the responsibility of creating meaning to the
words and placing the speaker's intention as secondary. In contrast,
Anvitabhidhana views meaning-making as an organic associative
act. For instance, in the sentence 'Dushyanta chased the black
beast', Dushyanta is the protagonist, and all other words act as
his actions, forming the basic structure of the sentence. Similarly,
in a story, the relationship between characters, their actions and
the situations mirrors this concept. The unfolding meaning of a
story hinge on the interplay of characters, actions and situations.
The success of a story's meaning depends on the amalgamation
of the three elements: Space (sthala), Time (kala) and Destiny
(daiva), coupled with Intent, Congruity and Setting. The aspect
of 'Destiny' may be a subject of controversy. Destiny's existence
remains invisible, its purpose mysterious, and some even argue that
meaning can arise without its presence. Yet, I can find no reason
for the story's Intent to possess a discernible meaningful purpose.
Unlike the simple unit of meaning in a sentence, the meaning
of a story involves numerous indistinguishable sentences. The
relationship between words in a sentence differs from that between
sentences in a story, suggesting that grammatical formulas for the
latter have not been fully formulated. In the spaces between words
within a sentence, the rules of grammar, along with Mammata's
Intent, Congruity and Setting, remain hidden—invisible to the
eye but perceptible to the intellect. Similarly, within the spaces
between sentences and in tandem with Space and Time, Destiny
also lingers.

In a story, the place is described, and time is indicated by
verbs. However, it is crucial not to overlook that the described
place and indicated time are also elements of meaning. Take
the sentence, 'Suffering from the summer heat, Shakuntala was
writing a love letter under the shade of the mango tree.' Viewed
as an independent sentence, Shakuntala is the subject and the

rest are her actions. The words 'summer' and the 'shade of the mango tree' refer to time and place, constituting elements of meaning. When considered in the context of Shakuntala's story, the sentence's meaning is intertwined with the broader narrative, gaining depth and breadth. In the context of the story, 'time' and 'place' represent the time and place indicated in the narrative, thus becoming elements in the meaning of the story. Apart from the time and place suggested in the story, there is also the time and place where the story unfolds, which may be termed as the space of narrative expression. The abstract meaning of the story finds concrete expression through time and place, and the space of time and place can expand or contract to facilitate meaning. The space given may vary based on the measures of meaning. Similar to the representation of land on a map, here too, it can be compressed in time and place. For instance, take the statement 'Rama was in exile for fourteen years'. If you ask what is the space given to express this unit of meaning, then there is no definitive answer. Its quantity might be small in a concise poem but significantly large in an epic like the Ramayana. If we try to imagine how many 'parvas' (chapters) are needed to describe the eighteen days of the Mahabharata war by taking into account the descriptions of it, we begin to realize how extensive the time and place built through the language of the story can be. This illustrates the distinction between 'Kavyartha' (poetic meaning) and 'Vakyaartha' (syntactic meaning).

In daily life, sentences are deployed for their practical usefulness. The interpretation of these sentences is specifically geared towards conveying that something has happened or will happen, and expressing what should or should not be done. From one perspective, it is not incorrect to assert that the meaning of language is its utility. However, the use of language in fiction occurs at a distinct level, referred to as 'Rasa' by the ancients. Unstained by the daily use of the word rasa, the literary term rasa remains detached from the various fluctuations in human life, sensual growths and degradations.

A few words should be mentioned here about 'Destiny', which represents the third principle in the story. In this context, no religious or otherworldly connotation is intended. The remaining five principles of katha—intent, congruity, setting, time and place—all align with logical and relatable aspects of conscious thought. The meaning inherent in language is also rational, allowing us to comprehend the meaning of a story much like we understand the meaning of a sentence. Anything that cannot be grasped in this manner is deemed absurd or incoherent. Therefore, what is meaningful also aligns with what is rule-bound. However, life always contains elements that are incongruous, absurd and mysterious. Language is constructed to comprehend these facets, but when grammatical rules are imposed, language becomes normative. What norms uphold is rule-based, as language is the art of capturing the unordered. The world, though not devoid of logic, also encompasses irrationality. Hence, the principle of 'Destiny' had to be acknowledged in the story, a principle also present in drama. It is often manifested through miraculous and unimaginable events in mythological or folk stories, with the tale of births in Bana's *Kadambari* serving as a classic example. The deepest point of the story is racial memory, and life across births provides rational framework and the logic to address the problem of human personality. The entire story is intricately woven to rationalize the irrational.

Bana's *Kadambari* is an exceptional narrative that incorporates all the principles of the art of storytelling. It is brimming with the intent of various storytellers such as the parrot, who narrates a tale to King Shudraka, as also Chandrapeeda, Mahasweta and Jabali. In the parrot's story, the details of the parrot's life are interwoven with the aspects of its previous human births. The parrot concludes its story, collapses before Shudraka and succumbs to death, highlighting the connection between the narrative and mortality. In the world of *Kadambari,* death is an incidental occurrence resulting from the narrator's intent. The storytellers retain vitality till the end of the narrative, and the congruity of characters is evident. Examining the relationship between Mahasweta's character and the story she narrates is essential. Mahasweta, born in a lineage of Apsaras created by the moon's rays, has Pundarika as her beloved, the son of Shwetaketu. They meet in the vicinity of Achoda Lake, and the symbolism of the colour white permeates Mahasweta's story. Bana has thus symbolically shown the connection between the narrative and the central character, establishing an analogous relationship. Unlike European stories, this relationship is not one of opposition. Bana deploys elements of opposition only when he is using pun. The figure of speech in the phrase 'Krishnopi Asudarshana' has, on the surface, an element of opposition, but beneath lies analogy. Any opposition in our literature is merely of the nature of paradox.

There is no doubt about the principle of 'Sannidhi' (setting) as Bana's prose flows incessantly like a stream. Bana's syntax stands out for being long-winded. For instance, a short sentence such as, 'Kimiva hi Duskaram Akarunanam?' ('What is impossible to the merciless'), is surrounded by long sentences running into four or five pages. An objection may arise that there is more description than narration in Bana's work, given his penchant for description. However, when considering the events of the story, the descriptions prove worthwhile. In Bana, description works in a different way. As mentioned earlier, story occurs in time, and the time within the story and the time of the story (i.e. time taken by the events of the story) are distinct. The pace of narration slows down the time of the story, allowing each moment to unfold vividly. In Bana, there is no description without colour. The story of Mahasweta features the colour white, the story of the hunter has the colour black, the story of the parrot introduces green as a colour, and there are diverse colours in the stories of Chandrapeeda and Kadambari. These colours symbolize the life values in the story. The order formed by these colours become a distinct language and construct a semantic framework of their own. Black in the hunter's life provides us with a fine illustration. He puts his hand into the parrot's nest, breaks the neck of the old parrot and throws it down. Bana's magical language separates the hunter's hand from his personality, granting it an independent persona. The hand's shape, colour, smell and sound imbue it with ferocity. To a parrot's eye, the hunter's body is not visible, only his hand comes into its arc of visibility. Hunter's personality belongs to a world unseen by the parrot. As the parrot had seen him before, it could make a connection between that personality and his hand. Only when the hand enters the nest does the parrot perceive it as a form of death, and the hand, unyielding to the old parrot's attacks, breaks its neck and throws it out. This distinction is feasible because the black colour of his hand evokes the image of a black snake's head. The statement about the hand is made for the sake of narrative harmony. The analogy with the snake's head sets it apart and imparts a distinct meaning to it. Another comparable symbol is the name 'Pundarika', Munikumar's name, which is associated with the white lotus. Despite changes in his personality across lifetimes, this connection remains unchanged, making his union with Mahasweta possible. Bana's prose, through such figures of speech, departs from the logic of reality and embraces a figurative logic that is characteristic of his narrative style.

We can briefly look into how 'daiva' (destiny) manifests in Bana's *Kadambari*. While it is true that Chandrapeeda goes in pursuit of Kinnara Mithunas in a quest for his personal destiny, this fact alters the course of the story. At the culmination of his search, Chandrapeeda meets Mahasweta, not Kinnara Mithuna. We are reminded of Dushyanta who pursues a blackbuck and ends up meeting Shakuntala. Dushyanta's meeting with Shakuntala decides his destiny. Similarly, the meeting with Mahasweta sets the stage for another narrative. Escaping the hunter's clutches, the surviving parrot finds refuge in the ashram of Jabali with the help of the sage named Haritha. The meeting with Jabali leads to another narrative. Thus, in Bana's *Kadambari*, the stories unfold through chance events, each leading to a new character. These characters play a crucial role in adding another dimension to the narrative, serving as the driving force of the story. Chandrapeeda, upon receiving Patralekha as his servant, from his mother Vilasavati, acknowledges her story; he learns from Mahasweta her and *Kadambari*'s stories which he also integrates in his narratives. After it finishes its storytelling the parrot dies, and Shudraka, its listener, relinquishes his life. This underscores the clear relationship between the story and its characters. If the story flows like a flood, the characters act as floodgates, indicating the current's speed and depth while serving as essential components of this narrative flow.

The story of *Kadambari* unfolds with the narrative of a parrot. The parrot, brought by Chandala, recounts its story to king Shudraka. Three-quarters of the work is occupied by tales narrated by the parrot. Having escaped the hunter's clutches, the parrot finds refuge in Haritha's care and joins Jabali's ashram. Observing the parrot's condition, Jabali learns about its previous birth and proceeds to narrate it to sages like Haritha. This, too, is a parrot's tale. Within Jabali's narrative, Chandrapeeda and Mahasweta's story commences. It is revealed that Pundarika (Mahasweta's beloved), Vaishampayana (Chandrapeeda's friend) and the parrot (the current storyteller to King Shudraka) are the same individuals, though separated by three births. Similarly, Chandrapeeda, who listens to Mahasweta's story in one birth, now in another, listens to the parrot's story as Shudraka. The perspective of the story shifts due to the roles of storyteller and listener. In one layer of the narrative, Chandrapeeda and Kadambari are the hero and heroine, with Pundarika–Vaishampayana and Mahasweta as supporting characters. However, this is a conventional view, as both stories are essentially the same, developing in parallel. Chandrapeeda and Kadambari lack the authority to narrate the story, remaining forever story-listeners. Chandrapeeda and Shudraka lack knowledge of other births. Pundarika–Vaishampayana, after taking birth as parrot, reach perfection. The parrot has experienced both the good and bad aspects of lust. But Chandrapeeda and Shudraka are indifferent to lust. Chandrapeeda and Kadambari have seen more separation than union. If Chandra is indifferent to Rohini, Chandrapeeda is indifferent to Patralekha. Shudraka, too, remains unmarried, avoiding the women of his court. However, this does not imply that Chandrapeeda follows the ascetic path and Pundarika follows the path of lust. The story's purpose is to unveil the unique rhythms of man's connection with their *daiva*. Defying Shukanasa's advice, Chandrapeeda pursues the Kinnara Mithunas, and thus meets his destiny. Vaishampayana, as Shukanasa's son, pursues the previous birth having sensed it. As his spirit is unafraid of curses he is not deprived of grace. Bana, through the pleasant narrative, exposes the harsh journey of these lives. To comprehend this comprehensive vision, Bana provides us with the viewpoint of a parrot standing on the summit of the third birth, or at the head of the Shalmalee tree.

The essence of consciousness in Bana's *Kadambari* remains somewhat elusive. Prior to Chandrapeeda's enthronement as Yuvaraja, Minister Shukanasa discovered him and delivered an extensive sermon, spanning four or five pages. Although he articulates commonly held policies, his bravery in exposing the weaknesses of kings to the aspiring prince is commendable. Similarly, Jabali, upon encountering a parrot in the ashram, engages in a lengthy discourse on sins and their consequences. He vividly illustrates the karmic path that yields the effects of perfection across different births. These two widely discussed stories are seen by some as the source of the story's essence, while others argue that Shukanasa's teachings and Jabali's reflections are flawed.

However, as previously mentioned, the story needs to be examined from the perspective of the parrot. Pundarika's third birth is as a parrot, but in the first two human births, his life was characterized by lust. Pundarika's eyes can see nothing but Mahasweta. For Vaishampayana, Chandrapeeda is the eye, and he has no independent existence. Only the parrot possesses the highest sensory capacity. Descriptions of Vindhyatavi, the Shalmalee tree, the sunrise, the evening at Jabali's ashram and the moon— all famous descriptions—come from the parrot's perspective. A parrot can distinguish ten different colours of sunrays and, contrary to Jabali's teaching, can perceive life by its own power. Even in its animal existence, it can reveal the strange destinies of human life. It must be said that the root of the consciousness of the *Kadambari* lies in the consciousness of the parrot, as no other parrot has the freedom of this parrot in the golden cage. A man cursed to become a parrot is a mythic trick—a way to escape from the confinement of personality. Since the personality of a man is an organization of many principles of action, the complexity of this organization is resolved through transformation in the Puranas. In the case of Ahalya, turned to stone by a curse, she is neither Gautama's wife nor Indra's mistress. She is just an entity—a state of release from archaic fetters, not independent. After being freed from Rama's feet, she becomes a free person. Similarly, the parrot is only a condition seeking its way out, and it is unclear what happens to the parrot after being freed from the curse—Vaishampayana or Pundarika. This dilemma makes a lot of sense. Shukanasa stands in front of Taruna, who has been released from the parrot's birth. Pundarika's father, Shvetaketu, is said to have entrusted his son to Shukanasa. Mahasweta is the same old Mahasweta, but her beloved is enriched by the experiences of three births. This represents a transformation—a technique particularly useful for indicating the essence of life.

This analysis had to be developed this much to show that Bana's *Kadambari* is useful in understanding the fundamental principles of the art of storytelling. Abounding in erudition, this mature work represents a profound adaptation of the once-popular folktale, encapsulating the basic tenets of the art of storytelling. The detailed exploration of this piece, which seamlessly merges folklore, mythology and *abhijata* (classic), remains beneficial even in contemporary times.

III

The novel is an important genre of modern literature, as it effectively portrays contemporary life. The genre encompasses various forms, making it challenging to pinpoint specific features. It draws on techniques from earlier epics and dramas, utilizing a range of techniques from descriptions to stream-of-consciousness narrations. True to real life, the novel is committed to capturing the joys, sorrows and thought processes of present-day existence. By creating an alternative world that mirrors or corresponds to the surrounding reality, novels attempt to address contemporary challenges. The artistic purpose of the novel lies in revealing the philosophy of contemporary life, which is also the goal of writing in contemporary period. Writing permeates every field from institutions, shops, law, journalism and education, ultimately extending to literature. The transition from speech to writing raises questions about semantic transformations, which require continued exploration. The impact of a guru's instruction depends on the disciple's needs, but this condition doesn't apply to the effect of a legal code in written form. In the realm of writing, which belongs to the world of the educated, the freedom found in speech, which belongs to the world of the unlettered, is rare. A careful examination of the distinction between sin and crime reveals that the history of our code of ethics has diverged into two strands. Ideas of sins and virtues belong to the unwritten world of mythical imagination, while criminal acts and good conduct belong to the written world of law. Sin lacks the specific form that crime has, just as crime lacks the depth of sin.

The nature of the novel serves as a testament to how literature has evolved, incorporating elements of both speech and writing. Poetry and plays, once purely oral genres, eventually transitioned to written forms. In Europe, the novel emerged from essays and other kinds of journalistic writings. While the stories used in novels have their roots in oral traditions, novels sought to document these narratives in writing, shedding light on various aspects of societal life. The genre aimed to address and rectify societal loopholes. Presently, the novel's vision appears to have returned to its original form. In Kannada literature, novels still uphold realism, social concerns and a humanistic outlook. A strong sense of history is deeply embedded in the essence of the novel, characterized by realistic depictions of human life, natural characterization, cohesive design and a contemporary outlook. If the world created by a novel does not align with the reality around it, the novel fails to capture the reader's interest.

What purpose does such a work serve? This question admits several answers. While one might derive pleasure from studying such works, the primary benefit is often perceived as the potential to offer solutions for the shortcomings and problems within society. The effectiveness of a work is subjective, and opinions vary on what constitutes effectiveness. Given that the objective of such literature is to engage with society, it should have the capacity to address the weaknesses within it. Historical instances, such as young people committing suicide after reading Goethe's novel, *Werther*, underscore the profound impact literature can have on individuals. In Karnataka, a man, moved by B.M. Sri's recitation of the poem 'Dukhkhasetu', publicly sought forgiveness in a crowded gathering for contemplating deserting his wife.

Some argue that incidents like these should not occur in the interest of social welfare. Another perspective asserts that the study of literature should nurture the heart and sharpen the intellect to discern the meaning of experiences, thereby enhancing understanding. This, it is argued, should be the primary benefit of literature. These are, in a way, efforts to rephrase and articulate the benefits of poetry espoused by Mammata: 'Sadyah Paranivrithi' ('immediate pleasure') and 'Kantasammita Upadesha' ('charming advice').

It is the reader who determines the merit of literature, exercising their moral right. While they may not articulate their opinions like critics, their preferences and disapprovals are evident in their choices of what to buy and read. This used to be the prevailing condition for literature in the past—a work appreciated by readers, lingering in their memory for years, later becoming the subject of scholarly commentary. However, in the modern times, the role of the reader has altered alongside the birth of the critic. The contemporary reader is often seen as a more dispassionate consumer, armed with the critic's literary formulas, contributing to a historical narrative of taste. The critic's duty is to elucidate the meaning of a work, but the reader should retain the freedom to embrace or reject it. While the role of the critic is undeniably important, they must also serve the needs and desires of the readers. Beyond focusing on the author's intent, literary rules, and the meaning of the work, the critic should consider the readers' preferences. In working on behalf of literature, the critic is equally obligated to advocate for the reader.

Shivarama Karanth's novel *Sarasammana Samadhi* (Sarasamma's Grave) was published approximately fifty years ago, and, in keeping with Karanth's other works, it prominently features his social ideas. The narrative revolves primarily around the failures of marriage, illustrating the discord among four couples: Thimmappayya–Janaki, Annappa Kamti–Sunalini, Hiranya–Bhagirathi and Sitarama–Nagaveni. The novel employs mild irony in portraying those who believe that praying to Sarasamma in the village's 'Masti' temple—a revered deity—would resolve their marital problems. Their disappointment is palpable when, despite fervent prayers and penance, no solutions materialize. In contrast, stark irony is evident in the depiction of Sarasamma's ghost, which exposes the hypocrisy surrounding Sarasamma's chastity. It is disclosed that Sarasamma had a coerced relationship with her ailing husband, Neelachalaiah. The unsettling revelation unfolds that, after her husband's demise, she was forcibly cremated on his pyre. Chandrayya emerges as the narrator who unveils this haunting story to the readers.

Chandrayya's character in the novel extends beyond its narrative purpose, possessing a profound personality. Among his friends, he is perceived as a cheerful individual, displaying a love for travel and an innate trust in others. Embracing both science and mythology, his thirst for knowledge becomes integral to the novel's development. Familiar with the works of authors like Sir Conan Doyle, Chandrayya eagerly seeks to unravel the secrets behind the existence of ghosts. In his pursuit of the supernatural, Chandrayya becomes a witness to the disaffection among all four couples. He has observed Janaki, Hiranya and Sunalini in Sarasamma's hut, witnessed the horror of Sitaram-Nagaveni's first night in Bekala's bungalow, and heard about the tragedy of Sarasamma's marriage directly from the ghost. Interestingly, Chandrayya remains unmarried, grappling with doubts about whether to wed Ramanna's daughter from Alampadi or engage in a relationship with Hiranya's wife, Bhagirathi, and Sunalini. The rich design of experiences woven by such a character serves as the essence of the novel.

From this perspective, it appears that the novel has successfully achieved its purpose. The novel also ironically portrays Chandrayya's faith. While all of this holds true, there exists another mythological aspect to the novel, encompassing Bellakka's ghost, Sarasamma's ghost and the narrative of Sarasamma's self-immolation in the funeral fire of her husband. Together, these elements contribute to the creation of a myth. The intellectualism within the novel challenges this myth, though not entirely debunking it. It is through Sarasamma's ghost that the falsehood of the story surrounding Sarasamma's fate is revealed. The novel refrains from detailing what happened to Chandrayya's faith upon discovering its falseness. Even if addressed, the 'ghost experience' of Chandrayya will persist as a real occurrence. If the ghost's encounter is deemed false, then so is the story it conveys.

What has been presented so far does not constitute a conventional criticism of the novel. It was necessary to choose a specific novel as an example, and this work serves to highlight certain narratological issues. The primary concern is the prominent role of mythology in the narrative. The principles governing humanist fiction differ from those of mythology, which, in this novel, adheres to its own set of rules. Sarasamma's ghost assumes a tangible form, embodying unsatisfied desire to the extent of becoming perceptible. The challenge arises as intellectualism dismisses the validity of mythic truth, deeming it irrelevant to our lives. However, mythology persists with its impact, portrayed here as acknowledging and ultimately surrendering to human intellectualism. Yet, the essence of Puranic truth endures.

Adjacent to this issue, another broader and more significant problem emerges. The novel explicitly emphasizes the importance of human intellect. Readers who embrace intellectualism will find it unsurprising if critics align with this novel's perspective. The narrative has already depicted Chandrayya's thirst for knowledge. If you can empathize with Chandrayya's character, then the

novel has succeeded in its mission. Chandrayya's comprehension
extends to understanding the world around him—he desires
to grasp everything. His ability to confront and converse with
ghosts, despite not being highly educated, renders Chandrayya a
hero, well-suited for the material of a modern novel.

This implies that Chandrayya assumes the role of the knower.
In a sentence, the verb encapsulates the intentions and actions of
the subject, transforming the world into an object of knowledge.
These activities are so commonplace that we don't pay much
attention to them. The act of knowing, ingrained in the living
individual and the world they comprehend, extends to the point
that even the act of dying is within their will. Observe the sentence
structure 'he dies', and it leaves no doubt in our minds that it is
within his control. This verse from the Adiparva of Mahabharata
should be taken into consideration:

Aditya Chandravanilonalashcha
Daurbhumirapo Hridayam Yamashcha
Ahashcha raatrishch Ubhe Cha Sandhye
Dharmashcha Janati Narasya Vrattam

The sun, moon, wind, fire, sky, earth, water,
Yama, man's heart, day, night, morning, evening and
religion know the conduct of man.

The moral code in this verse may not be relevant to us, but what
holds importance is that the surrounding world is an active,
dynamic, object of human behaviour with corresponding syntax.
Purana understood this, yet the story of man is still to be fully
understood. It is worthwhile to recall the words of the German
philosopher Wittgenstein (in *Culture and Value*, p.56): 'Don't, for
Heaven's sake, be afraid of talking nonsense! But you must pay
attention to your nonsense.'

IV

Sanskrit aestheticians have offered diverse definitions of poetry. While one asserts that poetry is the intertwining of words and meanings, another contends that form constitutes the essence of poetry. Anandavardhana identifies Dhvani (suggestion) as the soul of poetry, whereas Jagannath Pandita sees it as words with aesthetic meaning. Each of these definitions captures an aspect of the truth about poetry within its limited scope. When arranged chronologically, these interpretations reveal the evolution of poetic sensibility. Mimamsakas (scholars of hermeneutics), Naiyayikas (scholars of Nyayashastra) and other Shastrakaras (authors of scientific treatises) have also explored the nature of poetry from their perspectives, upholding its significance. That Shastrakaras have not overlooked poetry is significant from the point of view of culture.

Poetry has undergone significant transformations today. While defining poetry anew based on these changes would be simple if the challenges were consistent, the present uncertainty revolves around doubts concerning the philosophy and relevance of poetry. The current issue lies in our scepticism about the value of poetic representation, about the value of the imaginative truth proffered by poetry. We are unaware how this will impact the trajectory of our epistemology. Western epistemology posits the knower and the known as the two essential components of the process of comprehension. If either of these elements is flawed, comprehension falters. Just as one without eyes cannot see what is in front of them, a person with eyesight cannot see what is not in front of them. This principle extends to intellectual perceptions as well. Our ancient scriptures too reflect on these principles, emphasizing the roles of the knower (Jnatri), the known (Jneya) and the knowledge (Jnana). Additionally, a philosophy seems to have emerged after Patanjali's *Mahabhasya*, notably reflected in

Bhartrhari's *Vakya Padiya*, a significant grammar treatise. The following comments by Punyaraja, who has written an explicatory commentary on this work, provides valuable insights that warrant further exploration:

Trini Jyotinshi Trayah Prakashaha
Yoyam Jataveda, Yashcha
Purusheshu Antarah Prakasho
Yashcha Prakashasya Prakashayi Tha
Sabdakhya Prakashah
Tatretat Sarvam Upanibaddam

Three flames and three lights: One is fire; the second is the flame in the body of men; the third is word that illuminates even light; everything is subordinate to these three.

Three fundamental aspects of light are identified here. The first is Agni, the light that reveals the essence of things in the world. The second is the inner light within humans, the faculty of perception. The third is the illumination that allows light to manifest, namely language. The first two lights rely on the third for their existence. Here there is little confidence about understanding emerging from the shape and structure of matter and the insight and intellect of humans. The assertion made here, that comprehension is unattainable without the assistance of language, is remarkable. It only holds significance when the nature of understanding aligns with the object, referred to as 'meaning' in the context of poetry. It is this that poetry employs as meaning. The power of language is Janus-faced: it brings awareness of matter to humans from one direction and transforms matter into meaning in the other. Since this is an ongoing process, it may not be immediately apparent to us. In essence, language possesses the capacity to illuminate one's perception, influencing both the object of awareness and the intellect, imagination and emotions of humans.

For this reason, the debate over whether language is man-made or god-made persists. Language serves as a tool for understanding as also a norm for comprehension. It is for the purposes of the norm that the Vedas are considered *apaurusheya* (not having human origins). The radiant language of the ancient philosophy became a norm for the worldly language. A saying in the Nirukta (an ancillary treatise by Yaska connected to the Vedas, providing explanations to words found in Vedas) suggests that mantras are free of meaning, allowing them to assume varied meanings. In ancient times, there was a concern about human interference corrupting speech. In the Vedas, Agni symbolizes the power of speech, while in the Puranas, Goddess Saraswati, referred to as 'Sarva Shukla', is the goddess of speech. During that era, purity in speech was believed to correlate with purity in understanding. Bhartrhari emphasizes the importance of language by stating, 'Na sosti pratyayo lokay yah sabdanugamadrite. Anuvidhamivam jnanam sarvam sabdena bhasate.' The statement says that understanding is inseparable from language and that all knowledge is enveloped in language. He asserts that consciousness is verbal, and without the aid of language, understanding anything in the world is impossible. All understanding is imbued with language. Regardless of the nature of things in the world, the essence of our understanding is significantly shaped by language. Hence, words becoming norm is inevitable.

Bhartrhari's words are closely tied to knowledge, evident in his use of the term 'pratyaya'. Some may argue that in discussing poetry we need not concern ourselves with knowledge. In other words, understanding the nature of poetry requires exploring another principle in conjunction with comprehension. If the interplay of matter, meaningful language and human intuition aligns in a particular way, the pursuit of understanding unfolds seamlessly. The foundation of understanding rests on these three entities. However, are these elements alone sufficient for the creation of poetry? An episode in Bhavabhuti's play *Uttararamacharita* sheds light on this question. When Ramachandra's Ashwamedha (an emperor's ritual) horse enters Valmiki's ashram, a commotion ensues among the disciples. They are unable to recognize the horse since it is not a familiar animal. A disciple runs to inform Lava about the arrival of this unfamiliar animal. While Lava too has never seen a horse, he knows about it from military science. Lava's friend, lacking this knowledge, has now seen the horse first-hand. When Lava asks him to describe the animal, the disciple provides a visual description, but the essence of 'horseness' is absent. Does this imply a lack of connectedness in his understanding? In a grammatically precise language, the distinct features of the horse are not visible in the limited description. Lava has theoretical knowledge from books but lacks practical experience. On the other hand, his friend has observed the horse but lacks understanding. This scenario presents an image of the Ashwamedha horse advancing in one direction, symbolizing form, and in the other direction representing sound, eluding comprehension in either aspect.

It is natural that question arises as to what is erroneous in the response of Lava's friend. Bhavabhuti, in his play, did not explicitly address this issue. Alternatively, the overall structure of Bhavabhuti's drama could serve as the answer. After Rama and Sita are separated, Lava and Kusha are born in Valmiki's ashram, and from birth they are denied the lineage of Raghuvamsa. It is not that they were unfamiliar with Raghuvamsa; rather, their acquaintance with it was profoundly rooted in their study of the Ramayana. In essence, their experience of Raghuvamsa was through poetry. When Lava encounters the horse, he doesn't react with alarm as does his friend. Observing Rama's grief-stricken face, Lava intuits that the source of sorrow lies in the ill-fated connection with Sita. But they are unaware that Rama is their father. The case of Lava's friend is very different. He has seen an animal called horse, and describes it in an absurd manner, without obtaining a genuine understanding. His depiction, such as calling it 'the animal named horse, an angry ghost' falls short of conveying the true essence of the horse. The absence of meaning in this description stems from a misalignment in the relationship between matter, intellect and language.

There is no rule in language that an object must be physically present for meaning to emerge. The perceptual experience of an object can indeed give rise to the meaning conveyed in language. However, it is crucial to recognize that an object, in and of itself, cannot generate meaning. Meaning doesn't play a role in the inherent nature of matter; instead, the responsibility of creating meaning lies solely with language. The assertion that meaning is the potency of language holds true in this context. It is important not to overlook that Abhidha (literal), Lakshana (connotative) and Vyanjana (ironic), as identified by our linguists, are integral components of language. The key here is to recognize the difference between the word-level meaning as against the sentence-level meaning. Even the linguists who delved into various types of meaning, one suspects, may have overlooked this gap. Those who categorized Dhvani, ranging from word-level Dhvani to the discourse-level Dhvani, may have failed to realize that word-level Dhvani also cannot manifest without the support of sentences or syntax. A word essentially serves as a name for an object, capable of denoting an object even in its absence. However, this does not imply an independent, active sense. Ultimately, a word can transform into a conceptual representation of the object, preserving the form of the object.

The sentence's structure presents a different case. While it is accurate to describe a sentence as a group of words as our grammarians do, words alone are insufficient to create a sentence. Likewise, the sentence-level meaning is not merely a collection of individual word-level meanings. Rather, guided by the speaker's mental attitude—rules, regulations and preferences—words are organized into a specific order. One of the objectives of this process is to synthesize all the word-level meanings into sentence-level meanings. Practically all grammarians acknowledge this principle, which has served as a catalyst for the Sphota theory of language. However, it is crucial to remember that crafting a sentence is a creative endeavour. This notion holds true for every sentence we construct. Another vital point to consider is that a sentence establishes itself as an independent entity detached from the objects in the world. Unlike the meaning of individual words that may rely on the existence of the object, a sentence thrives through the speaker's 'discrimination' in assigning meaning.

The saying 'Nasato vidyate bhavo nabhavo vidyate satah' is derived from the Bhagavad Gita. It means that the existence of a thing and its essence are not distinct entities. The meaning of 'sat' or the existence of a thing is straightforward, and humans have a 'bhava' (feeling) about the existence of a thing. What is this feeling? Is it an understanding of the object? It seems not; although they might seem similar in general terms, there appears to be a subtle difference between them. According to the perceptive powers of the human intellect, understanding may vary among humans. Awareness can independently develop and evolve into a science, but the nature of 'bhava' is indivisible. Unlike awareness, 'bhava' is not abstract; neither is it beneficial like experience. One might question the need for this excessive analysis since, in reality, awareness, experience and feeling intertwine. However, in literature, it is feeling that proves valuable, making it essential to disentangle feeling from this complexity.

Careful consideration is demanded even when using the term 'feeling of existence' in this context. Bharata defines drama as the Bhavanukīrtana of three worlds, and later in the context of rasa, refers to bhava, vibhava and anubhavas. He does not explicitly address the dual use of the word 'Bhava'. Bharata doesn't find it necessary, but Abhinavagupta's renowned commentary does not touch upon this point either. The sense in which 'bhava' is used in 'Bhavanukirtana' is likely to be the same as its use in the phrase 'feeling of existence'. In subsequent verses, Dharma, Shilpa, Artha, Yuddha and others are mentioned, indicating they are not related to *sthayibhava* that the theory of rasa mentions. Abhinavagupta also acknowledges that dharma, yuddha, and so on, are various stages of life. Drama doesn't directly represent these situations but rather perceives their feelings and expresses them, a condition Abhinavagupta extends to all literature, including drama.

The crucial question here is whether language can effectively capture what is called 'bhava'—feeling. As previously mentioned, the primary function of language is to generate meaning, transforming matter into meaning. Meaning is broad enough to encompass feeling. All elements within the configuration of an object must be included in meaning. As I.A. Richards, a notable thinker, asserts, meaning cannot be divided into referential meaning and emotive meaning as linguistic meaning is indivisible. Despite differences in style, manner and effect, the meaning remains the same whether in a scientific statement or a poem that describes this using rhyme and rhythm. In the poem, techniques such as style, figurative language and humanization also serve to suggest meaning. It would be simplistic to say that what the first statement has is meaning and what the poem has is feeling; it would be a reduction of the meaning of meaning. While there are differences between science and poetry, prose and verse, these differences are to be found elsewhere, but not in linguistic meaning.

What is poetry? This is a question that must be revisited periodically. The answer is not fixed; a timeless question only elicits a temporary answer. The whole poetic tradition makes an attempt at addressing this question, offering numerous answers in the form of theories. Since the task of poetics is to depict the truth of poetry in a vivid manner, it engages in an ongoing search for fresh answers. It is beneficial for the vitality of criticism to recognize that, like poetry, it is also a game. Each artistic endeavour adheres to its unique set of rules, and with every new game, emerges a new set of rules, as rules essentially shape the essence of a game. Adhering to the rules and making the game meaningful is one form of creative expression, while breaking these rules and establishing new ones constitutes another form. As a result, definitions evolve with changes in rules, yet the fundamental truth of the game remains constant. Poetics engages in its own game within such a confined domain.

Poetry is an art that has language as its medium. The primary question is about the form of its manifestation in language. According to Jagannath Pandita, poetry presents aesthetic meaning. This definition while emphasizing the importance of the aesthetic 'meaning', seems to ignore the importance of the 'word'. The aesthetic meaning holds a technical significance, but is poetry solely word? The meaning that word possesses has already been explored, revealing that word-level meaning is not creative. Further, communicative intent is absent in word-level meaning. Such an intent exists in sentence-level meaning. The Sanskrit word 'vak', i.e. speech, is the origin of the Sanskrit word for sentence, 'vakya': we all speak sentences. A speaker's intent shapes a sentence into a structured form. Thus, poetry can be a sentence and not merely a word. From a linguistic standpoint, the sentence stands as an essential unit of poetry. Each word within a sentence contributes its meaning, creating a cohesive whole. This endeavour is creative. The three elements that Bhartrhari speaks of in his Jnana Mimamse also converge in the sentence. In various realms such as the Puranas, Shastras, philosophy and business, expressions like blessings, curses, rites, prohibitions, visionary ideas, compliments, praises and reproaches find form through sentences. These are merely a few examples. Like Trivikrama's foot, sentence envelops the entire universe. Therefore, poetry cannot be exempt from this reality. However, before delving into poetry, it is pertinent to understand the sentence's capabilities. A sentence can reveal the speaker's intention (vivaksha) and express it. Additionally, it can describe things and events in the world, highlighting the distinction between expressing and describing—an essential nuance in the functionality of language.

It is imperative to look further into the understanding of the sentence; to understand and to think about language means to use it properly. Wittgenstein, a German philosopher who firmly believed that the limit of language is also the limit of understanding, offers insights into the nature of sentences. According to him, a sentence is a logical portrayal of its meaning, a fact evident to the discerning eye. He further states that logic is concerned solely with reality, and in sentences, only insofar as they serve as pictures of reality. Each word in a sentence, except affixes, refers to an actual fact or object. From this perspective, a sentence transforms into a rational image of reality, representing meaning. Additionally, a sentence expresses rationality. For instance, 'he slept happily' depicts a picture of reality, being a factual sentence, whereas 'man's life is perishable' is an ideological picture and falls into the category of a logical sentence. The truth or falsehood of the first sentence is measured against reality which serves as the standard. Conversely, the second sentence relies on its internal logic and does not necessitate an external scale for evaluation.

Thus, if only these two types of sentences are considered, what happens to poetry is the question that emerges. While Wittgenstein's focus was on the language of philosophy, it is understandable that he didn't engage with poetry. Elsewhere he also states that logic must take care of itself, a principle applicable to poetry as well. Poetry should be conscious of the form and structure of the sentences it employs, along with their usage and the technical relationships between the words. Already, two types of sentences have been introduced. This distinction becomes evident in how Kalidasa described Parvati dressed for the worship of Shiva: 'Vasanta pushpabharanam vahantee . . . sancharinee pallavinee lateva!' Here, Parvati is portrayed as 'adorned with spring flowers, walking like a vine in bloom'. Is this a factual description of Parvati? There is no reality or logic in asserting that a woman is a walking vine. Therefore, is it a sentence or does it only appear like a sentence? We may say that the poet crafted this to express Parvati's beauty, so then the question arises: Why this complexity? Can't beauty be expressed simply and rationally? The answer poetry gives to these queries is that the purpose of poetry is the production of rasa, as asserted by ancient aestheticians. This response may not satisfy the modern mind, as the rasa theory is deemed obsolete. We are confronted with questions such as what does Rasanubhava in poetry or drama mean, how such an experience is obtained and what are its benefits. But, other than rasa, no fully satisfactory answers are available.

It has been stated that poetry is a form of a sentence, and now an additional layer is introduced—rasa. A sentence can function as a representation of reality or a rational image. Arguably, there exists a third type of sentence, a category that may be identified as poetry. This perspective finds support from experts such as Abhinavagupta, who employ a similar approach to resolve a distinct issue. Abhinavagupta considers the nature of the experience of rasa and argues that the experience of rasa is not a genuine experience and that it does not arise from a critical understanding. It is not a pretentious truth or an illusory experience; it is not falsehood either. He says it is a distinct kind of experience originating from art—Rasanubhava. Unlike real-life experiences, it lacks a historical context, causative background or subsequent effects. Rasanubhava begins and concludes within a poetic work. Vishwanath, in *Sahityadarpana*, elucidates the kind of Rasanubhava a reader attains, describing it as the 'Brother of Brahmasvada'. In this experience, pleasure is yielded by the excitement of the whole spirit. He further asserts that when

Sahrudaya's mind is immersed in rasa, it remains untouched by any other experience. In essence, Rasanubhava is a liberating experience, a sentiment that can also be attributed to poetry. If one were to inquire about the nature of this unique sentence, it necessitates a specific name. Fortunately, there is no need to invent a new term, as Vishwanath of *Sahityadarpana,* has already provided a name in his definition of poetry.

'Vakyam Rasatmakam Kavyam'—this is Vishwanath's definition of poetry. The purpose of our preceding discussion becomes evident when we recognize that the 'rasatmaka vakyam' (aesthetic statement) refers to the third type mentioned earlier. In such a sentence, there can be a depiction of reality as well as an idea. 'Tatha samaksam dahata manobhavam pinakina bhagna manoratha sati/Nininda rupam hridayena Parvati priyeshu saubhagyaphala hi charuta.' This verse from Kalidasa's *Kumarasambhavam* describes how Parvati, after witnessing Kamadeva being burnt, spurned by Shiva, curses her beauty wholeheartedly. Every detail in this description is realistic, and the idea that the fruit of beauty is the happiness of the beloved is also encapsulated. However, this is poetry, not a logical sentence. Parvati is preparing her mind for the demanding penance to win Shiva's love. In Shiva's absence, her penance must be more focused than in his presence. The untimely spring, the celebration in the forest, Parvati's unique dressing, Kama's incarnation, sudden burning down of Kamadeva and Rati's lamentation are events contributing to Parvati's current state of mind. Her own beauty is just one among these reasons. This narrative, crafted by the gods, typically results in the union of lovers. However, what Parvati's mind was set on remained unfulfilled. Kalidasa blends these factual details to convey that cause did not lead to action. Their purpose is also the production of Rasa.

'Priyaeshu saubhagyaphala hi charuta,' or 'the fruit of beauty is the affection of the beloved.' This seems to be an idea generated through a sceptical inquiry. The relationship of this sentence is logical, yet the meaning of 'true beauty is the affection of the beloved' resonates here. The love and beauty of the beloved strengthen the union of these elements with the compound 'Saubhagyaphala'. For that, Parvati curses her beauty and prepares herself to do penance to win her lover. Commonly, in the business of persuasion the gap between attempts and accomplishments is clear. Parvati's next endeavour is to bridge this gap. The climate, orchestrated by the gods, during the untimely spring were conducive to the usual romantic endeavours. However, when it leads to the burning down of Kamadeva, Parvati is compelled to seek the ultimate truth. The multilayered meanings embedded in Kalidasa's sentence transform it into poetry. This sentence operates with technical precision to convey its intended meaning. Particularly noteworthy is the appropriateness of the term 'manobhava' (mental state) to refer to the burning of Kamadeva witnessed first-hand by Parvati. Parvati's heartbreak and the burning of Kamadeva are parallel events—one external and visible—the other internal, and both caused by Shiva. The careful organization of these elements in Kavya is evident, demonstrating a meticulous approach akin to logic.

Kalidasa's cited verse is undeniably poetry. Not all poetry concludes within a single sentence; even a brief poem comprises several sentences. Just as the words collaborate to convey a singular meaning in a sentence, the multiple sentences in a poem work collectively to convey the poem's essence. Vishwanath, recognizing this, provides an example of an intriguing sentence in the form of a one-sentence verse and introduces the formula 'Vakyocchayo Mahavakyam'. He explicitly states that epics like the Ramayana and *Raghuvamsa* serve as examples of Mahavakya or epic sentence, just as a verse exemplifies a sentence. Hence, Vishwanath's theory proves to be comprehensive and internally consistent. It logically follows that the relational formulas governing words in a sentence, such as aptitude and aspiration, are also present among the sentences in epic poetry.

It is a historical fact that the theory of rasa has its origins in drama. It originated in the texts of drama, within the multifaceted performances of actors, in fine arts like music and dance, and ultimately in the empathetic responses of the receptive audience. The transition of rasa from drama to poetry is a captivating historical journey. It is significant that in arriving at the formula that rasa is self-evident like knowledge, the conclusion arrived at is that knowledge and rasa are on equal footing. Vishwanatha, in his commentary on the rasa Sutra, cites a verse from Bhartrhari, emphasizing how characters like Kamsa, established through words, become perceptible to the intellect of the audience and serve as instruments for the production of rasa as the Vibhavas in poetry. In this process, both intellect and experience are equally engaged. Often, these connections to lived experiences are not explicitly recognized; they are discernible only to the intellect. The act of experiencing is so immersive that even the mind becomes entwined in it during the experience. All the details of the experience become apparent in memory only after the action of that Bhava concludes. This reaction is natural in real life, as a deeply saddened person typically cannot reflect on their sorrow in the moment. The immediacy of experience will have cooled down by the time thinking begins afterwards. This is called 'satvodreaka' by Vishwanath. Bhartrhari suggests that this can happen also through the language of poetry. This seems to be the most important idea in the theory of rasa. In this context, Bharata's assertion about rasa holds true: 'Na hi rasadrte kaschidartham pravartate'—'poetry has no other purpose except the production of rasa.' Against this backdrop, Vishwanath's words, 'Vakyam rasatmakam kavyam' ('a sentence that has rasa in it is poetry'), gain even more profound meaning. The notion that this encapsulates the essence of understanding poetry comes to mind.

Let me summarize the ongoing discussion. Typically, language serves the purpose of conveying meaning, and meaning is intricately tied to the objects of the world. In other words, language imparts significance to the world, and this imbued meaning also renders language dynamic. The word, in this context, serves as a visible trace of linguistic activity. Philosophy and jurisprudence have one perspective on sentences, while poetry offers another. In everyday affairs, the reality of the world aligns with the meaning conveyed through sentences. In philosophy and legal doctrines, the logic of the sentence corresponds to its meaning, yet in both realms, language remains within the confines of meaning. Poetry, too, is a measure of its own meaning, but the language of poetry goes beyond merely conveying meaning; it responds to it. In the realm of poetry, words and meanings are interwoven, with one existing because of the other. Poetry, uniquely, allows for the possibility of words attaining a status beyond, yet there exists a condition that transcends words—the ineffable. Some poets venture into this uncharted territory, though the depth and breadth of the region of silence may elude complete comprehension through poetry. The dialogue between Allama and Muktayakka in *Shunya Sampadane* may be recalled here: 'In the devotee's mobility there is immobility, in speech there is silence.' Such a formula requires no further comment. For devotees, their experience is the standard to comply with; it is a state where the movement is the goal and the two are inseparable. Our world is fragmented into the void, the temples, the eyes and more; attempting to momentarily unite these facets through poetry seems a worthwhile endeavour. The role of the Rasika (implied reader) is to relish the poetry that comes to life and discern its form and characteristics. The poet, in turn, must articulate how poetry is conceived in the poet's mind. Post production, a critic can guide others on how to enjoy a poem, elucidate the benefits of such enjoyment, and evaluate the worth of the work. Critics have expounded on the nature of poetry in various ways, with one perspective emphasizing that poetry is essentially a sentence affording rasa. Language, as the medium of poetry, stands apart from other artistic mediums, where colour and tone may lack inherent meaning. Thus, the definition of poetry remains incomplete without acknowledging the unique capabilities of language.

V

We reserve a special place for Alankara (figures of speech) in poetry, which permeates three-fourths of our poetics. Aestheticians diligently categorize these Alankaras, aiming for their accurate interpretation. However, in the contemporary era, the significance of the Alankaras has diminished considerably. What captivates our admiration now is the simplicity of language and the unembellished style. While there might be a certain joy in unravelling the specifics of a figure of speech, like solving a riddle, such knowledge is not highly valued in present times. We firmly believe that recognizing Alankara does not constitute comprehensive criticism. This perception is primarily attributed to the entrenched habits of traditional scholars. If Mammata asserts that genuine poetry can be rich even in its unadorned form, we embrace this modern perspective with enthusiasm.

Nevertheless, it is not that Alankara are entirely devoid of utility. Not only do basic figures of speech such as simile, metaphor, paradox and allegory play a crucial role, but also more nuanced ones like *apahnuti* (negation), *sahokti* (twinning), *sandeha* (doubt), *vyajasutti* (criticism in the form of praise), etc., prove to be beneficial. When poetry unfolds in a straightforward and logical manner like prose, alankaras step in to redirect it towards evoking rasa. Primarily, the function of Alankara is to guide the connoisseur in experiencing the relevant subject matter through the use of seemingly irrelevant elements. For illustrative purposes, one can refer to a verse in *Kumarasambhavam*:

Harastu kinchit parilupta dhairyah
Chandrodayrarambha iwamburashih
Umamukhe bimbaphaladharoshthe
Vyaparayamasa vilochanani

Parvati, adorned with spring flowers, approaches
and seats herself before Shiva, worshipping his
feet with flowers. Shiva, too, experiences a momentary loss of
composure, fixing his gaze on Parvati's lips,
which glow red like a gourd.

While the metaphor comparing Parvati's lips to a red gourd
suggests a general sense of beauty, it lacks the depth to convey
more profound emotions, serving merely as an element of
Parvati's adornment. In contrast, the simile 'chandrambudhi
iwamburashih' possesses significant potency. The subtle shift in
Shiva's state of mind, where his mental control is slightly loosened,
is not immediately apparent. Given Shiva's role as the controller
of the system of nature, even a slight relaxation might disrupt the
entire system. The question arises: does the allure of Parvati's lips
possess the power to induce this loosening? The image of the sea
rising with the moonrise effectively captures this unique situation.
While the sea rising with the moonrise is a regular occurrence,
the analogy between the moon's soft influence on the ocean's
control and Parvati's beauty affecting Shiva's penance is poignant.
Above all, Shiva and Parvati's love affair transcends the ordinary,
leaping into the realm of the extraordinary. From the poem's
perspective, the crucial element is the portrayal of Shiva's mental
state. The moonrise and the seas, seemingly irrelevant, shed light
on the essential subject matter, making it a tangible experience.
Here, the distinction between the relevant and the irrelevant is
relative, determined by the poetic context. The combination of
both elements, the relevant and the seemingly irrelevant, serves to
deepen and enrich the poem's meaning.

Poetry, through its utilization of both the relevant and the seemingly irrelevant, exploits the common ground between the two. While this assertion is self-evident, deciphering the purpose behind this quest for commonality is no straightforward task. The nature of poetry inherently drives it to seek and construct analogies, a path it follows to make sense of human experience. The verse 'Tvam Jivitam Tvamasi Me Hridayandvidiyam; Tvam Kaumudi Nayanayoramritham Tvamange' from the drama *Uttararamacharita* vividly illustrates Rama's profound admiration for Sita. Rama's comparisons, such as describing Sita as 'you are my life, my second heart, the moon of my eyes, and the stream of nectar in my body', serve to deepen our understanding of Sita and his love for her. Analogies, like these, are inexhaustible, and poetry fulfils its purpose of evoking rasa through numerous such comparisons. It is worth noting that analogical relations are not confined to figures of speech alone; there are also meaning-oriented figures known as Artha-alankaras. Additionally, word-oriented figures such as rhyme and pun contribute to building analogies. Even when the lines of a poem resemble each other, a regular rhyme scheme aids in constructing analogies.

One particular figure, 'Arthantarnyasa', justifies the special from the general, the general from the special, the cause from the action and the action from the cause. Nagachandra's line 'abdiumorme kalavashadim maryadayam dantade?' ('doesn't the ocean too, if time ordains, transgress the boundaries?') exemplifies this figure, juxtaposing Ravana's extraordinary reaction to Sita's beauty with the common occurrence of seasonal high tides in the sea. This technique, favoured by poets like Kalidasa and Nagachandra, serves as a means to understand the facts of life.

While the name 'Arthantarnyasa' provokes further contemplation, a comprehensive explanation about its origin remains elusive. How can it be termed synecdoche (*arthantara*) when it leaps from the general to the specific? How does one ascribe an alternative layer of meaning to the ordinary interpretation of

a sentence? Upon contemplation, it appears that the underlying
purpose of all Alankara is synecdoche (*arthantaranyasa*). Through
these Alankaras, the exploration of a meaning distinctively tailored
for poetry takes place, surpassing the common understanding. In
poetry, the ordinary sense must transcend into the extraordinary
realm, directing the focus exclusively towards the creation of rasa.
This objective can be achieved through the unique beauty of
allusion, the intensity of hyperbole, or even through contradiction.
For instance:

> *Soumitre nanu sevyatham tarutalam chandanshujurmbhate*
> *Chandanshornishi ka katha raghupate chandrasyamunmeelati*
> *Vatsaitad viditam katham nu bhavata dhatte shurangam yatah*
> *Kvasi preyasi ha kuranganayane chandranane Janaki*

Bewildered by Sita's absence, Rama confuses the moon with
bright sunshine, instructing Lakshmana to seek shade under the
tree. Startled, Lakshmana says that there is moonlight and no
sunshine. In response,
Rama challenges him, questioning how he identified it as the
moon. Pointing out the mark on the moon, Lakshmana says, by
the deer mark on the moon. This reminds Rama of Sita's eyes
which are like those of the deer and he begins to lament.

In a sense, it is an artificial verse—the lovelorn mistaking moonlight
to be sunshine, being unable to distinguish sun from moon at
night, the mark of deer on the moon evoking memories of Sita's
eyes are all poeticisms that the poet weaves into an artificial world.
Here, the desire and heartache of the lovelorn converge to create
a personal world. In such a world it is no wonder if the moon's
coolness is mistaken as the sun's heat. This kind of poeticism has
a long tradition. As Dushyanta had once expressed, 'tava kusuma
sharatvam sheetarashmitva mindordvayamida mayathartham

shriyate madvidhesu.' In the realm of aesthetics, such a statement is known as 'asadakhyati', implying the assertion of something that isn't present. Its purpose is to convert a real scenario into an unreal one, conducive to the creation of rasa. If the moon's coolness turns into heat—if this magical transformation succeeds—then the world starts functioning by its own rules. Rama's absence in this verse holds the power to reshape the world. Feelings of Shringara, Viraha, Vipralambha (in both senses), delusion and more, emerge in succession. In the final line, when Lakshmana points out the deer's mark on the moon's surface, this reality pierces through Rama's illusion, bringing him back to a reality that is more poignant than the illusion itself.

It was only natural for memories of the deer-eyed Sita to flood into Rama's thoughts, when Lakshmana remarks about the deer-like mark on the moon. The recollection may have extended to the golden deer incident. However, the significance that stands out with the word 'Kuranga' (deer) is the enchantment of language. In this context, it is not the substance of meaning but the inherent value accompanying the sound that takes precedence. The term 'Kuranga' personifies the animal it represents, and the word thereafter revolves around that attached meaning. Liberation from the entwining of meaning and sound seems unattainable. Upon each repetition of the word, the associated meaning resurfaces, shaping the sentence that employs it. With the utterance of 'Kuranga', the remembrance of Sita, known for her Kuranga eyes, becomes an inevitable part of Rama's thoughts. What is noteworthy here is that the poetic experience emerges from within the language. In the context of this verse, this aspect also reflects the state of bewilderment Rama is in. Initially mistaking the moon for the sun, Rama finds himself enduring suffering in the moonlight, for that feels like the sun. This implies Rama is deceived. Similarly, he is deceived by the sound of 'Kuranga', connecting this deception with Ravana's treachery and the kidnapping of Sita. All these relate to the sensitive description in poetry. However, it is intriguing that this sensation arises and evolves from the mere sound of 'Kuranga'. Language not only triggers the emotion of the object, but the emotion takes a more active role than the object and these contribute to the production of rasa in poetry. Rama's separation becomes the singular essence of actual experience in this context, and this essence, propelled by language, is pivotal in the creation of rasa, giving rise to multiple sentiments. In this process, Alankara, like quirks of language, plays a vital role. This is how poetry transforms into an aesthetic sentence.

In the above quoted verse, various figures of speech such as doubt, illusion, response and recollection are evident. Identifying figures of speech in a poem is not a challenging task, but understanding how these figures are employed and the impact they have on poetry is crucial. One significant function of figures of speech is to aid in the development of poetry's technique, as demonstrated to some extent in the analysis of the verse depicting Rama's separation. Another meaningful Alankara from this perspective is the pun, considered a verbal analogy rather than related to meaning. For instance, Bana describes the leader of hunters as 'Krishnopi Asudarshana'. The simple meaning of this phrase is that the hunter was dark and unattractive. But the word 'Krishna' carries dual meanings of dark colour and Lord Krishna. Despite the hunter being Krishna—dark—he doesn't possess 'Sudarshan' (Krishna's iconic weapon as also handsome appearance). In this instance, Bana employs a linguistic play with two words, creating a clever manoeuvre. The contribution of such artistry to poetry is the enhancement of beauty. It is noteworthy to emphasize that this linguistic finesse is achievable even if overlooked in the business of language, emphasizing the creative potential inherent in language's ability to generate meaning.

Shree madhavana manoharada soundryamam
Ramana janakana kamaneeya lavanyamam
Ramachandrana raamaneeyakada roopamam
Taaltogeda sukumaarara.
Komalaangada sobaganabhivarnisuvarunte
Bhoomiyol chaluvige vasatanam madananam
Somanam padiyidal punaruktamappudane
Kushalavar kannesedaru.

Lakshmisha vividly describes the beauty of Lava and Kusha, born in Valmiki's ashram. The essence here is that Lava and Kusha radiate the beauty of Vasantha, Madana and Chandra. Yet, they are also the offspring of Ramachandra. How did the beauty of Vasantha become associated with Ramachandra? The answer lies in Rama's names: Vasantha is an alternative name for Vishnu or 'Madhava'. In one avatar, Rama is the father of Kama. Additionally, the moon is concealed within the name Ramachandra. Hence, it is not surprising that this beauty finds expression in Lava and Kusha also. This showcases how the language of poetry creates meaning. Both the verbal meaning and connotation can combine to generate various meanings, adding new layers to the language. Implied meaning is also a unique feature of language conveyed solely at the poetic level. For instance, in A.K. Ramanujan's poem, 'I came home in burning anger/the red champak tree was in full bloom,' we witness the richness of meaning these lines create. Only in the realm of language does the body burn with anger, and the flower becomes glowing coal. Thus, poetry emerges from the interplay of objects, their similarities and actual opposition, confronting reality as a challenge in the poetic experience.

The preceding discussion constitutes a review of poetics rather than the formulation of independent poetics. This endeavour seeks to breathe new life into age-old poetic formulas.

The development of poetry in any culture has been intricately linked to the prevailing intellectual order. The current perplexity stems not only from our use of Western poetics but also because we use it by divorcing it from its intellectual context. Western rationalism, at its core, is fundamentally dualistic. Consequently, Western criticism exhibits an ambivalent pattern, entangled in various dichotomies such as substance and form, meaning and sound, inspiration and artistry, classicism and modernity. We, too, have earnestly delved into these dualities without a thorough understanding of the historical rationalism underpinning them. Moreover, we have not scrutinized the extent to which a new rationality and philosophy have taken root within us. In light of these considerations, an attempt has been made here to rejuvenate the principles of ancient poetics in this discourse.

The success of this endeavour raises a pertinent question, and there are compelling reasons behind this inquiry. As mentioned earlier, the advent of the British ushered in a new awareness of history among us. Undoubtedly, Western influence played a pivotal role in shaping our historical consciousness. The impact of Muslim culture was also profound, leaving its mark on our customs, attire, literature and various other fine arts. This influence was so pervasive that even our deities appeared adorned in Muslim attire in the Rajput style of painting. In moments of uncertainty regarding the lexical and grammatical intricacies of Arabic and Persian, Muslim scholars sought the guidance of Nagar Brahmins from Gujarat. While this assertion might seem exaggerated, it holds merit, grounded in a significant rationale. Despite the influence of Muslim culture, it did not create intellectual confusion among us. However, the new historical consciousness instilled by English education not only heightened our awareness of being Indian but also reshaped the trajectory of our rationality.

There is no need to delve specifically into the advantages bestowed upon us by a sense of history. However, one of the most profound transformations brought about by historiography lies in the delineation of the present from the past. The continuous streams of time, once seamlessly intertwined, now stand divided, separated by embankments. While it could be argued that such a temporal division existed in the past by pointing to the Sanskrit words denoting past, present and future, the past was not a burden to a consciousness that embraced the interconnections and experiences across lifetimes. Now, such a situation doesn't exist. History, once recognized as such, transforms from an object of lived experience to a subject of scholarly study. The temporal awareness found in the ancient poets has become truth today. After shaping history through scholarship, we often fail to heed its words. After sifting through the historical material into fact, myth and legend, what survives must persist into the present. Even when history assumes the form of science or knowledge, its influence follows its own course. The numerous communal conflicts occurring throughout the nation are inspired by this historical language.

It is only natural for the past to weigh heavily on those who uphold the ideals of progress. However, gaining insight into the origin of the concept of progress, rooted in the eighteenth-century industrial revolution, can help alleviate our concerns. Progress is undeniably crucial for entrepreneurial success, but embracing it as an overarching life principle poses potential dangers. Adhering to this principle could lead to the belief that we have reached the pinnacle of evolution in this century. Taken to an extreme, such a perspective might elevate contemporary writers above literary giants like Kalidasa and Shakespeare. While these viewpoints are commonly held, they create a dichotomy in the cultural atmosphere. One path involves aligning with the current of progress, while the other staunchly upholds the belief that what is old is not necessarily outdated. The discussions surrounding the old and the new are inherently emotional, same as attempting to reverse the hands of a clock. A clock, however, is not a timeless monument but a measure of time's passage. Hence, the inevitability of being a trailblazer is emphasized by the dictum, 'Nanya Pantha Vidyate Ayanaya' ('no other path is available'), suggesting that there is no other path for the one seeking a historical trajectory.

A Critical Survey of Pre-Modern Kannada Literature

This essay serves as a preface to Kurtkoti's collection of essays titled Kannada Sahitya Sangati *(A Companion to Kannada Literature), published in 1995. The essays within this book offer critical introductions to major Kannada works, beginning with the earliest extant Kannada document, the* Halmidi Inscription, *and spanning several centuries up to the late nineteenth century. The 'Preface', translated here, provides a framework for the study of the various stages of Kannada literature. In presenting a historical survey, Kurtkoti also examines the implications of the transition from oral to written culture. He delivers a critical history of ancient Kannada literature, reflecting on various issues of evolution, significance, contexts and literary practices. This essay provides readers with highlights of Kannada literary history from the first millennium to the seventeenth century. In doing so, Kurtkoti offers insightful commentary on diverse issues of literary craft, evolving frameworks of literary composition, the philosophical and political resonances of literary texts, and their contexts. He explores and extends traditional figures of speech, and through comparisons and analysis, facilitates an understanding of the significance of the Kannada poetic tradition. Kurtkoti not only introduces readers to the canonical works of Kannada literature from the pre-modern era, spanning from the first extant Kannada text,* Kavirajamarga, *to the seventeenth-century Kannada writer* Lakshmisha, *but also to the genres, poetic forms and shifts in sensibility. He sets out to examine what constitutes canonical literary meaning and addresses it by examining the evolution of genres, forms, shifts in the deployment of words and meanings,*

the changing nature of the use of figures of speech, and transformations in
religious and social vision.

1

The earliest extant text in Kannada is Nripatunga's *Kavirajamarga*
(ninth century). Since this is a text about poetics, it can be
assumed that there were poetic compositions in Kannada before
this. Inscriptions date back to the fifth century, indicating that
writing in Kannada must have commenced around 1500 years
ago. For people with poetic sensibility to have existed during the
reign of Nripatunga, even without much formal study in the field,
('Kuritodadeyum kavya prayoga parinatamatigal') there must have
been a substantial body of folk poetry. It is likely that the Jain
poets played a significant role in transitioning poetry into the
written form.

Ear is crucial in the oral tradition because hearing is important.
Similarly, in the tradition of writing, eye is important as reading
is integral to it. Listening also holds importance in the ancient
Vedic tradition, where the Vedas are alternately referred to as
Shruti, meaning 'that which is heard'. However, it is essential to
acknowledge the significant difference between what is heard
and what is seen. The listener relies on another person, primarily
the guru. When the guru's speech becomes a mantra, its secrecy
becomes paramount. The power of a mantra lies in its secrecy.
Mantra represents a form of oral communication, proverbs,
riddles, curses and poetry manifest as other forms of speech. The
speaker's presence is necessary in oral communication. If poetry
is purely an oral expression, it becomes an art intertwined with
dance and music, finding its sanctuary in the human body.

The nature of writing is public, liberated from the human body
and attaining independence. A person reading a piece of writing
does not rely on that piece of writing. Needless to say, seeing

is a more independent act than hearing, posing a challenge in interpreting something expressed in language. If in speech, meaning hinges on the speaker's intent and perception, understanding writing necessitates adherence to established grammatical rules. While mantra embodies pure speech, inscriptions represent a pure form of writing—one religious, the other political. Spoken words end soon after they are uttered; writing is *akshara* (literally an alphabet, but also immortal). However, while spoken words are lively, writing lacks that dynamism. In our country, religion and politics have remained distinct for millennia, rendering the meaning of writing more precise than speech. A spoken word, lacking specificity, can encompass multiple meanings, unlike the specificity of meaning in writing where a word holds only one meaning. Though a word may have several meanings, they are specific and limited. An example is the famous saying 'Modakaistadayamam'. In a water sport encounter, a Sanskrit-educated princess addresses her uneducated lover: 'Ma udakai Tadaya Maam' ('don't hit me with water'). Misinterpreting the statement, the lover rushed to fetch 'modaka' (a momo or dumpling). When his error was revealed, he, embarrassed, committed to studying grammar. Regardless of the moral of this tale, the educated (abhijata) mind embraces a singular meaning. To the uneducated mind, word changes can yield myriad meanings. However, Abhijata Sahitya (literature produced by the literate population as against folk literature) lacks the disposition to accept the unexpected and unintended meanings. The goal of this kind of literature is the harmony between words and meanings, anticipating phenomena such as puns and other figures of speech. Abhijata Sahitya is produced keeping in mind a refined society and its gratification. A poet's imagination is creative, while the Rasika or the intended reader's imagination is receptive. This implies that both possess equal talent, meaning that no matter how exceptional Abhijata Kavya is, it cannot surpass these dual capacities. When such a culture becomes more prevalent, poetry takes on a more

secular nature. It appears that this is where the Abhijata poetic
tradition experiences impoverishment, aiming for the exploration
of imagination. Once imagination is explored, the desire to
transcend it no longer drives the language. Language is a human-
made construct, but when illuminated by the light of Shabda
Brahman (the Scriptures), it must possess the strength to endure.

The reason for discussing Abhijata literature at length is that
initially, Kannada poets looked to Sanskrit Abhijata literature as
their model. In the Badami inscription (dated to 700 ce), Ravi
Kirti asserts superiority over Kalidasa, while for the imaginative
powers of Pampa, Ranna and Ponna, Kalidasa is a challenge.
Sanskrit poets in the courts of Karnataka kings were engaged
in producing Champu Kavya. The sensibility of Kannada poets
was a bilingual one, and they had to view themselves through the
mirror of *Kavyadarsha* by Dandi, a southerner.

Perhaps the significance of *Kavirajamarga* lies in addressing
this issue. The phrase 'Naduvana Nade Nade Kannada Thirul'
('the region in the middle is the core land of Kannada') is
discovered in the translation of Dandi's *Kavyadarsha*, known as
Kavirajamarga. This marks the first identification of Kannada noun
forms, presenting the identity of the Kannada race for the first
time. This recognition led to the separation of Kannada from
other languages and, consequently, to the acknowledgment of
Kannada's oral traditions and efforts to establish a Marga tradition
(formally codified Sanskritic compositional style as against Desi,
the regional folk style) for Kannada. It remains uncertain if
Kannada boasted great works comparable to Sanskrit in the past,
but the opportunity for such masterpieces had to be provided.
Ancient Kannada (the three stages in the evolution of Kannada
that historians of Kannada language identify are: *palagannada* or
Ancient Kannada, roughly belonging to the period before the
sixth century; *halagannada* or Old Kannada, between the sixth and
late nineteenth centuries; and *hosagannada* or New Kannada after
late nineteenth and early twentieth centuries) had already lost its

communicative function, prompting the composition of literary works in Old Kannada. However, during that era, Karnataka did not represent a nation in the modern sense. The statement in *Kavirajamarga*, 'adarol bhavisida janapadam vasudhavalaya vileenavishada vishaya vishesham' ('the race in this region speak Kannada and is special in the whole world' [*Kavirajamarga*, 1:36]) indicate that by its time Kannada was not only a people or a state but an empire. By the time of Nripatunga's father, Govinda III, Karnataka had extended beyond (the present-day) Maharashtra and Gujarat, bringing both glory and the accompanying anxieties and complexities of the empire.

Nripatunga, a Vaishnava king, likely had Sri Vijaya in his court, who must have been a Jain. The prospect of uniting Kannada and Sanskrit implies the possibility of fostering amity between Jain and Vedic religions. As expressed in the verse, 'Kasavaramembudu nere sairisalarpode paravicharamumam dharmamumam' ('Gold is nothing but being tolerant to others' ideas and other religions' [*Kavirajamarga*, 3:126]), there are alternative ideas in other religions; one who can tolerate these ideas attains greatness. This verse, not a translation of Dandi's original verse, offers an example of Udatta Alankara. Inserting such pivotal verses in a translation is significant, even if not everyone recognizes them as Dandi's ideas. It is noteworthy that Dandi provides a platform for Sri Vijaya's verses. For the accommodation of Dandi's ideas in Kannada, there must also be tolerance for Kannada ideas by Dandi. Not only should the translation's mirror reflect the philosophy of poetry (Kavyadarsana), but also the ideals of poetry should reflect the image of Sri Vijaya. This sentiment is echoed by Durgasimha, who came later, affirming, 'Sri Vijaya's *Kavimargam* is a mirror and a lamp for the poets.' While the mirror reflects one's face, the lamp illuminates the path ahead.

Nripatunga's empire demanded sophistication as an empire requires Abhijata style. So, either Kannada must be developed as the Abhijata language or one must resort to Sanskrit, a language renowned for its refinement. Pampa's portrayal of Draupadi's Swayamvara evokes comparisons with the Swayamvara of Indumati in Kalidasa's *Raghuvamsa*, while Nagachandra's Rama, after the abduction of Sita, echoes Kalidasa's Pururava in his despairing cry, 'Talire Tavareye Madali Kulame' ('Deer, lotus, swarms of bees . . . ') All these elements serve to satiate the thirst for sophistication. Pampa turns to Kalidasa when sophistication is needed; yet in the episode of Shisupalavadha, when Shisupala rebukes Krishna, Kannada becomes inevitable, as the Sanskrit words of abuse pale in comparison to their Kannada counterparts.

The *Kavirajamarga* begins with a salutary verse, a feature absent in Sanskrit discursive texts. In the commencement of *Kavyadarsha*, a hymn to Saraswati is present, a practice adopted later in Sanskrit. Kannada texts invariably include hymns, and Dandi's translation of the Saraswati hymn stands as the third verse in the *Kavirajamarga*. In the preceding two verses, Nripatunga is alternately praised: 'Sri talturadol kaustubha/Jatadyuti balasi kandapatadantire/ sampreetiyinavananagalal' ('Vishnu's chest upon which a gem's radiance falls like light on a stage, from which Lakshmi never departs' [*Kavirajamarga*, 1:1]). Nripatunga is lauded under the guise of praising Vishnu, suggesting that he harbours Lakshmi in his bosom like Vishnu. The verse explicitly aims to praise the king by emphasizing that all the qualities of Vishnu reside in him. But how was such a poetic boldness possible?

In Sanskrit texts, when hymns are present, they are distinctly praises of deities. For instance, the first verse of Kalidasa's *Raghuvamsa* is Sivastuti, but there is no such hymn in his *Kumarasambhavam*, indicating the absence of a consistent rule in Sanskrit. Such a rule is exclusive to drama, where hymns appear as part of the prologue, and there too the hymns are dedicated to the deities.

The hymn in *Kavirajamarga* incorporates praise of Nripatunga, the king, forming a composite image. The two hymns unite to depict a composite image comprising king and god. Poetically, this relationship can be seen as analogous, suggesting that the king's personality is shaped by the glory of Vishnu. How is Lakshmi transferred from Vishnu's chest to the king's chest? If we interpret 'Sri' to refer to wealth and glory, it metaphorically indicates the presence of 'Sri' in the king. In a similar vein, the relationships of the remaining organs should be identified.

But is this merely a likeness? Comparing humans to deities is not uncommon, yet there is more to this image than likeness. Vishnu is the deity of Kshatriyas and war, and among his glories are Earth-saving prowess and his association with Lakshmi. Above all, Vishnu bears the responsibility for the salvation and welfare of the Earth—a concept accepted by the Vedic religion. Similar comparisons exist in the Sanskrit Mahabharata, though they remain analogical relationships. Even when we say 'a hero like Vishnu' and 'an archer like Shiva', they are different. A king cannot truly be Vishnu, even if the dictum goes 'Navishnuh Prithivi Pati' ('Vishnu is the King of the Land'). However, by the time of Nripatunga, not only had the glory of the emperor ruling a vast empire increased, but Jainism was also robust in the state. It is not surprising that the king serves as the god for Jains who do not acknowledge the existence of god.

If the king is deified in a single verse, its impact may not be far-reaching, as a change in meaning can limit its influence. The composite image implies an ideological shift, even surpassing the impact of the Vedic statement 'Matrudevo Bhava' ('the mother should be revered as god'). While the religious directive to treat mothers, fathers, guests and teachers as gods governs our social conduct, it draws distinctions between elders and the young, regulating the extent of this discrimination. The statement 'Matrudevo Bhava' lacks embellishment and its clarity becomes a limitation. In contrast, the hymn of *Kavirajamarga* presents different issues. The poem's ornamentation requires the reader to grasp its meaning by navigating through the embellishments. 'Matrudevo Bhava' is a straightforward statement; it is the advice given by the guru to his disciple. The effect of this instruction depends on the personality of the guru. Whereas the verse in *Kavirajamarga*, being a product of writing, is a text—as with any text, it has to be read and understood. It stands as a linguistic creation, and the impact of the statement can potentially alter the behaviour of a nation or its people. For an oral statement to be effective, human-to-human relationships must be alive, relationships between elders and the youth should be cordial. Moreover, there should be an organic relationship between humans and animals, with honesty found in nature mirrored in human conduct. Blood, heredity and friendship should prevail, fostering an environment where word of mouth can truly be impactful.

However, such a scenario cannot be expected in the political environment of an empire, as illustrated by examples in Kautilya's *Arthashastra*. The value of word of mouth diminishes due to the risk that a truthful tongue might also utter falsehood. In such circumstances, written communication becomes the pledge of truth. Writing, unlike speech, is not an immediate expression but a symbol of expression. Even if the symbol's meaning is not instantly clear, it is not inherently false—symbolism is inherent to writing. While oral communication relies on word, writing relies on symbols. If spoken words produce sound, written words remain silent. The words that produce sound indicate a lively existence. The silent letters in writing stand as monuments to this sound. In the absence of a speaker, these letters transform into words and sentences. The social implications of this distinction warrant deep consideration. Speaking, primarily serves communication, while writing's core purpose is to preserve spoken words. However, beyond these primary goals, secondary objectives emerge. Speaking is a responsible human act, and while this doesn't imply writing is irresponsible, it inherently lacks responsibility. Nevertheless, it can function as a norm—a quality appreciated in an empire because it endures without human presence, persists in absence and even outlasts death.

Inscriptions of Emperor Ashoka are also discovered in Karnataka. What is the connection between the inscriptions at Koppala or Maski and the deceased Ashoka? Pampa explores this connection. When emperor Bharata sets out to inscribe his triumphs on Mount Vijayadhra, he had to erase the inscriptions of preceding emperors using a diamond rod. The lifespan of a statute exceeds that of a king, yet even that is transitory—this is what Pampa wants to indicate. This ephemeral nature aligns with the transcendental truth perceived by Pampa, who observes the clash between this transcendence and culture. The truth of inscriptions is grounded in history, and Pampa's poetry is in pursuit of truth within this dualistic realm.

2

Mythology is an inheritance for Kannada literature. Episodes from the Ramayana and Mahabharata appear repeatedly. Once these holy narratives capture the imagination, escape becomes elusive. The Jain poets, however, discern no Jain scriptural significance in these tales. Pampa, from the tenth century, labels the mythological poems as 'worldly': 'Belaguvenalli Laukikamanilli Jinagamam!' ('I will illuminate the worldly with the light of the Jain scriptures' [*Adipurana*, 4:60]). Vrishabhanath's history too is a narrative; it is a story beyond history. This narrative is a convergence of meaning. The realm of meaning is available to contemplation. By adhering to the principles of this realm and putting them into practice leads to liberation from the cycle of births—an article of faith. Arikesari (not being a character from the Jain scripture) has no place here. His world belongs to the contemporary history, and he has a place within the secular tale of the Mahabharata. Arjuna and Arikesari meld into a singular persona. In contrast, the personas of Bharata and Bahubali remain untainted, their destinies rooted in the Agamas (Jain scriptures). Arjuna's persona serves as the vehicle of a metaphor, while Arikesari its tenor.

From a poetic standpoint, the relationship between tenor and vehicle is well-established. The role of a simile is to highlight similarities between disparate entities. Our aestheticians, keenly observing the subtle nuances in the realm of comparisons, have categorized various types of comparisons. However, when Arjuna's persona transforms into a vehicle for Arikesari, the realm of meaning opened by this metaphor is vast. Regardless of the status of vehicle in the external world, tenor lacks its independence. A vehicle serves as a yardstick. If Arjuna assumes the role of a vehicle, Arikesari becomes the tenor. Pampa's poetic approach is so nuanced that it melds the vehicle into the tenor. On the surface, what is apparent is the flourish of the vehicle, as in Arjuna's vision of 'Dugdabdhidavala shayyataladol malagida Mukundanam' ('Krishna reclining upon the bed of an ocean of milk' [*Adipurana*, 9:10]). In this instance, the 'ocean of milk' serves as a vehicle for Pampa; yet for the readers, it embodies a truth grounded in faith.

The truth of faith is an experiential reality, grounded in both experience and comprehension. Our ancient poets adeptly employ poetry as a potent tool to convey the understanding derived from these experiences. Poetry, in this context, holds the transformative power to convert understanding into lived experience. In that era, no one had any doubts about the truth of the mythological 'ocean of milk' and the authenticity of the Mahabharata. While Pampa acknowledges the Mahabharata's truth on a worldly plane, his transcendent truth lies in Jain mythology: 'Sanskriti Natakamam Amari Toridal Parividiyam' ('The celestial woman revealed the art of dance through her dance from beginning to end' [*Adipurana*, 9:45]). Much like Purudeva, Pampa too marvels at the truth revealed through Neelanjane's dance. Although Purudeva's perspective may differ from Pampa's, both share a sense of astonishment when observing the worldly truth of the Mahabharata. Pampa likely perceived the conflict between the

Kauravas and the Pandavas mirrored in the struggle between Bharata and Bahubali. The transcendental image appears to him as a worldly simile. Similarly, within the worldly simile, one can catch a glimpse of the transcendental image.

It is a common belief that Pampa translated Vyasa's Sanskrit Mahabharata into Kannada. But translation was not much in vogue during that period. What does it mean to say that all Jain poets wrote agamic (Jain scriptural) and secular poetry? Vyasa's Mahabharata and Valmiki's Ramayana, while containing historical and mythological elements, represent distinct categories. Historical facts pertain to events in the world, linking the meaning of history to this world. The relationship between the reader and the texts is well defined, and the meanings they elicit are experiential. However, the meanings of mythology are inherent to them. The significance of the term 'milky ocean' is confined to its mythological context; its meaning doesn't extend beyond the word itself. If the Mahabharata encompasses both historical and mythological dimensions, it becomes a synthesis of both meanings. A mythical meaning is deeply embedded in the collective psyche of the people.

Pampa grasped a composite image intertwining history and mythology—a symbol compounded of both understanding and experience. However, Pampa translated this intricate image, endowing it with the potency of language. Undoubtedly, the original image came alive with this linguistic energy, yet its meaning underwent a transformation. 'Idu Mahabharatakkadi yaytabjadalakshi kela samanyame bageye bhavatkesha pasha prapancham' ('Listen, Draupadi, whose eyes resemble the breadth of a lotus, that your tresses have engendered Mahabharata is no common matter' [*Vikramarjunavijaya*,12:156]). This is how Pampa's Bhima could depict Draupadi's tresses, a description unavailable to Vyasa's Bhima. Pampa's Bhima is aware of what Vyasa's Bhima has done because the poetic language employed by

Pampa is aware of the Mahabharata. As this awareness permeates Kannada and finds expression in its poetry, it blossoms into a unique experiential dimension.

'Karnana Pademathinol Pudidu Karnarasayanamalte Bharatam' ('Isn't Mahabharata narrative Karna-flavoured, filled with the renown of Karna' [*Vikramarjunavijaya*, 12:217]) is Pampa's valediction composed after Karna's demise in battle. The pivotal term in this expression is 'pademaṭu' (renown), a word Pampa utilizes in various contexts. Following the creation of the Mahabharata, countless individuals have likely extolled Karna's skill and charity. This is what Pampa means by 'Karna's renown'. Pampa embraces the image of Karna contained in this renown, resulting in a Karna distinct from Vyasabharata's portrayal of Karna. This distinction extends beyond Karna to encompass all the characters of the Mahabharata. This tells us why he calls the Mahabharata worldly. In this worldly verse, Pampa enjoys a freedom unavailable to him in the scriptural Agamic verse. The Mahabharata's mythology has no authoritative stance—it aligns more with history. Pampa wants to grapple with contemporary history, using the Mahabharata narrative, as a means to articulate his present. If contemporary history serves as the tenor, then past history becomes the vehicle. Pampa intricately weaves together these tenors and vehicles in his poetry.

'Viditam pratheethikam atisubhagam sundaram sooktigarbham mridusandarbham' ('This poem is accessible to all, pregnant with implied meanings, tender and pleasant, aesthetic, suited to the most sophisticated and soft situations' [*Adipurana*, 1:26]). These technical terms likely signify the rich and varied semantic landscape of Pampa's poetic language. This diversity encompasses meanings known in advance to the reader, those identified through language use and those revealed only in the context. Pampa's poetic language exhibits a multitude of variations. Despite this diversity, the challenge lies in amalgamating these meanings into a unified poetic essence within the work. Pampa's poetic endeavours are fundamentally grounded in the fusion of myriad meanings. Dualities such as scriptural–secular, mythological–historical, Kannada–Sanskrit, past–contemporary—aspire to coalesce in Pampa's poetic design.

The origins of Champu poetry remain shrouded in mystery. Dandi stands as the first aesthetician to discern the nature of the Champu genre. Even Sanskrit Champu poetry, including those crafted under the patronage of Karnataka's kings, pales in comparison to Pampa's creations. Sanskrit epics predominantly adopt a verse format, with works like *Raghuvamsa* and *Kumarasambhavam* serving as benchmarks for Kannada poets. The diverse metrical patterns distinctive to Champu poetry are absent in Sanskrit. Jain Puranas, too, adhere to the Anusthup metre. Kannada Champu poetry is a product of the creative cultivation by Kannada poets, who introduced the Yati form (line pauses), infusing Sanskrit metres with a Kannada flair. While the impetus behind this transformation raises natural curiosity, delving into the social, political or psychological factors remains elusive. Nonetheless, some observations can be made about the impact of this shift on the poetic form.

The fundamental tenet of our narrative heritage is continuity—an enduring principle not easily refuted. Whether in the genealogy of father, son and grandson, or in the seamless succession from one king to the next, where the eldest son ascends the throne, or even in the inexorable cycle of sunrise and sunset, the principle of continuity prevails in many facets of life. This principle is equally paramount in the realm of storytelling, constituting the very essence of a narrative. Culture's primary role is to steadfastly uphold this systematic order, as preventing disorder becomes a social responsibility. Stories, serving as cultural tools, play a crucial role in ensuring the unfaltering continuation of this process. In epics like the Ramayana and the Mahabharata, instances of disorder and their remedies are woven into the narrative—such as students seeking knowledge without a guru, youth pursuing happiness without marriage, or princes who are not the eldest in the family aspiring to conquer a kingdom.

It seems that Pampa is the first to disrupt the conventional continuity. His goal is to uniquely retell the entire Mahabharata, a monumental task that requires avoiding any misrepresentation. While the surface narrative and value system appear unchanged, subtle shifts occur at the core. When summarizing the Mahabharata, choices of characters and events are as much artistic as they are moral, and this responsibility lies with Pampa. In the concluding section of his work, Pampa highlights the protagonists of the Mahabharata, asserting that it is through them that the epic achieves universality. However, the exclusion of characters like Krishna, Draupadi, Vidura and others, raises questions. Does the Mahabharata solely revolve around figures like Duryodhana, Karna, Bhima, Shalya, Bhishma, Arjuna and Yudhisthira? This artistic deviation not only disrupts the narrative but also introduces a moral divergence. Regardless of a character's prominence, they should remain subordinate to the story's order. In traditional stories, the narrative shapes the character, serving as a witness to their actions, revealing the character's world and inner self. However, the characters highlighted by Pampa in the concluding verses stand apart from the story, characterized primarily by their triumphant yet out-of-order victories.

After the Pandavas emerged victorious in the battle of Kurukshetra, the question of succession to the throne of Hastinapura arose. Given Yudhishthira's status as the eldest of the five Pandavas, any lineage dispute seems unnecessary; his ascension to the throne is a natural course of events (as per krama), as depicted in the Mahabharata. However, in Pampa's narrative, victory (vikrama) is uniquely attributed to Arjuna, sparking commentary about Pampa's bias towards Arikesari. Literature of that era relied heavily on royal patronage, and it can be argued that Pampa's deviation (ati-krama) is influenced by this dependence. Nevertheless, the meaning of the work need not align entirely with this bias. Pampa's concept of 'vikrama' (victory/alternative order) goes beyond his indebtedness to Arikesari, and it is evident that this association cannot be entirely dismissed. With the expansion of the empire, the relationship between order (*krama*) and victory (*vikrama*) underwent a transformation. Adherence to order is expected from the general public, and they do so. The principle of 'Piriyannangeraguvadu' (bowing down to the elder brother) is valid, but when the elder brother seeks to enforce his seniority through force, the victorious younger brother is compelled to protest. In such a scenario, if one disagrees, the option is to leave the state, as only one individual can stand at the pinnacle of the empire, firmly grounded in 'vikrama'. The state wealth, as expressed in the line 'Bhata Khadga Mandalothpalavan Bhramariyappa' ('That which alters its loyalty under the influence of soldiers, swords and army' [*Adipurana*, 14:130]), is fickle, yet the allure of that status remains indescribable. One who recognizes its transience must embrace a Bahubali-like stance, as the option to either return or conform to the established order isn't available.

Yudhishthira willingly relinquishes the throne inherited by him, passing it on to the victorious Arjuna (Vikramarjuna) with the sentiment 'Prayada Pempe Pempemage' ('the majesty of youth is nobility to us'). However, Arjuna's majesty transcends this sentiment. Dharmaraja is undoubtedly virtuous, and his words are true. This is Pampa's way of establishing the theme of victory over order, where 'vikrama' prevails over 'krama'—a perspective emblematic of the empire. Therefore, it becomes necessary to speak of the victorious: 'chaladol duryodhanam nanniyolinatanayam' ('Duryodhana in determination and Karna in truthfulness'). This divergence from the Mahabharata is evident in Pampa's characters. Although the Mahabharata characters possess 'Vikrama', it remains subservient to the story's order. 'Nanniyolinatanayam': Pampa's portrayal of Karna's truthfulness shines purely. In contrast, Karna's truthfulness in the original story may shine sporadically or lose its lustre, dictated by the story's destiny. Even though born as the son of Surya (Inatanayam), Karna must endure the darkness of his birth, an inherent aspect of his destiny.

Pampa's portrayal of Karna's destiny aligns closely with the original narrative, yet Pampa's Karna exhibits a heightened awareness. This verse offers insight: 'Bidivasadinde puttuvadu puttisuvam bidi, ivangidu olpu, ivangidu biyam, ivangidu parakramam, ivangidu sava pangu, endu bidi samakatti kottode edeyol kudisal kidisal samartarar' ('Birth is governed by destiny; fate is the ultimate progenitor. When one is born destined to wealth, goodness, enjoyment, death, fame and prowess in all aspects, who possesses the power to disrupt or intervene in this predetermined course?' [*Vikramarjunavijaya*, 12:182]). It encapsulates a vision of victory, a perspective contrary to impersonal order. However, the anguish that accompanies victory is palpable. After the war's conclusion, Pampa's soldiers, stoically enduring, used tongs to extract arrow fragments from their heads, displaying no sign of pain. Karna's pain, in contrast, runs much deeper, separating him from the established order of the Pandavas or Kauravas. His personality becomes detached from the social context, including his seemingly incongruous friendship with Duryodhana. The original Mahabharata doesn't feature the verse beginning, 'Nettamanadi Bhanumati Soltode . . .' ('If Bhanumati loses in the game of dice' [*Vikramarjunavijaya*, 9:69]), undoubtedly contributing to Pampa's distinctive portrayal. Pampa's poetry leverages Karna's friendship with Duryodhana as a counterpoint to the friendship between Krishna and Arjuna. Since this is a creation of Pampa, its meaning must be explored within Pampa's context. The 'renown' of Karna doesn't explicitly mention this fact. Karna's truthfulness shines in such a context of the empire; within its political realm, the noble history of such victors assumes significant value. These individuals aren't merely products of history; their role as history-makers is a subject of debate. Facing history, they become heroes; turning away, they become yogis. Bharata and Bahubali share a fraternal bond, while Duryodhana, in the Pandavas' perspective, behaves as a villain. History's justice unfolds as he meets his end at Bhima's hands. However, the relationship between Karna and Duryodhana transcends the justice of history. Duryodhana granted shelter to Karna to cultivate a formidable adversary against the Pandavas, yet Karna's game of dice with Bhanumati isn't merely for the sake of the story. The grandeur of this friendship magnifies Karna's demise, making it even more profound.

Pampa's works craft personalities from one angle and history from another. His poetry illuminates the clash and interaction between individuals and history. Unlike a traditional story that unfolds explosively at its conclusion, Pampa's poetry doesn't demand patience until the story's end. Instead, it radiates like lightning within the ongoing conflict between individuals and history. An instance of this tension is seen when Duryodhana dispatches a war message, and Yudhishthira responds with a declaration that his elephants and horses are his relatives—an expression of both humility and pride. 'Poojisuvode ankada ane vajigalemagilla' ('We don't have military elephant and horses to worship' [*Vikramarjunavijaya*, 10:33]). Despite the Pandavas' impoverished and vulnerable state, their resilience in adversity becomes a profound testament to their personalities.

Both the politics as well as the otherworldliness of empire find apt representation in such figures. Duryodhana epitomizes the politics of the empire, and similarly, the victorious Arjuna, poised to become the next king, also embodies the politics of the empire. Pampa employs the metaphor of painting to depict such political manoeuvring, suggesting that political theoreticians can create illusions similar to skilful pictorial elevations in the same section of a picture. This artistry involves both deception and skill, and it remains a harsh irony of history to deem such political strategies essential for the prosperity of life and the welfare of the world. Although Pampa's poetry acknowledges this, it is not entirely liberated from the politics of the empire.

Commencing with Pampa's *Adipurana*, the subsequent scriptural poetry in Kannada (Agamic Kavyas) narrate the ascent of Jain scriptures (Jinagama). The pain of Bahubali's Vairagya, or detachment, is not found elsewhere. The soul of Bahubali, who was a hero, in a moment changes, and he is transformed into a yogi. In Pampa's vision, both the Veera (hero) and Yogi appear indistinguishable. The Vairagya within Pampa's portrayal of Bahubali defies further explication—it is ineffable. There is no narrative where the state of Vairagya is attained; for a story to exist, it requires the impetus of Digvijaya—triumph. The poet who explores this theme is the subsequent poet Janna, who brings forth the vital tenets of Jain Darshan, exposing its multifaceted nature. The central issue revolves around the fusion of the human body and soul.

The sages of the Upanishads conclude that the body is distinct from the soul, a notion exemplified in the tale of Indra and Virochana. When the body is mortal and the soul is immortal, their connection assumes an inherent opposition. Various Darshans (Indian philosophies), including the Nairatmavada (a philosophy that doesn't believe in 'soul'), have presented theories to elucidate this ambivalent relationship. However, translating this understanding into experiential knowledge proves challenging. While logical arguments can defeat opposing propositions and validate one's stance, this intellectual battle has unfolded continually in this country. Yet, what was understood intellectually didn't necessarily translate into a personal experience, and what was experiential often eluded intellectual grasp.

Yashodharacharite of Janna (twelfth century) begins its narrative from the end. Is Siddhi, or attainment, a novel birth divested of its previous memories? Perhaps, not entirely. Where does Siddhi stand when it relinquishes or forgets its potential? Unlike a baby born within a cocoon that eventually sheds the protection of its shell, Siddhi doesn't follow a similar trajectory. Janna initiates his story with the charm of Abhayaruchi and Abhayamati Kumara, and the narrative unfolds backward. What pain lies beneath their endearing qualities? In the words of the guard Chandakarma, 'Kumarara rupinge Thakkugondantirdam' ('Seeing the form of the boys, he was amazed' [*Yashodharacharite*, 1:58]), the term 'form' assumes great significance. Janna repeatedly employs this term to evoke a quality of the body. Additionally, in this sentence, he hints at the inseparable connection between violence and lust.

The forms of Abhayaruchi and Abhayamati, the form of sage Akampana that seems to have forgotten the physique, the visage of Amritamati's beloved Yashodhara, the form of Amritamati, who says, 'Olavadodane roopina kotale yavudo' ('In love where is the question of form' [*Yashodharacharite*, 2:43]), the repulsive appearance of Ashtavanka, the beauty of Sunande, who even when engulfed in fiery pyres arouses the desires of Chandashasa—each one binds the soul to the body. Janna reveals a disorienting vision of how the soul is tormented by the body. Furthermore, he illustrates the predicament of those who disregard their body. The scene in which the image of the disembodied soul enters the dough-chicken and creates paranoia leaves an indelible mark. The dough-chicken transcends being merely an image; it evolves into a symbol embodying the intricate relationship between body and soul. Delving into the image of a dough-chicken is futile without acknowledging the presence of a soul. Without there being a chicken body to the dough, the disembodied soul wouldn't have entered it. Once it enters the dough-body of a chicken, the disembodied soul should emanate cries like a chicken, and not as it pleases. When the soul enlivens the body, it is the body that governs the soul.

The dough-chicken and its inner essence symbolize not just the harmony of body and soul but evoke deeper meaning. This symbolism takes on a tragic hue. When the disembodied soul inside the dough-chicken screams, Yashodhara becomes aware of the horrors of the intended violence. The power of violence is not synonymous with the power of survival. What is the aftermath of the disembodied soul subsequent to its release from the chicken's body is unknown. Yashodhara, however, becomes ensnared in the web of sin. The disembodied soul possesses no body of its own; its sound is merely an eerie howl. Amritamati and Chandashas, are drawn to the power of the disembodied soul. There is potentially deception in the after-body state as well. Janna's world is permeated with experiences of heavenly and hellish states, all summoned by the cry of the dough-chicken.

The image of dough-chicken is termed here as an icon. But the distinction between the image (*pratime*) and icon (*pratimana*) needs clarification. A picture encapsulating any experience can be termed an image, serving the purpose of adding concreteness when employed in description. While an image can also be symbolic, representing abstract ideas, all metaphors and symbols fulfil their roles in poetry through images. Yet, the purpose of *pratimana,* an icon, differs from these; it is an experiential picture, just as an image. It can be used metaphorically, and like a symbol, it can embody abstract principles. Icon, however, distinguishes itself in another crucial aspect. ('Pratimana' with the meaning as explained here is a concept created by Kurtkoti, to supplement that of *pratime* or image.)

Just as images and symbols, pratimana or icon is inherent to poetry. In Vedanta and Nyayas like Ghatapatadi and Dehalidipa, these are employed to facilitate understanding of the subject. Dehalidipanyaya (a maxim referring to a lamp that lights either side of the door, referring to a single means with dual benefits) implies making the subject more comprehensible. However, the conventional meaning of Dehalidipa remains unexperienced; they are merely intellectual images. In contrast, *pratimana*, an icon, provides a tangible experience along with understanding. Furthermore, the experiences and understandings within an icon can collaboratively generate new meanings. Symbols and images do not directly or indirectly convey meaning; their existence does not cease after meaning manifests. If their structure is aesthetically pleasing and efficient, they can continue to captivate with beauty even after the meaning is unveiled. On the contrary, an icon creates meaning itself without explicitly revealing it. For instance, the symbolic significance of Janna's dough-chicken is continually reborn. This icon is formed for the purposes of creating new meanings. In a way, the process of icon formation is akin to the creation of riddles. Neither possess the ability to reflect or respond to worldly phenomena. The alignment between the dough-chicken and the invisible disembodied soul is not natural; it is a constructed relationship. This implies that it is not an inherently born entity but a product. The purpose of this construction is to generate fresh meanings. Philosophical meanings in poetry must be sought through such icons.

3

Ancient poets relied on narratives to convey their messages, using stories as a means of expression. These narratives, seemingly devoid of religious affiliations, found use among Jains and Buddhists who adopted Vedic stories, possibly giving rise to Jain and Buddhist versions of the Ramayana and the Mahabharata. What transpires when Vedic tales and Jain philosophy are juxtaposed? A story doesn't inherently embody a philosophy; it serves as both a way of life and as a fertile field for exploration.

While Vedic stories naturally unveil the Vedic vision, introducing another philosophy into this narrative may lead to confusion. However, there is also the potential for the story itself to influence and alter the underlying philosophy. Jain philosophy, for instance, has been known to transform the personalities of characters like Duryodhana and Karna, imbuing them with a more humane essence. The integration of Vedic deities into Jain philosophy, prompted by the acceptance of this story, has proved beneficial for poetry. The tale of Bharata and Bahubali mirrors the sibling rivalry seen in the Kaurava and Pandava narratives. Nayasena's *Dharmamrita* features a Jain story similar to the story of Chandrahasan in Jaimini Bharata, emphasizing the remarkable growth within the storytelling realm. The question of which story is ancient or new holds little importance; the marvel lies in the diverse narratives that can emerge within the domain of storytelling.

No nation can exist without stories. In ancient times, the creation of stories was a thriving enterprise. To understand the cultural politics of that era, a study of these stories is imperative. The strength of stories lies in their authenticity. Whether it is the worship of Shiva, the abandonment of such worship, observance of a *vrata* (a pious vow), or ritual, each has to have its own narrative. The efficacy of a vrata in the past determines its present popularity, and the *Panchatantra* stories exemplify how cultural education is predominantly conveyed through narratives.

Given that stories are a language in themselves, poets employed this language for their purposes. In Dasaratha Jataka, Rampandit attains enlightenment in a similar vein to Tathagata. Here, the significance of Bodhi relies on the significance of Rama's persona. The Vedics had Vedas, and the Jains had Agamas. While the Vedics had a Ramayana and a Mahabharata as their cultural resource, the Jains also require their own versions. The Jain Ramayana must be like the Vedic one, yet distinct. Stories, like humans, bear their unique imprints, and being Jain Puranas, they necessitate differentiation. Nagachandra (twelfth century) introduces a novel interpretation of Ravana's *dashamukhas* in his *Ramachandracharitra*. Ravana is named Dashamukha because his reflections are perceived in ten facets of a gem. In Nagachandra's *Ramachandracharitra*, Ravana indeed possesses ten heads, but they differ from those in the Vedic Ramayana. This offers a fresh perspective on the significance of Ravana's ten heads. Although the meaning is novel, the term 'Dashamukha' remains constant.

When a word's meaning changes without a change in the word, this needs to be interpreted in multiple ways. A new meaning has the potential to enrich a word, bringing forth fresh dimensions of interpretation. This enhancement is evident in the stories employed by our esteemed poets; works like Pampa's *Vikramarjunavijaya* and Nagachandra's *Ramachandracharita* deepen the meanings of the Mahabharata and the Ramayana. The alteration in Ravana's characterization, shifting from the Paulastya family to the Toyadavahana family, is not a cause for concern. Embracing this change is valuable when it allows exploration into the uncharted territories of the human mind, unravelling Ravana's infatuation and his vulnerability to Sita's form. The endurance, rather than their demise, of words through interpretation is a source of hope. Proclaiming utterances like 'Tatvamasi' and 'Ayamatma Brahma' as great, many philosophers in our country have offered diverse interpretations. Yet, the form of these sentences remains unaltered, as both stories and sentences endure without requiring changes in their forms.

However, there is another facet to this issue—one that carries the risk of altering the meaning of stories and asserting that the new interpretation is true while the old one is false. For example, the phrase 'Tatvamasi' could be construed to mean 'that is you', aligning with the Advaita view. Conversely, an argument can be made that this interpretation is incorrect, and the accurate reading is 'Tasya Tvam Asi', thereby supporting the Dvaita view. Oral tradition considered the potential for misunderstanding sentences as shocking. During conversions such tricks are employed. Texts like 'Dharma Parikshe' and 'Samaya Parikshe' efficiently navigate this terrain.

There is a lower likelihood of calamities when interpreting philosophical or logical sentences like 'Tatvamasi'. Understanding a philosophical theorem often aligns with worldly truths. During arguments, both litigants are well versed in rhetorical strategies, as in a chess match where both players engage in the same game. The outcome depends on the players' skill, but adherence to rules leaves no room for deception or cover-ups. In the post-Vedic era, the Vedics, Buddhists and Jains engaged in similar arguments with fair terms.

However, the approach to interpreting stories differs. Interpreting Shiva worship, which is linga worship, as a form of sexual ritual risks eroding the faith of linga worshippers. Unlike philosophical propositions, stories are experiential; if the experience turns bitter, it must be abandoned. To emphasize the taboo on linga worship, another story can be crafted to illustrate its pitfalls. The conflicts of the eleventh and twelfth centuries were essentially disputes over stories, rupturing the relationships between gods and humans.

What is significant in these episodes is the use of storytelling as a language, conveying essential messages through narratives. Jain biographies serve as depictions of the ebb and flow of life, each story independent yet interconnected. This narrative technique vividly portrays internal transformations, such as men having racial memory, understanding what the future contains and other such psychic episodes. This storytelling technique has also influenced poets of other religions. Nagavarma's (tenth century) *Kadambari* is also a story of life across births. Banabhatta's Sanskrit *Kadambari* is a unique work. Though Nagavarma's fiction *Karnataka Kadambari* is not explicitly Jain poetry, it must be understood within the context of Jain works. In contrast to the straightforward order of development in Jain biographical narratives, Nagavarma's fiction takes a more intricate narrative path.

The work's utilization of the concept of births, following the idea of 'kamasya vama gati', (The nature of desire is strange) is noteworthy. Pundalik's journey of births is depicted as convoluted, and the use of the image of births is pivotal. Life across births, a concept originating from Vedic religion, was embraced and brilliantly developed by Jainism. Unlike the Vedic notion of rebirth as a matter of faith, Jainism addresses the crucial inquiry posed by Nachiketa to Yama regarding life after death. The reparation of sins occurs over time, correlating with the cycles of births. The evolution of life holds paramount importance in Jain philosophy, giving rise to new insights. This cognitive philosophy, when combined with biographies, becomes a means of comprehending the order of biographies. This innovative concept also influences the theme of reincarnation in Nagavarma's story, serving as a conduit for unravelling the mysteries of friendship.

Texts such as Nagavarma's *Kadambari*, Durgasimha's (eleventh century) *Panchatantra* and Nayasena's (eleventh century) *Dharmamrita* reveal an alternative dimension of storytelling. Narration is fundamentally a communicative act, where a storyteller imparts a tale for the benefit of the readers. In Nagavarma's work, this principle extends to Bana's original story as well. A new character narrates a story, necessitating the audience to engage with Mahasweta's tale while events unfold in the story of Chandrapeeda's cousins. Chandrapeeda's act of listening to Mahasweta's story becomes an incident within his own narrative. In Mahasweta's story, the knowledge of Pundalika-Vaishampayana being Chandrapeeda's friend is solely derived through the narrative. This implies that the story and characters remain constant but assume distinct roles. Examining it from this perspective, the entire tale is a narrative recounted by a parrot in front of King Shudraka. The parrot shares its experience of transmigration, recounting the story of lust that intertwines heaven and mortals, life and trees, as well as animals and humans. Lust emerges as the maya permeating the world.

In *Panchatantra*, a story takes the form of a Drishtanta (fable), distinct from Vedanta and Siddhanta. Behind it lies life experience. Though it is not an experiential form, the structure of a fable creates its own experiences. Monkeys and crocodiles are not naturally friends, and while a betrayal is unexpected, this story seamlessly combines both friendship and betrayal, offering clarity to the reader's experiential perspective. The actions in these stories do not merely represent the karma of the characters. For instance, a Brahmin named Yajnadatta may carry a goat for a sacrificial function, but the thieves perceive it as a dog—an occurrence unique to stories. Every story, in essence, transforms into a parable.

Whether a grand narrative like the Mahabharata or a fleeting tale like the 'Story of Davaradakini' in the *Panchatantra*, the remarkable diversity of these stories is evident. The length of a story is significantly influenced by its intended purpose. It prompts contemplation on the unchanging nature of a story, regardless of its size. The reduction in the size of a story, according to its purpose, raises the question of what significance lies in this adjustment. The underlying motive is consistently philosophical or moral. A story, much like a compelling speech, can be wielded for good, as exemplified by the benevolent purpose of *Panchatantra* stories, elucidated by the teachings at their conclusion. In contrast, the stories in the *Samaya Parikshe* (Test of Time) were crafted to deride non-Jain religions. Whether in praise or criticism, it underscores that all these narratives are products of language. The impact of these stories remains unknown, as there are no records detailing their effects. However, the storytellers were solely focused on creating and nurturing stories, with the narrative technique unlikely to produce effects contrary to the story's intended purpose. Once a story comes into existence, it gains autonomy. If the essence of the story is substantial, it can wield an influence beyond the storyteller's initial intention. An exemplar of this is Janna's *Yashodharacharite*, originally extolling the virtues of Jivadayashtami's vow (a Jaina ritual, offering prayers to animals and other organisms), now serving as an enduring treasure trove of diverse meanings.

Kannada poets transformed the story into a poetic medium like language, not only enriching its essence but also expanding its artistic possibilities. They delved into profound philosophical themes through the narrative. Janna, speaking on behalf of all Kannada poets, asserted that 'Arididu Balabatte Paramagama . . . jarachoraveerara katheyalla' ('It narrates a holistic philosophy of life, not merely a tale of some libertines, thieves or heroes'). When the story has villainous characters, it becomes the storyteller's moral responsibility to ensure that the story does not become solely theirs. Additionally, the storytellers used the story as a means of education. Much like history, a story has the power to imbue any subject with a sense of antiquity and authenticity.

4

The Vachanas of the twelfth-century Sivasharanas (the Vira Saiva poets) raise several literary questions. It is now a historical fact that Sivasharanas from various parts of the region gathered in Kalyana, the capital of Bijjala. Basavanna was from the confluence of Bagewadi and Kappadi, Akkamahadevi from Uduthadi, and Allama Prabhu from Balligavi. Other Sivasharanas must have come from diverse regions. However, when we examine all their Vachanas together, uniformity in the language of the Vachanas becomes evident. These Vachanas have not adopted the varied regional dialects. While there is diversity in the imagery and style of the Vachanas, there is no diversity in language. Considering the substantial gap between the language of Vachanas and the language of the Champu poetry, it is natural to be curious about the language of Vachanas.

Criticism today posits that Vachana poets used colloquial language for their verses. If this assertion holds true, one would expect to find diverse elements of colloquial speech in the Vachanas. While the language of the Vachanas is close to colloquial, it falls short of being entirely so. It can be argued that they employed colloquialism with a sense of responsibility, conveying thoughts that writing would have considerably altered. It is evident that the Vachana poets did not engage in direct competition with their predecessors or contemporaries; to that extent they relinquished traditional poetry. Recognizing that they didn't share the religious sensibility of the Jain Agamic poets, they refrained from submitting to such poetic expression. In the Abhijata tradition, there is no scope for the experience of Anubhaava (experiences and ideas not amenable to logical explanation; ordinary experiences with extraordinary resonance; mystical). Even if Abhijata poetry addresses deities, its ultimate benefit is social. Existing within the social realm, it cannot disregard societal norms. Poetry, as a form of social narrative, directs its attention towards the educated class. Any neglect of lay readers by poetry may be attributed to the distinctions entrenched by the political system. The hierarchical division between superiors and inferiors serves as the political force of the empire. Showing respect for an individual's greatness exemplifies the benevolent power of the king. Abhijata poetry aligns itself with the social structure existing in the empire.

While the primary connection of the Sivasharanas is with their gods, a sense of sociality is still present, intricately intertwined with their personal faith. The practice of labour is devoid of any sense of superiority or inferiority for the Sivasharanas, as any form of labour can be an expression of Anubhaava. The Sivasharanas dedicate their labour to Linga (the deity), and only what is dedicated to the deity becomes the prasada (consecrated food) for the Sivasharana to consume. This philosophical practice, inherently linked to labour, extends into the social realm. Thus, there is a seamless alignment between actions and the utterances of the Sivasharanas, both carried out with the devotion to the personal deity. The inseparable relationship between labour and speech transforms labour into a metaphor for the worship of Linga. Take, for instance, Madiwala Machayya, whose profession involves cleaning clothes. Beyond the physical act, he cleans the mind, heart, and conduct. The poetics of the Vachanas can be discerned in this notion of labour, reflected in the austere simplicity of the language and the images employed. The value of labour has to remain at the level of external images. Similar to the minds of the Sivasharanas, their poetry appears to embrace a commitment to non-acquisitiveness—which is both social and asocial. It signifies a willingness to contribute to society without expecting anything in return, distancing itself from social obligations. A *jangama* (the Shaiva mendicant) exists within society while remaining somewhat detached from it, with only the mark of Sangamnatha (deity) adorning their body.

Sivasharanas are seekers of destiny, and the Linga-Anubhaavi possesses the ability to give form to the void, comparable to the poetic act of expressing silence. This helps articulate the unspoken. With the exception of Allama's Vachanas, the meaning in all other Vachanas is direct and accessible. One of the Vachanas of Basavanna states: 'If you speak, it should be like a necklace of pearls. If you speak, it should be like a crystal spear. If you speak, it should be like the light of a ruby. If you speak, it should be appreciated by the Linga.' This Vachana does not delve into the social aspects of speech. Necklace, pearls, ruby's light, and crystal spear are all used as ornaments to adorn god. Speech is a form of communication between god and the Sivasharana. If the Sivasharana speaks, it is for the Linga's approval. Whether this is achievable becomes irrelevant in this context; it is the Sivasharana's labour that can make it possible. The Linga's approval need not be known to others.

Kalidasa, in his depiction of the kings of Raghuvamsa, lauds them as 'Satyaya Mitabashinam': these kings exhibited moderation in speech, driven by their commitment to truth. The Sivasharana likely takes a similar oath, necessitating harmony in mind, action, and speech. Every Vachana, therefore, is meticulously crafted to preserve this harmony. However, a pertinent question arises: if Vachanas are intensely personal expressions, how can they have social significance? The dialogue between Muktayakka and Allama, while resolving philosophical issues, raises queries about its societal relevance. The contextual details of this conversation, including Muktayakka's search after Ajaganna's accidental death, remain unknown. Such an image of Muktayakka is vividly described by Allama in 'angaiyolondu aralda taleya hididu, kangala muttu pavanisuvake' ('holding a broken head in the palm and shedding the pearls of eyes, i.e. weeping'), which is available to us solely through Allama's words. This Vachana of Allama is included in one of the texts of *Shunyasampadane* (a compilation of the Vachanas and dialogues of several Vira Saiva Sharanas; there are multiple such compilations). This Vachana serves as proof of the incident, existing within a poetic context. The use of metaphors, such as 'broken head' and 'eye's pearls', emphasizes the metaphorical nature of the language of the Vachanas. Even if we agree that their goal was not creating poetry, the poetic expression of Vachanas has to be noted. Allama's response to Muktayakka's objection unveils the poetry implicit within Vachanas. When she complains that 'noisy talk is not apt', Allama responds, 'In mobility, a Sivasharana is immobile, in speeches, a Sivasharana is speechless.' The essence of Vachana poetry lies in this statement: What does it mean to be silent in speech? Every Vachana emerges from silence, and the void the Sivasharana seeks is also silent. The Sivasharana employs words to communicate with that silence, attempting to articulate the ineffable.

The relationship between silence and speech mirrors the opposition between the movable and the immovable. Contrary to the common belief that the movable is immortal, it is, in fact, perishable. On the other hand, when it is asserted that the immovable is immortal, a deeper truth emerges within this contradiction. Basavanna's words about the temple and the idol extend beyond physical entities; they embody conceptual ideas. In Basavanna's declaration, 'Enna dehave degula, kale kamba, shirave honna kalasavayya' ('My body is the temple with my feet as pillars and head as the golden cupola'), the focus is on the temple of the body, but not on its perishability. While the Shivalaya (temple for Shiva) constructed by the wealthy may perish, the idea that the body, if considered a temple, too is perishable. Against such a doubt, the concepts of sthavara and jangama (the immovable and the movable) provide reassurance. Vachana poets employ terms such as Kayaka, Prasada, Jangama and Sthavara, transforming them from mere terms into conveyors of meanings beyond their literal definitions. Through their artistic use of language, the poets transcend the limitations of words, expressing what words alone cannot convey. This ability arises from the profound, inexpressible silence surrounding the Vachanas.

A recurring tendency of the Vachanas is that of definition and redefinition. This is evident in the earlier discussion of the movable and immovable. When 'movable perishes', it challenges a traditional belief. Even declaring that the immovable is immortal presents an opposing viewpoint. The concept of the 'Temple of the Body' serves as an illustration of this duality. In the icon of the body, the immovable and the movable, join to strive to become something else. One becomes the definition of the other. If the temple is considered the body of god, then this Vachana seems to suggest that if the temple can become the body, there is nothing wrong with the body becoming the temple. It provides insight into the sense in which the body becomes a temple, emphasizing in what sense it is durable unlike the temple.

This Vachana by Basavanna captures his inner dialogue, an utterance that the Linga appreciates. However, the significance of this utterance extends beyond the personal and has a social dimension. The aspects defined and redefined in the Vachana belong to the world, where the term 'temple' carries a specific meaning. While the ancient understanding may have been that the temple is the body of god, the modern world might have forgotten this meaning. Basavanna's intent is to clarify the true essence of the temple. Even though this speech seems to be a conversation with the self, it attaches meaning to the temple. Basavanna's Vachanas are both dialogues and monologues. This equilibrium is a consistent feature in Basavanna's Vachanas. For instance, in the Vachana, 'Nara kennege tere gallakke, shareera gooduvogada munna . . . poojisu koodalasangamadevana' ('Before the cheeks and chin are wrinkled, before the body is all bent up . . . worship Kudalasangama Deva'), the focus is on an inward reflection, but it could be an advice given to the people. The Vachanas have a dual focus. The Sivasharana, according to Basavanna, should look within himself—a challenging task. As all our senses are focused on the externals, the mind too is focused on the external. Sivasharana's mind is not his soul: 'Geleya neenu, haleya naanu Kudalasangama Deva' ('You are a friend, I am old, Lord of Kudalasangama'). All Sivasharanas sought this soul, exploring the relationship between the soul and Shiva. Through their journey, they documented, or spoke, what they discovered, leaving behind numerous images and illustrations in their scriptures.

However, as expression too is focused on the externals, it cannot escape the relationship with the world. All Vachanas are creations of the Sivasharanas, and when a work comes into existence, it inevitably encounters the world. Conflicts may arise when there is incongruity between the world and the work. In the Vachana, 'Vedavanodidavara munde alu kandeya ele hota, shastravanodidavara munde alu kandeya ele hota' ('Do you weep in front of those who have read the Vedas! Do you weep before the ones who have read the scriptures, oh sheep'), meaning is indirect. If the victim, the sheep meant for ritualistic sacrifice, wishes to express its sorrow, it should do so in front of the pandits. However, crying before the pandits engaged in Yajnakarma (ritualistic sacrifice) proves futile, as their hearts, hardened by faith in the Vedas, remain impervious. The world would not remain unmoved in response to the revelation of a victim's grief contradicting the Vedas. Believing that 'mortality is the work of god', one must then work to cleanse the filth in this world—a task that carries its own significance.

The Vachanas offer their interpretation of everything in the mortal world. The Sivasharanas rejected the caste system and the associated discrimination. They identified the absurdity in considering the high-born as superior and the low-born as inferior, and rightfully protested against it. However, a contradiction persisted. While asserting that anyone engaged in reprehensible actions, even if a Brahmin, is deemed impure, it still left room for the distinction between Brahmins and lower castes. Erasing historical biases and establishing a new value system is a challenging endeavour, complicated by the unpredictable nature of historical events. History utilizes individuals for its ends and often discards them once its objectives are met. In the face of such uncertainty, the path of the Sivasharanas is to persevere. Allama, in one of his verses, anticipates the consequences of surrendering to the societal norms. The social responsibility embedded in Vachanas transcends time, and the true essence of a Sivasharana becomes evident in death, where the symbolic perfection of this truth is achieved.

5

Allama's Kadali, Basavanna's Kappadi Sangam, and
Channabasavanna's Ulavi stand as perfect symbols, seamlessly
aligned with their Vachanas. Vachana poets deliberately eschewed
the use of stories in their compositions. Their Vachanas are devoid
of narratives, and even parables like 'iriyada vira illada sobaga
helikonda' ('the non-aggressive hero boasted of absent valour')
are fragments rather than complete stories. While an image like
'Arisinavane mindu hondodigeyane thottu, purushana olavillada
lalaneyantadenayya' ('My condition is like a woman adorned in
cosmetics and finery, yet receiving no male attention') could
potentially give rise to a story, yet it remains a non-narrative.
Allama's verses mention seeing a musk deer, the companionship
of tigers and deer, and a hill catching a cold—elements that hint at
story seeds but are deliberately kept from sprouting into complete
narratives. Akka's verses, rich in personal experiences, might be
amalgamated to form a story, yet the Vachanas as a genre actively
avoid storytelling. They directed their attention away from the
past, placing emphasis on the present and future instead. Stories
were unnecessary for them, as their contemporaries engaged
in storytelling, while the Vachana poets sought a deeper truth
beyond the confines of narratives.

Subsequent poets found a renewed need for stories. The
world, time and again, craves stories, revealing its inherent desire
for narrative. However, the complete truth is seldom encapsulated
within a story; once found, the story concludes. The quest for truth
within stories is an ongoing journey. A similar pattern emerged
in Kannada literature. Post-Vachana poets, such as Harihara
and Raghavanka (twelfth and thirteenth centuries), discovered
narratives in the life stories of Sivasharanas, who had deliberately
steered clear of storytelling. The story of Raghavanka, whose
Harishchandrakavya brought about his humbling, is revealing.
From Harihara's perspective, the tale of Harishchandra is human

praise. Harihara's new vow was that praise should not find a place in poetry.

Harihara's vow stems from a determined intention to dismantle Jain and Brahmin traditions. He shows rebellious indignation at the tendency to include homage to the king in the opening lines of the poem, which consist of a panegyric to the deity. Notably, Harihara refrained from composing praises of god such as those found in Raghavanka's *Harishchandrakavya*. The work encapsulates a grand vision that transitions from pantheism to monotheism, devoid of any human praise. In this poetic narrative, Harishchandra, the hero, emerges as a Shiva devotee predating the Sivasharanas, belonging to the Puranic era. Although Harishchandra is not a Shiva devotee in the Puranas, Raghavanka's rendition transforms him into one. Perhaps this shift did not sit well with Harihara. However, considering Basavanna's transformation into Basavaraja as a Sivasharana, could Harishchandra not evolve into Shivsharana? Such confusions are characteristic of the fervour accompanying the inception of a religious movement.

However, the deluge of stories, once stemmed, surged with renewed force. Harihara, who had continued the Champu poetry tradition in *Girijakalyana*, did not continue the practice. Transitioning to Ragale, a distinct narrative genre in Kannada characterized by lines in the same metre but not divided into stanzas, Harihara severed ties with the traditional Champu genre. The linguistic nuances, structural elements and stylistic attributes of *Girijakalyana* differ markedly from those found in his Ragale compositions. Unconsciously, Harihara succumbed to the dictates of his poetic imagination, yielding to the inherent demands of his literary materials. This reality exerts considerable pressure on the poet's artistic prowess, compelling the synthesis of a fitting form for the chosen subject.

The narrative substance of *Girijakalyana* is derived from the Purana. The story of the marriage of Shiva and Parvati, initially found in the Shiva Purana, evolved into a majestic poem in Kalidasa's *Kumarasambhavam*. The exaltation of Lord Shiva, previously maligned by Jain poets, demanded rectification. In addressing this need, Harihara opted not to tread the path of Vedic mythology and poetry. Instead, he embraced the Champu genre pioneered by Jain poets. This approach mirrored the earlier endeavors of Brahmin poets such as Rudrabhatta, Durgasimha and Nagavarma. Harihara, it seems, found it necessary to respond to Jain poets in their own linguistic idiom.

Later, Harihara ventured into composing Ragale, hymns and Shatakas, exemplified in poems like *Nambiyannana Ragale*. While this one is a lengthy narrative compared to the others, it is evident that all Ragale compositions stand on an equal footing in terms of poetic prowess, a testament to Harihara's religious devotion. Unbeknownst to him, Harihara accomplished a significant feat— he unveiled the intricate relationship between poetic material and poetic form. The Champu form was available to him in the tradition, but he crafted the Ragale genre and introduced a prose form that possesses a compelling force. It is conceivable that he drew inspiration for the rhythmic structure of Ragale from folk poetry. Even within the Champu form, echoes of Ragale and Onakevadu (a folk lyric genre) metres occasionally surfaced. His genius seems to have recognized the suitability of the form of Ragale for the stories of Sivasharanas.

It is widely acknowledged that poetic form encapsulates poetic content, much like meaning concealed within words. If the poetic material represents the vachya (narrative), the poetic form becomes the vachaka (narrator). As mentioned earlier, Harihara transitioned from *Girijakalyana* to Ragale, recognizing the inseparable relationship between the vachya and vachaka. This shift likely unfolded amid these distinct poetic forms. For Harihara, *Girijakalyana* was the last work in Champu. Parvati, Shiva's consort, is also a devoted follower of Shiva. Her love and devotion transcend worldly norms. Although Parvati is

Sati's second birth, she wasn't mortal despite being the daughter of the Himalayas. The marriages, separations and reunions of Shiva-Parvati hold divine meaning. In line with this, Kalidasa demonstrates the separation and reunion, like that of word and meaning, in his poetry. What Harihara discerned in this narrative was Parvati's unwavering devotion. Shiva's excuses cannot stand up to the truth of her devotion.

Does it all end here? Should it end? What does devotion truly mean? There are numerous facets of Bhakti that remain unexpressed. This doesn't necessarily imply that Harihara experienced them all. Harihara wanted to forge a new narrative language; the inception of any legacy isn't always overt, because it is not a development that can be termed worldly. We assume a beginning for our satisfaction. In Harihara's *Nambiyannana Ragale*, these lines mark the outset: Shiva drank the poison from the sea's churning. A drop of poison lingered in his palm. Shiva's gaze fell upon it. That drop of poison commenced to 'quiver and stir'. Both verbs serve as metaphors. Shiva's gaze, far from being ominous, bestows life, causing the drop of poison to tremble and stir. The movement of the drop of poison within the palm evokes something profound. The convergence of the drop of poison and Shiva's sight engenders a new creation, comparable to the union of semen and ovum. The tales of Harihara in his Ragale compositions originated from a drop of poison in Shiva's palm, glittering darkly. Samudra Manthan (the churning of the sea) also narrates the genesis of creation from a particular perspective—a story born from the clash of deities and demons.

'The poison is trembling in the palms of Shiva': essentially, poison symbolizes death, not life. As a lethal instrument, it assumes the ultimate symbolic significance. However, the trembling drop of poison carries two contradictory meanings. Its mobility signifies life, yet its poisonous nature connotes death. What emerges from the conflict of these opposing meanings?

It gives rise to the dilemma of mortal life. Mortals live in constant fear of death. When Nambiyanna enticed Rudrakannika, Shiva instructed him to be reborn as a mortal. Being separated from Shiva was unbearable for Nambiyanna. He could not come to terms with living away from Shiva. Shiva urged him to have faith (the name 'Nambiyanna' has the Kannada word for faith—nambu—in it, thus the name signifies one who possesses faith). Faith forms the foundation for enduring separation. Thus, he had to depart, and the story originated from this dynamic. Yet, existence is a peculiar amalgamation of life and death. If Shiva's sight doesn't look after this drop of poison, life becomes unbearable. To endure, one must trust in Shiva's vision.

Poison, after all, is poison. Yet, this droplet, emblematic of death, has the potential to birth another narrative. Shiva, the Nanjunda, Mrityunjaya, has conquered time; even death cowers before him. Both trembling and stirring signify feelings of fear. Shiva, who transcends death's clutches, is worthy of trust. He assumes the responsibility of safeguarding Nambiyanna, now a mortal. To fulfil this, Shiva must accompany him discreetly. Shiva transforms into an enduring element in the fabric of Nambiyanna's life, becoming a character within his story. He disrupts Nambiyanna's marriage by revealing a document to show that he had left his son in Narasingha Mone's custody.

Everything Shiva orchestrates in Nambiyanna's narrative appears anti-life. He severs Nambiyanna's connection with Narasinga Mone, disrupting and thwarting his marriage, eventually relocating him. The only enduring relationship, according to Shiva, is the one between him and Nambiyanna. All other bonds are illusory and may entangle the being in death. The true connection between the devotee and the Supreme Lord should remain untarnished. Despite engaging in seemingly anti-life actions in the guise of old Maheshwar, Shiva imparts a deeper meaning beyond mere morality. This profound significance is a creation of Shiva himself. The essence of all our devotional poetry stems from god, and Bhakti alone offers resolutions to moral quandaries in Bhakti poetry. The name of the protagonist in *Nambhiyannana Ragale*, 'Nambiyanna', carries profound meaning, signifying one who possesses faith— an allegorical name emphasizing the role of faith over logical comprehension. If a devotee is to emerge from a droplet of poison, it transcends mere understanding; it becomes a matter of faith.

This Ragale satirizes the notion that truth can be manipulated through the power of doubt, as illustrated in one particular episode. During Nambiyanna's wedding, Shiva, assuming the guise of old Maheshwar, lays claim to Nambiyanna. While the world perceives Nambiyanna as Narasingha Mone's son, the old man produces a falsifying affidavit. The world places faith in certificates, and Shiva, as the creator of the world, can manipulate this principle. Shiva possesses the ability to shape the truth, creating a deceptive narrative for the world. This raises the question of what constitutes deception.

Placing faith in certificates implies confidence in the certificate system rather than the truth itself. The intriguing aspect is that certificates are believed, solely because they are in writing. In political contexts, written words are deemed true, while oral statements are considered false. Harihara's Ragale casts doubt on the credibility of the system. Although the phrase 'Hara is the truth, the truth is the Hara' is Raghavanka's, it is Harihara who concretely expresses this concept in his poetry.

'In Shiva's palms, poison is trembling' is a line from the Ragale. Another line immediately follows ('in Shiva's palms, poison is stirring') connected by rhyme with only one word changed. In a sense, it seems redundant, forming a rhyming pattern based on repetition. However, this rhythm is far from mechanical; while there's regularity akin to a heartbeat, it carries the organic essence of life's growth.

A line in a Ragale is rhythmic, as if it is a structural element, and it concludes due to the rhyme. This implies that the meaning of the sentence is discerned by observing a single line; no external line is necessary for comprehension. It represents a structure that commences on one end and concludes on the other. Simultaneously with its conclusion, a new line emerges. The moment between two lines—the juncture of one's end and another's beginning—is beyond the realm of language.

If the language of the poem represents a drop of poison, this silent moment transforms into a vision of Shiva. It is a moment that imparts meaning not only to the current line but also to those that ensue. The initial anxiety, the tremor, and the unease, along with the subsequent tranquillity and contentment, are all encapsulated in this moment. Here, sound and meaning diverge and then seamlessly reunite. In this convergence, when Nambiyanna is reborn as a mortal, he doesn't need to be his former self; for that transformation, his name ought to be 'Nambi'.

It can be argued that the Shatpadi emerged from Ragale through calculating its stress pattern, elucidating the design of the six-lined stanza. However, articulating its impact on the evolution of poetic sensibility remains a challenge. Sensitivity begins to germinate in language, unbeknownst to the poet. The convergence of Harishchandra's tale of truth with the narrative of Sivasharana leads to the birth of a stanza form such as Shatpadi. This poem emerges as a testament to the miraculous transformation of Harishchandra from a liar in the Vedic story to a paragon of truth. The historical reality of Harishchandra remains uncertain; the Vedic Harishchandra is distinct from Raghavanka's rendition. The poem grapples with the profound questions of truth and the equation with Shiva, serving as an intellectual element within its poetic realm.

Raghavanka's poetic sensibility seeks to assimilate Harihara's religious principles. While Harihara possesses a poetic sense, he doesn't actively pursue it. Raghavanka, on the other hand, is in search of poetry. This quest for poetic expression is evident in the section describing the forest in *Somnatha Charitre*, where the Shatpadi finds its genesis. All of Raghavanka's works are outcomes of such self-awareness, encapsulated in the query, 'Ee katharasada lahariyam bannisadaraaree dhareyolu?' ('Who doesn't wish to describe the essence of the story on Earth?')

The credit for utilizing the same narrative for a distinct purpose goes to Chamarasa's (fifteenth century) *Prabhulingalile*. The tales of both Harihara and Raghavanka share a common motif. The protagonist descends from Kailasa, undergoes separation in this realm and ultimately returns to Kailasa. The disparity lies merely in the personal aspect, as in style. However, the truth that emanates through the narrative takes the form of Shiva. It can be perceived as Shiva's divine sport (*leela*) from one standpoint. Despite the diverse nature of these divine sports, the essence of the experience remains intact, unaffected by the mechanism. Raghavanka expanded the expressions found in Ragale into Shatpadi. The length of a sentence is neither excessively brief nor overly extended; it can contract or expand through adjectives, adverbs or clauses. The inherent nature of language is to expand, and the language of Harihara's Ragale exhibits a flourishing quality. It has the ability to move back and forth like the dance of a marching band—mobile yet steadfast. Going into the technicalities of sentence construction may seem superfluous here, but inherent growth is embedded within it.

The story of Chamarasa's *Prabhulingalile* can be succinctly summarized in one sentence: Prabhu sought out those he desired, engaged in spiritual discussions, conquered Maya with his power, embarked on a conquest, encountered diverse Sivasharanas for discussions and ultimately returned to his native place. On the surface, it bears a semblance to Harihara's tales, yet it lacks the expansiveness found in Harihara's narratives. In Harihara's Ragale compositions, there exists one Sivasharana, one truth, and consequently, one sentence. However, this single element expands boundlessly. How long did Shankara dance in front of

Kumbar Gundayya? The answer is that his dance is perpetual—an eternal dance. While glimpses of it may be visible at times, the dance remains unseen for the majority. Harihara's fervent rhythm resonates with this concept of boundless continuity.

Chamarasa's work lacks the expansive quality seen in Harihara's narratives. While the protagonist, Allama, encounters a limited number of Sivasharanas, including Muktayakka, Siddharama, Akkamahadevi, Basavanna, Channabasavanna and Goraksha, the historical constraints impose a definite limit on their number. Chamarasa ingeniously employs this historical limitation, acknowledging that no exaggeration can surpass the boundaries of recorded history. In *Prabhulingalile*, the primary focus is on spiritual communication, with Allama actively seeking discussions. His hunger for conversation leads him to search for fellow Sivasharanas, engaging in dialogues, asking questions and pointing out any flaws in their thinking. This interaction represents an exchange of experiences, emphasizing that none of the Sivasharanas is deemed greater or smaller than the others. Their shared concern revolves around determining the appropriate approach to the Supreme Being.

The topic under discussion among the Sivasharanas is Anubhaava—a subject transcending the mind and language. Despite being an experience beyond verbal expression, communication necessitates the use of language. Chamarasa skilfully transforms the Sivasharanas who preceded him into poetic characters, positioning Allama at the focal point. The structure of *Prabhulingalile* is inherently intellectual, marking a unique instance where poetry unabashedly embraces intellectualism.

Sivasharana's Vachanas, Guluru Siddhaveeranna's *Shunyasampadane* and Chamarasa's *Prabhulingalile* are intertwined works, sharing a subtle philosophical lineage. The Vachanas of the predecessors are referenced in Basavanna's Vachanas, marking a form of inheritance where the words spoken in the traditional contexts are to be interpreted. The understanding can take various forms, and the context of Sivasharana's Vachanas was gradually lost to subsequent generations. The re-creation of such contexts is the contribution of the tradition of 'Shunyasampadane'. This work by Guluru Siddhaveeranna encompasses two types of expressions: the Vachanas of Sivasharanas and the prose of the author. This prose serves as a story, as well as commentary. Vachanas are essentially utterances. Guluru Siddhaveeranna's prose endeavours to encapsulate the meaning of the Vachanas, facilitating easier comprehension and provides chronology and context. This reconstruction is, after all, also a story and not history. The Vachanas fulfilled the needs of their time, and a new narrative is required to serve the philosophical objectives of a different era. Understanding the significance of Vachanas in various contexts is crucial. Not only the riddle-like Vachanas of Allama, even the more direct Vachanas of Basavanna necessitate knowledge of their context, which need not be solely historical. The historical accuracy of *Shunyasampadane* remains elusive over time, but imbuing these Vachanas with context, renders them meaningful.

Chamarasa's poetic interpretation offers a different lens to view these Vachanas. The poetic narrative unfolds with the introduction of Prabhu's parents, Nirahankara and Sujnani. Allama, once a historical figure, now exists merely as a name for us. The reincarnation of a historical figure should carry the essence of the name itself, allowing the personality to emerge from it. Allama, who was given the title 'Mayakolahala' (Grand Mystic), transforms into the embodiment of the nameless Parabrahman. However, Allama is also a Sivasharana, composing verses in the name of Guheshwara. In Chamarasa's rendition, Allama becomes a composite image of these two personalities, capable of providing solutions to various human predicaments. Additionally, personal salvation is not a concern for Sivasharanas;

their joys and sorrows do not impact them. The primary concern
for the Sivasharana community is contemplating the right path for
all human beings, influencing the fabric of poetic forms.

Chamarasa's Allama, Kumaravyasa's Krishna and
Ratnakaravarni's Bharatesa are three identical characters
embodying a fusion of human and divine elements. Allama,
in particular, professes allegiance to the truth, observable or
achievable by humans. The primary obstacle in the pursuit of
truth for humans is their ego, which persists as long as body, mind
and intellect are present. Allama, completely liberated from ego,
stands as a solution to this predicament, serving as an embodiment
of the egoless. This aspect of his persona represents the human
dimension. However, he is someone who is immobile in his
mobility and silent in his speech. This divine essence is articulated
in the narrative of Shivaparvati, validating Allama's divinity.

Chamarasa finds it necessary that Allama's character
encompass both human and divine elements. It was imperative
for him to infuse authenticity into the Sivasharana's words and
experiences. While Allama may personally deny the existence of
Guheshwara, he acknowledges the truth it holds, a divine egoism
equivalent to human egoism, which the Sivasharanas accept.

Kumaravyasa's (fifteenth century) portrayal of Krishna's
divinity requires no external validation. The cultural and religious
heritage of the country has already recognized Krishna's divine
status. He authentically brings forth the subtleties of moral
dilemmas in the human world. 'Rajakariyavaneegale tidduvenu
tolagisu sootashirava' ('I will fix political matter, do away with
Karna's head' [*Karnata Bharata Kathamanjari*, Karna Parva, 26:35]).
This perspective stands considerably apart from the truth of
human existence. Politics is a human affair; it is the humans who
have labelled Karna a sutaputra—slave-son; Krishna, conceals
this truth, directing Arjuna to kill Karna, a crucial plot necessity.
In the narrative realm, this cannot be avoided. Arjuna declines to

follow this diktat. But Krishna, though in response to Arjuna's declaration, felt pity for him ('Manadolu Marugidanu Muravairi') [Karna Parva, 26:31]) showed outward anger ('Keralidanu Bahiradali' ibid.); this pretence is an aspect of his persona and epitomizes Krishna's ability to apply accepted ethics to humanity and guide them in their actions, linking an aspect of his persona to the worldly realm.

'Do away with the head of Karna, the slave-son' ('Tolagisu sootashirava'): the dilemma surrounding the interplay of worldly needs and Krishna's otherworldly personality is stark and unforgiving. The Jain philosophies, in recognizing this cruelty, expressed compassion for Karna's tragic demise, an unavoidable fate. One way to mitigate this cruelty is through a narrative rewrite. In the past, Bhasa successfully experimented with such an approach in his play *Pancharatra*. This experiment, found in Bhasa's *Pancharatra* and *Karnabhara*, laid the foundation for all subsequent renditions of Karna in Kannada poetry. While Karna's death remains inevitable, the narrative allows for a momentary pause to contemplate it with empathy. Bhasa, Pampa, Ranna and Kumaravyasa exercised this narrative freedom. Despite the inevitability of Karna's death, his personality thrives. Krishna plays a role in Karna's demise through his words 'Tolagisu sootashirava', by concealing the truth about Karna, and justifying the act under Kshatriya arrogance that Karna is just a slave son. Krishna's utterances reveal his awareness of this, which, contrary to common perception, is not very direct. Kumaravyasa's work recognizes this nuance, where the cruelty in Krishna's words is less pronounced than in the statement 'Comparable to Rama, Bheema is a victorious warrior, who broke the diamond-like thighs of Duryodhana' ('Duryodhanorukshamadhura vajram . . . endabhivarnipem ranayasha sriramanam bheemanam'), an echo of old memories resonating in Ranna's words. Krishna's speech, emphasizing 'Tolagisu Sootashirava', carries an urgency inherent in the inevitable moment of the plot. Kumaravyasa's language use aligns with contemporary non-violent principles while reflecting rules of narration. This isn't Kumaravyasa's personal accomplishment but a reflection of the lessons his poetry has learned from tradition.

When Kumaravyasa undertook the task of rendering the Mahabharata in Kannada, he embraced its moral and metaphysical dimensions. This isn't to imply that moral issues aren't addressed in the story, but rather, they are compelled to find resolution within the realm of style. Kumaravyasa compartmentalized the context of the Bhagavad Gita into three facets, a motif reiterated for the third time during Karna's imminent demise. Arjuna's internal conflict before Karna's killing resonates in Kumaravyasa's language, as seen in the phrase 'Kannariyadirdodam karulariyade' ('What the eyes don't know, the heart does', *Yashodharacharite*, [3:44]). While the plot order of the story is inevitable, its sequencing can be manipulated.

Chamarasa asserted that his poetry isn't a chronicle of the deceased and viewed the Mahabharata as a narrative of 'fratricide'. This perspective reflects the belief that the story's indivisibility is as crucial as that of word and meaning. However, the disintegration of the link between word and meaning began earlier in Kannada literature. The meaning conveyed in the original Mahabharata and Pampa's *Vikramarjunavijaya* diverges. Kumaravyasa departed from Pampa's interpretation to create a distinct narrative, evident in his portrayal of Krishna. While Krishna's divinity stems from the Puranas, his humanity is enriched by contemporary history. Despite his divine detachment, Krishna's human side is deeply rooted in historical context.

Ratnakaravarni's (sixteenth century) character Bharatesha is very much like Allama in Chamarasa and Krishna in Kumaravyasa's narrative. His portrayal of Bharata significantly differs from Pampa's. While Pampa's Bharata briefly showcased imperial arrogance, Ratnakaravarni's Bharata is a connoisseur who flirts with the women in his court. His romantic attitude eases the political tension, altering the meaning of his triumph. The victory brings him more women. His worldly connections are enhanced. Ratnakaravarni strategically employs Jain mythology, portraying Bahubali as an incarnation of Madana. Kama, in this context, transforms into an allegory of Anubhaava for Ratnakaravarni. Anubhaava not found in any Jain poetry may be found in Ratnakaravarni's *Bharatesh Vaibhava*. There is a story suggesting Ratnakaravarni's conversion from Jainism to Virashaivism, and subsequent return to Jainism, though the historical accuracy remains uncertain. Nevertheless, his work stands as a tale of conversion. While there is hyperbole in his story about Bharatesha's little finger not moving even when a whole army has a go at it, it addresses the recurrent theme in Kannada poetry— the problem of the body—and offers a resolution. Bharatesha possesses a body yet transcends it. This aligns with the story about Allama being immobile in his mobility, Krishna's philosophical stance in Kumaravyasa's masterpiece, emphasizing a non-dualistic relationship between body and mind. Bharatesha's body exhibits a versatile nature, becoming a defining aspect of his identity.

For Bharata, the significance of the body extends beyond mere physical existence. On a particular occasion, the women of his inner palace present him with flowers—one offers a blue lotus, while others offer jasmine flowers. Each blossom serves as a unique expression of their emotions, using the language of flowers to convey sentiments. This floral language, more implicit than verbal expression, conveys a subtlety of emotions. The king's utterance about the jasmine that slipped, is a translation of the language of flowers into words. Romance necessitates a form of communication, and need not always be literal; language, however, remains essential. Bharatesha employs the body much like he does language. As Allama, he understands the importance of using language without it becoming a constraint. Upon discovering that his sons had renounced worldly life and departed, the betel nut he consumed turned bitter. Bharatesha, like spitting out the bitter tambula, cleanses his body—a reflection of his adeptness in utilizing both language and body to navigate life's complexities.

Following the splendour of Bharatesha, there was no comparable poetry in Kannada. *Bharatesha Vaibhava* is not imperial poetry; Sangatya (a Kannada genre comparable to ballad) is not recited in the royal court. What elements of folk poetry did Ratnakaravarni assimilate in his works is yet to be properly studied. Even the figures of speech used by Kumaravyasa and Ratnakaravarni are not purely Sanskrit. The novel principle of Kannada lies concealed within the similes and metaphors they employ. The refinement of the Kannada language evolved subtly, finding its culmination in Lakshmisha's (seventeenth century) *Jaiminibharata*. Lakshmisha's work provided a culmination to the poetic endeavours of his predecessors in one direction. However, Ratnakaravarni's Sangatya marks the initiation of another path.

In Harihara's fervent expressions, poetry started to explore a path towards independence from words. In Champu poetry, regardless of the significance or brilliance of an individual word, it must maintain a relational connection with other words, functioning within the structure of sentences:

Maleya mele tumbigala male terambholedade bere poo
Maleya leeleyamkedaki kekaramale shreeshamaleyam
Solise neela bahulate tola modal madananuragam
Salide sardu seete raghuvamshameruge male hoodida

(*Pampa Ramayana* by Nagachandra)

In this verse, the word 'Male' (garland) is reiterated six times, subtly weaving the metaphor of a garland another time. However, the term 'garland' doesn't stand out independently in the poem;

instead, it forges connections with the surrounding words. The garland entwines with Sita's creeper-like arms, Rama's appearance comparable to a tall tree. The four lines of the verse become a canvas for intricate semantics. The interplay of words holds great significance in ancient poetry. Words retain echoes of past meanings, constituting the verbal memory of poetry. This memory is intimately linked to the cultural memory from which poetry originates.

Over time, the language of poetry started to emancipate from linguistic memory, a shift evident in the work of *Bharatesha Vaibhava*. The metre employed in this poem mirrors folk poetry, allowing the words within this little metre to operate independently. Their brilliance and melody are striking, each word seeking its counterpart. Nrupati's expression, 'Mallige jaritu jaridarenadremmallige', showcases the importance of 'mallige' and 'emmallige' as central words. The essence lies not in the literal meaning but, in their repetition—in the Anubhava (experience) of words. *Bharatesha Vaibhava*'s Shringara rasa transcends the mere verses of the book, transforming the beauty within the work into the beauty of poetry—a form of beauty comparable to music, where tones create harmony, and in poetry, it is the beauty of words.

6

'The Preface' has become extensive, yet it offers valuable insights into the approach of this book, *Kannada Sahitya Sangati*. Our perspective on Old Kannada literature needs reconsideration. While it is commonplace to label ancient literature as conventional, suggesting a lack of room for independent vision, we must scrutinize what truly constitutes canonical literary meaning. With the advent of Navodaya (early twentieth century), lyricism gained acceptance, prompting literary criticism to seek this quality in ancient poetry. The prevailing view of old poetry as ephemeral constructions, lengthy descriptions, unreal events and unnecessary didacticism, has been shaped by the influence of Western literature and its accompanying rationalism.

There is no immediate need to question the validity of this rationale. The notion that all old poetry collectively as a tradition exerts power over us should be re-evaluated. Older works have served their purpose, and they don't linger as ghosts. The 1000th anniversary of Pampa and Ranna were celebrated recently in this century, marking it the first time a poet's birthday received such recognition in our country. If old poetic works endure, it is because they were relevant to the people, not because of any hegemony. Additionally, it was Western missionaries who edited and compiled old literature, presenting it in book form. Europeans, driven by the hobby of reconstructing and preserving history, wrote the history of our country and literary cultures. We are continuing in this tradition. Literature gains a historical meaning through the construction of tradition, and at times, this historical weight can significantly impact the present.

Yet, we are no longer emancipated from history, let alone the historical sense. Delving into detailed accounts of the political and social conditions of yesteryears seems implausible. What we have now is literature—imbued with Jain, Vedic and Vira Saiva influences. This literature, once a conduit for comprehension, should not be reduced to a collection of bare descriptions. Ancient poetic techniques have undergone revision, a facet deserving our attention. The ensuing articles strive to illuminate one dimension of this comprehension. Our literary practices have undergone substantial changes, rendering contemporary commentary on old works unfeasible. Previously, elucidating the semantics of poetry sufficed. Criticism has now evolved into an independent art, manifesting in the essay form. The benefits of this evolution are self-evident.

If criticism is considered a literary genre, it should be subject to the same rules as literature. Criticism endeavours to uncover and elucidate the meaning within literature, contributing to the ever-changing interpretation of literary works. Literature, a product of imperceptible forces, allows the poet to realize their intentions within the work. Discerning the poet's intent, implicit in the work, is not a formidable task, regardless of whether the poet explicitly states it. However, these invisible forces, rather than the poet's intentions, shape the nature of literature. These forces may be religious, political, social or other, which a literary critic aims to identify. As mentioned earlier, literature serves as a medium of understanding. In ancient times, it was believed that rasa embodies knowledge that can only be derived from experience.

Apart from literature being shaped by imperceptible forces, the same holds true for literary criticism. A critic might not consciously acknowledge this fact, but their work is also a product of these subtle influences. The essence of the work may manifest in the critique, and correspondingly, the critic's perspective should be transparent in criticism. This necessity intensifies with the magnitude of the work. For instance, when critiquing a poet like Kalidasa in contemporary times, the critic arises to meet the demands of the present. There exists a distinction between understanding whether Kalidasa can be contemporary and understanding his work in the present day.

This observation is also applicable to the critiques within this book.

Emergence of New Literary Practices in Kannada

This essay is the preface Kurtkoti wrote for a collection of essays titled Nooru Mara Nooru Swara *(Hundreds of Tunes from Hundreds of Trees), a companion volume to the previously mentioned* Kannada Sahitya Sangati *and published in 1998. This collection features essays on major Kannada writers of the modern era, spanning the late nineteenth century to the late twentieth century. The 'Preface' offers a broad introduction to modern Kannada literature, commencing with the publication of Reverend Kittel's* Kannada–English Dictionary *and tracing the inception of translation along with the development of literary cultures influenced by colonialism. Kurtkoti begins the 'Preface' by reflecting on the significance of Rev. Kittel's dictionary within the colonial context of Karnataka. He proceeds to discuss the transformations induced by the epistemological structures of colonialism, elaborating on the disparities between the concepts and practices of translation in our culture compared to Western culture. His detailed examination of translation within the historical context of Kannada not only addresses issues of language relations but also draws comparisons with translation practices in Sanskrit. Kurtkoti remarks on the sensitivity of a language to translation, particularly in literary discourses, highlighting it as a matter of choice. Additionally, he explores the contrasts between Western and Indian approaches to translation and attitudes towards the past. Furthermore, Kurtkoti discusses the disparities between history and the novel, as well as the historical emergence of drama, fiction and poetry in Kannada during the colonial period. In his overview of the historical emergence of the novel in Kannada, he examines the distinctions between history and the novel. Similarly, in delineating the*

154

emergence of drama in Kannada, he engages in a discussion of epic and drama. This essay serves as a comprehensive introduction to the emergence of new literary practices in Kannada under the impact of colonialism.

1

Rev. Ferdinand Kittel's *Kannada–English Dictionary* was published in 1894, but similar endeavours had commenced much earlier. In 1840, Sir William Jones presented the English translation of *Manusmriti*, and during the time of the former Governor-General Warren Hastings, an English translation of the Bhagavad Gita was published. The British authorities acknowledged the Bhagavad Gita as the Hindu holy book, equivalent to the Bible for Christians. It was mandated for oaths in courts. While Shankaracharya interpreted the Bhagavad Gita in the light of advaita, the British authorities viewed it through the lens of 'kayada' or legality. They classified it as a religious and holy book for Hindus, demonstrating how religious scriptures could be employed for political ends. The narrative of *Manusmriti* takes a different trajectory, which is beyond the scope of our discussion.

In contrast, Kittel's *Kannada–English Dictionary* is neither a scripture nor a literary work; it serves a distinct purpose in the realm of science. Religious and literary works have their intrinsic purposes, but a dictionary operates as a scientific text with the pursuit of knowledge as its goal. Patanjali, in his *Mahabhashya*, asserted that a true Brahmin must study the Vedas with no express purpose. Kittel's intentions were similar. This 'scientific' dictionary was a pioneering effort not previously attempted in Kannada. The contrast between Sanskrit's *Amarakosha* and Kittel's dictionary underscores this distinction. Leveraging the scientific method he acquired in Germany, Kittel demonstrated remarkable success. While there might be gaps in capturing all Kannada words, ongoing efforts to produce improved versions of the dictionary can address this limitation. Kittel's approach to specifying the meanings of Kannada words was meticulous and scientific. He diligently examined thousands of texts, visited the Dharwad market every Tuesday to collect words from common people, and considered both the geography and history of words. Kittel stands as an exemplary lexicographer in our eyes.

It is undeniable that the Kannada people have greatly benefited from such a scientific book. This valuable resource is indispensable for scholars. However, it is worthwhile to consider this work from another perspective. Kittel's mother tongue was neither Kannada nor English. While a Kannada–German dictionary might have served the German language, he chose to write for English-speaking officers. He was initially met with scepticism, but the British government eventually provided financial aid, a feat also attempted by individuals like Dr. John Faithfull Fleet and Dr. Hermann Mogling. Kannada scholars indeed owe gratitude to Kittel, but even more, the British authorities.

Though Kittel's dictionary primarily serves the study of the Kannada language, we have treated it so far as a Kannada work. With the help of Kittel's dictionary, the forgotten aspects of Kannada were recovered. Friedrich Ziegler (1888) and William Reev (1858) had undertaken similar efforts before Kittel, as also Gangadhara Madivaleshwar Tooramari, who compiled a dictionary around the same time. Kittel thought them unscientific. The significance of Kittel's dictionary lies in its scientific methodology. However, it must be recognized as a European work written in Kannada which will forever remain in Kannada. Nearly a century later, Mariappa Bhat revised and released its second edition, solidifying its place in our curriculum. We have realized the importance of dictionary in the study of a language. We now understand that language authenticity is proven through the dictionary, and even if we challenge the meaning of a particular word, we have come to accept that it should also be done in the European manner. While it is possible to argue that Kittel's dictionary gives an inaccurate meaning for a particular word, or that a distinct meaning is found in a text that was unavailable to Kittel, the scientific methodology of the dictionary remains unquestionable.

As Kittel's dictionary is also a text, it has another level of meaning. The meaning of a work extends beyond its material form, especially in works post the nineteenth century, emerging from various historical contingencies. Kittel's dictionary was born amid historical circumstances, coinciding with the establishment of the British Empire in our country. At that time, understanding Indian culture was considered an aid to conquering India. Kittel's dictionary originated in Dharwad, where detailed maps of every lane and house are still preserved in the collector's office. In 1840, the *Bombay Karnataka Gazette* was published as part of the *Imperial Gazette*, and translated into Kannada by Venkatarango Katti. Surveying was widespread—of land, cities, villages, language and literature. Kittel's dictionary, along with Dr. Fleet's collection of inscriptions and Rice's *History of Kannada Literature*, contributed to this cultural mapping, mirroring geographical and political maps in its comprehensive scope.

It is through maps that knowledge is acquired. In one of Jane Austen's novels, *Mansfield Park*, the heroine is considered ignorant as she could not even read a map of Europe. For the empire to expand, maps must be read, and the desire and methods of conquest should be instilled through the education system. Conquering a language is like conquering a country. Despite creating a perfect dictionary, Kittel wrote poorly-received religious songs in Kannada. The reason lies in the fact that while Kittel conquered the Kannada language, he did not establish a connection with it. Those in power often struggle to connect to the people! While the Kannada people and the Kannada language benefited from Kittel's dictionary, neither the German nor the English language did.

Another perspective on the Kittel dictionary is the exchange of meaning between two vastly different language cultures. The meanings of Kannada words are provided in English. A similar ancient example is the Kannada grammar written in Sanskrit. Kannada grammar may have been composed in Sanskrit because famous grammar texts, in those days, were in Sanskrit. However, no Sanskrit scholar would have learnt Kannada through that book; Sanskrit served merely as the language of grammar. The compilation of Kittel's dictionary might have shared a similar purpose and it is undeniable that Kittel's work did elevate the status of the Kannada language. Viewing meanings through the mirrors of two languages is a unique experience.

This work triggered a remarkable process of translation. The primary aim was to make Kannada accessible to English speakers and to resolve confusions, doubts and contradictions about meaning. Ultimately, Kittel's dictionary remains a work of translation. The term 'translation' should be understood not only in its literal sense but also in its figurative sense. All the transformations that occurred in our country after the British can be considered translations. Educated individuals learnt the English language, missionaries converted people, lands were divided and incorporated into systems like zamindari and ryotwari, new means of transportation and roads were established, and administrative systems like post, telegraph and court offices emerged—all forms of translation. This translation process was necessary, even inevitable, for the firm establishment of the British Empire in our country. Since studying the English language was indispensable in the educational system, the translation process gained unprecedented power and speed.

An argument may be made here that the ancient literature of Kannada is also a translation of Sanskrit. Famous poetic works like Pampa's *Vikramarjunavijaya*, Kumarvyasa's *Karnata Bharata Kathamanjari* and Nagachandra's *Ramachandracharitapurana* are also translations. However, it is crucial to note the difference between these ancient works and our contemporary translations. Ancient translations do not claim to be faithful to the original work. When Pampa says, 'Vyasamunindra rundra vachanamrita vardhiyaneesuven' ('I will expand on the expansive work of the Sage Vyasa' [*Vikramarjunavijaya*, 1:13]), he doesn't mean to create a faithful translation of Vyasa's work. The value of translation here is not dependent on the original work. Efforts to compare translations to the original work are relatively recent. The sole intention behind such 'translations' is that if there is a Mahabharata in Sanskrit, there should also be one in Kannada. Therefore, these works are rewritings and not translations. Like there is a Venkateswara (Balaji) temple in Tirupati, there is also a temple in Soratur in Gadag district, surrounded by the row of seven hills of Kappatagudda. There is a legend that Lord Venkateswara appeared in a dream and stood on a rock there because the Desayi of Soratur could not travel to Tirupati. All our old translations are like this. Now they have to be valued based on how much they differ from Sanskrit.

However, translation is now recognized as an art and science, with extensive discussions about it and many theories emerging. Translation is a relationship between two languages, and its quality is measured by its faithfulness to the original work assuming that the truth lies in the original work. A successful translation is one that finds and expresses this correctly in another language. Regardless of its success in this task, a translation cannot equal the primacy held by the original work. If the original work is an image, the translation is its reflection; if one is sound, the other is an echo.

A translation, no matter what, cannot be an original work. Yet, translation is as necessary as it is inevitable. In the past, thousands of translations of scriptures such as the Bible were prepared during proselytizing work, leading to further translations into other languages. Many translations were not done from the original language, and as a result, the meaning changed from language to language. The story of the last days of Jesus was written by Kittel himself in Bhamini Shatpadi, in metrical language. Reading the story of Jesus in English provides an experience not available in the Kannada account of it. Even Kittel's Kannada is not natural Kannada; if it were, the original meaning would have changed further. Yet, such a natural translation could have remained a part of Kannada literature. When we read the English translation of the Bible, we feel that Jesus of Judea must have been speaking in English. Similarly, the characters of 'Pampa Bharata' forget Sanskrit and speak only Kannada.

Like the spread of religion, the expansion of an empire demands translation. When the rule of the East India Company was established in this country, the English language had to stand alongside vernacular languages, fostering either dialogue or dispute. There is a significant difference between foreigners learning our language and our learning English. Foreigners learnt our languages for a purpose, and scholars like William Jones and Max Muller learnt Sanskrit, translated and explained the meaning of our literature. However, they left Sanskrit here. While we initially learnt English with scepticism, we later engaged in a romantic affair with English literature. English became a standard language for us, permeating all fields, including law, administration, science, technology, literature and art. The number of Indian literary, religious and scientific texts translated into English is more than the number of English works translated into our languages. This is because, after learning English, we no longer need these translations, and the learned can directly read those texts. The gift of the Empire to us is the book, and at the beginning of this century, everyone posing for a photograph had a book in their hand, symbolizing culture.

By the time Kittel's dictionary was published, the history of insurgency at Naragunda near Dharwad became an old story. It was a period marked by waning hostility towards rulers and a growing acceptance of their authority. Simultaneously, the resounding triumph of the British Empire echoed globally. Influential British thinkers like Carlyle, Ruskin, Mill, and poets such as Tennyson extolled the glory of the empire and its moral responsibility. The Empire realized the Vedic dream of uniting nations across oceans. In the seemingly barren soil of barbarism, the Empire fervently sowed the seeds of culture. Western knowledge, flowing from three universities in the country, enriched the entire land. During this period, translation work persisted consistently. The initial phase of this process involved translating economic exploitation as a system of trade. An illustrative example of this translation is the journey of cotton cultivated in India and Egypt, reaching England through the Suez Canal. The cotton was transformed into cloth at the Manchester mills, and returned to Egypt and India— also a form of translation. In a metaphorical sense, this translation symbolizes a hidden aspect of culture: the transformation from cotton to cloth, highlighting that while cotton can evolve into cloth, the reverse transformation from cloth to cotton is not possible. It underscores a symbolic representation of culture's nuanced dynamics. The subsequent stage in civilization tends to move towards destruction rather than a return to nature.

Those who embraced British rule didn't hesitate to express their allegiance, a sentiment often conveyed through translation. A generation of students sang, 'Victoria emba Maharaniyavaru/ Yuktiyindali nammanalutiharu' ('Maharani by the name Victoria/ rules us and rules cleverly'). Many years later, another generation sang, 'Dhanya Dhanya Vibudhamanya Sarvabhauma Nripavara/ Ananga Sundara' ('Blessed, blessed is the enlightened sovereign King/Disembodied and Handsome'). Both songs, independent compositions, not translations, reflected a sense of unfamiliarity turning into familiarity through addressed titles. Post 1857, the official recognition of Queen Victoria's 'Yukti' rule unfolded, providing insight into her governance. The second song's

'Sovereign King' referred to Edward VII. When did he attain 'enlightenment'? And what is the significance of labelling him 'Ananga Sundara'? It is not untrue that unbeknownst to poems, sometimes meanings are concealed in poetry. We have a tradition of depicting kings using poeticism, and that is precisely what the poet employs in this song. However, in doing so, Edward is translated into our poetic language. From the poet's perspective, this portrayal may be accurate within the poetic tradition. Yet, in the eyes of Edward and his compatriots, this depiction may cast Edward as a clown. Much like Ashoka, and Chandragupta, Edward was a king and an emperor, though the cultural language of these emperors is distinct. Initially, British writers referred to Napoleon as an imperialist, not a king. The British Empire, it was believed, was distinct in its approach and aimed at spreading civilization in India rather than plundering the country. They created a sense of history in this country, where it was absent. However, the history they crafted was their own, not India's. Through translations of works like the Bhagavad Gita and *Shakuntala, Manusmriti*, they tried to shape an India they envisioned.

Translation serves various purposes, driven by motives like friendship, disdain, suspicion, desire to win, and attraction to culture. In the clash of cultures, common purposes may be absent. The educational system emphasized mutual understanding, with foreigners creating dictionaries and grammars while learning languages like Kannada and Sanskrit. Unlike them, we learnt English from the very beginning. People like Kittel did not learn Kannada this way. Foreigners learnt our languages since a man of advanced intellect can learn other languages. Hence, the quality of translations varied. In the educational system, translation was a necessity for language learning, but once learnt, its continued use diminished. Presently, English learning among children is primarily driven by career considerations in fields like engineering, medicine and technology.

The work of translation went on implicitly, with the Indian education system being a translation of the Western education system. Similarly, all other public institutions mirror one another through translation. The essence of translation lies in the exchange between two languages. However, if one language is robust while the other is weak, if one holds meaning while the other lacks significance, or if one is patronizing while the other requires nourishment, such translation is bound to fail. This failure stems from the underlying notion of victory inherent in colonialism. Imperialism's origins can be traced back to continental exploration, with English explorers venturing into America, Africa, Australia and Asia. The conquerors of these lands were deemed cultured, while the conquered were labelled uncultured. In response, the term 'sanskriti' was coined from Sanskrit to denote culture. The word 'culture' carries connotations of both self-respect and contempt for others. Colonists labelled the locals as uncivilized, leading to the creation of systems such as settlement to keep anti-social elements at bay. The residence of British officers was distinct from the town, emphasizing a separation between the two. In this area, the concept of culture was perceived as a structured system. The translation work began with the term 'sanskriti' itself.

When the principle of 'culture' began to haunt us, we set out to translate. It is our history. Translation became a novel method of comprehension, aligning with the ancient desire to grasp the supreme principle encapsulated in 'Yasmin vijnate sarvam idam vijnatam bhavati' ('that which, if known, can illuminate the entire world' [*Munduk Upanishad* 1.1.3]). This method, starting afresh, reflects humanity's responsibility to acquire knowledge from the beginning, a principle followed by religions, arts and sciences. In the clash of two cultures in the modern era, translation unexpectedly emerged as a mode of understanding. Kannada began assimilating what it desired from other languages.

Translation vividly highlights the similarities and differences between the two cultures. Yet, in the realm of languages, one serves as the giving language while the other functions as the receiving language. Kannada, in this context, played the role of the receiving language. Although every language possesses the capacity to receive, this power is not boundless. Moreover, a language doesn't receive content exactly as it is given; the received content undergoes changes. In the latter part of the nineteenth century, two Kannada translations of the Sanskrit *Abhijnana Shakuntala* were published. Basavappa Sastri's translation adheres closely to the original, employing the 'Kanda' metre with efficiency. On the other hand, Churamari Seshagiriraya's translation takes a different approach by placing *Shakuntala* in the Kannada folk environment. This form of translation is also acceptable. While Basavappa Shastri wrote with court theatre in mind, Churamari translated with a focus on folk theatre. Through these translations, the Kannada language showcased its ability to embrace works from other languages in diverse ways.

Kannada inherently possessed such power. Despite Sanskrit being distinct from Kannada, the cultural interaction between the two languages didn't manifest conflicts. Kannada and Sanskrit share a history of both proximity and enmity. Over time, Sanskrit had to adapt and survive through Kannada, learning elements like alliteration (*padamaitri*) and verbal figures of speech (*shabdalankara*) such as Adiprasa (initial rhyme) from Kannada prosody. It was Kannada grammarians who asserted that *padasandhi* (combining words) should not lead to *srutidosh* (error in pitch).

The relationship between Kannada and the English language is nuanced. While history attests to Kannada accepting and welcoming English, the simplicity of their connection raises questions. If queried about whether contemporary writers have engaged with English in the same profound manner as our old poets did with Sanskrit, it becomes difficult to answer affirmatively. Kalidasa profoundly influenced our narrative poets, each poet striving to surpass him. However, with the emergence of Vachana literature, Kalidasa's name faded and translations had to wait until the nineteenth century. Kannada, as a language, discerns the distinctions between Sanskrit and English, recognizing that English is more distant than Sanskrit.

Understanding the sensibilities of languages is crucial when discussing translation. The rules of translation are contingent on a language's sensibility, considering the proximity or distance between two languages. For instance, translations of Kalidasa into Kannada have been published, as have translations of Shakespeare. However, Shakespeare's works did not significantly influence Kannada literature like the Ramayana and Mahabharata did. Despite repeated attempts at translating Shakespeare, Kannada hasn't fully developed a medium for expressing his plays.

The earliest translations of Shakespeare took the form of adaptations, with Hamlet becoming Hemalata and Romeo transforming into Ramavarma. Such adaptations were inevitable when embracing a different culture. Direct translations have persisted over time, yet the rhythm of Shakespeare's language and his symbolic images haven't fully been translated. Achieving the uniqueness of Shakespeare in translation seems elusive. Perhaps a successful translation of Shakespeare would only be possible if Kannada evolved into the English language of the Elizabethan era. However, if Kannada remains true to itself, the desire to fully capture Shakespeare in Kannada may need to be relinquished. From a certain perspective, this compromise for Kannada can also be viewed as a victory. Kannada selectively absorbed what it needed from English, flourishing as Kannada.

The Shakespeare example highlights the language's sensitivity, emphasizing that the language itself should determine the need for translation, particularly in literary contexts. This observation is relevant primarily to literary translations. In the initial stages of our curriculum, all textbooks were translations, including Kannada textbooks at the primary level. The poem 'Ahaha Chandanadua'

('Let Us Play the Ball') featured in the Kannada textbook, and when Marathi school boys in our neighbourhood sang 'Wahawa Wahwa chendu Ha' ('Oh, wow, this is a ball'), we mocked them for seemingly appropriating our song. Surprisingly, the same song appeared in a Gujarati textbook. It is conceivable that these three songs were translations of an English poem, fulfilling curriculum requirements. In the old education system, the teacher possessed the book, while the new system necessitates students having their own books, designed for easy comprehension. Education, like medicine, follows a rule of doses, leaving little room for the sensitive responses to language.

One unequivocal truth emerges—the new curriculum universalized the process of translation. Textbook construction was not merely the construction of knowledge; early textbooks warrant revisiting. The Empire's pervasive history was taught directly and indirectly through each lesson. In one lesson, there was a description of 'dombarata' (an acrobatic performance) a topic seemingly unrelated to the Empire's history. However, within that lesson, a boy sends a half-day leave slip to the teacher to witness the dombarata in his locality. The holiday chit was one of the many administrative schemes of the British Empire. Though the cause wasn't visible, the action revealed itself clearly. Even though the British emperor is far away in England, his authority, issuing from a magic wand as it were, permeated the length and breadth of Indian villages. Translation through textbooks served as a medium for expressing and perpetuating this system.

2

In the realm of literature, translation takes on various forms. When we assert that the medium of literature is language, we recognize that something is conveyed through this medium. While language is termed a medium, it often implies that there is no distinction between history and literature, except technical differences.

Literary language, however, transcends being a mere medium—it is dynamic and not inert. Unlike a medium, literary language is not passive; it is a phenomenon that embodies its meaning. Literary translations, although they exist, fall short when they constrain the depth of meaning. A successful literary translation entails an equal exchange between the two languages, with both giving and taking. In the early part of this century, all our students read Marsden's *History in Kannada*, in which the passivity of language in translation is striking. In this context, Kannada serves as a neutral medium. However, this cannot be said about any literary work.

A significant characteristic of a literary work is its ability to generate not only meaning but also a tradition of meaning. Beyond the literal meaning, a work may harbour connotations and implications, and its significance may evolve over time. The language of the work, and the world that speaks that language, possesses the freedom to interpret it, even to alter the meaning while evaluating it. Ancient writers categorized meanings into Vachyartha (verbal), Lakshanartha (connotative) and Vyanjakartha (suggestive), all of which are meanings revealed by the work itself. Additionally, depending on the context, other meanings may emerge. The meaning illuminated when reading Kalidasa's *Abhijnana Shakuntala* may differ when witnessed on stage, comparable to a form of translation involving linguistic switch and interpretation.

A literary work can encompass various meanings, but a distinction should be made here. The literal and figurative meanings exist within the work, making every word inherently 'meaningful'. Connotative meaning, like literal meaning, is embedded within the word itself. However, the remaining meanings extend beyond the word. Analysing any sentence reveals that it attempts to create different meanings by combining the meanings of the words within the sentence. As the passive meaning becomes active, additional meanings emerge. A literary work, though, is not a container filled with all these meanings. In the verse of Lakshmish,

a pun can hold more than one meaning, and these meanings are
always implicit in the verse itself. There is no distinction between
the literal meaning of the verse and the pun within it, as the pun
itself serves as the meaning. Each reading of the verse progresses
only after addressing this embedded meaning. Yet, this meaningful
verse can combine with other verses to unveil an additional layer
of meaning.

It would not be inaccurate to assert that the characteristic
of a literary work lies in its diversity of meanings. The
perception of Lakshmish's *Jaimini Bharata* by his contemporaries
remains unknown to us. As the author crafted his work for his
contemporaries, the intended meaning of the work is directed
towards them. Lakshmish expressed his thoughts about
contemporary readers in his own words, 'Kavyaman keldu mathisi
janisida padarthamam tilidu nodade vinootana kaviteyendu
kundittu jaredode peldavanolavudoneyam' ('Without hearing
the poem and understanding the material produced therein with
adequate consideration, if it is derided as a fancy new poem,
such a comment won't hurt the poet . . . ' [1:7]). Although he
doesn't explicitly mention what the 'material produced' is, the
only 'material' he refers to is the intended meaning of the work—
'Punyamidu Krishnacaritamrutam': the purpose of his work is to
illustrate how the pious history of Krishna is woven into poetry,
and it suffices for contemporaries to comprehend this much.

However, poetry has the potential to surpass the intended
meaning. The meaning of Lakshmish's *Jaimini Bharata* may
appear different to us now. When one seeks to understand the
contradictions in poetry, new meanings may surface that were
previously unnoticed when focusing solely on the intended
meanings. A tradition of meaning is established through a creative
dialogue with a poetic work, prompting the need for reviews in
this context. What one critic perceives may differ from another,
yet both comprehend the meaning of the work equally well;

only the nuances of the meanings vary. This divergence could be attributed to the critic's perspective or his historical context. Essentially, a plethora of potential meanings surrounds a work, but the foundation for all these interpretations remains rooted in the text of the work itself.

Kannada literature underwent a transformation during the peak of the British Empire. It is now an accepted historical fact that Kannada literature, starting with translations, gradually evolved to achieve an independent form. Numerous nuances are involved in this process. Initially, the new literature neither praised nor disparaged the Empire, signifying a meaningful silence. An illustrative example is the occasional poem 'Shukrageete' by B.M. Shrikantaiah. The poem concludes with the lines, 'Let the dying be dead, the departing be gone, may the divine rule be established.' Penned during the silver jubilee of the Mysore University, this poem reflects a liberal-minded culture born during the imperial period. The generosity of this culture lies in keeping an open mind to any philosophy, idea or practice that could excel in the world. For such generosity to thrive, an agreeable system must be in place. The Mysore state was benign enough to allow for ideological generosity. The peace and order of Mysore contributed to the emergence of another empire that ruled from outside the state with regulatory power.

The ideological generosity conveyed in 'Shukrageete' prompts a question. 'When did the opposition to god begin? When will the opposition to god end?' The answer to this question is not structured within a political framework. Even if the diverse philosophies of the world can be reconciled, the challenge of 'opposition to god' remains unresolved. The creation of this poem may not have occurred if this question had not surfaced. Even though it emerged, it might have remained merely an occasional poem—everything about it, from its form to language and substance, seemed to be in conflict. As mentioned earlier, this is an incidental poem, born during the silver jubilee of Mysore University. While the episode held significance then, it may not be as relevant now. Its structure aligns with the rigidity of our aarti (ritual songs), yet the intricacy of the poem's weave is notable. Quotations from religious sayings worldwide are woven into the poem, preserving Vedic mantras and translating Biblical sayings. Both the act of quotation and translation are not merely poetic ideas; they represent the interweaving of others' ideas with one's own. The word 'text' is connected to weaving. Consequently, new questions arise within the knots of interlacing personal and external ideas, emphasizing the importance of attentive listening to the poem's message.

However, poems like 'Shukrageete' do not stand as representatives on their own; there are others that contradict its sentiments. Notably, Bendre's (D.R. Bendre, 'Ambikatanayadatta', 1896–1981) poem 'Bidugade' (Freedom), likely composed around 1924, was written in defiance of imperialism during our national movement. Some of its lines read as follows: 'Neck is bound to a yoke/Breaking it off is good for life/Mother is crying within/Until then, the world is a prison/Let us go, off towards freedom.'

This poem unequivocally communicates the longing for freedom when the pain of oppression becomes unbearable. Unlike the density found in many of Bendre's other works, this poem adopts a straightforward approach, serving as an alternative statement to the action suggested in 'we are off towards freedom'. The simplicity is interrupted only by the phrase 'Till then the world is a prison', which aptly portrays the natural consequence of living under foreign rule. The entire poem comes alive in meaning because of this one sentence, laying bare the frightening reality faced during the independence struggle. The term 'song of agitator' might seem contradictory, but the agitator's singing becomes a symbolic declaration of freedom. Singing is equal to proclaiming freedom, emphasizing the shared experience between the prisoner, and the policeman waiting for him; both cannot escape each other. The activist is prepared for anything when freedom is regarded as the supreme value.

These two poems, 'Shukrageete' and 'Bidugade', present contrasting perspectives. One notable advantage of imperialism is the unification of the entire world. Lines like 'Vritra Kali Mara Ahi Ahriman Saitan' (listing the names of characters from myths of diverse countries) likely could not have been written in the twelfth or thirteenth centuries; the empire brought together different cultures. Another significant aspect of Empire is the emphasis on system. After resolving political and social issues within this system, the empire provides the mental tranquillity to ponder otherworldly questions such as 'when will there be the end of opposition to god'? One of the aspirations of the 'Model Mysore' during that time was to emulate the British state system and translate it into its own context to construct a civilized society.

Bendre's poem conveys a completely opposing sentiment. 'The bird finds a path in the sky/Fish in water/River flows even on the hills/Why we alone are in chains?' The aspiration for freedom is symbolized through images of nature. Despite any joy, the 'yoke on the neck' brings pain. The only way is to rush forward without dwelling on the pros and cons. Additional violence may be encountered, and even after gaining independence, chaos might persist. The history of nationalism is rife with treachery, fraud and deceit. Poems like these envision a new era beyond such turmoil. Kuvempu's (K.V. Puttappa, 1904–94) poem also reflects a similar spirit: 'Let the head roll/Let me bleed and collapse/Yet the heart insists/on seeing the sun rise.' It emphasizes charging ahead without concern for the future.

An examination of the themes of these poems reveals a contradiction, embodying the perplexity arising from conflicting perspectives and experiences. It may now be perceived that these poems encapsulate the choices confronting the country's political consciousness at that period. The populace had to navigate between these opposing ideologies, recognizing that, in history one side triumphs while the other faces defeat. Yet, these victories and defeats are not the final verdict. Instead, they serve as testaments to our country's evolving sense of history. The quest for our history began with the onset of British rule, and for Karnataka, Alura Venkatarao's *Karnataka Gatavaibhava* ('The Glories of Karnataka's Past') marked an early exploration into historical consciousness—a vision of history.

History unfurled vivid depictions of the past before our eyes, providing an avenue to escape the degrading circumstances of the present. The urgency for historical study intensified with the failure of the 1857 war of Indian Independence against the British Empire. Excluding works explicitly expressing our historical consciousness, we must explore how history has indirectly moulded our literature. The sudden transformation of literature in the latter part of the nineteenth century, diverging from its unique trajectory until then, warrants persistent inquiry. The prevalent notion attributes this change to the influence of English literature.

While this traditional belief holds some truth, crediting the birth of a new literature solely to the individual efforts of educated writers seems less credible. The innovation in Navodaya literature is somewhat distinctive. Kuvempu compared the freshness of the sunrise to the novelty of new literature, proclaiming, 'A new dawn is breaking on the virtuous eastern horizon of the country' ('Naveena'). Writers of that era collectively endorsed the idea that literature should be as refreshing as the sunrise every day. Rejecting the old in favour of the new was logical. 'Trampling on yesterdays/Tying the tomorrows to the head/A new day has arrived,' sang Anandakanda's (Betageri Krishnasharma, 1900–82) vision of novelty in a somewhat ironic and ludicrous manner. However, at that time, little consideration was given to the meaning of the 'newness' that had encompassed one's personality. Exploring how this 'newness' revitalized our language remains a challenging question.

A little reflection on these reveals the intertwined relationship between history, translations and modernity. Western scholars translating Indian works into English for our educated populace contributed to their growing admiration for history. The uniqueness of English literature also captivated them, initially defining our identity. Above all, translation became a pursuit for the educated. 'Discourse' has become a popular term in English in recent times, yet an equivalent Indian term is yet to emerge. In Kannada, it could be referred to as 'nirupane'. Diaries, letters, scriptures and poems all became forms of discourse. 'Translation' too transformed into such a discourse for our educated individuals. During a certain period, all college-educated individuals wrote in English, and editors penned forewords in English for new editions of our old poems. There was a university mandate that students studying Kannada literature should write their PhD theses in English. While not conventional translations, these constituted translations of unwritten Kannada discourses. The bilingual sensibility of the educated sought a form of unity through translation. Writing an English preface to an old Kannada poem represented a novel approach to studying that poetry. A more traditional method involved offering a detailed commentary on the poem, as seen in Durgacharya's commentary on Yaska's dictionary, now included in Yaska's expanded dictionary. However, the new type of study featured distinct authorship and editing. Even if the critique centred on the work itself, it stood as an independent work. This scientific method was imparted by Western scholars of the East.

Such translations provided us with a sense of history, introducing us to modernity. History is not merely knowledge of the past; it involves seeking the roots of present problems in the past and envisioning tomorrow's dreams through those solutions.

History represents the consciousness of unbroken time, and historicism emerges as a concrete principle in this context. Historical time differs from natural time, and the principle of history transcends the laws of nature. A Western scholar posits that if god created the world, then man created history within that world. Regardless of the existence of god, for humans to live as humans, a sense of history is essential. Historicism indirectly asserts that the full responsibility for humanity's sins and virtues, right and wrong, wisdom and foolishness, lies with humans. Even religion, which once shed light on these matters, has now become a part of history. History does not disprove religion, but the vibrant sensibility of religion has become a thing of the past. This principle of historicism is the reason humans have lost both nature and religion, with no mysteries remaining according to historicity.

At the outset of this discussion, a fact was presented: an idol of Venkateswara manifested on a black rock in a forest near Soratur in Gadag district. God appeared in Soratur Desai's dream, revealing the fact of His incarnation. The next morning, Desai went to the location, lifted the rock, discovered the idol buried beneath the refuse and ritually installed the deity there. Many years later, a sadhu named Brahmananda went to the site and erected a temple, which still stands. Buildings for pilgrims have since surrounded the area, where Venkateswara is worshipped throughout the year.

How does history perceive this fact? Both Soratur Desai and Beladadhi Brahmananda, who erected a temple, are historical figures. Brahmananda was born in 1859 and buried in Kagwad in 1918. History acknowledges these details. However, neither Desai's dream nor Brahmananda's devotional service to god can be captured by history. It does not assert that the god within Tirupati is enshrined in the stone in Soratur. Even at that time, people accepted that god appeared on a rock at the foot of the hill. Perhaps, similarly, in the household of a poor Brahmin priest, there should be an incarnation of a great devotee like Brahmananda. There is no causal relationship between these two facts.

Historically, this is a legend, true only from a devotee's perspective. History extracts the factual aspects of this legend, leaving the rest behind. Soratur Desai is a family known to history, one that participated in the 1857 war of Indian Independence. Hammigi Desai joined forces with Bhimaraya of Mundaragi and aided Babasaheb of Naragunda. Brahmananda was born into a poor priest's family in Gadagoli near Badami. Having learnt the scriptures from different gurus, realizing that even the admiration of scholarship could hinder devotional asceticism, he sought the guidance of Brahmachaitanya of Gondavali and propagated Rama bhakti. Interspersed among these historical facts are the details of legends such as the order given by god in a dream, the appearance of an idol of the deity under a rock amid refuse and Brahmananda's epiphany. History will assess the significance of each of these elements.

History is an all-encompassing force, amalgamating disparate principles, assigning them their rightful places and constructing a system. The primary objective of history lies in crafting a distinct period, diverging from the notion of seasonal periods. Unlike natural time, where nothing is truly new or old, the categorization of old and new occurs inherently within historical time. Although not as systematic, a form of historicism began to emerge in our country in the nineteenth century. A significant reason for labelling our history as unsystematic is the lack of access to proper media. Every European country possesses its own history, following a narrative path marked by continuity. By adhering to a similar trajectory, India's history became synonymous with the history of north India, relegating the history of south India to a mere footnote. The approach to history needs a transformation.

Simultaneity should arise by disrupting the unified narrative of history. A history encompassing multiple languages and diverse cultures must be forged, accompanied by a shift in perspective.

Despite the historical chaos, 'newness' emerges organically from history itself. The combination of history and translations has played a pivotal role in shaping our modernity.

3

When discussing the modernity of the new Kannada literature, the focus must be on the emergence of new literary genres. The beginning of our new literatures with historical novels is not accidental. The introduction of history as a literary theme itself was novel. B. Venkatacharya played a pivotal role in bringing to Kannada the novels of Walter Scott-inspired Bankimchandra. As the onset of British rule was in Bengal, English education gained traction among the Bengali educated class. Notably, figures such as Keshab Chandra Sen, Ishwar Chandra Vidyasagar and Bankim Chandra Chatterjee were part of this intellectual milieu. The introduction of the English language and Western culture triggered conflicting sentiments of attraction and repulsion. Keshab Chandra Sen deeply engaged with English literature, undergoing a complete immersion and conversion. He regularly delivered speeches in both Bengali and English. In contrast, Ishwar Chandra Vidyasagar and Bankim Chandra Chatterjee were contemptuous of the British. This period saw the translation of classical Sanskrit poems into Bengali. The novelty of the English language was a sort of challenge to Sanatan Dharma. In this context, Bankim Chandra's historical novels were produced. Both Keshab Sen and Bankim Chatterjee represent fragments of our blended social sensibility. Achieving an undivided sensibility beyond these divides was only possible for the international mindset of an aristocrat like Rabindranath Tagore. However, that is a separate story.

Hari Narayana Apte, a Marathi writer comparable to Bankim, shared a similar historical backdrop. Bengal and Maharashtra witnessed decisive battles against the British, and after the Peshwa's downfall in 1818, the East India Company's rule was firmly established. Sir William Bentinck's governance marked a period of fundamental reforms. This era played a crucial role in shaping the history of India, providing writers with a historical canvas.

Bankim Chandra's *Anandamath* and Hari Narayana Apte's *Kamalakumari* stand out as representative novels with a shared objective—the liberation of the country from foreign rule. *Anandamath* depicts an army of committed young men led by a monk, advocating readiness for any sacrifice for the nation's liberation. In *Kamalakumari*, Apte portrays Shivaji's conquest of the Kondana fort and the sacrifice of Tanaji Malasure, Shivaji's favourite commander, illustrating the theme of sacrifice for the nation's cause. These works play a crucial role in the formation of nationalism, emphasizing the readiness for selfless commitment to society and country.

While the subjects of *Anandamath* and *Kamalakumari* belong to different eras, their shared goal is to voice opposition to the British invasion. The methods employed in *Anandamath* for the freedom struggle exude an air of mystery, with disguises and transformations creating an enigmatic atmosphere. Members of the organization use a secret language, communicating through verses from Jayadeva's *Gita Govinda*. The devotional and beautiful verses of *Gita Govinda* are laced with political overtones, exemplified in lines like 'Mlechchanivaha Nidhane Kalayasi Karavalam/Dhumaketumiva Kimapi Karalam' ('Appearing like a comet, carrying a terrifying sword for bringing about the annihilation of the barbarians at the end of the Kali-yuga' [*Gita Govinda*, 1:10]). This verse conveys a clear meaning, intertwining Purana with disguised history and presenting a novel historical philosophy. In the face of political crises, the novel suggests that when war becomes the only solution, violence becomes inevitable. However, the violence is carried out in the name of a monk, shrouded in secrecy, to keep the enemy unaware.

Kamalakumari also portrays war, where a hero like Tanaji must fight to conquer a fort held by the warlord Udayabhanu. In this novel, violence knows no limits, and Tanaji's death, though causing grief to Shivaji, is deemed inevitable. The fort is named 'Sinhagad', becoming a memorial for the hero Tanaji. Such conflicts are not uncommon between outsiders seeking settlement, and the locals. When outsiders aim to obliterate the 'culture' of the locals, the locals strive to preserve it. Under these conditions history invariably rises to become the Purana. The underlying sentiment here is that the outsiders are all 'mlechas'. If they conquer our forts, we must fight to reconquer our forts.

The term 'mlecha' is religious, representing all non-followers of Vedic principles, whether Muslims or Christians. Protecting religion, daughters' chastity and cows are deemed a sacred duty. Although these sentiments may not be novel, they underscore the age-old theme of protecting one's faith and culture. The novel form allows for humorous situations, as seen in Kerura Vasudevacharya's *Aurangzeb*, where widows in the city of Bhagya flee with their pickle jars when attacked by Aurangzeb's soldiers, turning a historical event into a comic episode within the novel's atmosphere.

The purpose of these novels was to discover historical parallels to the contemporary situation of alien rule. Another motive, whether known or unknown to the author, was to infuse realism, a rarity in our country's literature. European literature, drawing inspiration from Greek literature, sought to develop a connection with reality. Aristotle's timeless statement, 'Art is an imitation of reality', underscores the duty of art to follow, imitate and reflect the real truth. Greatness in art lies in its imitation of reality, prompting a significant question: Does art, which imitates reality, have an independent existence? This question has sparked debates since the time of Aristotle. While some argue that art is not mere imitation but a representation or re-creation of truth, the moral validity of truth remains unquestionable. Philosophers may offer different definitions of truth, but the sovereign power of truth governs not only art but all sciences. Philosophers may discuss truth, but the role of art is to embrace the authority of truth and proceed. Recently, there have been statements suggesting that 'reality imitates art', in contrast to Aristotle's view. Nevertheless, regardless of one's perspective, the connection between art and reality remains unmistakable.

Similar debates have surfaced in our culture as well. Rhetoricians have questioned the significance of 'Rasanubhava', the experience of rasa, contemplating whether it is true, false, illusory or metaphorical. The nature of human wisdom tends to categorize experiences as true or false, and even if there is a slight suspicion that what art conveys isn't true, art strives to affirm its truth. Literature takes pride in the belief that truth can be encapsulated in the all-pervading net of language. Western philosophy shares the belief that the nature of truth is hidden and must be revealed, making the pursuit of truth integral to all arts and sciences. Instruments must be innovated and refined continually, while processes and concepts need to be rediscovered. It is an ongoing quest. The nature of truth can take on historical, scientific and occasionally even artistic dimensions. In instances of conflict in scientific methods, another method can be crafted to rectify it. The objective is methodological perfection, a concept that is the essence of technology.

The construction of the Venkateswara temple by Soratur Desai brings another dimension to this discussion. In addition to Desai and Brahmananda, another character in this narrative is Sakhabai of Shirahatti, who, after her husband's death, invested all her money to build a room in this place and devoted her life to god's service. Living in a small house in the forest with her daughter,

Sakhabai helped pilgrims whenever they arrived. Ultimately, Soratur Desai, Sakhabai and Brahmananda transformed this place into a sacred temple.

When presented in writing, all these details might resemble a historical account or the opening chapter of a novel. Yet, can both these genres—history and fiction—effectively convey events like Venkateswara Desai's dream-ordained instructions or the episode of god manifesting in stone? History remains silent on such matters. Unlike a novel, history is a linear narrative, restricted from taking detours. A novel, on the other hand, can weave multiple perspectives into its plot. The Western novel, from its inception, has remained loyal to reality. Additionally, individual consciousness has taken precedence over collective consciousness. In the eighteenth century, as individuals became increasingly detached from their societal bonds, autobiography emerged as a literary form. The difference between Saint Augustine's autobiography and Rousseau's autobiography is quite pronounced in this context. Saint Augustine placed paramount importance on his relationship with god. Augustine's individuality, like the individuality of our narrators, is engaged in an ongoing dialogue with god. His relentless pursuit is to embody the ideals of a perfect Christian. Conversely, Rousseau's autobiography takes an opposite stance. Rousseau posited the idea that a person, born in a state of purity, becomes constrained by society's moral regulations and gradually loses moral freedom. This period seems to signify a time when individuals become estranged from the society that nurtured, raised and educated them, akin to the separation of a growing child from their parents, both physically and mentally. This shift had a profound impact on literature, particularly evident in the emergence of the voice of individual freedom in the romantic literature of Europe.

In Jane Austen's novel *Mansfield Park*, the theme of individual freedom is subtly interwoven. Fanny, the protagonist of this tale, departs from her father's house to live with her aunt. Fanny's mother, facing the challenges of supporting numerous children in poverty, leaves her at her sister's residence. Fanny is compelled to grow up obediently under the care of her aunt and elder sister. She dutifully serves and tends to their needs, displaying a submissive demeanour to everyone. Her uncle's authority is absolute and unquestioned, at least for a few years. However, the daughters of her aunt eventually act according to their own desires and enter into matrimony. Edmund harbours deep affection for Fanny, though he refrains from openly expressing it. Another suitor, Crawford, also becomes enamoured with her. When Fanny's elder sister urges her to marry Crawford, Fanny decides to leave for her father's house, citing her inability to comply with the proposal.

Both Fanny's compliance and defiance are driven by her prudence. While she has sought refuge in her uncle's house and has been favoured by them, she considers it her duty to obey him, primarily to fulfil his wants and needs. Whatever tasks her uncle assigns, she dutifully carries them out, recognizing them as her responsibilities. However, she maintains her independence when it comes to her work, listening to no one's instructions. Even when Henry proposes to her, she is the one who decides how to respond. While obedience can be deemed a commendable quality, it is not an inherent trait; rather, circumstances often compel individuals to obey. However, the unique freedom lies in the individual's power to decide whom to obey, when and to what extent. Faced with disappointment, Henry seeks advice from Fanny on what he should do next. In response, she says, 'Listen to your heart, everyone should act according to the dictates of his conscience.' The essence of individual freedom is encapsulated in her statement, reflecting her desire for knowledge to guide her. It is noteworthy that this perspective doesn't have a spiritual meaning. It is a perspective opposite to customary views.

With the advent of the novel, came the practice of writing autobiographies and biographies, all distinct forms of history. This period coincided with the emergence of Walter Scott's novels, blurring the lines between narrative, history and fiction. Thinkers like Carlyle and Emerson contended that history was essentially the biographies of great individuals. While fiction seamlessly integrates geography and history, historical writing often centres on the intimate details of notable lives, creating a symbiotic relationship between historical novels and the broader historical narrative.

This consciousness can be considered the driving force behind the inception of historical novels in Kannada. In historical fiction, the coexistence of fictional characters with historical figures is a distinctive feature. Galganatha's (1869–1942) novels, which are adaptations of Apte's Marathi works into Kannada, showcase numerous fictional characters within the historical context. Crafting a character in this manner serves to establish a unique perspective of consciousness. In K.M. Munshi's novel *Gujaratano Nath*, two characters, Kakabhatta and Manjari, take centre stage, reconstructing the history of medieval Gujarat. Kakabhatta's gaze is all-encompassing, traversing Gujarat from Khambhat to Kachchh on his horse. His mission involves locating the Nath of Gujarat. Subsequently, Kakabhatta imparts knowledge to Siddharaja Jayasimha, the king of Gujarat. His understanding of medieval Gujarat's history surpasses that of eminent statesmen such as Munjala, Udayana Mehta and Tribhuvanapala. Kakabhatta possesses a mystical vision, seeking to unify these diverse elements and transform the disparate factions of Gujarat into a cohesive nation by realizing their innermost essence. Additionally, Kakabhatta serves as the narrator in this novel and its sequel, Rajadhiraja.

However, the question arises: What authority does Kakabhatta hold in this novel? Unlike historical figures, he is a fictional character. While only a handful of individuals are remembered from Gujarat in the Middle Ages, their collective contribution alone cannot construct a state. Hence, the novelist introduces additional characters. In Betageri Krishnasharma's novel,

Mallikarjuna, numerous fictional characters exist, yet they remain confined within their individual roles. Kakabhatta, however, assumes a central role in steering the narrative. Therefore, the legitimacy of his authority within the novel prompts inquiry, and the straightforward answer is that he is a fictional character within a novel.

This question warrants a more detailed examination. We can also consider M.S. Puttanna's (1854–1930) novel *Madiddunno Maharaya.* Sadashiva Dikshita, Sita and Kittajoisa are fictional characters in the novel, not historical figures. However, Mummadi Krishnaraja Wodeyar appears in this work as a character, attending Sita's wedding and blessing the bride and groom. While the novel undoubtedly depicts life in Mysore during Mummadi's reign, the query arises: Is Mummadi's role merely indicative of the period? It seems that Mummadi's character is responsible for all the events, both positive and negative, in the novel, putting the statement 'Raja Kalasya Karanam' ('the king is the cause of the times') to the test.

Although Kakabhatta in Munshi's novel and Mummadi in Puttanna's novel are both characters in novels, a significant difference sets them apart. Mummadi is a historically accurate character, whereas Kaka is a fictional creation. Mummadi's identity can be traced back to history, a claim that cannot be made for Kaka's character. Kaka's persona solely belongs to the novel's world, nourished by its air, light and water. It can be described as a portrayal of possibility or something similar. The author envisions such a character and places it within the novel's realm. Since Kaka must be born and raised in Gujarat during the Middle Ages, his attire and mannerisms should align with that historical period. This rationale for adaptation must reside within the author, a concept Aristotle refers to as the logic of the plot.

While it is true that the logic of the plot is an author's responsibility, the author has the liberty to waive it if deemed inconvenient. An author, free to create any character that can interact with the historical world, can take even greater liberties. Another Kaka from the twentieth century might enter the historical world, making Kaka a modern character in disguise. This introduces the possibility of the intermixing of time or anachronism. Shakespearean plays are rich with examples of such hybridization of time or anachronism. This attempt aims to scrutinize history through the lens of contemporary reality.

When it comes to a literary genre like the novel, the way our authors approach it varies as much as their talent. M.S. Puttanna's novels, despite being filled with reality, differ significantly from those that followed him. In Puttanna's novels, the world within the narrative isn't confined to the consciousness of the protagonist. *Madiddunno Maharaya* lacks a hero character, with Sita occupying the central role. However, her consciousness is limited to her way of life, rendering the world she inhabits somewhat without a protagonist. Even the magician who resurrected the deceased Sita arrives and departs by the end of the novel. In Mummadi's enervated regime, vices such as murder, extortion, theft, rape, cheating and fraud abound. The novel deals with the predicament of virtues and sins, a theme more pivotal than the conventional notions of good and bad. It ponders the secret behind Sita's virtue provoking Siddappaji's sin, presenting a unique perspective compared to subsequent novels. Puttanna's novel infuses reality bestowed by history, depicting life in historical places like Mysore and Sanjawadi. The places are disrupted, extinguished and revived by forces invisible to conventional history. The novel explores the intricate relationship between the unseen system and the visible chaos of life.

In a similar vein, one can contemplate the mythological novels of Devudu Narasimha Shastri (1886–1962). Devudu's experimental approach is apparent in works like *Mahabrahmana* and *Mahakshatriya*. A distinction arises between the imaginative realms of the novel and the Purana. While a Purana creates an uncanny object, a novel fashions a familiar world. The rationale of the plot, prevalent in the novel, is absent in the Purana. Puranic figures may endure for thousands of years to fulfil their destiny, transcending temporal and spatial limitations. The rules governing the Puranic world are the same as the rules governing poetry.

Purana, history and fiction represent three distinct forms of storytelling. The Purana genre underwent transformation within our epics, with works like the Mahabharata encompassing all three narrative forms. This multiplicity is evident in the Mahabharata's three types of beginnings. First, after completing the Panchaka Samanta Yatra, reminded of his ancestors, Suta Puranika, embarks on narrating the story of the Kauravas and Pandavas. This aligns with the old historical route. Second, a sacrificial event is described, presenting a narrative structure that commences and concludes abruptly, like a description found in a novel. Last, the third chapter unfolds the story of the feud between Garuda and the son of Kadri, which is the mythological path. The Mahabharata adeptly incorporates these three openings, showcasing its diverse storytelling elements.

Devudu skilfully adapts the narratives from the Puranas into the novelistic form, as evident in *Mahabrahmana*. The tale of Vishwamitra found in the Vedas, Upanishads, Ramayana and Mahabharata is meticulously gathered by Devudu and shaped as a novel. An illustrative instance is the character of Vamadeva. Although Vamadeva is a Vedic sage, the novel doesn't provide a basis for his amicable relations with Vishwamitra or his aid in Vishwamitra's pursuits. Similarly, there is no grounding, as Vishwamitra received Rudra's blessings with Vamadeva's assistance. Devudu openly acknowledges in the novel's foreword that these elements stem from his personal experiences. Another example is the treatment of the Menaka episode. The dynamics between Vishwamitra and Menaka, amusing in contemporary society, are elevated to a superhuman context within the novel. It is crucial to emphasize that there is no glorification of Vishwamitra and Menaka's romance. Instead, the novel suggests that if lust awakens in the heart of an ascetic like Vishvamitra, there must be a divine plan or intention behind it. This nuanced perspective is exclusive to the novel, showcasing the dynamic interplay between Purana and fiction in Devudu's work. Before *Mahabrahmana*, Devudu honed his craft through the creation of numerous novels. In works like *Antaranga*, he explored the theme of lust in a similar context. While this vision of lust differs from Sigmund Freud's, it serves, like Freud's vision, as a tool to delve into the mysteries of life. The novel's realm provides a vivid and empathetic exploration of human experiences. His novels, steeped in Rasanubhava, offer rich material for understanding modern literature's emotional experience. The realm of the novel, as envisioned by Devudu, encapsulates vitality and empathy, providing a rich source for understanding Rasanubhava in modern literature. Devudu's novels offer a captivating exploration of the transformation of Puranic symbols into novelistic characters. In *Mahakshatriya*, the primal conflict between Indra and Vritra assumes a distinct significance. Devudu portrays Indra not merely as a god but as a character embodying a principle, the lord of the gods. To establish this point in the novel, Shachi's character undergoes a reconstruction mirroring that of Indra's. If Indra symbolizes the deity of the senses, Shachi assumes a parallel role as the deity of the fundamental elements. Employing the Panchikarana Vidya from the Upanishads, Devudu masterfully recreates these characters. Vritra, in this narrative, emerges as another principle disrupting the established order of creation. Driven by aspirations to become a mystic, Vritra, the son of Vishvarupa, introduces a complex network of relationships within the novel. This intricate interplay unravels the mysterious universe of mythological meaning. Significantly, it is within the novel's confines that these diverse meanings converge, giving rise to a poetic and nuanced image.

An exploration of the meaning of Devudu's works might not be pertinent here. However, Devudu's adept utilization of the newly emerged novel form is remarkable. Despite being a scholar with a command of the Vedas and Upanishads, along with his own claims of mystical experiences, Devudu's true talent manifested as that of a novelist. He successfully navigated the realm of social novels with works like *Antaranga* (The Mind), *Eradaneya Janma* (Second Birth) and *Malli*. The essence of his novels lies in breathing life into the mystical figures of the Purana, making their significance tangible. An examination of the episode depicting the invocation of Rudra through mantra and the subsequent realization vividly illustrates Devudu's imaginative prowess. These works demonstrate the possibility of crafting novels distinct from Western counterparts.

Devudu's novels are extraordinary, grounded in a purely worldly vision. Few elements captivated our emerging author more than reality itself. The ultimate benefit was the revelation that the reality of our country lay untapped, like an uncultivated field. Novels like *Kanuru Heggadati*, *Marali Mannige* and *Gramayana* derive their essence from this unexplored reality. Novels and short stories adeptly harness this inexplicable yet richly textured reality.

4

Before examining new dramas in Kannada, let us re-examine the relationship between drama and epics. Whether in the Greek tradition or in our own, dramas have sustained themselves by drawing subjects and characters from the epics. Six of Bhasa's thirteen dramas find inspiration from the Mahabharata, while some draw from the Ramayana. Yet, disparities exist between the narratives presented in these epics and Bhasa's dramas. In *Pratima Nataka* there are episodes such as Bharata entering the hall of statues or Rama pursuing the blackbuck (rather than the golden deer) during Sita's abduction which are absent in the original Ramayana. Similarly, in the play *Pancharatra*, there is no depiction of the battle between Kauravas and Pandavas. The reasons behind these differences remain elusive. From an artistic standpoint, these alterations may seem to convey something. In *Pratima Nataka* on the day of Dasharatha's death anniversary, when Rama seeks Brahmins, Ravana appears in disguise before him. Ravana, posing as a Brahmin, imparts hunting skills to Rama and subsequently kidnaps Sita when Rama departs. This modified episode brings attention to an underlying issue in the Ramayana. Ravana asserts that it is easy to abduct the wife of Rama, who is not a king, just as demons are able to seize fire, when it is unconsecrated by mantra.

The history of Raghuvamsa intertwines family and political ties. Kaikeyi opposes Rama's kingship, insisting he should go to the forest, even though Rama agrees to relinquish the throne. Bhasa, cognizant of the enigmatic power of kingship, highlights the distinction between managing a family and governing a kingdom. In Valmiki's poem, Rama loses Sita due to Ravana and Maricha's deceit. However, in the *Pratima Nataka*, Rama loses Sita as he is not the king. Rama withdraws from politics but loses Sita in a dramatic irony. Kaikeyi, triumphant in politics, suffers the loss of her son. Ayodhya remains guarded solely by the vacant shrine of the Raghuvamsa kings for fourteen years.

Taking the liberty of criticism and delving deeper, Bhasa's *Pratima Nataka* appears to convey significant insights about the genre of drama itself. The play narrates the saga of the Raghuvamsa kings, beginning with Dileep, followed by Raghu, Aja and Dasharatha. This lineage is the essence of the story. Dileep, empowered by Nandini's grace, begets a son; Raghu achieves great conquests, expanding the kingdom's borders; Aja dies after the death of Indumati; and Dasharatha, steers his chariot in ten directions. However, none of his three wives bear children, and eventually he begets three sons, but also the curse of a sage.

Bhasa subtly reveals this understanding through a minor incident. Rama, required to dress up as a young man for his coronation, shows reluctance and engages in other activities. He dons the attire intended for a drama, turning himself and Sita into characters from the play. Rama, expected to embody a prince, assumes the role of a sage. Rama feigns ignorance of the crisis facing the dynasty's history. This act disrupts the lineage's historical continuity, termed a disturbance of order in the play. Kaikeyi was the first to break this order. As the lineage's history unfolded, the relationship between the individual and the lineage remained intact. The prosperity of Dileep or Raghu mirrored the prosperity of Raghuvamsa. However, Rama now distances himself from Raghuvamsa. His exile, Sita's abduction, and his victory over Ravana, become personal accomplishments. Despite this, Rama belongs to the same lineage. In Nandigram, when Bharata comes to see him, Sita mistakes Bharata's voice for Rama's, highlighting their close bond. Rama leaves his parents and ventures into the forest with Lakshmana, while Bharata waits for him, refusing to rule in Rama's absence. Rama's shoes replace him, and deceased kings are immortalized as statues. If Rama is not Kaikeyi's son, she is Bharata's mother but not a nurturing mother. Bharata elucidates the difference in meaning between the words 'Jananee' and 'Mata' to her.

In Rama's absence, his footwear assumes the role of king, Bharata becomes the regent, and the mother loses her nurturing essence, signifying a breakdown in the connection between words and meanings. According to Bhasa, when one entity transforms into another, it embodies drama. Laxmana contends that if a king—a warrior, does not bequeath the kingdom to his eldest son, rebellion is justified. The truth that the eldest son should be the king deserves protest against anyone who distorts this fact. If the eldest son, now the king, embodies truth, then the footwear representing the king becomes a symbolic truth. Perhaps, symbolic truth takes precedence in drama. Symbols allow for description, and their truth can be ascertained, even though the world around them is vast. Allegory, symbol, metaphor, simile, and other figures serve as tools to render invisible truths visible. In Bhasa's play *Madhyam Vyayoga*, he explores various meanings of the word 'Madhyam'. While Bhima embodies meanings like 'middling' and 'great,' Kesavadasa's middle son suggests opposing meanings. Only by being the middle one does he become a replica of Bhima. However, the means of conveying the truth is not in itself the truth.

Epic narratives such as the Ramayana and the Mahabharata predominantly address issues of kingship and anarchy. From this standpoint, the eldest son assuming the role of king aligns with order. Yet, this is a complex issue. In the Mahabharata, there are elder sons who renounced the kingdom for various reasons, making it challenging to define the eldest son. Bhasa revisits this question in his plays. While an epic is audible poetry, drama is visual poetry—what the eyes see, the ears cannot hear. Both the eyes and ears must remain attentive during the play.

Our criticism of Sanskrit dramas often centres on their frequent reliance on material from the Ramayana and the Mahabharata. However, comparing Bhasa's *Pratima Nataka* and Bhavabhuti's *Uttararamacharita* reveals distinct dramas. Classical dramas, in essence, lack a singular subject. For instance, if one inquires about the subject of Sophocles' play *Oedipus*, the response would involve the character Oedipus, laden with various meanings. Similarly, Rama's character presents a different set of problems in *Pratima Nataka* compared to *Uttararamacharita*.

The tradition of Sanskrit drama ended in the seventeenth century, ushering in a new direction during the Bhakti period. Notably, the experience of drama became a shared endeavour for both actors and the audience. The poetics of the Bhakti period classified worldly rasas as 'rasabhasas' (appearance of rasa), asserting that Bhakti was the sole genuine rasa. Jayadeva's *Gita*

Govinda exemplifies the idea that Shringara is also a devotional device. What holds greater significance is the absence of distance between the play and the audience, who collaboratively piece together a puzzle. In this context, the audience doesn't evaluate the play solely based on the experience it imparts. Classical drama, in contrast, maintained a separation, with the audience reverting to their daily lives following Bharatavakya. When they recite 'kale varshathu parjanyah prithivee sasyashalinee' ('may it rain timely, may the Earth be plentiful with crops') the audience is likely to be reminded of their own concerns pertaining to rains and grains, and their farms and houses.

However, the old drama served as a socially motivated temporary organization, necessitating performances at fairs and festivals to reach a broader audience. Due to the absence of dedicated theatres, drama remained an improvised institution. The auditorium was erected just like the temporary arrangement on the eve of the wedding and was dismantled after the performance. As a result, theatre did not evolve into a distinct profession.

Professional theatre made its debut in India with the arrival of the British, marked by the emergence of Parsi theatre as the country's first professional stage (these came to be called 'company drama'). Predominantly featuring mythological plays, their repertoire also included historical dramas and Urdu translations of Shakespeare, introducing a new principle of reality into Indian drama. In these plays, reality manifested in a distinct form; for instance, the portrayal of Jayadratha's severed head flying from one wing to another. What was once a symbolic performance transitioned into a tangible one. The realism that emerged, from Ravi Varma's paintings to contemporary cinema, stripped mythology of its symbolic essence, a departure from the symbolic expression found in poetry, dance and traditional drama.

It is crucial to recognize that the disparity between Sanskrit drama and company drama extends beyond literary aspects.

While it is true that the literary brilliance of figures like Kalidasa or Bhavabhuti may be absent in company dramas, a more significant loss lies in the diminishing dramatic quality of our performance methods. Consequently, the Rasanubhava delivered by contemporary drama becomes artificial. In the realm of Rasanubhava, experience and understanding are interwoven; understanding does not distort experience. If, for instance, Jayadratha's head appears to fly directly before our eyes, acknowledging it as an artificial construct becomes necessary. Unique experiences require unique modes of comprehension. Company plays often eliminate any room for the audience's intellectual or imaginative engagement, emphasizing simplicity in comprehension and sensory experience.

Perhaps, it is for this reason that a new theatre movement began in protest against company plays. Among our new dramatists, only 'Samsa' stood outside this protest. It would be premature to comment on Samsa's theatre without it being staged a few times. Nonetheless, his dramas could potentially endure even on the company stage, provided they are supported by a well-trained cast. Consider, for example, Doddi, who, upon seeing Ranadhir asleep, must deliver a four-page speech; she must possess the skill of speaking effectively on stage. Similarly, the actor portraying Randhir must have mastered the art of acting while lying down, complementing Doddi's dialogue delivery. Company plays did have such skilled actors. Undoubtedly, drama training is indispensable for professional theatre, to ensure that the audience receives value for money.

The accomplishment of theatre companies is commendable. The primary allure of these dramas lies in the actors themselves. The list of notable actors is extensive, including Varadacharya, Gangadhar Raya, Gubbi Veeranna, Subbaiah Naidu, Nagendra Raya, Handiganur Siddaramappa, Hiranyaiah, Adrisyappa Manvi, Garuda Sadashivaraya, Vamanarao Mastar, Shirahatti Venkobaraya,

Lakshmeshwarada Bachasani, Guledagudda Gangubai, Sonubai Doddamani, Basavaraja Mansoor and many more. After Shivaji and Lokmanya Tilak, Balgandharva is the most celebrated name in Maharashtra. It is no coincidence that such actors sparked fervour for drama among the audience. These actors may not have been highly educated, and the specifics of their training are unknown. However, studying their performances can contribute to the development of the art of acting. Despite theatre and cinema being new mediums, these actors adapted to both very well. It is worth noting that many early actors in our cinema hailed from Parsi theatre. Although theatre and cinema were novel mediums for these actors, they adeptly learnt how to perform for these forms of entertainment.

However, these actors cannot be credited with creating the language of acting. Even when the actor is interpreting the playwright's work, they infuse their performance with their own language. Some of Balgandharva's acting moments surpassed the talents of Khadilkar. In the hands of a musician, a raga achieves perfection with vivacity. A genuine actor is one who explores all the possibilities inherent in a playwright's work. If confined to the performance of a single actor, such a production ceases to be a true drama, and the actor cannot be considered an authentic actor. Nonetheless, some actors in the company had this remarkable power.

However, our drama culture did not evolve in this manner. The reason is the sudden separation of company plays from our folk theatre. A certain civic class consciousness developed among the actors. Consequently, the actors in amateur theatre groups constituted a distinct category. Even in amateur theatres, there are no formally educated actors. Although they may be educated, their understanding of drama and performance is not profound. Due to unnatural acting in company plays, they approached acting from a different perspective. Some actors are oblivious to the notion that they should transcend their individuality and embody their characters. Furthermore, a new wave of actors trained at the National School of Drama (NSD) emerged. The director, serving as a new guiding principle, shapes the play according to their vision. However, actors in this setting do not always enjoy complete creative freedom. It is crucial to recognize that the one who must stand on the stage and execute the play is the actor, not the writer or the director.

Kannada dramatic literature has matured through the works of notable playwrights such as T.P. Kailasam, Samsa (A.N. Swamy Venkatadri Iyer), Sriranga (Adya Rangacharya), D.R. Bendre, Jadabharata (G.B. Joshi), Shivaram Karanth, Girish Karnad, P. Lankesh and Chandrasekhara Kambara. Their successful experiments in dramatic literature indicate that these plays will endure as literary works. Influences from Western dramatists like Bernard Shaw, Henrik Ibsen, Anton Chekov, Luigi Pirandello, Albert Camus and Jean-Paul Satre have also left their mark on Kannada drama. While this cross-cultural influence is inevitable in the twentieth century, the extent to which Kannada drama has impacted others remains a question. Translations of Sriranga's *Kelu Janamejaya*, Karnad's *Tughlaq* and Kambara's *Jokumarswamy* are popular across India.

Given the recognition of Kannada dramas in the world of dramatic literature, they deserve to be considered as literature in their own right. Sriranga's (1904–84) works serve as a representative example. With approximately fifty full-length plays and over a 100 one-act plays to his credit, evaluating his works often requires a broader understanding gained from his novels. Sriranga's first novel, *Vishwamitra Srushti*, published in 1934, intricately portrays the birthing pains of the Navodaya movement. Narayana, the novel's protagonist, embodies a consciousness that strives to dismantle the old world to usher in a new one but fails to fully develop as an individual. The characters encountered during train and bus journeys, individuals like Kulkarni Ranganna, Tulaji and Narayan's father, along with the Acharyas who accompanied him, represent people entrenched in the old world, resistant to change. Narayan, on the other hand, is characterized by impatience, depicted through numerous images in the novel. In this narrative, Narayan grapples with the unfamiliar language of the old world. The incident of Kalamma searching for a railway ticket in her bag, only to discover it in the folds of her saree, is more than just a comical situation; it highlights the complex web of meanings that signs acquire in this world. The dropping of the Saligrama from Kulkarni's hands during the puja prompts contemplation on the potential chaos in the world of meanings. Symbols such as Kulkarni's old house, his sit-out and the village tea shop have lost their original significance. Narayan, armed with a BA degree but lacking employment, struggles to connect with the villagers' conversations, while they, in turn, find it challenging to comprehend Narayan's expressions.

From *Harijanwara* to *Sandhyakala*, Narayan serves as the central consciousness in all the plays. The plays depict the old house, the authoritarian father, the bloodsucking Acharya exploiting religion, and the girls wasting their lives in the kitchen or delivery room. The protagonists in these dramas share the common thread of unemployment, leading to the theme of their struggle between home and the outside world. Much of the drama unfolds in isolated settings, such as the heartland of the grand Raya house in *Harijanwara* or the battlegrounds in *Prapancha Panipat*, where wandering lanterns attempt to dispel darkness, and the desire for the future conceals the present darkness.

In 1947, Sriranga published *Purushartha*, narrating the tale of four young men who pledged national service on the day of Lokmanya Tilak's passing in 1920. All four reunite in 1947, at Madhu's house. For some, the national movement symbolizes loyalty, while for others, it is a means to attain an elite social position. Madhu ultimately sacrifices himself for the freedom movement, dying on August 15 while holding the national flag. Notably, the novel predates Mahatma's assassination, but

Madhu, a sincere follower, passes away on the day the country gains independence.

The novel portrays the disappointment and failure of the dream of freedom. Examining the changes brought about by freedom in our lives, it becomes evident that the emergence of a new class of politicians is the only significant transformation. The narrative unfolds as a poignant exploration of loyalty turning into betrayal, hinting at a subtle relationship between creative moments and history. While not explicitly referring to Mahatma's assassination, works like Sriranga's *Purushartha* subtly contemplate the dynamic between creative moments and historical events. It suggests that death does not necessarily mark an end. For instance, Gandhi emerged from the death of Lokmanya Tilak, illustrating that death doesn't conclude with the realization of a dream. Sriranga's later plays, focuses on the political reality post 1947 and grapples with the theme of death. The death of Jayaraya in *Shokachakra* echoes the theme seen in Purushartha—death brings no sense of completion or creativity. Both characters, Madhu and Jayaraya, represent individuals who, in their righteousness, have detached themselves from reality, leaving the world orphaned by their departure.

In Sriranga's later plays, apart from a few like *Jarasandhi* and *Shataya Gathaya*, characters remain nameless. The earlier plays emphasized the conflict between individual consciousness and the environment, showcasing the blossoming of personalities in challenging circumstances. However, the immediacy of the rebel, more painful than the disillusionment of the idealistic rebel, results in the destruction of personalities through acts of betrayal. Sriranga's last plays may not perfectly capture the political reality, and some have faced criticism, but it is noteworthy that the playwright persisted in his efforts until the end. During the performance of *Harijanwara*, there were instances of people pelting stones and halting it. The play *Samsariga Kansa* went unnoticed, while *Shokachakra* elicited tears from the audience. Subsequent plays failed to make a similar impact, with the audience remaining indifferent. Until the end, Sriranga, known also as Adya Rangacharya, remained a figure whose language was not fully understood by the public.

A play, as a literary work, possesses the potential for being explosive, as evident when the performance of *Harijanwara* was met with stoning—an acknowledgment of the confrontation with reality as in a novel. While poetry can engage with reality, it often prevails with its unique imagination. The dynamics of drama, especially Western-style drama, are distinct. The spotlight on the stage in a theatre brings to life everything hidden in the darkness of real life. Works like *Harijanwara* can provoke the world on multiple fronts, creating impactful headlines. The interplay between a satirical work and an angered world often benefits only the writer, enhancing the meaning of the work when the world reacts with anger.

However, Sriranga's later works struggled to establish a connection with the world. It is challenging to determine whether Sriranga's dramas failed to incite the world or if the world remained indifferent to the dramas. The underdevelopment of theatre as an art form might be a contributing factor. In contrast, visionaries like Girish Karnad (1938–2019) and Chandrashekhara Kambara (1937–) envisaged alternative relationships. Karnad's dramas exhibit an intellectual refinement found in Western dramas, gaining acclaim as they appeared at the onset of modernism in Kannada. Despite *Tughlaq* delving into religious and political themes, its brilliant structure and innovative characterizations convey nuanced messages beyond these connotations. *Tughlaq* stands out as one of the most successful Western-style dramas in Kannada, a statement made without irony. On the other hand, Kambara's *Sirisampige* achieves success in a different sense. Analysing these plays suggests that our modernity derives inspiration from either Western models or folk traditions. While the dramas of Sriranga and Kailasam resonated with the educated middle class, their success did not endure. Comparisons to plays like *Tughlaq*, *Hamlet* and *Caligula* come to mind. Tughlaq is not Hamlet or Caligula; historically, he may be Mohammed, yet he is a character battling in vain against Aziz. Aziz's victory represents the harsh reality of the world, and for that reality to triumph, it must follow Tughlaq. Consequently, Aziz's pain becomes more profound than Tughlaq's frenzied suffering, bordering on the ridiculous. In their pairing, Tughlaq and Aziz embody the historical interplay between leader and follower. The rich dilemma of meaning at the play's conclusion resonates with the enduring shadow of Aziz and Muhammad uniting—a shadow stretching across centuries in our history.

Kambara discovered modernity in his pursuit of folk theatre, employing folklore as a language to connect with the world. It is through language that one engages with the world, and Kambara, by embracing folklore, established that connection. The saying 'man loses himself and gains the world' reflects the acceptance of language, and Kambara, through the folk legend of Ramgonda and the play *Sangyabalya*, found a means to connect with the world. The events of *Sangyabalya* unfold in Bailawada, a place that still exists, portraying a story that uproots the families of Kattimani and Lagali. The characters in the play align themselves with the justice system of the British government, placing the play on the cusp of contemporary history. Kambara seems to have learnt from folklore the art of transcending history while acknowledging it. The folk song's tune lacks historical meaning and embodies a primitive tonal structure. While one interpretation of *Jokumaraswamy* lies in the government statement that 'the tiller is the owner of the land', it fails to capture the poetry of the play. The image of the present fleetingly reflected in the play's mirror is like a picture erased before it is drawn. For a drama to endure, it must possess the quality of poetry, yet it is inevitable for the work to align with current trends. Present-day writers often infuse reality into their writing, and to prevent this reality from becoming overly natural, a conscious sense of poetry must prevail. Folk poetry furnished Kambara with metaphors, images and superhuman elements, and he accepted them gratefully, constructing a drama that reflects contemporary life.

5

By the latter part of the nineteenth century, prose and verse in Kannada literature had already diverged. In ancient literature, prose was also a form of poetry, and scientific compositions were also written in verse form. These two types of writing differed only in the way of writing. Poetry did not have a distinct field of experience, a unique emotional world, or a specific kind of coherence. However, the writing style and word deployment were distinctly different. Every poem possessed a metrical structure, constructing a field of meaning for the senses, much like the tonal extension of a raga affording a meaningful rasa-bhava. This indicates a relationship between the uniqueness of poetry and its metre. The story of Kraunchavadha ('The killing of the mating birds') suggests that the Anushtup metre used by Valmiki was born out of the pressure of his emotions. Yet, how did that metre express all the emotions of the Ramayana? This was possible because the Anushtup metre became the poetic language of the Ramayana. Metre becomes a distinct language employed by poetry, serving as a unique medium for the expression of emotions as in Kraunchavadha; it can also become a common medium like language.

The idea that metre shapes the poem structurally and, like language, becomes the medium of the poem, is somewhat complicated. However, this is a factual observation. Kumaravyasa's

Bhamini Shatpadi (a six-lined metrical form) can be seen to change from verse to verse while retaining its figurative meaning. Each verse becomes unique due to the weight of words, the shifting pauses and the fluctuation of rhythm. Metric regularity prevents this uniqueness from becoming arbitrary and thus metre itself becomes a medium. The ultimate benefit of metre is like the benefit of grammar—both serve to make the meaning easy to understand. Shabdalankara (figures of speech related to words) combine with metre, with rhyme playing a crucial role. Rhyme holds a place in shabdalankara like simile in arthalankara (figures of speech related to meaning); while simile shows similarity between two different things, rhyme indicates similarity between two different words. Poetry capitalizes on analogy on many levels. Similarly, contrast functions as the opposite of analogy, yet technically, it serves the same purpose as analogy. In ancient poetry these two principles combine to form poetic structure.

There was a time when prose and verse served as equal mediums for both poetry and science. However, today, both prose and verse have their own defined fields and materials of expression. The realm of prose is vaster than that of verse. An unwritten rule today dictates that all journalistic and scientific literature should be written in prose. In literature, novels, short stories, essays and criticism, primarily use prose as the medium of expression. Poetry and, to some extent, plays are now the primary forms expressing through verse.

However, in modern times, metre has lost its earlier magic in prose. The magic in the metre of Abhijata kavya (elite poetry) has also diminished. The metre of elite poetry once served as the language of social communication. Only when poetry in vernacular languages began to flourish did metre come into special favour and attempt to regain its lost magic. This is why the magic of Vedic metre persists in folk poetry. Magic, in a sense, is a very ancient principle. Metrical arrangement held this preference during times when deities were believed to be visible through mantras. In one of his modern poems, Bendre describes poetry as, 'this is a mantra; a technique of taming meaningless words.' If deriving meaning from an object indicated by word is a characteristic of ordinary language, magical words create their own meaning.

In Kalidasa's *Meghadutam*, however capable the Mandakranta (a metre commonly used in Sanskrit poetry) may be, it is not indispensable. On the other hand, Kumaravyasa's Bhamini Shatpadi is indispensable for his poetry. Here, I am not discussing evaluation of these works. Kannada poets went a step further than Sanskrit poets in making the divine charge heard in poetry. While Champu poetry was modelled after the court poetry of Sanskrit, the poetry of the late twelfth century, Vachanas, rejected Sanskrit poetics. It is in our Vachanas that the intimacy of word and meaning is broken.

In modern times, metre has once again lost its magic. The reason for this is that literature now has become the craft of the educated middle class—the reason also for realism being an established mode in literature. While the realism found in stories and novels may not be present in poetry, when the sense of reality starts working in poetry, poetic meaning becomes more significant:

Love and pity are God, he says
A cool new way to Bhakti.
I am the daughter of a Shanubhog
I have to have my Gauri.

In this poem by K.S. Narasimhaiah, the young wife talks to a neighbour about her husband's rationale. Her husband embraces modern ideas, questioning the need to worship god when love and mercy are the true gods. However, being the daughter of a Shanubhog, this girl does not give up the worship of her deity Gauri. The poem paints a clear picture of real life, suggesting a close relationship between the new humanism and reality. When love is considered god, the position of faith changes. There is no need to seek god through worship; instead, one finds love and compassion when seeking god. Therefore, god is deemed important, not worship and penances.

There is not much distance between this attitude and that of the new poetry in Kannada. Poetry holds the same importance for new poets as god does for the husband in this poem. Poetry is considered more significant than figures of speech and metre, as these elements merely constitute the external features of poetry. Emerson, an influential American writer impacting our new literature, offered a fresh perspective on poetry:

> For it is not meters, but meter-making argument that makes a
> poem—a thought so passionate and alive that, like the spirit
> of a plant or an animal, it has an architecture of its own and
> adorns nature with a new thing. The poet has a new thought; he
> has a whole new experience to unfold; he will tell us how it was
> with him . . . For the experience of each new age requires a new
> confession, and the world seems always waiting for its poet.

—'The Poet', Ralph Waldo Emerson,
The Major Prose[2]

According to Emerson, a poet's new idea or experience should bring its own metre. The poet's experience is unique, contributing to the enrichment of the world. Each age awaits its poet, reflecting the ambition of new poetry. This view underscores the eagerness to abandon pre-existing models of poetry and create new ones, making metre and figures of speech constraints to poetry.

---

[2] Editors Myerson and Bosco (London: Cambridge University Press, 2015), p. 205.

Romantic poetry is characterized by its demand for freedom and its vision of new models within that freedom.

Our poetry has also recognized that metre can be a constraint. In his collection *Samudra Gitegalu*, published in 1934, V.K. Gokak remarked, 'Shatpadi should not be prescribed to a sea.' Even before that, Bendre had expressed a similar sentiment, stating, 'Beauty without bond/Is the cleanest beauty.' B.M. Srikantaiah experimented with new metre in his *English Gitegalu*. Bendre in his *Gari* collection incorporated about twenty recognizable Shatpadi poems. Some poems attempted to break the Shatpadi and give it a new form, introducing new tunes like those using the syllable structure of matra ganas. He even used Sarala Ragale (a poem without stanza structure) and the sonnet form. This departure from old metres and adoption of new ones emphasize that metre belongs to the exterior of poetry—it is not an intrinsic or essential principle of poetry. While new poetry in Kannada (Navodaya) hasn't completely abandoned metre, it firmly believes that poetry doesn't necessarily require it.

Lyric poetry has become a major form of new poetry. Despite having a rich tradition of songs, our predominant poetic form was narrative verse. The emergence of lyrical poetry is a new development, influenced by Western trends. This shift is not merely about the distinction between old and new; it involves a profound consideration of poetics and the ethics inherent to poetry. The essence lies in breaking free from old constraints and assuming responsibility for constructing its own technique as an independent form of poetry. If metre and figures of speech constitute the exterior of poetry, the focus should be on exploring the interior of poetry, prompting a reconsideration of poetic language and the intricate connection between words and their meanings.

This shift in poetic form holds great importance. Joint families have given way to smaller family units, mirroring a crucial social transformation. It is essential to recognize that comparing the numerical size of family members in different setups oversimplifies the intricate web of relationships within joint families—a complexity akin to the relationship between words in a sentence. It is through this relationship that a sentence is understood as a whole. The interplay between words in a sentence finds its echo in the connection between lines in a narrative poem. The consolidated qualities, both positive and negative, of an individual are intertwined in the enduring characteristics of a family. A Kannada proverb encapsulates the moral fabric of a joint family: 'She who has money covers her vitiligo; She who has a large family covers her adultery.' Joint families serve as protectors for the vulnerable—lunatics, disabled individuals, orphans, widows and sinners—and bear responsibilities for at least half of society. Language use in this context is inherently social, evident in both soliloquies and asides.

Because the connection between words in a sentence is social, society can understand the sentence. All comprehension revolves around meaning. Meaning is established through norms. It is not coincidental that the word 'artha' (meaning) also signifies 'money'. Like a meaningful word, money also operates according to established norms. The social nature of language is apparent in this. The language of our ancient narrative poems also mirrors this characteristic. They expressed themselves through metres like Shatpadi, Chaupadi (four-line stanza), Tripadi (three-line stanza) and Sangatya (a quatrain variation), combining poetic uniqueness with a prosody similar to prose. For instance, the Chaupadi in 'Govina Hadu' ('Ballad of the Cow') achieves poetic excellence while narrating a story. However, lyric poetry offers limited scope for prose expression.

Netrapallaviyinda sutrgombihanga
patra kunisyana olumige/ dina dina /
jatriyenisitta janumavu

With his eyes, he is making me perform like a puppet,
    day by day, life is beginning to feel like a fair.

Sarvajna employed a modified version of folkloric *tripadi* (tercet),
opting for the regularity of Matra Gana over the pace of Ansha
Ganas. The tripadi quoted above is by Bendre, characterized by folk
language and metre, yet possessing a remarkably modern syntax.
The line 'Netrapallaviyinda sutrgombihanga patra kunisyana'
captures the lover's audacious creation of the beloved's character
through the language of his eyes. The interaction between language
and the dancing character takes on a modern hue. Furthermore,
the 'feeling' evoked by utilizing tonality over literal meaning is
entirely novel. The term 'Netrapallavi' itself is a recent invention,
a mysterious language confined to the realm of dance. Yet, the
significant aspect lies in the transformation of public elements
like language, drama and fairs into personal experiences. Each
figure in this poem is on the verge of encountering its opposite.
A puppet dances to the dictates of the eyes, embodying a
convergence of opposing actions. It is this inherent contradiction
that renders the experience exceptionally unique. The resolution
of this opposition is manifested in the use of rhymes—Netra,
Sutra, Patra, Jatre—these alliterations become similes perceptible
to the eyes and audible to the ears.

Bendre's mastery in tercets is truly astonishing. The structure
of the tercet in folk poetry lacks such precision; it resembles a
fragment of a fertile poetic field where experiences can be sown
and cultivated. While numerous poets may work in this field,
Bendre's approach stands out. Even though his tripadi adheres
to an old form, the arrangement of imagery, the transformation
into metaphors and especially the use of rhymes are distinctive.
This perfection signifies a departure in the evolution of the tercet.
Among contemporary poets, Bendre's experimentation with
rhymes sets him apart. In addition to Akshar Gana, Ansha Gana
and Matra Ganas, he also delved into Vedic metres. However,

what emerged from these various genres was the new form of lyric. His line 'Arthavilla Swarthavilla Bariya Bhav Gita' ('no sense, no selfishness, just a good song') encapsulates the essence of lyricism. This new lyric introduces a fresh tone of expression, going beyond the mere interweaving of words and their meanings.

The size of a lyric is significantly shorter than traditional poetry, impacting its overall performance. Kuvempu's poem centred on the 'Heere Hu' (the ridge gourd flower) exemplifies this shift in focus. Exploring such a small and seemingly insignificant flower becomes an attitude in itself. The poet is alone without his family, contemplates the flower in the courtyard, creating a poem about it. This act elevates the seemingly useless 'Heere' flower to the status of a poetic subject. The poet and the flower, standing face to face, collaboratively construct a new world through words—a world unrelated to the mundane. This poetic endeavour, though seemingly unrelated, bears a distant connection to the upliftment of the poor. The choice of the overlooked 'Heere' flower becomes a symbol of the wisdom inherent in poetry, revealing that this neglected flower is no less than the champa or rose.

The techniques employed in this poem to discuss the attributes of the 'Heere' flower in the courtyard are modern. To draw attention to a flower overlooked by everyone, the poem must isolate it from the other flowers, from nature, and from the world at large. It resembles a botanist examining the flower under a microscope. While the scientific purpose is distinct from poetry, the relationship between poetry and the world is inherently symbolic. It is as if the pictorial real world here serves another purpose. The flower, initially part of diverse nature, takes on the same meaning as nature but, in the poem, is extracted from its natural context and introduced into the poetic realm. Whether poetry employs an object from the natural world as a symbol or not, its connection to the object is inherently symbolic.

It becomes necessary to re-examine the metaphorical and symbolic relationships here. Consider a line of verse where poet Lakshmisha describes Krishna: 'Atasee Kusumagatranam Kamalanetranam'. Krishna's blue complexion is likened to the butterfly pea flower. While Krishna's complexion is reminiscent of the flower, he does not literally become a flower. The relationship between Krishna's face and the butterfly pea flower is metaphorical. In Kuvempu's poem, however, the 'Heere' flower is the focal point. Yet, the poem isn't intended to provide information about the flower; it engages with different senses. Given the poem's concise size, the flower remains singular, serving as a symbol.

We accept similes in a metaphorical relationship as literal. For instance, when we say 'Chandramukhi', implying that the moon has bestowed its beauty upon the face, the moon retains its own beauty without diminishing. After conveying the intended meaning in the line, the moon seamlessly rejoins nature. However, a symbol must maintain its symbolic essence. A symbolic relationship is arbitrary, subjective and often associated with the otherworldly. In contrast, a metaphorical relationship always involves a connection between two objects. While the analogy between the moon and the face enhances poetry, they don't relinquish their natural attributes. A symbolic relationship links the direct to the indirect, with no requirement for the indirect to possess spiritual qualities. In Kuvempu's poem on the 'Heere' flower, there is no overt spirituality. The apparent 'Heere flower' is connected to the indirect, and what the direct points towards is left to the reader's interpretation.

In the past, when poetry told a story, readers may not have grappled with this issue. Even in religious literature, prevalent in our old literature, there was a connection to the indirect, yet indirectness wasn't perceived as problematic. It is like a lady's plait with three strands, where only two are visible, and the third, though present, remains unseen. This exemplifies the subtle presence of indirectness in old narrative poems. In these poems, the direct had a close relationship with the indirect. Deities like Shiva and Krishna, when directly involved in the story, become visible in the language, albeit indirectly. In contrast, god in Tagore's *Gitanjali* is presented as abstract. In 'Shravan', the devotee, even though present in the boat while crossing the stream, remains unseen, and god's indirectness becomes the focus of the song. Everything in old poems is evident. For instance, the word 'Shunya' appears seven times in one of the verses of Pampa's *Adipurana*. Taking it a step further, Bendre suggests there are eighteen 'shunya' that an eye can catch in that particular verse. Manifesting 'shunya' is like manifesting indirectness, according to Bendre.

The quest for the essence of poetry is unavoidable for the new poetry, particularly lyric, which has abandoned the external elements of poetry such as metre and figures of speech. This quest is evident even in the subject matter of many new poems. On one occasion, Bendre stated that old poetry contains meaning, while new poetry is imbued with feeling. Both 'Artha' (meaning) and 'Bhava' (feeling) are ancient words, but their meanings have evolved over time. When confronted with the question of the meaning of new poetry, Bendre, despite relinquishing the old poetic meaning, interpreted it as the 'symbol of truth'. While it is not incorrect to attribute this meaning to the word 'Bhava', derived from the element 'Bhoo', the relationship of this word with truth becomes symbolic, surrounded by an aura of indirectness. 'Matu Matu Mathisi Banda Nadada Navneetha' ('Poetry is the butter produced by the churning of words') makes this indirectness visible, prompting contemplation on how words should be wielded. Speech appears to authorize meaning, yet the word transforms, becoming both old and new. This process poses a significant challenge for new literature. The power that rejuvenates the old word, breathing life into it, lies in the realm of imagination, but the extent and scope of imagination remain beyond our control.

A question arises: Should a word convey meaning or evoke feeling? If the meaning of the word is the father, then feeling is the mother. Bendre, recognizing this duality, views poetry as the mother's domain, harmonizing both elite and folk manners. In Chandrasekhar Kambara's *Chakori*, the hero is exclusively nurtured in the mother's domain, absent of a father figure, and the mother functions as both father and mother Earth. The language that witnesses this form of motherhood becomes capable of singing. Even prose sings in *Chakori*. This work is devoid of darkness, bathed in moonlight. The sun, the progenitor of twenty-seven forms of knowledge, becomes the moon's rival and foe. The goddess of song, Yakshi, is appeased by the mother and son. The image of Yakshi parallels the image of Bhava, resilient against the hammer's blow, concealed in the created world, if faith is absent. Yakshi, lusting after the devotee Gudda, tirelessly works to arouse his desires. Although Chandrasekhara Kambara labeled *Chakori* an epic poem, it lacks the conventional epic's continuity. Instead, it presents a continuous musicality without coherence, capturing the vast expanse of time and conveying a sense of infinity. The form of the song encompasses aspects of mantra, witchery, medicine, worship, chanting and meditation.

The form of poetry undergoes constant evolution over time. Kannada Navodaya Poetry, influenced by Western romantic poetry, explored the relationship between the direct and the indirect through feeling. Conversely, Kannada Navya poetry assumed a distinct trajectory under the influence of Western modernist poetry. Navodaya poetry faced accusations of drifting away from the real world into the dreaminess of old poetic ideals. Adiga's poetry embodies a strong determination to construct a new poetic realm. A detailed discussion on the nuances of Navya poetry may not be essential here, but it is crucial to acknowledge that even in Navya poetry, the relationship between the direct and indirect remains symbolic. As the enthusiasm for Navya poetry wanes, poetry is striving to be pro-people. However, there is a concern that poetic populism might become merely a stylistic choice.

Roland Barthes, an authority on Western modern poetry, once remarked about modern poetry: 'These poetic words exclude men; there is no humanism in modern poetry.'[3] While it is accurate to say that modern Kannada poetry doesn't use Sanskritized Kannada like its older counterpart, the purpose of using vernacular language in poetry is primarily to serve the interest of poetry rather than to cater to the people. In poetry, the relationship between words is not inherently social. B.M. Shri, a translator of English lyrics, aimed to rejuvenate Kannada poetry and infuse it with a new spirit. He composed his own poems in Old Kannada, which stand as a testament to his experimentalism and mastery of the traditional style. His work *English Gitegalu* marked the inception of the new Kannada poetic tradition. Although translation has introduced a fresh essence into Kannada, it also created a division between the old and the new. The new phase is not a seamless continuation of the old, departing from the historical trend where the new used to be an extension of the old. Presently, we find ourselves engaged in both making and continuing history.

However, a crucial point must be emphasized here. It has been fifty years since the British departed from India, leaving behind the remnants of their Empire. Every empire leaves its mark in the form of ruins. Just as language has a mouth, it also has ears. Yet, when the spoken language differs from the language being heard,

---

[3] Roland Barthes, *Writing Degree Zero*, translated by Annette Lavers and Colin Smith (London: Jonathan Cape, 1967), p. 56.

translation becomes a necessity. Ours is a language that has been attuned to the echoes of Empire.

As we bid farewell to the century that will conclude in four years, it is evident that poetry has undergone transformations. The poetry born in this century has been meticulously examined and explicated, and the success of its various theories has been scrutinized. Numerous statements exist on what constitutes a new poetry. Moving forward, there arises a need for a poetry that can explain these concepts to our people.

Vachana: Language and Structure

This essay is taken from the collection Kannada Sahitya Sangati. *In this concise introduction to the Vachanas, Kurtkoti explores the longstanding debates regarding the language and structure of these compositions—specifically, the simplicity of the Vachanas and their categorization as 'utterances'. By examining the intentional efforts of Vachana composers to avoid Sanskritized Kannada and narrative elements, he contends that the fundamental poetics of Vachanas is related to 'Kayaka' or labour, and to the idea of one's conduct matching one's speech. Kurtkoti also contemplates the significance of context in comprehending Vachanas, as well as the emergence of genres such as 'Shunyasampadane' and other similar forms within the Vachana discourse.*

A prevailing perception regarding the language of the Vachanas of Sivasharanas is that it is notably simple. When comparing the Vachanas to the prose found in Kannada Champu poetry, the simplicity of the language of Vachanas becomes apparent. The prose of Champu poetry is Sanskritized, while the language of the Vachanas is predominantly Kannada. If one deems Sanskrit as difficult and Kannada as accessible, the argument holds. However, even for those to whom Kannada is their mother tongue, Sanskrit is not a foreign language. The complexities or simplicities of language appear to depend on a principle different from the intimacy of language. Consider, for instance, how few people can truly comprehend Allama's verses, even though they are in Kannada. The language of the Vachanas indeed appears simple, and the reason for this simplicity needs to be explored.

212

From a historical standpoint, the Kannada found in Halmidi Inscription represents the language in its infancy. However, the Sanskrit verse at the outset of the same inscription displays linguistic maturity. So, what do these variations in maturity and immaturity within the inscriptions signify? The inscription doesn't serve as evidence for the poet's intellectual prowess. Similar to the development of the human mind, the evolution of language isn't strictly historical. A thousand years ago there were wise individuals, just as in the twentieth century there are those who are fools. Numerous historical factors contribute to language development. From the tenth century onwards, Jain poetry played a pivotal role in shaping the growth of Kannada language, allowing it to thrive alongside Sanskrit. This evolution encompassed storytelling, mythology, literature and poetry, all serving the ultimate purpose of understanding the world and its truths. As individuals learn to perceive the world through the medium of language, a natural dependency on that medium ensues. With increased reliance, individuals distance themselves from direct experiences of the world, translating those experiences into language, which then shapes their understanding. In this context, language can be seen as a convenience. Through language, humans access elements like memory, thought and imagination, enhancing the benefits of human experience through the power of grammar. However, as these conveniences multiply, so does human dependence. Language, inherently meaningful, is the medium through which we all communicate. A fascinating definition of meaning says— when everything else fades away, what endures in language is meaning. This observation holds true significantly.

This may have been the challenge confronting the Sivasharanas. They had to purify the language, utilizing it without its previous traces and seeking a truth beyond the language itself. A glimpse of this idea surfaces in the conversation between Allama Prabhu and Muktayakka. Ajaganna, her elder brother, served as her guru.

When she mourns Ajaganna's death, Prabhu argues that genuine companionship doesn't necessitate a guru. In response, she dismisses him as a mere talker, emphasizing that Ajaganna, her teacher, transcended verbal discourse as his knowledge surpassed the limitations of language. As Allama Prabhu communicates, Muktayakka questions his knowledge, remarking, 'Speech crowded with words is not appropriate, Prabhu.' Allama's reply is precise. He asserts that the Jyotirlinga is an utterance of a Sivasharana, evident through both conduct and speech. This resonates with the Vedic concept: 'Vak mei manasi prathishita, mano mei vachi prathishitam' ('May my word be one with my thought and my thought with my word'). Such is also the view of Allama. If one speaks, it should convey an authentic experience; otherwise, silence is preferable. As Allama puts it, 'A Sivasharana is immobile when in mobility, and silent while speaking.' One could argue that the most remarkable accomplishment of the Sivasharanas was the transformation of words into non-words and language into non-language. Like penance, meditation and karma, language serves as a bond for Allama. If one breaks that bond and then speaks, they are no longer bound by it. As he eloquently states, the wind remains untouched by dust.

Basavanna in one of his Vachanas speaks about the transparency of language: 'If you speak, it should be like a necklace of pearls. If you speak, it should be like a crystal spear. If you speak, it should be like the light of a ruby. If you speak, it should be appreciated by the Linga.' Pearls, rubies and crystals do not conceal; instead, they illuminate the objects. Language, according to Basavanna, should not reveal itself, but be luminous enough to showcase the other. If you speak, the Linga that is beyond speech should also appreciate. In Basavanna's Vachanas, the destruction and creation of language are intertwined.

The form of Vachanas is also distinctive. As it stands, the Vachana is neither prose nor verse. Moreover, this literature is not conventional writing. Sivasharanas relied on their spoken words to express their Anubhaava (mystic experience). Writing serves to preserve the past for future generations. It seems there was a system to transcribe the oral expressions of the Sivasharanas. Without this system, their Vachanas might not be accessible today. However, this is not a crucial point. The Vachanas of Sivasharanas primarily exist in the form of utterances. Traditional literature relied on writing, but Sivasharanas do not even inadvertently reference those writings. This divergence is a key reason why Vachana literature is entirely distinct from its predecessors.

The Vachana discourse may serve as an expression of experience, an explanation of experience, a question or an answer. When viewed from this perspective, some individuals have discerned a similarity in structure between the Upanishads and the Vachanas. However, there exists a distinction in the way the question-and-answer format is used in the Upanishads and the Vachanas. The Upanishad poses questions like 'Whose is this creation?' and provides an answer: 'Brahma, the Prajakaman, created food and life, which in turn, keep the creation going.' Yet, this answer does not negate the question; alternative answers may be found within the same Upanishad or elsewhere. The task of the question in the Upanishads is to seek and find an answer, as questions tirelessly seek. However, the nature of questions in the Vachanas is different. The questions in Vachanas serve multiple functions, with obtaining answers being just one of them. Their primary function is to continually question the provided answers.

While the Upanishads incorporate stories, often employing storytelling as a philosophical technique, Vachanas, in contrast, abstain from narrative elements. However, a unique aspect emerges as Vachanas evolve into biographies of their composers. A story in the Kenopanishad illustrates this point. To dismantle the deities' ego, Brahma challenges each deity to demonstrate their power using a blade of grass. Fire fails to burn it, and the wind cannot shake it. Umadevi intervenes, revealing Brahma's identity. The tale aptly highlights spiritual challenges arising from pride in divine or human power. Surprisingly, every detail of this Upanishadic story finds parallel chronicles in the interactions between Allama Prabhu and other Sivasharanas. Allama subjects Sonnaligeya Siddrama, Muktayakka, Akkamahadevi and Basavanna to similar tests, liberating each Sivasharana when their formidable personalities become impediments. What was a story in the Upanishads transforms into a biography in the context of Vachanas. Consequently, the connection between Vachanas and history is intimate. Each Sivasharana is engrossed in Kayaka (labour), not merely as physical action but as a potential spiritual act. Consequently, while studying Vachanas, one must consider the transformation of abstract philosophy into narratives, biographies and works that manifest spiritual experiences—all occurring on the same level.

Vachanas abstain from storytelling, making their interpretation challenging. The meaning extracted while reading Vachanas doesn't encompass their full significance. Understanding the utterances of Allama Prabhu or Basavanna on specific occasions requires contextual awareness. Additionally, Vachanas were instrumental in shaping and evolving a religious tradition, resulting in rich terminology and symbols. The term 'Bayalu' in Vachanas denotes 'Shunya', yet its contextual usage imparts a nuanced meaning. Allama Prabhu's riddle-like Vachanas also defy grammatical norms. Consequently, various versions of Shunyasampadane and works like Kallumatha's *Prabhudevara Lingalilavilasa Charitrya* emerged, categorizing Vachanas by subject and reconstructing their historical context. These treatises provide invaluable assistance in understanding Vachanas. Despite the colloquial appearance of the Vachana language, it serves as a purposeful metalanguage—a conscious language that is aware of its objective and functions accordingly. Sivasharanas eschew riddles for expressing philosophical insights, opting for straightforward, uncomplicated accounts of experience. Consequently, the expositor must sift through Vachanas, interpreting their meaning while considering the background. To truly grasp Vachanas, one must understand them in the context of specific situations, such as the conversation between Allama and Muktayakka or Siddarama, or the episode where Basavanna is engrossed in Shiva puja while Allama waits outside.

Vachanas endure due to the prevailing strength of oral traditions in our country, distinguishing them from written ones. It is crucial to discern the disparity between speech and writing. Writing carries an inherent meaning, requiring the reader's effort for comprehension. Once written, it gains autonomy from the author, with the text's meaning subject to the reader's interpretation. In contrast, the meaning of speech hinges on the speaker's intent. In the realm of writing, a singular author prevails, whereas the world of speakers is diverse. The speaker's duty lies in fulfilling the listener's desire. Meaning emerges from the interplay between speaker and listener. Despite the use of questions and answers in writing, these are fundamentally oral communication techniques. Beyond the speaker and listener, a silent audience exists in the world of speech. Muktayakka reflects on Ajaganna's speechlessness, while Allama's teacher, Animishaiah, remains silent. The Anubhava Mantapa likely harboured others in silence. This silence surrounding speech is significant. In contrast, the silence around writing is antagonistic to speech, like the darkness beneath a lamp. Writing cannot embrace the essence of silence as effectively as speech. 'If you speak, it should be such that the Linga too appreciates.' The Linga, being speechless, is moved by the Sivasharana's speech, making the Linga's silence responsive.

The Vachana Poets

This essay is also taken from the collection Kannada Sahitya Sangati. *It showcases Kurtkoti's analytical fervour. Through his analysis of Vachanas, he provides both historical and theoretical insights. Kurtkoti addresses certain issues concerning the meaning of Vachanas, elaborating on their spiritual essence, their challenge to hierarchy and their dedication to truth. As a result, the essay acquaints readers with the historical contexts of the Vachana composers, the philosophical essence of their discourse and the poetics that emanates from their compositions.*

More than 200 Sivasharanas gathered for the Anubhaava congregations in Basavanna's Mahamane (great house) in the town of Kalyana during the reign of Bijjala (1130–1167 ce) of the Kalachuri dynasty. Notably, these meetings included both male and female Sivasharanas. The formation of a distinct religion took shape here, fuelled by a unique devotion to the pursuit of truth without ritualism. In these gatherings, devotees came together to express their feelings, their own experiences and their philosophies through Vachanas. As poetry may not have been their explicit goal, they did not formally address their stance on poetry. However, it is evident that they were profoundly aware of the challenges in verbally expressing the indescribable truth. The impact of this knowledge of the Vachana composers on the awareness intrinsic to Kannada language is remarkable. Therefore, the Vachanas warrant examination from a literary perspective.

Kannada in the Halmidi inscriptions of the fifth century aspired to become a textual language. Over time, it evolved, constructing its grammar, cultivating figures of speech, recognizing rasa-bhava, and creating poetry and poetics. The language which matured through the assimilation of new knowledge, not totally dissociating from the influence of Sanskrit, inevitably progressed to its culmination. Language serves as another world that we construct to make sense of the world itself. This linguistic world may function as a replica, a symbol or even an independent entity. The meaning we attribute to language shapes our understanding of the world, influencing all human affairs conducted within its realm. As we rely on language for our connection with the real world, we perceive truth through its lens. Yet, the tragedy lies in the realization that what we come to know is language itself. The narratives we create in language, such as literature, poetry and drama, aim for the realization of truth. However, the truth is only perceived within these narratives, leaving us entangled with the narratives themselves. Jain poets and writers embraced Vedic religious narratives, modifying them to generate new meanings. Despite subjecting Vedic deities, stories and rituals to sharp criticism, their forms endured. Similar to literal language, form possesses the ability to shape meaning, persisting even in the fragments of a statue. Jainism, in response to Vedic religion, developed its philosophy, literature, mythology and poetry. While successful in this independent creation, its victory also revealed a defeat in terms of attacking the other.

Interestingly, the sole surviving Vedic deity outside of Jainism is Shiva. In Andaiah, Kama emerges victorious while Shiva suffers defeat. In Brahma Shiva's *Samaya Parikshe* (Test of Time), Shiva's form undergoes distortion to the point of irony. Brahma Shiva invokes the name of Jedara Dasimaiya, the most ancient of Vachana poets. It is remarkable that Shiva after being burned down by the fire of satire is reborn from the ashes of Shiva.

The Shiva extolled by the Vachana poets under various names differs from the Vedic Shiva. While deities are immortal, their verbal forms undergo transformation over time due to historical calamities. Moreover, Allama's Guheshwara is distinct from Basavanna's Kudalasangama Deva. Each Vachana poet realizes the unique meaning within their composition, grasping the divine in Linga form. Even if the adage 'God is one but has many names' holds true, the undeniable truth of multiple names arises because the Absolute Linga is devoid of meaning. When attempting to describe the indescribable aspect of Linga, one must consider the verbal aspect of the indescribable.

When studying Vachana literature, numerous such dilemmas surface. As far as Jain literature is concerned, it could independently convey meaning, thanks to the patronage it received. The preconceived notion that quality diminishes with royal support is irrelevant in this context. The word derives its significance from state power—a principle that remains pertinent even in today's democratic society. While we naturally perceive an inseparable connection between word and meaning, it is crucial to recognize that non-communication through language is also possible. Kalidasa, in the opening verse of *Raghuvamsa*, likens word and meaning to Parvati and Parameshwara, emphasizing inseparability. This may hold true for him, but Bhavabhuti, in the play *Uttararamacharita*, engages in a reassessment of the link between word and meaning. Jain poets in Kannada, adhering to Jainism's disdain for certain concepts, avoided using the image of Ardhanarishvara to symbolize the confluence of word and meaning. Within the three forms of narration—Mantra, Shastra and Kavya—the Vedics clung to Mantra (chant), leaving the other two for secular purposes. Shastra (science), places less emphasis on language as the meaning and didn't delve into linguistic concerns. However, in Kavya (poetry), where both word and meaning are crucial, the inseparable relationship of the two becomes inevitable.

The relationship between words and meanings isn't always as seamless as desired. Despite their close association, shadows sometimes cast doubt. Poetics must be meticulous in tending to this relationship. Grammar tightens its rules, only to loosen them again, to facilitate easy understanding. However, interpretation, often beyond the control of sciences, presents challenges. The era of Vachana composition faced such complexities. As mentioned earlier, Jain poets enjoying royal patronage didn't grapple with this issue. The interpretation of Pampa's *Vikramarjunavijaya* hinges on whether it relies on Pampa or Arikesari. If Pampa composed the poem at Arikesari's behest, one might assert that Arikesari is the master of poetry—a perspective dear to us. Alternatively, Arikesari might have embraced the meaning created by Pampa, driven by the virtue of Gunarnava. It was Pampa who envisioned Gunarnava, and the poetry emerged from the friendship between Pampa and Arikesari.

However, this convenience was not accessible to the poets of the twelfth century. Jainism, arriving from north India to the south, carried a historical legacy, unlike Vira Saivism, which lacked such advantages. Vira Saivism was the religion that developed before Basavanna's eyes. The royal patronage that Basavanna had was distinct from the one that Pampa had. While there wasn't mutual distrust between Basavanna and his king, their relationship was characterized by mutual neutrality. Consequently, Basavanna's palace evolved into another power centre in contrast to Bijjala's palace. Speculation arises on what might have transpired if Bijjala and Basavanna had been allies—a matter open to historical possibilities. In the harmony of word and meaning, the shadow of historical possibilities looms large.

An example illustrating this is found in the episode of Haralayya and Madhuvarasa's relationship. Haralayya belonged to the untouchable caste, whereas Madhuvarasa was a Brahmin. However, as both were Sivasharanas, they transcended caste distinctions. Logically, there should be no obstacle to their children marrying. Inter-caste marriages were not unprecedented, and there were those who became Sivasharanas after breaking the bonds of caste. Despite this, their wedding offended some people. Prompted by slanderers' words, Bijjala blinded both of them in a swift and historic event, with far-reaching consequences in the future.

What is relevant here is the impact on the interpretation of the narrative. It is the Sivasharanas who supported this marriage. This Vachana by Basavanna sheds light on the matter

Vipra modalu antyaja kadeyagi
Shivabhaktaradavaranellanonde embe
Haruva modalu shvapacha kadeyagi
Bhaviyadavanonde embe

Where the high-born is placed first and the low-born last,
I assert that all devotees of Shiva are the same.
Where the Brahmin is favoured over the outcaste,
I hold that all followers of Shiva are one.

This portrayal effectively captures the caste-based discrimination in a system where those of the priestly caste are deemed superior to the lower caste. Basavanna vehemently rejects this distinction among human beings, envisioning a narrative of humanism. However, even if this distinction is erased, the demarcation between Sivasharana and Bhavi (those who are not followers of Vira Saivism) remains. Basavanna's view is fundamentally religious, and its meaning is unambiguous from that perspective. There is no room for misunderstanding. Yet, the challenge lies in the fact that understanding does not solely rely on the narrative text. One narrative challenges the meaning of another, engaging in a battle where new meanings emerge through this churning. This complexity is inherent when language is utilized for communication.

However, there is another possibility. Sivasharanas supported this marriage for their own reasons, and Basavanna's narration sheds light on these motivations. On the opposing side, there were those who rejected this union, but unfortunately, we are unaware of their narrative. They may be termed Sanatanavadis or by some other name, yet historically, their stance remains elusive. What is evident is their ability to resist and penalize the marriage. Essentially, the unspoken narrative of this opposing group shapes the meaning of Basavanna's narrative. This indicates that the shadow between word and meaning is cast by history. This might explain the profound intensity in the language of the Vachanas.

Considering the circumstances, Sivasharanas appear to have had two available paths. One option was to align with the Avadhuta sect, acting indifferent to history, as Allama did. The alternative was to cultivate a resilience that refrains from bitterness even in full awareness of the tragedy, a sentiment touchingly conveyed by Harihara in one of his verses:

Jagadolagella noduvede satyame teevi tulukutirpudai
Bagedode bhaktanorvanadarol nere satyavanalatane
Pageyenisirpudekela? Asatyame ta piridageyentadam
Bageyade satyamam nudiyutarchisutirpudu Hampeyaldanam

The whole world is full of truth,
Yet when a devotee tries to embrace truth, why is he hated?
When untruth dominates, without worrying about it,
One must worship the Virupaksha of Hampe without deviating
from truth.

The answer to Harihara's question about why a truthful devotee might be hated is not simple. Harihara finds it paradoxical that a devotee speaking the truth would encounter hostility, despite the abundance of truth in the world. However, acknowledging this in a poem is simpler than recognizing it in reality. The notion that dialogue between truth and falsehood is futile also must have struck Harihara. Nevertheless, Harihara emphasizes that a devotee should worship god by adhering to truth and avoiding falsehood. Although these words are not explicitly about Basavanna, they unveil his inner turmoil.

As noted earlier, Vachanas are religious narratives rather than historical ones. In certain Vachanas of Basavanna, history surfaces as an antidote, intensifying emotional impact. Vachanas are not constrained by past recollections. No Vachana narrates a story or reminisces about one. Basavanna mentions Bijjala in some Vachanas, Allama Prabhu recalls his guru Animishaya, and Muktayakka mourns the loss of her guru and elder brother Ajaganna, and Akkamahadevi frequently reflects on the child she left behind. However, through these Vachanas it is not possible to reconstruct the life story of these Sivasharanas. We will have to make do with the narrative bits that can be derived from the oral tradition. It is crucial to recognize that the path of Vachanas diverges from the narrative style.

Comparing history to a story often leads us to the conclusion that a story is a product of imagination, while history is closer to reality. However, from another perspective, history can also be considered a form of storytelling. It doesn't fully reveal itself until it transforms into a narrative. It can take the shape of a Vachana, much like history evolves into a story. Allama's Vachana exemplifies this transition:

Duration was dead, period lingered, truth integrated with the truth, listen, oh Basavanna. A true Sharana has no future in Kali Yuga. Go and join Kappadi's Sangayya. Channabasavanna, you meet your end in Uluve. Madivalaiyah, you too. Soddala

Bacharas and all the Pramathas should also seek the absolute truth . . . Proceed to Kailasa. The guidance to all of you is to be free of your body. I will confront truth in Kadali. This is the order of our Guheshwar for you all.

—Allama's *Vachanchandrike*, p. 255

These are the words of Allama Prabhu to the other Sivasharanas, at or shortly before the time of the tragedy of Haralayya and Madhuvarasa's captivity. However, the historical reason behind Allama's directive to Sivasharanas to end their lives and fulfil their duty can only be speculated upon. This Vachana does not provide that information. Nevertheless, it unequivocally conveys the idea that a Sivasharana must embody their truth, even if it leads to their true death. Allama also alluded to his meeting the Truth in Kadali, emphasizing that there is no future in Kali Yuga. The time had arrived for the words of the Sivasharanas to manifest as reality. That duration ('avadhi') has concluded, and what remains after the 'duration' is over is the 'period' ('vyvadhana'). A period is a defined duration, and it has its end. The challenge lies in the reality of the flowing time. If one incarnates in time and looks back, only time endures. According to Allama, the meaning of a word rises and falls in the current of time. Vachana and Sivasharana are inseparable. If time rises, it should arrive; it must depart before it sinks. The freedom of a Sivasharana is genuine freedom.

Allama discerns a distinction between spiritual truth and historical truth. He identifies 'Avadhi' (duration) and 'Vyavadhana' (period) as two temporal dimensions. According to Allama, if a Vachana is a narrative, its meaning is contingent upon the time when it is articulated. Any narrative is tethered to its temporal context and unfolds within its constraints. If a narrative persists through time, it risks losing its significance. Allama addresses this intricacy explicitly in his statements. As he asserts in

another context, 'There is no escape from the deluge for that
which has become an idol.' There is an inherent contradiction
in this discussion. Attaining an understanding of the timeless
'real' means being contingent to the time and place. Without
undergoing such temporal transformations, it lacks meaning, and
his very characteristic also limits its lifespan. Allama highlights
the paradoxical symbiosis of the immortal and the mortal in his
Vachana: 'Adiya lingava medinige tandu martyadolage mahamaneya
kattida Basavanna' ('Basavanna first brought Linga to Medini and
constructed a palace in the mortal place'). Allama, acquainted
with the Sivasharana's life history, hints at the culmination of
their historical journey. There is no ambiguity in Allama's words
and understanding. Allama's narration does not mirror that of
a prophet. While a prophet envisions beyond the constraints of
time, Allama's 'chronology' is distinctive. The temporal realms
appear illusory to him, and his struggle is against Maya.

However, Basavanna's stance appears to differ. Basavanna
doesn't refute Allama, yet he doesn't sever ties with history like
Allama. He is the son of Madiraja Madalambike of Mundage
as also the initial incarnation in seven births as a devotee of
Shiva. Perhaps the association with Kudala Sangama predates
even this! 'You are a friend, I am old, Oh, Kudalasangama Deva'
encapsulates Basavanna's inner truth. In Basavanna's persona,
ancient and contemporary principles coalesce. This self-reflection
by Basavanna illuminates the inseparability of old and new aspects
in his character.

Honnu hennu mannemba karmada baleyalli saluki
Vrutha barudore hoha keduka haruva nanalla
Haruvenayya bhaktara barava gudikatti
Haruvenayya sharanara barava gudikatti
Koodala sangam deva vipra karmava bidisi
Ashuddana shuddhana maadidanagi

I am not the Brahmin who futilely prances
Ensnared in the karmic web of gold, woman and land;
I await the advent of devotees
I await the arrival of the Sharanas
Kudalasangama has liberated me from priesthood
Transforming my impurity into purity.

This narrates the historical account of Basavanna's life, where
Kudalasangama Deva freed him from Viprakarma (priestly work).
The historical interpretation succinctly declares the transformation
from impurity to purity. The crucial term in this Vachana is the use
of the word 'prancing'. (The Kannada word here is Haruva, which
means prancing and is also a derogatory slang for a Brahmin).
Originally derived from the meaning of 'rishi', the word took a
different connotation as Brahmins began making much ado about
purity and lost philosophical power. Here, Basavanna employs
the same term in a new context: the Brahmin here is the one
awaiting the devotees, the Sivasharanas. This reflects a historical
progression from the waning significance of knowledge rituals to
the redemptive power of devotion. It signifies that 'flying' never
departed from Basavanna; it evolved. Basavanna's earthly duty is
to uplift the fallen, purifying the impure—a task accomplished by
Kudalasangama Deva.

The historical significance of Basavanna's persona is
undeniable. While hundreds of Kayaka devotees engaged in
spiritual discussions within Basavanna's palace, their collective
Kayaka also enriched the life of Kalyana town. If Bijjala wielded
political power in Kalyana, the Sivasharana Kayaka possessed a
formidable influence no less potent. The central power of the
palace rested with Bijjala, whereas the Great House's nucleus
was Basavanna. However, Bijjala lacked the brilliance inherent
in Basavanna's character; his prowess lay primarily in political
organization. This disparity hindered the development of mutual

understanding between the two power centres. Although the
'Shunya' throne in the Great House failed to evoke the throne's
authority, its mere presence acted as a challenge. Basavanna's
resilient personality served as the strength to overcome this
opposition. The conventional image of a king depicted in Vachanas
lacks glory, as articulated by Basava Dandanath: 'The corpse of the
king is not worth even the price of a nut.' Basavanna's life appears
to harmonize opposites, a testament to his unique duty. However,
maintaining such equilibrium demands constant vigilance. It
seems that Basavanna was that vigilant figure in Kalyaṇa who did
not sleep. Undoubtedly, not everyone requires such commitment
to navigate the mortal realm as they see fit; Allama Prabhu, for
instance, holds no interest in this. Yet, Basavanna's way of life set
him apart, embodying a distinctive duty:

Dharaniya melondu hiridappa angadiyanikki
Harada kullirda Mahadeva setti
Ommanvadare odane nudivanu; immanavadare nudiyanu
Kaniya sola addaganiye gella
Jana nodavva namma Koodalasangamadeva

Establishing a grand emporium on the earth,
Our Mahadeva, the astute trader, positions himself.
In agreement, he promptly speaks; in disagreement,
he remains silent.
Neither a penny more nor a half-penny less
does he accept.
My Lord Kudalasangama is truly sagacious.

Kudalasangama Deva is wise, but he also carries the responsibilities
of a business. This same sense of responsibility is ingrained in
Basavanna's persona. Just as one cannot abandon the shop while
being in the shop, business must be conducted with integrity,

ensuring no loss or gain of a fraction. Only Mahadeva Setti comprehends the inner turmoil in a merchant's mind—speaking when he wishes to speak and maintaining silence when he chooses.

Basavanna was not in Kalyan when Bijjala's murder occurred at the Royal Avenue in Kalyan. He had departed Kalyana three months earlier to go to Kappadi Sangama. Serving as his replacement, Basavanna's nephew, Channabasavanna, held the ministerial position. The perpetrator of Bijjala's murder was Mallideva—these are the documented details surrounding the incident. While Bijjala's murder holds historical significance with its attendant consequences, there exists a dimension beyond the historical context. The palace endured. Post Bijjala, Sovideva assumed the title, but Mahamane remained empty. Sivasharanas likely discovered their truth, as stated by Allama. In various locations—Basavanna's Kappadi Sangam, Channabasavanna's Uluve, Allama Akkamahadevi's Kadali in Srishaila—spirituality endured, although obscured for a period. The defeat of the Sivasharana echoed the defeat of human life, casting a shadow on our existence.

However, the narrative intricacies persist. The language employed in the Vachanas and their distinctive nature, compel repeated readings.

Section 2

Literary Theory

Speech and Writing

In this essay from the collection of titled Panditara Tappu *(Scholars' Errors), published in 2001, Kurtkoti examines a recurring theme present in some of his other essays: the comparison between oral and written literature. Here, his focus is on highlighting the potential for multiple meanings inherent in oral communication, contrasting it with the more precise delineation of meaning achievable through writing. Kurtkoti's fascination with the multifaceted nature of language is evident once again as he emphasizes the richness of meanings that language offers.*

I recall a tale from a village wherein a young man planned to sell flowers at a nearby fair. Being unemployed, he saw this opportunity as a means of making ends meet. Venturing to the village's flower garden to purchase his stock, he came across a young woman who tended the garden alongside her husband, their basket brimming with blooms. When he requested some flowers, she jested, 'If you humour me by calling me your wife, you may have the flowers without charge.' Contemplating his dire need for the flowers and the unconventional proposal, he did not object to addressing the young woman as his wife. Yet, mindful of her husband's presence, he carefully responded, 'You my wife I your husband, can go to the fair together.' This reply elicited a joyful response from the young woman, who readily gave him a basket filled with flowers.

There is no need to debate the authenticity of this tale. It serves as an illustration of verbal creativity, a light-hearted account

of a young man adeptly navigating a verbal puzzle presented by
the young girl. While seemingly unremarkable at first glance, the
young man's response prompts deeper reflection. If transcribed,
his sentence would convey a singular meaning: that the girl selling
flowers, his own wife, and he, along with the husband of the flower
seller, could together attend the fair. However, the nuances of
speech—intonation, vocal inflections—are lost in written form.
The pause between 'You my wife' and 'I your husband' imbues
these two clauses with distinct interpretations. In languages
like Kannada, where the verb typically concludes the sentence,
the meaning must be encapsulated within the verb itself. When
reading a sentence, our eyes instinctively seek out the verb, the
key to unlocking its meaning. To decipher a written sentence, we
must approach it with scrutiny, adhering to the rules of grammar,
often unfamiliar to us.

Understanding what was said necessitates understanding the
speaker's intent. Humans communicate driven by an inner urge
to express something. In the anecdote mentioned, the young
man's response corresponds to the young girl's query. Questions
inherently seek answers, each question serving as a guidepost
to its corresponding answer. In every dialogue, one's words are
intricately linked to the others. The meaning of a single word
often hinges on the context provided by another. Engaging in
conversation is a weighty responsibility; numerous challenges in
life stem from neglecting this duty.

This may explain why the speech of children was disregarded
in olden days. Young children lack a sense of responsibility. During
Draupadi's harrowing ordeal, elders like Bhishma and Drona
remained silent even as the youngest of the Kauravas objected.
Although one of them clearly recognized the injustice, the elders
remained silent. Effective speech requires authority from the
speaker, a poignant irony evident in this Mahabharata scenario:
those in power remain silent while those who speak lack authority.

This irony is compounded by the fact that the Mahabharata is an epic of our oral tradition. A prayer from the Vedas expresses the aspiration: 'May my speech be noble in thought, may my thoughts be noble in speech.' True honesty in speech is achieved only after a lifetime of endeavour.

As previously stated, the interpretation of spoken words hinges upon the speaker's intent, with their meaning reaching those who listen attentively. This exchange between speaker and listener straddles both the public and the private realms, governed by specific linguistic conventions for public understanding. A word serves as a sign of meaning, wherein sound and meaning meld to produce word. For semantics to function effectively, the precise meaning of a word must be established. Adherence to these rules renders linguistic transactions public affairs. Yet, within the confines of private conversation, a unique meaning may emerge, known only to the interlocutors. The speaker's motive may likewise remain undisclosed, possibly bound by a tacit agreement. In this linguistic exchange, like the covert gestures and signals of cattle traders, a similar game unfolds, shrouded in secrecy, as participants clandestinely convey messages.

Another irony in the previously cited tale lies in the clever use of a single sentence to convey two contradictory meanings: the young man artfully crafted his words to suggest the designation of a stranger as his wife while avoiding its actual implication. Such ambiguity, where two conflicting interpretations coexist within one sentence, leaves the choice to the listener to discern which meaning to embrace. This technique, inherent in oral traditions of villages, serves as a means to imbue language with layers of meaning through narratives, proverbs and riddles. The capacity for a word to evoke its opposite meaning is truly remarkable.

For those who utilize language solely for practical purposes, a single meaning for a word suffices. When spoken words effortlessly convey their intended message, achieving clarity becomes paramount—a kind of fulfilment. Such simplicity in communication always finds supporters. In instructions, in laws and statutes, in government directives and in the media while disseminating news, straightforward language is required. In such instances, writing proves more expedient than speech. An episode in the Bible recounts God's transmission of commands to Moses, instructing him to deliver them to the people. Subsequently, Moses is directed to Mount Sinai, where he discovers two stone tablets inscribed with these commands. Enraged by his followers' idolatry, Moses shatters the tablets, only to later receive further instructions from God atop the same mountain, which he then commits to writing. It may not be incorrect to say that the genesis of religion lies in this act of writing.

God communicated with Moses, though Moses could not behold the face of God; only His back as He turned away. God selected Moses as His intermediary, delivering His commands through Moses to the people. Communication with God was exclusive to Moses; others did not have this privilege. Moses was filled with light upon encountering God, who bestowed upon him His authority.

Perhaps for similar reasons, there exists a necessity for inscriptions on stone—a decree from God Himself. Although God remains unseen, His law embodies His authority. Even Moses did not witness God in person, but rather heard His voice and transcribed His words. Nevertheless, these inscriptions serve as symbols of God's presence. It is undeniable that such symbols have shaped the religion and culture of nations. Perhaps the gap between speech and writing carries a similar weight.

The Visual and the Aural

In this essay from his 1996 collection of essays Rajasparsha *(Royal Touch), Kurtkoti starts off by exploring the contrasting modes of perception embodied by the visual and the aural. However, he swiftly transitions from a linguistic analysis to a broader cultural commentary. Kurtkoti's thesis revolves around the educational systems of ancient India and modern India, with an implicit assertion of the value of the aural, or traditional, means of education in relation to the visual, or modern, counterparts. This shift in focus underscores Kurtkoti's overarching perspective on the significance of traditional modes of learning in contrast to contemporary devaluation of them.*

Human beings rely on their five senses to perceive and comprehend the world around them. Among these senses, vision and hearing play crucial roles in the educational process. Our eyes capture the world in visual representations, while our ears absorb the multitude of sounds within it. Experience, garnered through these senses, forms the basis of understanding. Language serves as an indispensable tool to translate this experiential knowledge into comprehension. Language is readily available to individuals who endeavour to grasp the intricacies of the world. The educational journey commences with language; language acts as both a conduit and a means of understanding. Unbeknownst to us, we acquire language even as we utilize it to comprehend our experiences.

Language is apprehended through our senses, prompting a question: Do we perceive language visually or aurally? When language is represented by alphabetical symbols, it is visible and can be read. Conversely, when articulated verbally, it is audible and can be heard. Throughout the annals of civilization, these two modes of expression have intertwined, forming an inseparable and layered connection. The term 'Shabda' (word) connotes sound, rooted in aurality. However, when transcribed, it transforms into a visual image. Thus, understanding language through hearing necessitates familiarity with its visual counterpart, and vice versa.

Listening to sounds with the ear should not be conflated with listening to music; these are distinct processes often confused with each other. However, appreciating music requires specialized education, including an understanding of vowels, consonants and the seven tones. While it is advantageous if words are sung in tune, it is not a strict requirement; what matters is the ear's perception of the sound's meaning. Moreover, the presence of the person producing the sounds is essential during listening, as it is through them that the sounds emanate. This presence gives birth to the personality of the teacher or guru, who embodies the teachings even when discussing texts authored by others. The guru, in essence, becomes the book, and the disciple, in turn, 'reads' or listens to the guru, absorbing knowledge through the ear. This tradition of transmitting secret knowledge from guru to disciple underscores the social contract between them. In ancient educational institutions, scholars were known as 'Bahushruta', indicating their extensive learning from a single teacher in various disciplines.

On the opposite end of the spectrum lies the acquisition of knowledge through sight—reading written words. It is believed that Jains and Buddhists introduced reading and writing to our region. The term 'Alekha' first appears in Buddhist scriptures, and Pampa's use of 'Alaka' likely serves as a synonym. Despite a guru instructing numerous disciples, the Guru-disciple relationship remains personal and private. Speaking, whether in public or private, retains a personal touch, yet the creation of books and writing assumes an objective public quality. Unlike speech, written words lack the mystery inherent in language; however, their silence yields understanding. Books act as inexhaustible sources of wisdom, capable of enlightening countless individuals without depletion.

Despite the distinction between hearing and seeing, both serve as avenues of understanding. However, the significance of this disparity becomes evident when viewed from another perspective. A disciple who listens to the guru must acknowledge and accept the guru's authority; their social contract remains unchanged. While a disciple has the liberty to select their guru and embark on a quest to find them, upon becoming a disciple, they must submit to the guru's authority. Disputes may arise between the two, and students are entitled to pose questions and voice doubts. However, ultimately, only the guru possesses the authority to provide answers and propose solutions. The transmission of knowledge through the lineage of gurus, known as 'Sampradaya Vidya', flows from one to another akin to a relay of compassion and understanding, embodying the principles of 'Daya' (compassion) and 'Deya' (bestowal).

When the guru is likened to a book, the stringent nature of rules tends to soften due to the inherent humanity of the guru. Rules within any domain—be it religion or law—are typically rigid, yet books lack the inherent understanding that social rules need not be as stringent as natural laws. Readers often perceive this sternness in books, leaving a lasting impression. Moreover, unlike the disciple who accepts the guru, readers of books are not obligated to embrace the text in the same manner. From this perspective, readers enjoy a degree of freedom. Reading a book is not a social contract but rather an individual act; therefore, readers can freely express their will. If readers are influenced by books, it is a testament to the genius within the text, rather than the formation of a personal relationship. However, the possibility remains that just as a guru can become a book, a book can also become a guru. Just as numerous gurus have encapsulated the essence of countless texts, so too can books attain the stature of a guru. While guru-centred religions demand faith, scripture-centred religions advocate independent thinking. If the ear perceives through faith, the eye can independently perceive the world. These two modes of understanding have coexisted throughout history, often leading to conflicts. However, in our country, despite occasional conflicts, a balance has been maintained between these approaches. In the British era, with the advent of universities, the educational system underwent radical changes, altering the social status and existence of both guru and book.

Othering

In this essay taken from the collection of essays titled Rajasparsha, *published in 1996, Kurtkoti demonstrates how literature serves as a tool for elucidating complex ideas. Here, he inquiries into the concept of 'Others', exploring its cultural dimensions and substantiating his arguments with literary and historical examples. Kurtkoti's overarching thesis asserts that while the fragmentation of humanity into smaller groups is inevitable, despite humanist ideals advocating for a unified humanity, and despite efforts to cultivate sensitivity towards others, human cultures tend to harbour scepticism and prejudice towards 'others', rooted in historical experiences of the perceived threats posed by outsiders.*

A millennium has elapsed since Pampa's proclamation, 'Manushya jati tanonde valam' ('The human species is all but the same'). Scientists such as Darwin confirmed this notion long ago, establishing its validity in terms of physiological evolution. History further demonstrates that even individuals within the same country often fail to unite harmoniously, let alone humanity as a whole. It appears inherent for humans to splinter into myriad groups. This fragmentation may serve numerous noble intentions. Cultural advancement thrives best within small, cohesive communities. Insisting on a singular culture worldwide would resemble a vast farm cultivating only one crop. Perhaps this historical apprehension is not distant from the widespread Westernization observed in this century. However, this issue warrants separate consideration.

An inherent weakness of small groups lies in the creation of an 'us versus them' or 'Self versus Others' mentality. This division is not confined to national boundaries; rather, it encompasses all those from different cultures, who are designated as 'Others'. In ancient times, the Vedic people labelled foreigners as 'Mlechchas' and 'Niragnis'. 'Mlechcha' refers to those whose speech is incomprehensible, while 'Niragni' denotes those who do not worship Agni. The English terms 'barbaric' and 'savage' carry similar connotations. Those whose speech resembles birds chirping are barbaric, while those residing in forests are deemed 'savages'. This perception was echoed by local Brahmins in Saurashtra when they encountered Brahmins from Uttar Pradesh who had migrated to the region, derogatorily referring to them as 'foresters' due to their dishevelled appearance after the long journey, as against their self-perception as cultured or 'Nagari'. Consequently, this led to the creation among Brahmins of a group called Nagar Brahmins.

As man's ego evolves, so does his consciousness of Self and Others. Everything encompassed within the boundaries of his ego is automatically categorized as 'Self', while anything outside is relegated to the realm of 'Others'. Even a stranger in close proximity can provoke discomfort. Reflecting on the constituents of 'Self' reveals several truths. The ego's expansion, spanning from oneself to one's home, street, town and country, often lacks sensitivity. However, within this geographic consciousness, man retains his sanity, leaving room for generosity. Yet, self-awareness extends beyond geographical boundaries; it encompasses race, caste, religion, language and nationality, rendering this realm highly sensitive. Many of the insults we employ stem from these categories.

This is because race, caste, religion and language are as intrinsic to human identity as is complexion. The categorization of 'Others' serves as evidence of this assertion. The Chandogya

Upanishad recounts the tale of Indra and Virochana, illustrating
that one lacking self-awareness is considered an 'asura'. For the
'asuras', the body itself is the soul, leading them to adorn the
body of the deceased with sandalwood and other offerings, even
providing food and treats before burial. Additionally, the critique
extends to the practices of other religions even when propagating
philosophies. Intense religious and linguistic fervour often
triggers blind aggression, fuelling pride within self-groups. The
communal riots in our country serve as poignant examples of
this phenomenon. The horrific violence during such unrest brings
shame upon both parties involved.

However, hatred towards 'Others' doesn't necessarily
culminate in violence; mistrust of foreigners persists even
during times of peace. In peaceful times, we often criticize the
religions and languages of foreigners, leading to bizarre beliefs.
For instance, the Egyptians believed that Romans ate people's
noses, as depicted in Bernard Shaw's play *Caesar and Cleopatra*,
where Cleopatra holds her nose while conversing with Caesar.
Countless examples illustrate the mutual misunderstandings
between different human groups, yet we remain unashamed of
our prejudices.

Our biases, disdain and reservations towards 'Others' find
profound expression primarily in drama. A prime example is the
character of Shakara in the play *Mrchchakatika*. His name was
'Sansthanaka', but as he pronounced the sound 's' as 'sh', he is
nicknamed 'Shakara'. Shakara possesses only partial knowledge
of our country's myths and is portrayed as vile, wicked and
avaricious. While these traits may be accurate, the disdain he
provokes primarily stems from his status as an 'Other'. Similarly,
Shylock's role in Shakespeare's *The Merchant of Venice* exemplifies
this sentiment. As a Jewish pagan, Shylock is vilified without
justification. For Elizabethan audiences, the mere presence of a
Jew on stage was sufficient to elicit contempt and amusement,

even during his trial scene. The suffering of strangers fails to evoke empathy within us; we refuse to acknowledge that 'Others' are equally human and possess human sensibilities.

The portrayal of foreign characters in plays often reflects our perspective towards them. In the ancient dramas of Bengal, all English characters were depicted as villains, like characters such as Ravana and Duryodhana from the epics. Since the arrival of the East India Company in Calcutta and the subsequent establishment of their rule under the guise of trade, Bengalis have harboured a deep-seated animosity towards them. The Bengalis witnessed first-hand the destruction of industries in Murshidabad and the devastation of their city, providing a historical basis for the animosity depicted in these dramas. In contrast, English characters in historical dramas from Kannada literature, such as *Kitthura Chennamma* or *Naragunda Muttige*, are often portrayed in a comedic light. This differing portrayal stems from the indirect influence of the East India Company on us.

Despite mutual misunderstandings, the coexistence of two cultures is often inevitable. Christianity, for instance, had to coexist with Greek and Roman cultures. Throughout history, one culture often intimidated or absorbed the other, leading to the formation of today's European culture. The amalgamation of two cultures may stem from either hatred or love, yet it remains a fusion nonetheless. As the saying goes, 'Prema Dhritarashtranappige Bhagna Balabhima' ('Dhritarashtra's loving hug, destroys Bhima') signifying that ultimately, only one survives the conflicts between cultures. It is worth noting that the Greeks and Romans had their own religions, although Christianity has become omnipresent. Nonetheless, the humanism of the Greeks remains a significant element in the evolutionary trajectory of European culture.

From the outset, foreigners have been attracted and challenged by our country. Muslim rulers arrived in waves, establishing kingdoms that left a lasting cultural imprint. However, Islam itself underwent transformation, as seen in the poetry of Sufi saints, with Muslim singers making significant contributions to Indian music. Likewise, painting and architecture underwent innovation under their influence. Subsequently, the English arrived, ushering in an era of Westernization characterized by new education, governance and economic policies—all directly influenced by English culture. Yet, this influence was not devoid of misunderstandings, leading to lingering mistrust, fear and misunderstandings towards foreigners. The potential outcomes of the close interaction between these two cultures remain uncertain, as civilization is replete with contradictions, rendering any conclusive statements difficult to make.

Civilization has devised numerous strategies to mitigate the fear of alienation, yet the metaphor of alienation itself is evolving. There is no inherent rule dictating that an alien must always be perceived as an enemy; they can also be viewed as guests. The duty of the host is to respect the guest and accommodate their beliefs, just as the guest's duty encourages harmony with the host's beliefs. It appears that the roots of this approach lie in fostering new humanism. However, success is not guaranteed. While temporary guests may be easily accommodated, if they overstay their welcome or develop inappropriate intentions, tensions can arise, and the alien remains estranged. Our behaviour often differs from the ideal, especially when personal interests are at stake. Although the concept of a free society is gaining traction globally, the extent of this openness remains uncertain. Answering this question definitively is challenging, leaving us no choice but to await the verdict of history.

Consciousness and Environment

'Consciousness and Environment' is an essay taken from the collection of essays titled Rajasparsha, *published in 1996. In this piece, Kurtkoti explores the conflict between the individual and society, prompted by the advent of modern education in India. He scrutinizes the ramifications of this phenomenon, pondering on whether there exists an alternative to the inevitable clash between the two entities. What distinguishes his approach is his adeptness at dissecting these inquiries through literary analysis, drawing insights from a variety of literary works spanning different languages. It is this capacity of Kurtkoti to integrate knowledge from diverse literary cultures that elevates him as a prominent figure in the realm of comparative literature.*

The title of this article is not mine; it originates from a book written by Dr. U.R. Ananthamurthy long ago. The influence of Jean-Paul Sartre on that book is evident. According to Sartre, man creates the world of meaning through his actions and experiences. The history of mankind is shaped by the negotiation and conflict between individuals and worlds, essentially a conflict between self and others.

However, the focus of this article is different. Due to the advent of new education in this century, there is a separation between the individual and society. It is a historical fact that an educated person often stands apart from the uneducated society that surrounds them. Similarly, the French Revolution brought about a similar social upheaval in Europe, resulting in the separation of the individual from society. Many literary depictions of this phenomenon can be found in novels from that period. Jane Austen's *Mansfield Park*, for example, can be interpreted as an allegory of this revolution.

The protagonist of this novel resides in her uncle's household, where she adheres to the authority of everyone around her. This obedience maintains order within the household, providing a sense of security for all its inhabitants. Chaos only ensues within the family when the uncle's authoritative presence is absent; order is swiftly restored upon his return. However, the girl remains consistently obedient throughout, until the latter part of the novel, where she defies her uncle's wishes regarding her marriage, displaying a newfound awareness of her individuality.

A hallmark of individuality is the acceptance of responsibility, where the individual becomes their own teacher, navigating through life guided by their conscience and shaping their own world. It becomes inevitable that personal beliefs diverge from societal norms, leading to ideological conflicts evident in later European literature. While ancient literature often depicts conflicts between individuals as forces of good and evil, modern literature grapples with ideological clashes. For instance, in Henrik Ibsen's work, conflicts arise as Nora's husband doesn't have the same beliefs as her. The modern individual asserts their right to judge what is right and wrong. The process of psychological and religious separation from one's parents, symbolizing the transition to independence, is a relatively recent development in history.

A similar transformation began in our country as a consequence of modern education. Regardless of the lessons education imparts, it liberates us from the past. The consciousness of a well-educated individual became valuable, devoid of any experiential background or seniority. This consciousness disregards experience and authority in one swoop, leading to conflicts where experiences and understandings diverge, giving rise to new dilemmas. In such instances, experience often clashes with consciousness, yet consciousness tends to prevail in this conflict. Even if experience emerges victorious, our sympathies typically align with consciousness. Consider Sarat Chandra's novel *Devdas*. The central sense of justice in the novel dictates that Devdas should marry Parvati. However, societal tradition triumphs over this justice in the narrative. Parvati ends up marrying an older man, while Devdas, consumed by despair, succumbs to alcoholism and dies at her doorstep.

Sarat Chandra's artistry shines through in the poignant portrayal of this episode. Devdas's sapphire ring and his and the town's names tattooed on his hand serve as signs of recognition. Mahendra, Parvati's eldest stepson, was the one who discovered Devdas's body. He is the one who informs Parvati about the death. The narrative is filled with numerous twists and turns of irony. The final twist stands out as the most profound. The repercussions of Devdas's death continue indefinitely, leaving behind an enduring legacy. His lifeless form emerges as perhaps the most poignant symbol in modern literature. All these tragic consequences could have been avoided if he had married Parvati. The closure of this alternate path fills us with frustration.

The underlying consciousness driving all this art is the urge to dismantle and reconstruct the social order. This consciousness exudes confidence in its creative power, capable of unveiling an alternate reality. The world depicted in the novel *Devdas* is etched in our memory, suggesting the possibility of an unseen yet inherently just world.

In Kannada literature, such novels exist as well, though examining each is beyond the scope of this discussion. Sriranga's novel *Vishvamitra Srishti* (The Creation of Vishvamitra) serves as a striking illustration of this theme. Here, there is a concerted effort to highlight the potency of individual consciousness. Throughout the narrative, Narayan, the protagonist, stands as the sole educated figure amid a populace of illiterates. The backdrop, characterized by barren plains devoid of rain, scorching summer sun, dust, uneducated villagers, obstinate priests and powerful elders, seem to conspire against the assertion of individual consciousness. Despite these formidable challenges, Narayan fervently maintains that his individual consciousness can prevail over such adversity. His unwavering resolve reflects the prevailing ethos of the era. Titled 'The Creation of Vishwamitra', the novel posits that humans bear responsibility for both the positive and negative aspects of Vishwamitra's creation, contrasting with the creation attributed to god.

Yet, a lingering uncertainty persists: Must everything else be rendered irrelevant for individual consciousness to prevail? Does the spirit of consciousness render all else inert, or is there room for a different perspective?

The Nature of the Lyric

This essay is taken from Kurtkoti's collection of essays titled Nooru
Mara Nooru Swara *(1998). In this essay, Kurtkoti historicizes the
genre of Kannada lyric, known as 'bhavagite', and speculates on its
poetics. He illustrates how the Kannada bhavagite emerged as a distinct
literary form during the early twentieth century, diverging from traditional
Kannada songs, under the influence of English lyric, particularly that of
English Romanticism. He also notes their divergent paths, particularly
concerning their attitudes towards nature. Notably, Kurtkoti observes a
fresh exploration of the interplay between words and meanings in the new
Kannada lyric.*

The term we now use in Kannada for the English word 'lyric'
is 'bhavagite'. When B.M. Srikantaiah (1884–1946) translated
English poetry into Kannada, he titled the collection *English
Gitegalu* (English Songs). It is likely that the word 'bhavagite'
was borrowed from Marathi. Nevertheless, the fundamental
structure of a bhavagite is that of a song. Songs have been around
for long. However, poetry, distinct from song, has evolved its
own rich significance, as evident in the contrasting rhythms of
elite poetry and songs. While ancient poems like the Ramayana
and Mahabharata were indeed sung, it was more a case of music
complementing poetry. Whether sung or not, poetry evolved in
close association with storytelling.

In the context of Kannada, excluding Haridasa songs
(devotional poetry by the Vaishnavite saint poets) and Sivasharanas'

250

verses (Vachanas by the Shaivite poets), the majority of poetry was narrative. Our poets, perhaps unwittingly, embraced the conventions of storytelling. Narrative poetry represents one form within the spectrum of literature. The essence of a poem flows through the sequential lines, culminating in a resolution. The devatastuti (invocation section) at the beginning, and the mangal verse (benediction section) at the end, serve as the frame of poems, akin to the *nandi* (opening) and *bharatavakya* (concluding) sections in a play. This, in essence, forms the foundational structure of our ancient poetry, providing poets with the flexibility to shape their works within these boundaries.

Another advantage of narrative poetry lies in its seamless incorporation of both prose and verse forms. Kannada poetry in particular boldly embraces prose. In the poetic genre of Champu, prose takes on the role of another form of verse. Prose, known for its expansive style, enables the inclusion of numerous elements within descriptive episodes. In Champu, there seems to be no limit to the use of prose. In Harihara's Ragale, prose retains its distinct prose identity, whereas in his use of the Shatpadi genre, it seamlessly transforms into a verse. In many ancient poems, prose and verse are so intricately woven together that they cannot be easily separated. The highs and lows of the poetic landscape are a result of this seamless blending of prose and verse.

In contrast, a modern lyric lacks both narrative and prose elements. In ancient poetry, the 'gite' (song) had developed its own independent format, but due to its limited scope, a comprehensive poetic presentation was not achievable within its confines. The new 'bhavagite' (lyric) enjoys greater freedom than the old gite, without the constraints of primary and secondary refrains. Despite the brevity of the new lyric, its open structure allows for elaboration. In other words, there has been confusion about the nature of 'bhavagite' due to the mistaken notion that it is similar to the old 'gite'. The evaluation of what has been lost and gained during the adaptation and shortening of the old song is still incomplete. This does not imply that there is no element of song in the new lyric; indeed, many modern poets have written beautiful songs. However, the primary focus should be on understanding what poetry has forfeited and acquired through this transformative process.

While it is true that this new poetic form emerged in Kannada after the publication of B.M. Srikantaiah's *English Gitegalu* (English Songs), this account warrants careful consideration. In fact, it might be more accurate to say that the quest for a new form of poetry began with this publication. The lyric form was prevalent in English literature also, even before Wordsworth, but prior to him, the accepted poetics of lyric, whether long or short, was rooted in the epic tradition. The poetics based on lyric began with Coleridge, who identified the power of imagination as the source of lyric poetry. Coleridge drew on lines from old poets like Shakespeare to articulate his theory, suggesting that elements of his theory were already present in the works of those poets. B.M. Srikantaiah, in illustrating the lifeblood of the new lyric, referenced four verses of Pampa describing Banavasi. Considering all these factors, it must be acknowledged that the quest for new poetry is an ongoing process.

In Wordsworth's poetry, the terms 'emotion' and 'feeling' are significant. Perhaps the term 'bhava' must be employed in Kannada to reflect these English concepts. D.R. Bendre noted in one of his statements that while old poetry is rich in meaning, new poetry is replete with feeling. Wordsworth stressed specific situations in life evoking distinct feelings, asserting that the feeling is more crucial than the situation for a poem. This shift in perspective likely began after the French Revolution in the latter part of the eighteenth century, when individuals became aware they were distinctive from society. When an individual is an integral part of society, their sensibility aligns with that of society. It is a relatively recent development in history for individuals to attain individuality by breaking away from the protection, nurturing, restrictions, ethical norms and religious rules imposed by society. This is similar to a child establishing individuality by being physically and mentally separated from their parents.

In such a situation, emotion becomes detached from its context. How does one express a divorced emotion? Vakrokti (deviant expression/indirection) holds a special place in poetry, favouring the indirect over the direct. In narrative poetry, it is through the story that poetry is conveyed. In the case of lyric, even the story becomes poetry. How does emotion, separated from situations, integrate into a story that is inherently filled with situations? Perhaps this is why an American poet once claimed that poetry is an irresistible yearning for metaphor. Poetry must search for something distinct from itself in the world, a resemblance that is different yet shares similar characteristics. Our rhetoricians have also stated 'upamanishtha kavayah' ('poetry is committed to comparison'). Like comparison, poetry also explores opposition. If the resemblance of two different things is a simile, poetry can also delve into the difference between two similar things. Poetic deviance can find expression through simile and antithesis. As the story fades in the lyric, all that remains is the individuality of the poet. There was individuality in earlier devotional poetry as well. However, the individuality dedicated to god would lose its mental tumult and seek god. The individuality expressed in modern poetry is different. The subjectivity of the individual must be connected to the objectivity of the world, fostering dialogue and conflict. It becomes necessary to build this relationship through language and through poetry formed in language. The artistry in language varies from poem to poem.

In what sense is the word 'bhava' used here? This question is crucial. Are the *sthayi* (stable) and *sanchari* (transitory) bhavas transformed into rasa? Or is it a simple feeling that corresponds

to the English words—feeling or emotion? For Bendre, 'feeling'
means the image of truth raised in the psyche of the poet, the
form of the experience of awareness of existence. The word
'bhava' is an important term that has taken on different meanings
for the new poets. In this new age, poets opened their eyes to
see the world anew. After realizing that the subject of the poem
does not have to be an old story, they experimented freely in the
celebration of freedom. Kuvempu wrote a poem about the 'Hire
Hoovu' (the ridge gourd flower). It is not merely a descriptive
poem but also a symbol of rebellion. By writing a poem about this
flower, a part of the world that poetry had not seen until now came
to be illuminated. This idea is evident in one of Bendre's poems

> *Halu beelu padavu banje*
> *Hakklokkalellavoo*
> *Vyaptavaytu hoova hoova*
> *Rasalilegellavoo*

> Every nook and cranny of the land,
> Fallow, barren or waste,
> Was enveloped
> In the grand dance of flowers
> (Glory of Shravana)

In the first two lines, except the word 'halu', all other words
are new in Kannada poetry. Each of these words identifies and
describes many types of land. What is represented here is that
what is infertile becomes fertile. With the magical touch of
Shravana rain, grass grows and flowers emerge on the ground.
This does not appear to be a realistic description of the Shravana
season. This poem deals with the characteristics and forms of
creativity. The rains make the land fertile in the Shravana season.
The details of this phenomenon remain invisible. In the barren

land scorched by the summer sun, the rains of Shravana engender
abundant flowers. An invisible force is at work behind the visible
details of this phenomena. This is how words like beelu, pada,
hakkalu enter poetry and perform their rasalila—play of rasa.
What happens to these flowers after Shravana is over? This poem
doesn't think of that. As in natural creation, there are many hidden
elements in literature. What is meant to remain relevant, remains
so. The rest will perish. It is essential to capture the magical power
of Shravana.

Once the power of creativity was recognized, its influence
on our poets was such that they disregarded the skill of poetic
composition. The process of fertilizing the soil by the Shravana
rain does not require any skill. These lines from one of Bendre's
poems are convincing: 'If you sow, you will sow the grain; do
not sow pearls and jewels and spoil the farm.' Seeds of flowers
should be sown, not pearls. What does it mean to sow the seed?
Poetry is not ordinary. The aspiration of the new poem, the lyric,
was to convey extraordinary meaning in ordinary language. The
expression of Anubhaava was an irresistible urge of Navodaya
poetry. The form of a lyric is a form that facilitated the expression
of Anubhaava. The nature of creativity was also spiritual
like mystical experiences. Therefore, the poetry of mystical
experiences and the mystical experience of poetry were exploited
poetically by the Navodaya poets. This fact also reveals the secret
of the influence of Aurobindo and Tagore on our poets.

Many of the new lyrics focus on the beauty of nature. Even
in old poetry, there was ample description of nature, but the
beauty of nature appeared as a stimulant (*uddipana*) and not as a
foundational factor (*alambana*). The description of seasons in old
poems was merely a background to human life. The details of the
description of nature in Kalidasa's *Meghadutam* remain fresh even
today. However, nature was given a personality in the new lyric.
The context for poems like Kuvempu's 'Tenehakki' (Lapwing)

or Bendre's 'Belagu' (Dawn) is the subject of those poems. The poem does not provide any understanding about the lapwing bird. Rather, the reader's own understanding of the lapwing helps him understand the poem. The bird in the poem is both a bird and a metaphor. If it is only a metaphor, the poem takes the form of a riddle. The poet's intimacy with the lapwing tells a story of the history of poetic sensibility.

The poem 'Tenehakki' is in the form of an address. The poem speaks to the bird, regardless of whether the bird knows what it is saying. The poem hopes that the antics of the bird teaches the poet a philosophical vision. 'Teach me to first walk calmly beyond the hot and cold, so that I may finally be able to attain the land and the sky.' Here is an account of a new idea that attempts to turn the worldliness (*pravrutti*) into renunciation (*nivrutti*) due to the imperfections that attend the inclinations of worldliness and renunciation. The relationship between a lapwing and such a philosophy is the relationship between tenor and vehicle. The relationship in symbolism is essentially the same. The attempt of the poem is that the bird should not lose its true form even when it is about to become a symbol. Even beyond this philosophy, the lapwing should sing. Only then does it become 'alambana' rather than 'uddipana' in the poem. As it becomes a symbol, it also becomes a carrier of meaning. The creative power of the new lyric performs its function through the poem by making nature the medium of significance. It also gives a new poetic understanding of nature.

There is no doubt that the love of nature among Navodaya poets came from English Romantic poetry. Wordsworth's influence on the poets of our country surpasses that of other poets. However, a point must be emphasized here. Our poets did not treat nature as a book, as seen in English Romantic poetry. They did not read nature like reading a book. While one or two lines, such as Kuvempu's 'As God put his signature, the poet looked on captivated', may be found, our poets do not view nature as a book of knowledge. For them, nature is a treasure-house of beautiful images. Even though poets like Kuvempu attempted to extract morals from nature's icons such as the rainbow, cuckoo and clouds, it does not seem to have brought about a profound and radical change in the outlook of life.

The question, what constitutes true poetry, arose as the bhavagite became customary. It is natural for such questions to emerge when the form of poetry undergoes changes. This question needs to be answered with patience. However, the new lyric appears to be inclined towards a continual quest for poetry. The fact that new poetry differs from old poetry has led to a heightened self-consciousness about poetry. Both in poetry and criticism, new debates on the relationship between the poet and poetry, the relevance of poetry in the contemporary world, the nature of poetry, poetic language, etc., began to emerge. It is commonplace to pose such questions in criticism and critics have offered solutions they deemed fit. Poetics must be constructed anew from time to time. However, one phenomenon in the new lyric is that poetry itself becomes the subject of poetry. Many of Bendre's poems revolve around the birth and development of poetry, the benefits of poetry, and the power of poetry. Modern poets (Navodaya poets) wrote about the changed form of poetry, the decline of the influence of old poetry and the adoption of different poetic attitudes.

This is the first line of Bendre's poem 'Garudiga' (Wizard): 'It is a mantra, a technique of taming words that do not make sense.' Here lies the response to the query—what is poetry. The manner in which the poem articulates its message holds greater significance than the message itself. It is not a specific answer to a specific question; rather, it is as if the question is an assault, and poetry, in defence of its existence, must respond. It is like the question that death poses to life. In response, the poem must make a sound, asserting its presence, and loudly proclaim its significance. The 'technique of taming words that do not make sense', but denotes the role of meaning in poetry and also signifies the current dynamic between words and their meanings. Every poet is compelled to confront and engage with this challenge.

Though bhavagite is concise, it is ready to raise such profound questions.

Purana, History and Novel

In this essay, taken from his collection of essays Nooru Mara Nooru Swara, *Kurtkoti once again attempts theorizing the emerging new genres in Kannada literature. He engages in a discussion of the continuities and discontinuities among three interconnected genres belonging to various temporalities: Purana, history and the novel. Through this discussion, he highlights some of the distinctive features of the novel. As elsewhere, here too we witness his incorporation of a comparative framework and his efforts to historicize conceptual terms and writing practices.*

At one point, history, Purana and poetry seamlessly coexisted within the same narrative framework, as exemplified by the Mahabharata. Functioning as the dynastic history of the Chandravamsa kings, it weaved together tales of sibling rivalry, similar to the story of the rivalry between eagles and serpents, transforming them into a Purana. Simultaneously, in its portrayal of random reality, it is comparable to the novel. Similarly, Pampa's *Vikramarjunavijaya* intricately entwines history, Purana and poetry.

The divergence of these three narrative modes appears to have occurred mainly in the twentieth century. Works such as *Mudramanjusha* emerged during a period when our historical sense was so distorted that it ventured into creative realms. In this work, history isn't divorced from Purana, yet it is distinctly aware of its independent identity. Purana, in this context, isn't rhetorical. Both Purana and history serve as languages that consistently articulate the experiences and phenomena of the world. Poetry, as the imaginative sculpting of words and meanings, assumes the role of an art form within verbal language.

Purana, fundamentally non-realistic, thrives on its deviation from reality. Characters, events and situations in Puranas don't mirror reality but attempt to grasp both worldly and supernatural truths simultaneously. The intermingling of history and Purana necessitates careful disentanglement. Until the nineteenth century, these narratives coalesced to create the cultural fabric of our country. Puranic language, intimately known to us, served as the most familiar linguistic medium. Shakara's intermixing of Puranas in Shudraka's play *Mrcchakatika*, resulting in humour, attests to the familiarity of this language. While its grammar might be unfamiliar to us, the manner in which Puranic language imparts meaning significantly differs from literal language. The language of the Puranas shapes meaning in a manner similar to the lac house constructed by the Kauravas in the Mahabharata. Typically, a house is a dwelling for humans. If we consider 'house' as a word, it signifies a place for living. However, the material and function of the lac house alter its essence, turning it into a site of violence and death. Puranic symbolism holds inherent meaning precisely because Puranic language doesn't mirror the truth of the world. The sign itself becomes the means of understanding the sign, signifying that Purana is not immutable. Its poetics change, not its mythology. In the Mahabharata, Duryodhana is portrayed as evil, but a poet may present him as good. However, the essence of Duryodhana lies beyond whether he is good or evil; it resides in his role as Yudhishthira's brother and adversary.

History operates on distinct principles. Historiography observes the unfolding events in the world from a fixed standpoint, where everything inevitably ages with time. History scrutinizes the roots of each event and organizes them into a different sequence, an order intrinsic to history itself. The Mahabharata war, although mythologically recurrent, transpired historically only once.

History scrutinizes its causes, subjects its effects to examination and, given the temporal distance, elucidates the reasons behind this ancient conflict. The enduring impact of this war on our lives remains profound, as history continues to test this fact.

This divergence stems from history's unwavering focus on the reality of truth. The meaning history seeks to convey is grounded in reality. Unlike Purana, history lacks an inherent, meaningful external form. The Mahabharata acquires its Puranic character due to the historical backdrop of Chandragupta Maurya. Chandragupta Maurya's birth mirrors the controversy surrounding the Pandavas' birth. The Nandas become the Kauravas and Chanakya embodies Krishna's political strategies. This intertwining gives rise to the history of the Mauryan dynasty and imparts meaning to historical narratives. Purana and history have developed in tandem, accepting each other's significance. While the twentieth century saw the independent development of the sense of history, our understanding of history continues to be shaped by our Puranas. Puranas serve as a symbolic system that interprets our history, a system that we are yet to thoroughly examine.

The novel genre is a relatively recent addition to our literary landscape, originating in the West and spreading from Bengal to other languages. Bankim Chandra's novels drew inspiration from Walter Scott's works in terms of form. Initially, the social nature of English novels held limited appeal. However, the historical novel opened up new possibilities. Novels such as *Anandamath*, *Durgeshanandini* and *Vishavriksha* kindled our historical consciousness. Harinarayan Apte wrote similar works in Marathi. The final acts of history in Bengal and Maharashtra were evolving into tragedies, indicating that history was still dynamic. People know every word of the conversation between Shivaji and Ingale's Sagunabai at the fort's gate. When the historical novel emerged, at least a few who witnessed the looting of Peshwa's Shanivarwada were alive. Although history wasn't yet a science,

the novel, as a form of literature, possessed the ability to create
meaning. This, perhaps, explains the proliferation of historical
novels in our literary landscape.

A historical novel fundamentally adheres to the structure of a
novel. While history and fiction may differ in substance, the novel
faces no such limitations. The statement 'Peshave's reign ended
in 1818' conveys an understanding, but the novel's realm is one
of randomness and meaning. In Keruru Vasudevachara's novel
Bhratrughataka Aurangzeb, the penultimate chapter vividly describes
Aurangzeb's procession to humiliate his elder brother Dara Shikoh.
The realistic details of this procession suggest that, in fairness, Dara
Shikoh should have ascended to the Mughal throne, which could
have potentially altered the course of history. Aurangzeb disrupted
this possibility, becoming the king himself. The novel meticulously
recounts these events to unravel the senseless hatred between the
brothers, providing an experiential depth that historical facts alone
cannot supply.

The novel's world is inherently random, prompting critics
to explore its connection to the external world. One common
interpretation posits that a novel reflects human life. While this
assertion is simple to state, its acceptance can be challenging. In
Kerura Vasudevachara's novel *Indire*, the clown character Madhura
Natesha accidentally falls from a bridge in Srirangapatna and
dies. The statement 'Alas, Savithramma's lineage has come to an
end!' resonates emotionally with readers, showcasing the novel's
impact. Yet, this statement is purely fictional. Savithramma, a
widow, is socially tied to her husband's lineage, although the novel
does not disclose his name. This ambiguity prompts the phrase
'Savithramma's lineage'.

Although characters like Savithramma and Natesha may appear
realistic, they remain confined to the novel's pages, absent in real
life. This deviation from regular rules contributes to the novel's
narrative freedom, embraced by authors like Kerura Vasudevachara

and Galaganatha. In the novel *Marathara Abhyudaya*, Afzal Khan of Bijapur comes riding a horse, which is compared to a moving mountain, and encounters a vegetable seller on the way—a lone farmer who, frightened by Khan, spills his vegetables. The soldiers find it amusing, and the frightened farmer abandons his basket, fleeing among the trees. Later, it is revealed that this fleeing farmer was Shivaji. This incident lacks historical basis. The forested Sahyadri region remains unchanged; Afzal Khan could have traversed the same route, and Shivaji, aware of Khan's reputation, likely devised plans to eliminate him. These elements coalesce to form an imaginative story, blending historical events and fictional narratives. This blending became a legacy in the early historical novels, fostering a unique style of storytelling.

A novel is not a representation of actual events but a realm of possibilities, entirely belonging to the domain of language. Within the principles of language, encompassing sound and meaning, a novel emerges as a distinct creation. Much like a poem, it is a construct woven from the web of words.

Literature and Feminism

This essay is taken from Kurtkoti's collection of essays Nooru Mara Nooru Swara. *It offers a concise reflection on literature and feminism. Originally written as a newspaper column, the essay is brief. However, it is surprising that Kurtkoti has not attempted here elaboration and theorization of Kannada women's literature through textual analysis. Despite its brevity, the essay is insightful.*

The entry of women into the Kannada literary sphere gained momentum during the 'Navodaya' period, with Thirumalamba, the author of Sati Hitaishini Granthmale, being a notable pioneer. Subsequently, writers like Gouramma from Kodagu, Janakamma from Belagere, and Shyamaladevi Belgaonvkar made names in the literary landscape. However, their early works lacked the voice of opposition. The realization that women, too, faced oppression like Dalits, came later. In examining the ostensibly cordial relationship between men and women, one cannot help but suspect that it might be another manifestation of male selfishness. This parallels a historical situation in Europe, where women were at the forefront of demanding political and economic freedom. As the opportunity for obtaining these freedoms arises, a critical question emerges: What comes next? This juncture necessitates a reassessment of the philosophy underpinning male–female relationships. In the Biblical narrative, God initially created man and then woman, granting men primacy of power. God is portrayed as masculine, the father of the world. However, the

Bible also introduces a paradox with Jesus being the Son of the Mother. The key lies in determining which of these contradictory mythological facets finds acceptance in history.

A notable characteristic of European history lies in the decisiveness of any conflict. Similar to our country, Europe initially experienced matriarchy before the ascendancy of patriarchy, which led to the gradual disappearance of the former. Curiously, remnants of this matriarchal past have endured uniquely in our society. Transformation of meaning poses a significant challenge in understanding these dynamics in our culture. While Goddess Shakti embodies the feminine, historical narratives often render women 'powerless'. This paradox is exemplified by Manu, who, on the one hand, states, 'Yatra naryastu poojyante ramante tatra devata' ('Where women are worshipped, there reside the gods'), but on the other hand declares 'na stri swatantramarhati' ('a woman is not fit for independence'). The inherent contradiction between these statements is not incidental. Despite these explicit proclamations, a subtle reality of male supremacy persists in history. Notably, rules dictating women's social behaviour have historically been formulated by men, a fact challenged and subverted in the contemporary era.

The women's movement is still in its nascent stages in our society. Over the course of this century, a considerable number of women have engaged in literary pursuits, expanding from fiction to poetry. Their confident voices bear witness to the influence of the ongoing movement. Unlike Western culture, where objections to women's creativity were prevalent, our literary landscape has generally embraced women's contributions. Philosophers here have not echoed the notion that women possess the power of retention but not creation. Despite this, the full fruits of feminist awareness are yet to materialize. Such awareness requires time to yield meaningful results. M.K. Indira's novels, such as *Tunga-Bhadra*, *Gejje Puje* and *Phaniyamma*, offer intimate glimpses into women's lives. However, these novels could have been written even by those with limited literacy. The portrayal of a woman's motherhood often tends to be sentimental. In the past, the joint family system provided support for widows, and deserted individuals and the childless. The home, at that time, served as the moral foundation for women. With the disappearance of such structures, women embark on a new adventure, entering the tumultuous male-dominant domain. As women navigate this challenging terrain, they must accept history's challenge. Currently, truth is perceived through a masculine lens. For it to become a foundation for women, history must undergo transformation. Until then, the struggle will persist. Like Krishna Sobti in Hindi or Mahasweta Devi in Bengali, Kannada writers have yet to delve into the history of men and expose its ignoble legacy. The example of Rani Lakshmibai of Jhansi, while commendable, is insufficient. Lakshmibai achieved what figures like Nana Saheb could have accomplished. The significance lies in women accomplishing what men cannot. Only women can discern the true nature of this challenge. It is imperative to construct a history that points towards a future alternative.

The Fear of History

This essay is taken from Sanskruti Spandana, *a collection of essays published by Kurtkoti in 1986. In this piece, Kurtkoti delves deeper into the exploration of history and Purana, distinguishing between the two and elaborating on the concept of Puranic consciousness compared to historical consciousness. He then extends these concepts into an analysis of Pampa's* Vikramarjunavijaya.

The weaverbird builds its nest in a distinctive manner. Even if we examine hundreds of nests, they all appear as if built by the same bird at the same time. That is why there is a belief in our age that nothing new transpires in nature. In contrast, change is the fundamental rule in human history. While the weaverbird may have been building its nest in the same way for a thousand years, the architectural designs of human houses undergo constant evolution.

Our interest in human history is relatively recent. Modern assertions like 'God created the world, man created history' underscore this point. The fundamental distinction between nature and history lies in the fact that, unlike history, which carries meaning, nature has existence but lacks inherent meaning. Moonlight, for instance, can illuminate the world, provide solace to tired minds and bodies, and evoke romantic sentiments. However, this entire set of meanings is a human construct, as moonlight itself lacks the intention to achieve these effects. Moon, deemed goddess at one time, got devalued after man landed on it, but it is our history, and not that of the moon.

Nonetheless, change and progression remain the defining characteristics of history. The recognition of this truth has permeated the modern mind, ushering in a new principle of progress. The question of what constitutes the goal of progress remains unanswered. Scientists and philosophers are actively quantifying the depletion of resources in the present world, from petroleum, to the air we breathe. While nature and life continue to follow their inherent order, we find ourselves living in the shadow of history, giving rise to a sense of fear.

Purana: History

Ancient man harboured no fear of history, as the concept of progressive history was alien to him. History never evolved as systematic knowledge in our country; it was the contact with the British that introduced us to a sense of history. The creation of history comes with its own set of rules and philosophy. In our tradition, the ancient accounts did not transform into history; instead, they became Purana (mythology). Purana, too, adheres to its own rules and philosophy. However, the truth presented in Purana differs from historical truth. History seeks truth within the conflicts, and harmonies between man and his environment, documenting the rise, peak and decline of man-made value systems. Although the objectives of Purana are similar, it does not follow historical chronology. The chronological sequence from Krita Yuga to Kali Yuga is not historical. Placing it within a historical framework poses another problem. History does not accept the idea that the seed of Krita Yuga remains unmanifested in the decline of Kali Yuga. It rejects the notion that a decline in religion is the opportune time for the incarnation of god. Thus, the value system of history starkly differs from the Puranic worldview.

Yet, history and Purana find a momentary but significant intersection. Life gains meaning when the perspective of historical truth is illuminated by the insights of Purana. As the layers of historical personalities unfold, Purana Purusha (mythical persona) emerges. Even the lesser-known heroes of our ancient history find themselves accommodated in the Puranic paradise, surrounded by nymphs and a dwelling in the divine world. Those who safeguarded village cattle from enemies or tigers, the girls who jumped into wells or ponds, or those who sacrificed themselves to construct temple towers—all these individuals find a place in our Purana. It is our folk, it is Desi.

Puranic Consciousness

However, the Marga is not very different. Both our Marga and Desi are grounded in our Purana consciousness, giving meaning to our world. Purana does not merely denote something ancient; it is an ever-present reality. Tulsi's marriage, celebrated annually, symbolizes all marriages in the material world. This divine union is self-contained, a state without growth or momentum, representing the ultimate goal of our material life. Yet, the physical world and the other world are not mutually exclusive; they are intricately connected. This interconnection is why history aspires to be myth.

I believe that our ancient poetry should be analysed with this perspective. Pampa's *Vikramarjunavijaya* stands out as one such remarkable endeavour. Pampa was deeply immersed in the activities of his contemporary life, with a clear vision of the value system prevalent in that militaristic age. He articulated this value system in various ways: 'Chagada Bhoga Dakkara Geyada Gottiyalampinimpugalagaramada Manisare Manisar' ('Those men who know how to derive pleasure from sacrifice, indulgence, learning, music concerts are the true human beings'). Whether or not we agree with these values, it cannot be denied that Pampa, responding to a tradition steeped in values, was fervent about life.

In his poetry, he interprets such a world. However, this was not
the sole purpose of Pampa's poetry; its intent was neither simple
nor straightforward.

One of Pampa's verses asserts: 'Poetry should embrace
innovation, woven with soft sounds, designed in the pure Kannada
style, and harmoniously blending with the richness of Sanskrit
style.' In Pampa's poetic vision, merely expressing a new material
or an idea eloquently was not a noteworthy achievement. Pampa
introduces two additional nuances: Desi and Marga. The meanings
of both these terms have become unclear in contemporary usage.
Concepts such as Kannada–Sanskrit, folk–urban, and the like
are evolving. Desi implies indigenous or Earthly, while Marga
denotes supernatural or transcendent. Anand Kumaraswamy has
elucidated this spectrum of meanings in one of his essays, drawing
from various sources. It becomes evident that Pampa endeavours
to amalgamate Dharma (righteousness) and Kavya Dharma
(poetic principles) with these two concepts. This verse marks the
commencement of the construction of Kannada poetic heritage.

Effortlessness

Yet, in all these endeavours, Pampa displays no signs of fatigue.
Poetic efforts should not make us break out in a sweat. In the
latter part of the verse mentioned above, Pampa conveys the
seamless nature of poetic creation through the metaphor of a
bountiful harvest. What is the underlying principle of spring that
infuses vitality into every aspect of poetry? How do the elements
of poetry come together effortlessly, like the beauty of a mango
tree, the melodies of cuckoos and the hum of bees emerging
naturally with the arrival of spring? This, precisely, is Pampa's
poetic vision and his poetic prowess.

Critics find Pampa's Arikesari to be a source of irritation.
They argue that had Pampa not felt compelled to equate Arikesari

with Arjuna in his poem, he might have produced even more exceptional poetry. After all, Arikesari wasn't an emperor but a vassal—how can he be comparable to Arjuna? Furthermore, Pampa's audacity in asserting that 'even if the story is expansive' he will write in a way that 'its essence is not lost' (*Kate Piridadodam Kate Meylidaleiyade*), adds to the critics' discomfort.

Our Heritage

It should be evident to us that Pampa elevates history to the level of Purana. What Shakespeare achieved in *Henry VIII*, Pampa accomplishes even more successfully in *Vikramarjunavijaya*. This is the tradition of our country. Researchers have recently begun to unravel the proportions of history, mythology and imagination even in the Sanskrit Mahabharata. The true worth of pure poetry that emerges from this research remains to be seen. From this critical standpoint, very little may seem to remain in Pampa's poetry. However, Pampa's religion, Purana and history, were not our religion, mythology and history. The significance of his poetry becomes more apparent when Pampa's crisis is understood. We need the patience to listen to what this classical (*vastuka*) poetry conveys. Our dialogue with Pampa has not yet commenced. In his world, one must grasp the meaning of birth and death, the material world and heaven, the ordinary and the causal, the individual and the environment. If these aspects are forgotten, the entirety of Pampa's rendition of the Mahabharata may be reduced to the four verses written about Banavasi, savoured only as pure poetry.

The Story of Stories

This essay is taken from Sanskruti Spandana, *a collection of essays published by Kurtkoti in 1986. Here, Kurtkoti endeavours to theorize storytelling, drawing insights from both Indian and non-Indian traditions. He examines the use of symbolism, and the reciprocal relationship between stories and communities. Additionally, he examines how stories convey values, incorporate human and non-human elements, and the unique methodologies employed. Following his characteristic style, he elucidates his perspectives through a meticulous analysis of Bana's* Kadambari.

The habit of recounting past events as a story, appears to be as ancient as human memory itself. Memory continually revisits events of the past, and a story essentially involves narrating something preserved in memory to someone new who has not experienced it. Even before stories took on a proper literary form, they existed. What truly matters is the act of telling and the act of listening to these narratives. This exchange likely transpired continuously before stories were curated into a collection of memories. As this collective memory evolved into a shared cultural treasure, available to all, stories assumed a literary form. Countless narratives have emerged, serving as an indispensable cultural necessity for human existence, like the elements of nature—land, water, air and sky. The realm of life-values is constructed through stories.

Symbolism

Traditional stories often commence with the phrase 'once upon a time'. The vagueness of time is essential when transforming history into a fairy tale or myth. A mere trickle from the flood of time can nurture a story into a towering tree. The 'Parva' and 'Kanda' terminology of our Puranas are remnants of the forest imagery embedded in our cultural stories. A narrative flowing from an undetermined time into the present creates a lush backdrop for life. Despite its indistinct nature, the story unfolds in a chronological sequence. The chronological order in stories adopts a mystical symbolism, detached from actual timelines. For instance, if the tale mentions that the prince embarked on a quest, walked for seven days and nights, and eventually went to sleep in exhaustion, the chronology presented is not realistic. The requirement for him to traverse a specific duration becomes one of the symbolic elements of the story.

Not only time but also the overall atmosphere in stories is symbolic. Each character in these stories is inseparable from its environment, living within the same narrative. Descriptions serve to construct this atmosphere, with narration and depictions crafting a unique world for the characters to inhabit. In this sense, the worlds depicted in stories are 'not bound by nature's rules' (Mammata's concept). Characters like Kumbhakarna would find no place in modern novels. The storyteller crafts a perspective that aligns with the story and then begins the narrative, assuming a role as a character. Whether it is the Suta narrating ceaselessly to Shaunaka and other sages in Naimisharanya, Shahzadeh sharing stories under the Arabian night sky to stave off death, Gulliver recounting his experiences in the tradition of sailors' strange tales, or Vishnu Sharma, the Brahmin of the Panchatantra, guiding foolish princes on to the right path—these characters are timeless and immortal.

The Significance of Community

When such a storyteller begins narrating a tale, the entire community pays attention. However, a crucial aspect must be kept in mind: a story relies on a community just as the community depends on narratives. Though it may sound like an exaggeration, it needs to be emphasized that a story cannot come into existence if the community doesn't persist as a unified entity and is fragmented into isolated entities. In modern novels from Europe or America, a discernible plot is often absent. If there is one, it is usually found in the novels authored by individuals from Jewish or Black African backgrounds. This statement requires no further elaboration. Stories thrive wherever communities retain their organic unity.

It is for this reason that the essence of the story has not relinquished its folk character. Fundamentally, all stories are folktales. Even epics like the Mahabharata and the Ramayana trace their roots to folklore in their original forms. One of the most refined works in our country is Bana's *Kadambari*, but its origins are also rooted in folklore. The fact that the Ramayana, Mahabharata and the great narratives have given birth to the entirety of Sanskrit literature underscores their folkloric nature. The folkloric essence of the story becomes evident when considering that half of Bana's narrative is conveyed by a parrot. This characteristic is not limited to Chandrapeeda, who pursued the Kinnara twins (mythical hybrid beings—half human, half horse); it extends to all heroes in pursuit of their fortune. Activities such as hunting and travelling are emblematic of the protagonist's perpetual quest. For fortune to favour him, the hero must venture away from his current location. 'Charati-charato bhaga', 'from a small worm to the Supreme Lord, everyone seeks fortune', is a perspective rooted in folk traditions, where values become objective and transform into principles. Illustratively, a village girl placing cow dung on a boulder outside the village to dry, asking why it isn't drying, unfolds a traditional narrative: the cow dung hasn't dried because sunlight has not shone upon it, which is due to the grass having grown tall, which is because the ox is not brought for grazing, which is because the cowherd has not reported to work, which is because the old woman did not give him a roti, which is because the old man did not bring millet, which is because the government has not paid the salary, which is because the queen's (Queen Victoria) order has not come. This seemingly nonsensical tale, crafted to amuse children, effectively captures the intensity, complexity and vitality of human relationships within a community.

Representation of Values

It is challenging to attempt a condensed account of the values conveyed by a story, as a literary form, and the manner in which they are conveyed. The diversity in the forms of stories, their illustrations, and some deeply ingrained yet inconspicuous features warrant deep consideration. Questions arise: Why does the adventurous prince consistently receive aid from his grandmother during his exploits? Why is the heroine frequently in captivity? Why does the life force of a demon reside not within him but in the neck of a parrot beyond the seven seas, in the egg of a duck, in the jewel on the head of a serpent in the underworld? Why does the prince always choose the stepdaughter struggling day and night after losing her mother? Why are the first two of the king's three children deemed bad, while the last one is considered good? These aspects appear to symbolize dualities such as the god–human effort, truth–untruth, strength–cruelty and beauty–orphanhood. However, these questions persist as questions. The hybridization of values prevalent in life, causing sufferings, continue to hold true today. The equilibrium of justice in the world remains inherently unstable. The primary objective of these stories is to establish and reinforce this justice system. It is undeniable that all our animal stories serve as moral tales. Yet, the potent irony of expressing the values of human life through animal behaviour remains impactful.

Human–Animal Relationship

A more profound impact emerges when the contrast between human and animal life is meticulously established and earnestly explored. The tale of Shuka in Bana's *Kadambari* is a quintessential example. As the parrot recounts his life story to Shudraka, he begins with the history of his lineage. The Vindhya forests, the towering shalmalee tree (Indian silk cotton tree) that stretches towards the sky, hosting thousands of parrots in its branches, and the aged parrot nestled within the nest with its blunt beak and filial affection—these details unfold a vivid picture. The narrative progresses to describe the frenzy of hunting, the last hunter extending his hand like a snake's head into the nest, the demise of the old parrot, the rescue of the young parrot, Haritha's mercy and Jabali's conscience. These intricacies seamlessly converge, turning the parrot's life into a captivating narrative. Bana, with a unique dramatic power, captures the emotions and mysteries of life through extraordinary descriptive details. A hunter climbs a challenging tree, thrusts his hands into the nests, plucks the parrots as if harvesting fruits from a branch, breaks their necks and hurls them down. The horror embedded in these details evokes profound sadness, especially considering that it is the parrot narrating the story. The colours of the small parrot, the hues of the old parrot, the shades of leaves and fruits, the colour of the hunter's hand resembling the head of a black snake, the colour of the white lotus stem that he devours akin to how Rahu swallows the moon—all these colours amalgamate to create a canvas of analogy, contrast, harmony and, ultimately, appropriateness.

The intriguing aspect here is that while the parrot's narrative is brimming with avian experiences, it also resonates with human emotions. A protracted and unprecedented description of the sunrise would be superfluous if it were just a parrot's tale. However, the juxtaposition of the romantic, tender sentiments in that description, against the brutality of the hunters' frenzy hints that human history is sombre. A parakeet, nestled warmly beside its father in the nest, is suddenly gripped by mortal fear. It quivers like life caught in an unguarded dwelling, heaving a sigh of relief as the group of hunters moves past without approaching the tree. Yet, disheartened by the unsuccessful hunt, the hunter returns; he appears death-like to the parrot. He effortlessly scales the tallest tree, and the hand entering the nest is more terrifying than the hunter himself. 'Kimiva hi dushkaram akarunanam'? ('What is impossible to the merciless'), another truth of human life is unveiled. The hunter's hand, resembling the head of a snake casting its shadow, knows only to kill. Plunging it into the nest, he breaks the old parrot's neck and hurls it down. The fledgling parrot escapes due to its proximity to its father, a fortuitous breeze guiding it downwards and a cushion of fallen leaves beneath the tree. It eludes the hunter's gaze as he descends. Subsequently, it finds care in the hands of a benevolent sage called Haritha. The reason for this lies in its destined forty-year lifespan. This brief episode unfolds the intricate web of the enigmatic conflict between life and death, mystery, karma and divine providence.

Peculiar Procedure

As the evening descends, Sage Jabali, having bathed and now resting under a tree in the ashram, is approached by his son Haritha, who presents the parrot to his father. Jabali's revelation that the parrot is undergoing the karmic repercussions of past lives piques the disciples' interest, setting the stage for the parrot's tale. With an unexpected turn, the parrot's role assumes significance in Bana's expansive work, where numerous stories interweave to construct the fabric of the narrative. The stories of nymphs' daughters, cursed deities' sons, and their unique sagas of love, desire, marriage and adventures, converge and diverge throughout the narrative. At the epicentre of these tales lies the parrot's story. Celestial beings like Gandharvas, Devas and Apsaras, as well as sons of celibate sages, enact lives mirroring human experiences. The parrot's story, however, preserves the essential humanity within them, offering insightful commentary on others' lives. This narrative unfolds a peculiar journey of life's consummation. Pundarika, who woos girls with a parijata flower in his ear, falls victim to Mahasweta's charm, meets his demise and is reborn as Vaishampayana. Cursed for the same lust, he eventually takes the form of a parrot.

This is more than just a parrot story. It is not a technique merely showing a distorted reflection of human life, as seen in the stories of the *Panchatantra*. In *Panchatantra*, the connection between human life and animals remains random until the moral of the story is grasped. The tragic tale of the friendship between the monkey and the crocodile beneath the plum tree, even when the monkey departs seated on the crocodile's back, doesn't alter our emotional response. Despite marvelling at the monkey's intelligence when it says, 'I forgot my heart on the plant', the emotional tone remains unchanged. The monkey's wisdom serves as a response to the crocodile's foolishness, ensuring that the monkey escapes the perils of friendship. Undoubtedly, this story serves as an effective metaphor for understanding human morality. The initial scepticism about the friendship between the crocodile and the monkey is dispelled by the assertion that this is not a casual friendship. The critical aspect for us here is identifying the aspects of human life represented by the crocodile and the monkey. They become human in characteristics only in external actions such as lifting and climbing. They converse like humans, and friends are invited to their homes. This deliberate mismatch between man and animal is essential, as without it, the necessary irony in the story would be lacking.

Bana's parrot story lacks such inaccuracies. The parrot behaves as a parrot should. It resides within the shalmalee tree. Its father, the old parrot, has lost feathers, possesses a blunt beak and lacks the energy to fly. Even after entering the court of King Shudraka, the parrot's nature remains unchanged. The food fed lovingly by Shudraka's queen consists of plums resembling the eyes of a plump cuckoo or pearl-like pomegranate seeds that have fallen from an elephant's trunk. The joys and sorrows that occur in a parrot's life also befall it. Yet, among the thousands of parrots residing in a shalmalee tree in the forests of the Vindhyas, no other parrot shares his fate. They lack this parrot's vision and talent. The parrot sees the world through the eyes of a poet like Bana. It beholds the captivating colours of the morning sun, is repulsed by the despicable life of hunters, Haritha's mercy brings tears to its eyes, and it observes the evening, like a red-eyed hummingbird, ripening into moonlight as it roams around Jabali's ashram.

Story and Curiosity

This implies that the parrot is in the process of evolving into a human, awaiting its fortune to unfold like that of human beings. In one of its previous births, its father is named Shukanasa. Trans-birth experiences accumulate in the parrot's short life. In *Panchatantra* stories, analogies between animal and human life serve a specific purpose. When the purpose is met, an animal remains an animal and a human remains a human. However, in Bana's work, the spiritual essence of animals, humans, Gandharvas, nymphs, gods and goddesses is portrayed as identical. Humans assign names like Shukanasa, Kapinjala, Vaishampayana, etc., to birds. Bana's analogy bridges the inert and the sentient. A notable example is the extensive description of the shalmalee tree, likened to an ancient man of a thousand years. The tree's old age serves as a reminder that the world is ancient. The life of a parrot effectively reflects the divine and human aspects, as a shared spirit permeates all of creation. The story originates from the interconnectedness of all entities—animals, humans, gods and goddesses—in this world. It is the tale of Pundarika, born from the union of Shvetaketu and Lakshmi, and Chandrapeeda, who incarnates in the form of Chandra due to a curse. The grander the story, the more it incites interest and curiosity. The listener's curiosity never wanes. If it does, the story dies. Storytellers like Bana keep people alive by narrating never-ending tales. The most significant purpose of a story lies in the expression that when someone has passed away, we say their 'story is over'—a poignant figure of speech!

Narrative Technique

This essay is taken from Sanskruti Spandana, *a collection of essays published by Kurtkoti in 1986. Through an analysis of the narrative structure of the Mahabharata, Kurtkoti examines issues related to the structural aspects of narratives. It is noteworthy that Kurtkoti elucidates the complexities and curiosities inherent in the Mahabharata, such as its multiple beginnings, diverse storytellers and the fundamental quest of human existence, within the narratives.*

The connection between the story and the narrator is enigmatic; for those who find the word 'enigmatic' unsuitable, let me describe it as ambiguous. Regardless of the story's immediate objectives, its ultimate aim is to unravel the meaning of human existence within the broader context of the world. Upon the unveiling of the story's realm, a delight similar to discovering an unforeseen trove of emeralds in a witch's cave ensues. The Pandavas may have filled the void of their twelve-year exile with the rich experiences found in old stories. Consider this mind-boggling illustration in Rudrabhat's *Jagannath Vijaya*.

Kateyam kelele kanda hum raghujanembam hum sakantam vana
Stithanadam gurupele hum dashashiram kondoyda na ramana
Satiyam tanene purnaman neneyum hum kolladukkopa hum
Kritiyam maduthumoundugarchi kisugannitta chyutam ranjikum

(*Jagannath Vijaya*-Tritiyaswasa-61)

Yashoda narrates the story to avert Krishna's mischief. He listens intently, punctuating the tale with occasional 'hmm' sounds. However, a particular incident in the narrative—Ravana's abduction of Sita—triggers a recollection of a past life, provoking his ire. The story's philosophical significance lies in Krishna absorbing the account of his own life as though it were someone else's. Under the narrative's influence, Krishna's consciousness, fragmented across lifetimes, becomes unified. Krishna, of course, possesses divine consciousness. Even us mortals, lacking such consciousness, may recall past lives while engaged in storytelling, as long as we remain immersed in the narrative. Without this engagement, the relishing of rasa becomes impossible.

A Quest for Essence

Let us set aside the theatrics of this situation and delve into the fundamental principles of the story. Yashoda assumes the role of narrator, but what connection does she have with Rama's tale? She didn't author the story of Rama; it's a narrative she recalls, one from an era long past. Unaware that the protagonist of that time is now reborn and is attentively listening, she recounts a story that has traversed time. Had it been an expression of personal experience, the approach to storytelling would differ. Yashoda doesn't create the story; the story creates her. Moreover, it shapes Krishna, who listens with a spectrum of emotions from pride to anger. The storyteller's imagination doesn't give form to the story; due to the temporal gap between the story and the storyteller, the narrator's prejudices do not colour Yashoda's tale. She accepts what the story has wrought and complies.

These observations consider both Yashoda and Krishna as active characters in another grand narrative, a story within a story. This is a recurrent theme in our country's literature, where subplots and side stories often evolve into substantial narratives. In the realm of our country's storytelling, each tale has been disseminated through myriad voices. This phenomenon serves as a necessary technique in many of our great narratives. Stories take shape through the act of telling and hearing, a pattern evident in the growth of our Puranas. A Romanian folklorist once visited a village to collect songs and stumbled upon a rare ballad. The tragic love story it narrated unfolded thus: A young man in love with a village girl, set to marry the next day, was deceived by elves in the mountain who took him to the hilltop. Pushed off the hill before daylight, his corpse was discovered by shepherds at dawn. The village mourned; his lover wept, and he was cremated with respect. When the folklorist inquired about the authorship of the ballad, he learnt that the incident occurred only forty years ago, and the heroine of the song was still alive. The song's plot was straightforward: the boy and girl were about to marry, spending the night together. On their way back, the boy slipped down a hill and tragically died. This simple incident metamorphosed into a poignant story in the form of the song.

The incident didn't appear as straightforward to the poet who penned the verses. The tragic demise of the young man on the eve of his wedding suggested a fate steeped in sorrow. The involvement of elves in the hills hinted at a mysterious connection. While the natural cycle involves living and dying, the rupture of life's formula implies an underlying reason, perhaps beyond our awareness. A life prematurely ended might find a more abundant existence in another realm. This narrative verse emerged to encapsulate these notions and beliefs. Seen from one perspective, it is a legend, and a community devoid of such legends could be deemed sterile. Myths and legends are crafted to immortalize the extraordinary and grand facets of human life, yet their cultural exploration remains incomplete in our country.

The Mahabharata as a Legend

A legend is a narrative transmitted orally, and we have significant works that specifically employ this technique. Among them, the Mahabharata can be considered as the most profound work. Recent research on the Mahabharata suggests that it originated as a small poem and gradually expanded to its current size. According to these studies, this poetic epic has been evolving over many centuries, with the contributions of various poets evident in its composition. It is suggested that eighteen disciples of Vedavyasa may have added their own ideas to this monumental work. The Mahabharata mentions figures such as Vedavyasa, Sauti, Vaishampayana and Jaimini within its narrative. There has been an attempt to produce a purified version of the Mahabharata by removing fragments, but the success of such efforts is yet to be determined. The Mahabharata stands as a collective poetic effort that has evolved remarkably over time, and perhaps it is better to preserve it in that form.

In the Mahabharata, various characters take on the role of storytellers. Suta Shaunakadi is said to have recounted the narrative to sages in Naimisaranya, but Vaishampayana initially shared it with Janamejaya. Other instances include Vidura narrating to Dhritarashtra, Narada and Bhishma to Dharmaraja, Sanjaya to Dhritarashtra, Dhaumya to the Pandavas in the forest, and so forth. There is no strict rule dictating that all the stories they tell must share identical characteristics, nor do they necessarily facilitate the present situation meaningful. However, this storytelling technique is a fundamental aspect of the Mahabharata. For instance, the extensive narrative of Nala and Damayanti unfolds in the context of other kings experiencing exile similar to that of the Pandavas. The connection goes beyond a mere analogy between the Pandavas' exile and Nala Damayanti's experience of exile, revealing a more profound interrelation. Both stories share the theme of gambling leading to exile, yet Nala's tale introduces additional essential details. In Nala's story, symbols such as the serpent and fire hold significance, like the broader symbolism in the Mahabharata. Nala and Damayanti undergo a philosophical rebirth following a snake bite. However, unique elements in Nala's narrative set it apart from the Mahabharata. The separation of Nala and Damayanti is not a fleeting episode typical of Sringara kavya. The solitude of Nala's consciousness, severed from Damayanti, surpasses even the narratives of Rama and Sita. The disintegration in Nala's personal life is extraordinary in every aspect. The symbolic situations, including Nala's external disfigurement after being bitten by the venomous snake, Karkotaka; Rituparna's charioteering and the exchange of knowledge, warrant further exploration. Nala's story unfolds as a unique journey where, after losing his identity with Damayanti, he undergoes a transformative process, harnessing latent powers embedded in the depths of his personality and thereupon receiving divine grace.

The intricate life design of Nala's story doesn't directly correlate with the current predicament of the Pandavas. However, this extensive narrative serves as a diversion for the Pandavas, allowing them to momentarily forget their own situation and immerse themselves in another realm of experience. The Mahabharata itself doesn't explicitly detail how the Pandavas were affected by Nala's story. Yet, when the narrative of Nala is intertwined with the circumstances of the Pandavas, the combined impact of both cannot fail to resonate with the reader. Amid the highs and lows of Nala-Damayanti's lives, navigating between sins and virtues, karma and misdeeds, the shadow of divine influence, at times clear and at times enigmatic, consistently looms over them. Within the constraints of Nala's character and the unrestrained nature of Damayanti, whose beauty captivates even the gods, their lives find completeness only in union. It is against the backdrop of this

narrative that the personalities of the Pandavas, complete in their
anonymity above, are evaluated.

The Three Beginnings

The significance of the narrative strategy in the
Mahabharata extends beyond a singular beginning. The beginning
of this epic is fraught with inscrutable complexities, resulting
in three distinct versions. Prompted by a visit to the Samanta
Panchaka site, Suta commences with the extensive history of the
Chandra-vamsa, recounting the events of the battle between the
Kauravas and the Pandavas. The second version of the beginning
arises within a different context—the tale of the three disciples of
Sage Daumya. The final disciple, Uttanka Janamejaya, impels the
king to perform the Sarpayajna. However, the narrative abandons
this thread, pivoting to another scenario. The Mahabharata's
narrative truly unfolds with an ancient myth, steeped in the stake
of Kadru and Vinata, her son Garuda delivering nectar to the gods
to liberate Vinata, and the subsequent enmity between serpents
and Garuda.

Such a beginning may initially appear perplexing, particularly
when juxtaposed with Homer's poetry, where it seems to lack
the same orderliness. Analogous to the story of Ellora, where
ancient sculptors embarked on carving rock, only to start anew
if the initial attempt proved unsatisfactory, the Mahabharata
embraces a grander vision. Achieving precision and refinement
doesn't necessitate superhuman abilities or extraordinary morale;
it is the craftsmanship of skilled artists. Had the Mahabharata
been solely a poem, its beginning would likely have been more
straightforward. Yet, the Mahabharata is not confined to mere
poetry. In the beginning, Suta's visit to Samantha Panchaka,
evokes memories of the past war, hinting at its historical nature.
Indeed, some commentators classify the Mahabharata as a

history. As the sequential history of the Kuru dynasty neared an impasse due to impotence, a great war became inevitable, stemming from the conflict between gods and humans. Janamejaya's performance of the Sarpayajna (serpent sacrifice rite) and his subsequent hearing of the entire historical account from Vaishampayana can be perceived as a strategy to fulfil his paternal obligation. Nonetheless, the Mahabharata also serves as a poetic wellspring, providing sustenance for generations of poets to come. Janamejaya, despite being aware of his role in the serpent sacrifice, sought to hear the familiar history from another's perspective. Vaishampayana, disconnected from that specific history, elucidates the poetry composed by his guru Vyasa Maharshi, extolling its influence, benefits and overall glory.

From another perspective, the Mahabharata assumes the status of a Purana. Within the annals of the Kuru dynasty's history, numerous elements of divinity weave through the design. Ancestors of the Pandavas harboured a fervent desire for heaven. Some aspired to attain the status of Indra but met with failure, while others sought heavenly bliss on Earth, striving for immortality. The lineage boasted illustrious kings like Pururava, Yayati, Dushyanta and Nahusha. However, the predicament faced by the Kauravas and Pandavas is unparalleled in the extensive history of the Kuru clan. At its core, the Mahabharata grapples with the fundamental issue of sibling rivalry—a profound dilemma. Solving the enigma as to why siblings, sharing similar sensibilities, battle as bitter enemies, is tough. This quandary encapsulates one of the myriad mysteries of human existence. The origins of the rivalry between the Kauravas and Pandavas has to be traced back to a much earlier mythology, glimpses of which are discernible in the narrative of the serpents and eagles. This story mirrors a form of sibling rivalry between giants and deities. They are equals, and hence the gods prevail sometimes, and the giants, at other times. The conflict between the sons of Kasyapa's two wives affects the world order. Serpents and eagles are the offspring of Kasyapa's two other wives. Vinathe and Kadru engage in an argument over the colour of Indra's horse's tail, resulting in the former becoming the latter's slave. Kadru has hundreds of children while Vinathe has only one—a friend to the gods. This son, the Garuda, brings them nectar and with their help frees his mother from slavery. There are many similarities between this story and the sibling rivalry story of the Kauravas and Pandavas. Hence, the myth of Garuda is the source of Mahabharata.

Triveni Sangam

In this way, history, poetry and Purana intertwine to shape the structure of the Mahabharata. Consequently, the beginning of the story is intricately layered. The Mahabharata holds significant responsibility for the enduring spirit of truth among the people of our country. Our cultural symbols, expressions, celebrations and evocations, collectively form our cultural psyche, all deeply influenced by the Mahabharata. This fundamental influence underscores why the story of the Mahabharata is, in essence, our own narrative.

Elite and Folk

This essay is taken from Sanskruti Spandana, a collection of essays published by Kurtkoti in 1986. The term 'Abhijata', translated here as 'elite', could denote urban, classical, educated or sophisticated. Recently, it is used to refer to written literature in contrast to the oral tradition of folk literature. These terms also correspond to a significant dichotomy explored in Kannada poetics—Marga and Desi. Kurtkoti highlights their shared attributes before contrasting the abstract principles inherent in elite literature with the context-specific nature of folk literature.

The continuous flow of our folk poetry, which once ran for hundreds of years, now appears to have dried up. However, the efforts to conserve, study, and promote folk poetry and arts, are underway. The contradiction between these two facts demands serious consideration from the perspective of our culture. What are the reasons behind the cessation of the creation of folk poetry, which used to flow as naturally as breathing without the need for patronage? In which cultural milieu does the creativity of folk poetry originate? What is the nature of the consciousness that shaped the various poetic forms, both small and large, such as songs and *tripadi*? Folk art and poetry thrive when the creation or appreciation of poetry is not just an intellectual inclination but a fundamental aspect of one's sensibilities. Yet, why did our people lose this inherent sensibility?

Folk poetry thrived until recently, up to the time of India's first war of independence. The battles of Srirangapatna, the riots

289

at Naragunda, Kittoor and Mundaragi gave rise to numerous
ballads that still linger in our memory. Figures like Sangolli
Rayanna, Sindura Lakshana, Surapurada Bedru, Naragunda and
Kittoor Chennamma existed in a world that seems vastly different
from ours today. However, what distinguishes the characteristics
of that era from our own? The valour of these heroes who
resisted the British East India Company likely inspired the
talents of folk poets. While this assertion holds merit, it raises
a question: Why did Mahatma Gandhi's movement not leave a
similar impact? The essence of folk poetry is notably absent in the
songs of 'Prabhatpheri' (morning marches) sung during the non-
cooperation movement. Could this be attributed to the fact that
individual bravery of the past has transformed into a collective
movement today? The salt satyagraha at Dandi, a potentially rich
subject for heroic ballads, failed to capture the attention of folk
poetry. Gandhi's act of making salt on the seashore, a gesture
that rallied the entire nation against the British Empire, did not
resonate with the consciousness of folk poetry. Between this
historical event and folk imagination falls the shadow of our well-
documented history.

Popular Literature

In the pre-Independence period, folk consciousness could have
illuminated this shadow. Following independence, the country
became ensnared in the grip of materialism leading to dissipation
of values. In a society where power and wealth reign supreme,
popular literature is born—that creates dreams and seeks to
fulfil them. Similar to the cheap literature, movies and television
prevalent in Western countries, these trends have also made
their way to us. Folk literature is a collective art, and it does not
strive for the objective refinement or eloquence found in elite
literature. However, folk literature can have a profound effect

on a different level. It satisfies the innate need for artistry buried deep in the heart of the common person, often without their conscious awareness. Popular literature initially stirs desires and then seeks to fulfil them and failure to recognize the fundamental difference between folk literature and popular literature can lead to confusion. The enduring appeal of epics like the Ramayana and the Mahabharata for thousands of years suggests that the tastes of the common person are far from low.

Epic poems like the Ramayana and the Mahabharata stand as representations of the highest values cherished by our people. Additionally, they serve as a source of entertainment for those residing in remote regions. In contrast, popular literature tends to lose its currency quickly. The allure of constant innovation, once it takes hold, proves difficult to shake off. The transformation of art into a business inevitably leads to the demand for novelty. This phenomenon is evident in the plethora of bestselling works in America today. Consequently, genuine art often finds itself compelled to distance itself from such forms of popular literature. The impact of high realism in photography on the realm of painting provides an illustrative example of this dynamic.

At one point, there existed a tradition of categorizing arts into Marga and Desi. Both types of arts differed in their materials and modes of expression. This classification likely dates back to Vedic times, although its essence has been largely forgotten. The reason for this forgetfulness is the gradual merging and development of both types over time. While revisiting the history of this classification is not pertinent here, it is essential to note that they have become enriched by each other, erasing the opposition between them. Even now, the distinction between our Marga and Desi music lies not in their effects—they do not belong to different strata. This assertion holds true for poetry as well. Folk poetry may be more accessible than elite poetry, but it does not differ significantly in terms of poetic technique and values. On the contrary, popular art and literature contribute to the development of individuality among human beings.

Abstract Truth

It has been highlighted that the connotative meaning of folk poetry differs from that of elite poetry. Despite the concrete experiential material and technique of elite poetry, its emphasis lies on abstract philosophy. The reason behind this is the impersonal nature of the abstract. There is no need to elaborate on why higher capacities are required to comprehend and express abstract concepts. An illustration from Kalidasa's *Kumarasambhavam* may be pertinent here:

Harastu kinchit pariluptadhairyeh chandrodayarambha ivamburashih
Umamukhe bimbafaladharoshthe vyaparayamasa vilochanani

Siva's unusual restraint loosened a little due to the arrow of lust, and, like the sea losing its courage by the time of moonrise, Siva became anxious. He gazed at Parvati's lips, resembling a ripe fruit.

The details of the description, such as the simile of the sea, lack abstraction individually. However, their collective effort strives to reveal an abstract truth. For Kalidasa, Siva's desire and restraint symbolize creation and cataclysm, unveiling an abstract truth around these details. The harmonious interplay of this comparison, signifying the beginning of creative power at the dawn of the moon, is truly remarkable.

Nimbiya banadaga nindarasabyada haragola
Nitivantara magalu, Ambigaranna,
Holeya datiso bega.

Baleya banadaga bhalottu madabyada
Balevantara magalu, Ambigaranna,
Holeya datiso bega.

Linger not around the lemon groves
O boatman, I am the daughter of the righteous
Cross the stream quickly.
Linger not around the banana groves
O boatman, I am the daughter of the virtuous
Cross the stream quickly.

Both the form of expression and the benefits of folk poetry are tangible. Folk poetry has the ability to dissolve abstract philosophy into concrete experiences of life. It ensures that ways of life and truths are unveiled through the specific colours and smells of real-life encounters.

The girl crossing the stream on a boat is a young virgin, though not innocent. She discerns the boatman's hesitation to quickly cross the stream, observing him lingering along the edges, stopping briefly in the lemon grove and pausing near the banana grove. Despite her awareness, realizing her vulnerability as she is alone, she politely requests him to ferry her across. The term 'Ambigaranna', meaning 'brother boatman', delicately suggests a newfound 'brotherly' connection with him. Asserting that she is the 'daughter of righteous people' serves as a shrewd strategy to navigate the potential danger. While the words 'Niti' and 'Balve' (principled, virtuous) allude to abstract values, their usage here is palpable. The descriptive details in these verses aim to visually convey the integrity of the scene—the stream, boat, lemon plants, banana trees, the natural bond between ground and water, and the pervasive solitude. This scene distinctly shapes the characters of the girl and the boatman in the poem. The boatman's behaviour is influenced by the girl's underlying disadvantage and her reaction is a direct response to this situation.

Unique Contribution of Culture

The preceding examples illustrate elite and folk poetry, emphasizing a nuanced gap in poetics rather than cultural values. Kalidasa's moral values align with those held by folk poets. Labelling elite poetry as civilized and folk poetry as uncivilized is a biased accusation. Associating culture solely with languages like Sanskrit or urban settings is a simplistic notion lacking substance. Poetry, in all its forms, represents a distinctive contribution of culture.

The question arises: Are there no profound, meaningful distinctions between these two poetic forms beyond the technical gap? The primary distinction is in language. Kalidasa's language is not colloquial, a concept swiftly grasped by those acquainted with poets in recent times, who use a colloquial style. Sanskrit, initially colloquial, evolved into a literary language, a remarkable development in history. Conversely, folk poetry exclusively emerged in colloquial language, though this isn't an absolute truth. Comparisons between Kalidasa's Sanskrit poetry and Kannada folk poetry serve as extreme examples for this examination. Concluding that Kalidasa's poem is artificial due to its Sanskrit composition, while folk poetry, in colloquial language, is natural, oversimplifies the matter. A contemporary poet might discern the nuances of a verse crafted in colloquial language.

> *Mattagajagamini nee etta horatevva*
> *Suttalu janaru barutara | adaraga*
> *Matte kamigalu iratara*

> Where are you off to, with a stately gait,
> People throng around here, among them
> There will be lewd men too.

In this poem, both language and rhyme adhere to folk traditions, yet the poem itself transcends the folk genre. The flamboyant morality usually found in both elite and folk poetry is absent here. If meaning is the essence of language, this poem is crafted using that very power.

Expansiveness of Consciousness

From this perspective, elite and folk poetry assume profound significance beyond mere meaning. Elite poetry, while acknowledging meaning, constructs a rasa that surpasses it. Folk poetry, at times, disregards meaning yielding to 'bhava', sentiment. Here, 'rasa' and 'bhava' (in a non-static sense) are used in a limited capacity. 'Rasa' is a subjective experience even from the standpoint of the manuals of literary criticism, while 'bhava' denotes an experience rhythmically manifested. The use of language in these poetic forms varies due to their distinct expressions. Elite poetry employs the full spectrum of language to achieve its unique advantage. We do not harness all forms of language expression in our transactions; a word can function as a statement, rule or prohibition, and questioning and doubting can assume diverse forms. These linguistic forms may not align with our experiences. The phrase 'Krishnapi Asudarsanah', describing the lead hunter in Banabhatta's *Kadambari*, indicates that the hunter's black and ugly appearance is a realistic account. However, the statement 'Krishna, though he was an asudarsana' uses paradoxical language, not a mere linguistic trick. (The pun in this phrase relates to the two words used to refer to Krishna—the first word Krishna also suggests dark complexion; Sudarshana is another name for Krishna as well as for 'handsome'. But in this case, the prefix 'a' implies 'ugly'). Elite poetry allows the planning and development of numerous ideas, manifesting not only realistic but also verbal and figurative experiences, ultimately expanding consciousness.

Reliance on Colloquial Speech

Only folk poetry hinges on colloquial speech, where language is alive, audible and a form of living speech. However, it is not a mere tool for the exchange of ideas, as in mundane transactions. In the example provided earlier, the interaction between the girl and the boatman is a genuine exchange, but the expression doesn't need to be as elaborate as in this song. The daughter of the righteous and virtuous encompasses more than just these virtues; it extends to being humane. The original rhythm of this poem is complete and takes on new life with each repetition. Elite and folk configurations are essential components of culture, distinct from popular ones.

Puranas

This essay, taken from Kurtkoti's 1993 book, Uriya Nalige *(The Flaming Tongue), offers another glimpse into his reflections on Puranas. Here, he underscores that Puranas transcend mere fanciful tales, asserting their role as a means of understanding. He suggests that before disparaging or dismissing Puranas, we must thoroughly comprehend the diverse dimensions of their significance.*

Have we forgotten our Puranas? Will future generations be able to remember them? It is difficult to satisfactorily answer these questions. Puranas are forgotten if we try to protect them for sentimental reasons, or maybe it is better that they are. We perhaps do not hesitate to take another's life in the bewilderment we would be in when our faith is under attack. Our Puranas do not need the protection of our heroism. We need to understand them. In misconstruing Puranas to be histories, we may lead to further bloodshed. Instead, we need to find intellectual methods to understand the Puranas.

My friend K.V. Subbanna keeps saying that the stories of both the Ramayana and the Mahabharata are in fact two languages. This proposition makes a lot of sense to me. Perhaps this does not apply to any other epic poetry in the world. Unlike the canonical religious texts such as the Bible and the Koran, these are not scriptures. Yet, millions of people seek to understand the mysteries of life with the help of these languages. Only with the help of language can we give a form to the understanding of the world. The Ramayana and Mahabharata are not pure mythological stories; they encapsulate elements of history and poetry. Each of these components, mythology, history and poetry, constitutes distinct yet integral channels of acquiring knowledge.

The importance of Purana is that it is a more perfect means of knowledge than history and poetry. Our race has now lost the power to create Puranas. At one time this mythic genius was prominent in our race, not only creating Puranas but cultivating them to imbue them with other meanings. An example of the development of Puranas is still before our eyes. God's avatars, which were only four at first, gradually increased to ten. As all that had to be said in these ten incarnations was completed, the Purana of Dashavatara did not develop further. A Purana once born can transform but not die. They come and haunt the depths of man's consciousness.

Meaning of Purana

The work of interpreting the Puranas was also undertaken in earlier times. Yaska's *Nirukta* and Sayana's *Vedabhashya* are two examples. Yaska's *Daivatakanda* is a very serious attempt at this model, in which, based on the ancient myth of Indra and Vritta, he asks fundamental questions and tries to find answers to them. There is no difference in the interpretive techniques of Yaska and Sayana. Both try to arrive at the meaning through the words of Puranas. Among these two, Sayana distinguishes himself by constructing a realm of significance through the exhaustive enumeration of a word's diverse meanings within its contextual milieu. The enduring impact of Yaska and Sayana as seminal interpreters of the Puranas persists, with subsequent exponents invoking their contributions.

Now, we need to discover alternative interpretive methods, a prerequisite contingent upon dispelling prevalent misconceptions about the Puranas. We must recognize that Puranas are never meant to reflect reality. Therefore, a statement such as, 'Sagararaja has 60,000 children', should not lead to questions about the plausibility of such a phenomenon. Puranas employ distinct techniques, including transformation, boon bestowal, the metaphorical application of time and the exchange of youth for old age. For instance, Kindama Rishi does not 'celebrate' like a beast; rather, he becomes a gambolling beast. The metaphorical constructs inherent in poetry assume the form of metamorphosis within the purview of Purana. Purana itself is a language. But for those who use it, concepts like curse and time become its dialects. It is very important to pay attention to what meaning the Purana conveys by using all these techniques. We should not accept only one meaning which is convenient for us and thereby forget the structure of Purana. Doing so invites the question of what the form of the story implies.

As an illustrative case, the narrative of Dhruva in the Bhagavata Purana merits consideration. Dhruva, an esteemed devotee, undergoes a transformative journey as a young boy subjected to indignities by his stepmother. Empowered by a mantra given to him by Narada, he engages in rigorous tapas and attains the singular privilege of witnessing the manifest god. This narrative is ostensibly tailored to underscore the pre-eminence of devotion; however, it harbours additional facets warranting exploration. The nomenclature associated with the characters—Dhruva, Uttama, Uttanapada, Sunithi, Suruchi, among others—evinces distinctive narratives of their own. Notably, Suniti's progeny assumes the name Dhruva, while Suruchi's offspring becomes Uttama, a potential indication of the dichotomy between religious and cultural paradigms. An interpretive thread may be discerned, positing that virtue does not inherently attain divinity; rather, devotional practices, symbolized by tapas, constitute the sole avenue to attain Dhruva, connoting eternity. Dhruva's aspiration extends beyond a mere visual encounter with the manifest god. Despite being conferred the status of Dhruva, signifying the eternal, he returns to his kingdom, where a relieved Uttanapada installs him as its ruler. Subsequently, Dhruva is enraged by the killing of his brother Uttama at the hands of northern Dasyus (demons), leading him into a battle with Kubera and the subsequent vanquishing of numerous Yakshas. A necessary intervention by his grandfather Swayambhuva Manu is needed to guide Dhruva through this tumultuous phase. Following a prolonged reign, Dhruva attains celestial eminence, aligning himself with the Pole Star (Dhruva), an object of veneration for the seven sages who circumambulate it. This connotes that Dhruva's devotion constitutes merely a segment of his life, prompting further examination into the uncharted dimensions of his existence.

Calculation of Time

Dhruva's genealogy can be traced back to his grandfather, Swayambhuva Manu. Significantly, the chronological framework of Manvantara, comprising lunar eras, transitions into the solar era commencing with the 'Vaivasvata Manvantara'. The current Manvantara necessitates a fixed and unchanging reference point, a role fulfilled by Dhruva—the Pole Star—for the calculation of time. The philosophical underpinnings of time, as expounded in this context, exhibit polar and dynamic attributes. Dhruva's consort is named Bhrami, and their progeny include sons named Kalpa (symbolizing four ages) and Vatsara (representing years), along with descendants named Pushparna, Tigaketu and others. The marriage of Pushparna to Prabha (day) and Dosha (night) yields offspring named Patra, Madhyandina, Sayam, Pradosha, Nishita and Vyashta, thereby contributing to the systematic beginning of the calculation of time. The altercation between Dhruva and Kubera, the ruler of the north, acquires meaning in this context, suggesting the requisite conquest of the northern direction in the narrative tradition. Ravana, who fails to achieve this, comes to the south, another Purana story, the rational implications of which also need to be studied.

The narrative extends to the Shishumara, an entity positioned beyond Dhruva akin to an unborn child, serving as an embodiment of primordial time. Analogously, the motif of a coiled snake with its tail in its mouth, prevalent in the philosophical traditions of ancient Europe, also symbolizes time. If we remember that Dhruva's wife, Bhrami, was the daughter of Shishumara, the intrinsic correlation between Dhruva's narrative and the overarching philosophy of time becomes clear.

As of now, this exposition remains a preliminary analysis of the mythological narrative, necessitating a more exhaustive and nuanced examination. I intend to write another article to give a complete analysis of a Purana story. Purana stories are not just anecdotal tales. They encompass layers of nuanced meanings. Just as archaeological excavation of half-an-inch of Earth can help us go back thousands of years in our knowledge of the past, so is the story of Purana. New meanings have been added to them from time to time. All of them have to be taken into account. It is also a completely scientific system, so one has to proceed with caution.

Word and Meaning

This essay is taken from Kurtkoti's 1993 book, Uriya Nalige *(The Flaming Tongue). It showcases his adeptness in extracting fresh insights pertinent to contemporary literary studies from ancient Indian poetics. Here, he elaborates on Indian poetics and philosophy's perspectives regarding the correlation between word and meaning. Kurtkoti accomplishes this by delineating three categories of words and their varying relationships with meaning. Despite its brevity, the essay is remarkably concrete and enlightening.*

Scholars from the past have categorized speech into three types: Mantra, Shastra and Kavya (the incantatory, the scientific and the poetic). Interestingly, these three forms of speech continue to be recognized. While the significance of Mantra has waned in the present age, Shastra and Kavya have retained their relevance and importance. Despite the transformation of their original forms, their significance remains unabated. The depth and breadth of our understanding hinge upon Shastra and Kavya. Due to the close connection between Mantra and religiosity, the import of the Mantra fluctuates with that of religion. Consequently, Mantra is not an unfamiliar or forgotten phrase; rather, the Mantras employed for meditation and chanting are familiar to all, regardless of their efficacy. This underscores the enduring and widespread recognition of these three forms of speech.

The explanation provided by our scholars regarding these three types of speech is fascinating. They assert that in Mantra, the word is significant and meaning secondary; in Shastra, meaning takes precedence, while the word is considered insignificant. However, both word and meaning are deemed important in Kavya. The allure of poetry, where both elements carry significance, has captivated the minds of people to such an extent that the prominence of the other two forms has remained obscured. While Mantra and Shastra have become subjects of scholarly contemplation, Kavya has evolved into a cherished form of expression for the people. Behind the elaboration of poetic ideas through concepts such as rasa, dhvani and alankara lies a rich history. Nevertheless, the principle of classifying the three types of speech—Mantra, Shastra and Kavya—has been forgotten today. The extensive contemplations on the relationship between word and meaning, as found in ancient texts, have faded from our collective consciousness. The significance of the relationship between word and meaning cannot be overstated. If disrupted for any reason, it results in a disconnection of our experience and knowledge, leading to a form of cultural confusion. Given that such a time has dawned once again, it is only right that we engage in a healthy discussion on this matter.

Let us consider the first of the three forms of utterance—Mantra. What does it mean to say that in Mantra, the word is important, while meaning is insignificant? When Yaska composed his *Nirukta*, debates surrounding the meaning of Mantras were already underway. Yaska references the phrase 'anarthakah mantra', claiming Mantras to be 'devoid of meaning' an exaggeration. Every Mantra does indeed carry meaning, but the emphasis on that meaning is not as crucial. Merely acknowledging the meaning and neglecting the words won't yield any benefits. Hence, it is asserted that in Mantras, the word holds more significance than the meaning. The effectiveness of a Mantra lies in its practical application. Each Mantra should ideally be associated with its respective rishi, devata, chandas and viniyoga (sage who has given

the Mantra, deity to whom Mantra is addressed, metre in which
the Mantra is composed and the application for which the Mantra
is intended). Notably, the mention of viniyoga at the end holds
significance as the subsequent step is the siddhi (accomplishment
of the intended in the Mantra). Thus, the true meaning of a
Mantra is nothing but the accomplishment of what it seeks in
stating it.

Herein lies the crux of the issue. Understanding the concept
of meaning becomes incomplete if we equate the word 'gold'
solely with the metal. The essence of meaning doesn't reside in
the metal itself, but is inherent in the word 'gold'. We don't need
to physically point to the metal every time the word is uttered. It
becomes clear if we associate the meaning of gold with a power
intrinsic to the word 'gold'.

It implies that the power of the word in a Mantra is heightened
through the interplay of shabda, shakti, rishi, chandas and devata.
Unlike ordinary words, which merely serve as names for things and
function as symbols, the words in a Mantra can generate meaning.
However, this isn't a predetermined or commonplace truth. For
instance, when we encounter a building named 'Vidhana Soudha',
it triggers familiar meanings related to its use, political history,
laws enacted there, political influence, respect, hatred, contempt,
disgust, humour and various other emotions. The term 'Vidhana
Soudha' becomes meaningful as it encompasses these collective
meanings. The meanings that arise in this context are not solely
literal; they are connotative and symbolic also. In contrast, the
meaning derived from a Mantra is distinct. The word within a
Mantra has the power to create a visible and audible meaning.
However, the meaning it evokes remains concealed in the realm
of potential. The unseen becomes visible due to the power of
the word, leading to the assertion that the words in Mantras are
'meaningless' in the sense that their meanings are yet to be born.
In this sense, their 'meaninglessness' (meaning as a yet-to-exist,

inherent potentiality) itself is perhaps the power of the word in Mantra. In Bhavabhuti's play *Uttararamacharita*, there is a statement: 'Rishinam Punaradyanam Vachamarthoanu Dhavati'. The essence of this statement is that in the realm of worldly language, if the word follows the meaning, in the divine language of venerable sages, the meaning follows the words. This proposition holds true within the context of the drama *Uttararamacharita*, where the legacy of the message transmitted by Vasishtha—the Rishi Vachana—is enacted as the entire play.

There is a crucial point to be mindful of: the potency of words in Mantras extends beyond the religious realm. While it is true that chanting the Gayatri Mantra may yield some siddhi, and individuals with unwavering faith might attain such accomplishments, the influence of words in a mantra is not confined solely to these religious aspects. Bhavabhuti, in the drama *Uttararamacharita*, vividly illustrates the far-reaching impact of word. The power of the word, as portrayed in the drama, is responsible for Sita's defamation, Lakshmana's departure, Rama's solitary existence, and Lava and Kusha being deprived of the history and legacy of Raghuvansha. Each character therefore undergoes its share of tribulations. This narrative serves as an elaboration of Vasishtha's message. It underscores that meaning isn't preordained, existing independently before the word and that the word is not a mirror reflecting this fixed state of meaning, but that world and language interact to shape this realm of meaning.

In contrast, in Shastra (the scientific form of language, the second of the three forms of speech), meaning takes precedence. Language serves as a conduit for conveying this sense to us, and it is crucial to remember that language constructs meaning. Through language, we connect with the external world, and the truth we apprehend is rooted in this meaning. In Shastra, understanding the form, shape, colour, smell, effect and destruction of this meaning constitutes its primary objective. Consequently, our emphasis is

not on the language deployed. The word here functions as a sign
representing experience, form and object. A study of Shastra
doesn't introduce a new dimension of meaning in language;
instead, it is remarkable that language is necessary to Shastra.
It is universally acknowledged that knowledge emerges from
the interplay between the knower and the known. But because
knowledge cannot be had without the help of language, the need
for language is seen in the study of Shastra.

The third form of speech is Kavya (the poetic form), where, it
has been noted earlier, both word and meaning carry significance.
Poetry is an art primarily conveyed through language, but for some
poets it manifests only as a play of words. Rhetoric is the poet's
prerogative, enabling them to capture the musicality of words
or deploy words in unique ways to create unexpected meanings.
Consider a line of verse from Lakshmish's *Jaimini Bharata*, which
illustrates this: 'Vimalasumatiyam Tayenege Taye Nagegudi
Nodi.' Here, despite the similar sounds (tayenege taye—'give me
mother'), the words are distinct, each carrying a different meaning.
We can consider the *shlesha-alankara* (pun) in our ancient poems.
Shlesha means embracing. When the two meanings residing in the
same word are opposed to each other, the beauty is greater. The
secret of this figure of speech is that words manifest themselves
as if two meanings are in an embrace. Besides this embrace there
is another embrace too, which also is important—the inextricable
embrace of words and meanings. In Kalidasa's play *Shakuntala*,
a line reads: 'Anaih dvijaih parabritah balu poshayantee.' The
word 'dwija' holds dual meanings—Brahman and bird. Similarly,
'Parabritah' signifies both a cuckoo and a harlot. Dushyanta is
aware of only one meaning: that cuckoos get their young nurtured
through other birds. Yet, there is another meaning, unfamiliar to
him or perhaps forgotten—the tale of Menake, a divine harlot,
leaving her daughter, Shakuntala, in the care of Sage Kanva. The
poem is unique because the same words encompass both these

meanings. The author of this play, Kalidasa, in another instance has expressed, 'Vagarthaviva sampraktau vagartha pratipataye/ Jagatah pitarau vande Parvati Parameshwarau' ('Salutes to Shiva and Parvati, the parents of the whole world, who are intertwined like word and meaning'). Shiva and Parvati represent the mother and father of the world. The clever twist lies in the same word 'Pitarau' having two meanings—father and mother. Thus, word and meaning play a vital role in the texture of poetry.

Sculpture

This essay is taken from Kurtkoti's 1993 book, Uriya Nalige
(The Flaming Tongue), *where he contemplates the importance of visual
depictions of deities. He highlights the symbolic significance inherent in
sculptural methods of divine representation. While the essay laments
contemporary departures from traditional divine symbolism in favour
of innovation, it also serves as a concise reminder of the foundational
principles underlying visual representation in Indian culture.*

Public festivals have become increasingly perplexing and intricate
in recent times. The initiation of communal festivities poses not one
but many problems. The quintessence of our festivals lies in their
temporal regularity at designated intervals each year. Enveloped
within the fabric of time, we welcomed and commemorated these
festivals with fervour. While there exists a normative framework
prescribing a degree of consistency in celebratory practices, certain
deviations prove inevitable. One notable tradition involves the
veneration of Gauri, symbolized by the depiction of her image on
a clay pot. However, urban dwellers face difficulties in securing
traditional clay pots, and even if procured, using chalk colours for
the portrayal of Gauri becomes impractical. Consequently, people
in cities have shifted to the use of copper and silver vessels, upon
which the desired images are intricately drawn. Furthermore, the
observance of Gokulashtami previously entailed the meticulous
creation of a domestic replica of Gokula, replete with essential
elements, such as a flute, a fortress, a fortified gateway, a scholarly

priest engrossed in reading, a fruit vendor, a matron with ample bosom, Nanda and Yashoda, and effigies of the thumb-sucking Krishna and Balarama. This tableau sought to evoke the ambience of Krishna's divine birth within the sanctified wombs of the nocturnal realm. However, today, prefabricated, coloured sculptures of Krishna and Balarama are available in the market, thereby altering the traditional craftsmanship associated with Gokulashtami celebrations.

Nature of Soul

These reflections direct our attention to the discipline of sculpture. Essentially, our religious practices encompass the veneration of idols, rendering the creation and display of statues as a culturally accepted norm. Consequently, a systematic approach emerged to materialize our divine entities through sculptures fashioned from stones, clay and metals. While a comprehensive examination of this artistic and religious science is beyond the scope of the present essay, a pertinent issue here is the challenge of representing imperceptible deities in sculpture that is, inevitably, a medium of visual senses. A customary practice invokes the mental imagery of deities through the repetitive recitation of meditative shlokas. These are then translated into mental impressions and tangible sculptures. This practice, in essence, is an easy method of representing deities. However, if we ask where the meditative verses got the intricate details from tradition offers no answers.

The Upanishads engage in an exploration of the intricate relationship between the body and the soul, a thematic concern with its roots in the narrative of Indra and Virochana as elucidated in the Chandogya Upanishad. In this foundational myth, Brahma instructs both of them to observe their reflections in water and tell what they found there. Strikingly, both discern only the corporeal form. The ensuing narrative unfolds with Indra's dissatisfaction, leading him to embark upon an extended period of penance, culminating in his profound realization of the authentic nature of the soul. What is significant about this narrative is that there is a rejection of the truthfulness of reflection. In Western philosophies of art, the mirror and its reflective properties assume a pivotal role.

The absence of a comparable emphasis on mirrors and reflections within Indian metaphysics prompts us to wonder, while it is possible to represent a corporeal body like a mirror's reflection, is it possible for visual arts to encapsulate the formless principle of the divine or the soul? It is noteworthy, however, that such artistic considerations do not amount to a wholesale repudiation of the materiality of the body. Indra's acknowledgment within the same narrative, that the mortal body serves as the locus of the soul, underscores the need for a nuanced perspective on the coexistence of the corporeal and the spiritual. The Upanishads assert a philosophical stance that posits both the soul and god as entities residing in a state of existential nothingness. Allama Prabhu asserts that calamity befalls those who have been transformed into idols. The overarching philosophical discourse within the Upanishads converges upon the relations between the idol and the annihilation.

Our sculptural tradition unfolds within this philosophical framework. The absence of a predilection for realistic imitation within secular art precludes any expectation of its manifestation in religious art. Faced with the impracticality of capturing the transcendental verity of god in a realistic manner, artistic expression gravitated towards symbolism and imagism. Each deity in our culture is represented in similar form but was endowed with distinctive attributes. A parallel is discernible in the portrayal of heroic human beings. An episode in Bhasa's *Pratima Nataka* is notable. Bharata, having arrived in Ayodhya from his maternal uncle's residence, pauses at a shrine situated beyond the town limits. Within this sacred space, he discovers the effigies of his forefathers and asks the shrine's attendant about their identities. The attendant enumerates the names of the three statues successively—Dilip, Raghu and Aja. However, upon the introduction of the fourth statue, the attendant abruptly halts. This newly installed statue portrays Dasharatha, who had recently died. Bharata, unbeknownst to the news of his father's demise, remains unaware of the identity of the newly erected statue. A pivotal aspect of this scenario lies in Bharata's inability to recognize the statue as that of his father. The convention of representation of deceased forefathers in a like manner is the reason behind Bharata's inability to recognize the statue of his father. The attendant eventually reveals the identity of Dasharatha's statue. Notably, the countenance of Dasharatha's statue diverges from his living visage. This narrative serves as the underpinning for the adage asserting the similarity in form between forefathers and deities. It must be underscored that this phenomenon transcends the confines of Vedic religious practices. Buddha statues exhibit uniformity, while differentiation among the statues of Tirthankaras is predicated not on facial features but on distinctive attributes. For instance, Parswanath is characterized by a serpent emblem, while Chandraprabha is identified by a moon emblem, facilitating the discernment of Tirthankaras beyond facial expressions.

The recognition of deities in art necessitates the discernment of characteristic features. Marks such as Varuna's noose, Yama's staff, Brahma's kamandal (pot) and Saraswati's necklace, alongside the animals serving as their vehicles, become instrumental in this identification process. For instance, Durga is associated with a lion, Ganapati with a mouse and Indra with Airavata. Facial features also play a crucial role, with distinctive characteristics such as Garuda's nose, Tumburu's horse face (a Gandharva in Kubera's court, a mythical being with horse face and human body) and Narasimha's lion face serving as distinctive identifiers. The trunk of Ganapati, in particular, emerges as an indelible feature. These observations collectively underscore the adherence to the prescribed conventions, wherein each deity is characterized by specific weaponry, ornaments, vehicles and handprints.

Victory of Art

Ganesha's iconographic representation serves as a seminal source of inspiration and a challenge to our sculptural endeavours, embodying distinctive features such as the elephant's face, prominent belly, truncated limbs, fractured tusks, a serpent band and a trunk, collectively coalescing into a visual Purana. The amalgamation of these attributes poses a formidable challenge to the artist tasked with the creation of aesthetic beauty. Notwithstanding the inherent difficulties, sculptural representations of Ganesha in places such as Goolur, Idagunji and Gokarna, are beautiful. It is noteworthy that the beauty discerned in the depictions of Lakshmi are also found in these Ganesha sculptures, which we may consider as artistic triumph. However, the beauty of iconography found in such sculptures is currently jeopardized by extraneous additions made to Ganapati idols.

The erosion of sculptural beauty can be attributed to the underlying principle of innovation, which has ushered in a departure from traditional artistic norms. One kind of profit can be obtained if Chaturbhuja Ganesha is worshipped; another type of profit requires the worship of Ashtabhuja Ganesha. While variations in artistic representations may arise for technical exigencies, the contemporary trend reflects a departure from established artistic conventions. The depiction of Ganesha with the facial features of Nehru, Saibaba or a police officer, for instance, lacks justification either from an artistic or religious standpoint. Unlike humans, deities do not undergo developmental stages, as they are inherently immortal. Consequently, artistic representations of deities assume symbolic significance, transcending the confines of human growth. As avatars, Rama and Krishna have childhood, youth and old age, yet their sculptural representations serve distinct purposes within the sculptural lexicon: the purpose of Balakrishna's idol is different from that of the youthful flute-playing Krishna's idol. As symbols, deities encapsulate the ineffable aspects of divine power, necessitating a symbolic language to convey their profundity. The symbolism inherent in the idol of Ganesha, despite attempts at explication, remains veiled and enigmatic.

In the context of our civilization, characterized by a proclivity towards idolatry rather than iconoclasm, recent developments in idol worship exhibit a transformation in this age-old tradition. When followers of other religions destroyed idols, people decorated the stones found on some hill to use it as the idol representing their divinity. The evolving landscape of idol worship seems to signal a diminishing presence of divine symbolism amid the proliferation of myriad idols.

Translation and Rewriting

This essay, sourced from Kannada Sahitya Sangati, *published in 1995, revisits a theme previously explored by Kurtkoti. Here, Kurtkoti offers a fresh perspective on the practice of translation as a form of rewriting in Indian culture. He emphasizes the significance of this rewriting as a deliberate act of transformation, providing new insights into old tales. Drawing examples from Bhavabhuti, Pampa, Nemichandra and Ponna, Kurtkoti highlights the translation process as a form of rewriting, deeply rooted in a tradition that imbues old tales with fresh layers of meaning.*

The beginning of Kannada poetry is intertwined with the art of translation and rewriting. Pampa articulates the challenges inherent in this poetic pursuit, stating, 'Kate Piridadodam Kateya Maigidaliyade Samastabharata manapoorvavagi pelda kabbigarilla' ('The story of the Mahabharata is huge; no poet has been able to retell this story concisely without harming its basic structure'). His perspective underscores the difficulty of preserving the structural integrity while transposing a narrative into another language. Whether a lengthy tale should be condensed or a concise one expanded, is not just a deliberate process, but one imbued with significance. For the poetic tradition to endure and accommodate new layers of meaning, the size of poems must undergo alteration. The deliberate elimination of unnecessary and irrelevant elements, when condensing a larger narrative, or the addition of fresh perspectives and meanings when expanding a shorter one, becomes integral to this evolutionary process.

This intentional transformation is not confined to the realm of written poetry alone; it echoes through the oral tradition, where stories continuously contract or expand based on the storytellers' discernment. In the folk context, the adaptability of stories is contingent upon the audience, who infuse their creativity to enhance the narrative's presentation.

Kannada poets were attentive to the Sanskrit Abhijat Kavya (classical Sanskrit poetry). In ancient times, poetry went beyond being a mere manifestation of rasa-bhava; it served as a medium for expressing knowledge. The knowledge of the age of Abhijata Kavya is evident not only in refined scientific treatises but also in poetic works. Varahamihira, for instance, incorporated Kalidasa's poetic style into his scientific writings, while Kalidasa drew on knowledge from Varahamihira's scientific works in his poetry. Essentially, the domains of religion, politics, literature and arts during this period were fashioned by kings for their education. A profound disparity exists between the knowledge systems of the age of the Abhijata Kavya and the knowledge systems of the Brahmans. The latter, drawn to the truths of Vedanta philosophy, developed theories of Karmasiddhanta and Karmamimanse, recognizing the possibility of rebirth for humans. In this context, the poetry of the age of Abhijata Kavya was secular, though not anti-religious. Notably, the language employed was Sanskrit.

However, as the influence of Buddhist and Jain heritage began to permeate diverse poetic forms in various languages, the continuity of Abhijat Kavya likely faced challenges. During Chandragupta's time, the intersection of south and north India spurred cultural divergence. By the era of Pampa and Ranna, figures like Kalidasa and Bana had likely demonstrated the feasibility of embracing ideals beyond religious ones. In the realm of Kannada Champu Kavya, a significant endeavour was to unlock the chests of ancient knowledge and claim the treasure within. The Kannada poets did not shy away from elements of Abhijat

Kavya that diverged from their religious beliefs. Nonetheless, the
technical significance of the rewriting, and translations initiated
by these Kannada poets, warrants examination.

In the act of rewriting, old perspectives intertwine with new
ones, paving the way for fresh meanings. A concise illustration
of this phenomenon can be found in a particular episode from
Bhasa's play *Dutavakya*. In this scene, upon learning of Krishna's
impending negotiation visit, Duryodhana schemes to keep him
at bay. He summons Kanchuki and instructs her to procure
the painting depicting Draupadi's disrobing. Upon its arrival,
he meticulously examines the painting, offering his assessment
in the end: 'Aho asya varnadyata. Aho bhavopapannatha. Aho
Yuktalekhata. Suvyaktamalikhitoyam Chitrapatah' ('Such rich
colours! Such fine expressions! What a perfect composition!
It really is a picture well done'). This painting serves multiple
purposes. Duryodhana's fury intensifies upon encountering the
Pandavas in the image, triggering the audience's recollection
of the Mahabharata episode and arousing curiosity about the
unfolding future.

But what does Duryodhana's analysis of the picture signify? To
him, terms like 'varnadhyate', 'bhavopapannate' and 'yuktalekha'
are technical expressions. Duryodhana assumes the role of an
art expert, an aspect seemingly unnecessary in the Mahabharata
narrative. However, in Bhasa's rendition, Duryodhana transforms
into an art connoisseur—a cunning individual who transforms art
into a political weapon. This introduces a novel dimension to his
character, even though the underlying story is age-old. It is not
the tale itself that is new, but rather the fresh understanding that
Bhasa injects into it. This verse from the thirteenth chapter of
Pampa's *Bharata* may be considered:

Sangataneetishastravidarapparavandira tamma tamma
kajjangala meygalol pusidadam kadu nanniye madi torparu

ttunga susukshma parshvakrishakomala nimna ghanonnata
pradeshangalama samana taladalliye torpavol chitrakam
(Chs 13–21; 367)

Just as a painter shows the higher and the lower, the thin and the
tender, the thick and the delicate regions on the flat surface of a
picture, so do those who know politics will make the falsehood
of their actions the absolute truth.

Pampa's analysis of the painting surpasses Bhasa's in both
technical depth and insight, yet it is crucial to acknowledge their
shared purpose. In Bhasa's portrayal, when Duryodhana wields
the painting as a political weapon, it transforms into an icon
embodying both comprehension and critique. (It is worth noting
that the term 'image' [pratime] differs from 'icon' [pratimana].
While abstract concepts can be conveyed through images, an icon
serves as a tool for evaluation, standing on the rational capacity
of humanity!) Pampa employs the same icon in his interpretation.
Subsequently, a multitude of Jain poets also incorporate the icon of
painting into their works. Nemichandra adeptly employs the icon
of music in his *Lilavati Prabandha*. In a conversation between the
clown and Kandarpa, the harlot sings the Hindol raga, described
as an incarnation of spring. The clown remarks, 'Ee ragamargam
Hindola   raganga   sambhavamappa   deshiya   hindolamidu
shringarayuktamappudarim . . . ninage keltakkudu' ('This raga that
follows the path of Hindola, is Desi Hindola with its emphasis
on Shringara'). This dialogue underscores the clear distinction
between Marga and Desi, as well as between understanding and
experience. It suggests that Marga is intellectual and theoretical,
while Desi is experiential. This dichotomy between Marga and
Desi, serving as an icon, defines the two primary types of art.
Ponna, in describing the beauty of a garden in Videha, articulates,
'Cheeraghattiye   bareditta   chitrada   banakkeneyaytu   banam

videhadol' ('In Videha, the garden resembles a pretty picture drawn by a painter'). Whether it is feasible to find the beauty seen in the picture in nature is a separate question. However, the remarkable phenomenon of a picture evolving into an icon to portray the beauty of nature is truly astonishing.

Music, dance, painting, poetry and ethical sciences offer a distinct category of icons—tools of understanding. This ensures clarity and avoids misunderstanding regardless of the occasion. However, there are also mythological images that borrow icons, repurposing them in new contexts. Through the process of rewriting, these icons take on different meanings. Over time, the accumulated interpretations coalesce, unravelling and reconstructing the Puranic archetype—essentially dismantling it and giving rise to a new creation.

Consider the story of Sita's abandonment in the Uttara Ramayana as an example. In the original Ramayana, the people of Ayodhya discuss Sita's character openly, and the accusations gradually reach Rama's court. Respecting the opinions of his subjects, Rama decides to leave Sita. Subsequently, Lakshmana takes Sita to the forests on the other side of the Ganges. The meaning of this episode is explicit in the Ramayana; it marks the initial step towards the dissolution of Rama's incarnation. Following the loss of Lakshmana, Rama ascends to heaven as mandated by Time.

In the Ramayana, a moral dilemma arises for Rama when he must choose between satisfying either Sita or his subjects. This episode inherently presents a moral quandary. Subsequently, figures like Bhavabhuti in Sanskrit, as well as Lakshmisha and Muddana in Kannada, revisit the same incident but interpret it differently. Each provides a distinct rationale for Sita's abandonment. Folklore elements, such as the story of the launderer, might have infiltrated the narrative, adding further complexity. Amid these diverse rewritings, a creative debate unfolds, centring on the conflicting themes of Rama's love for Sita and his duty as a king. Deciding which takes precedence becomes a challenge, ultimately reflecting the spirit of the times. However, the consistent use of Puranic icons underscores a crucial point: their employment fosters community discussions. Furthermore, the Purana itself serves as a catalyst for intellectual development within the language.

Marga and Desi

In this essay from Kannada Sahitya Sangati, *published in 1995, Kurtkoti provides a clear exposition of two concepts central to Kannada poetics. Drawing on Ananda Kumaraswamy, he expands the conventional understanding of these twin words, elite and folk. Additionally, he highlights the practice of ancient Kannada poets like Pampa, who integrated the two, arguing that evolutionary contingencies mandated the combined utilization of Marga and Desi styles.*

The meaning of Pampa's words, 'Bage posadappudagi mridubandhadolonduvadondi desiyol puguvudu, pokka margadole talvudu, taltode kavyavoppugam' ('With novel ideas and manners, it should be composed with sweet words, arranged in a Desi manner, then fashioned in Marga manner, for the poem to succeed'), seems somewhat unclear in contemporary terms. The present-day literary criticism has assigned different connotations to the terms Desi and Marga, now synonymous with folk versus Abhijat (classical) and Kannada versus Sanskrit. While this narrowing of meaning is understandable to some extent, it is not very useful to understanding the endeavours of poets like Pampa.

Pampa belonged to the tenth century, a period when Sanskrit literature was in decline. Moreover, even during the zenith of Abhijat literature, Sanskrit poetics remained entirely secular. Despite its secular nature, it also carried a religious aura simply because it was in Sanskrit—the language of the gods, with Devanagari script. Consequently, other languages lacked this inherent sanctity.

Ananda Kumaraswamy has looked into the concepts of 'Marga' and 'Desi' in one of his articles. During the Vedic period, the arts were categorized as Svargya and Asvargya. Seeking the hidden light of the divine principles not visible to the eye was a path known as 'Marga'. In other words, art could be born of religious longing. Conversely, 'Desi' denotes art primarily aimed at entertainment, concerned with the joys and sorrows of this world. Since the purpose of 'Marga' isn't to entertain the masses, it may not sustain the desire for beauty, whereas beauty is crucial for 'Desi'. Taking these arguments too literally could render art rigid and meaningless. Pampa's aspiration is that these two paths should be united for art to be vibrant. Pampa's words express a sincere desire, indicating that such integration was not commonplace. His view serves as an ideal, and this ideal should be inherent in languages. If the desire is not embedded in the language, can the poet's poetic intention alone fulfil this ideal?

For any language to qualify as a poetic language, it must embody this particular ideal. Kannada has attempted to claim the Abhijat status. The reasons for Abhijat-*ness* (high or sophisticated quality of poetry) lie hidden in history. Every language seeks refinement (Abhijat-*ness*) through its poetry. The terms 'Marga' and 'Desi' in Kannada have undergone shifts in meaning due to historical factors. During Pampa's era, anything composed in Sanskrit was considered Marga. Kannada poets strategically employed Sanskrit to surpass their Sanskrit counterparts. Additionally, since Sanskrit is not a mother tongue, Kannada poets experimenting with Sanskrit found it challenging to write in Sanskrit as Kannada was their mother tongue. The Sanskrit employed by Kannada poets lacks the intrinsic resonance of that language. This becomes evident when comparing Ranna's Samasa (word compounding) to Kalidasa's. The proficiency of Kalidasa in creating Samasa unveils layers of meaning beyond the grasp of grammar, while Ranna's efforts at Samasa reflect merely a mature utilization of compounded words. Nevertheless, the connection with Sanskrit was unavoidable for Kannada poets, at least for the sake of competition. The oath of 'Kalidasanginnurmadi' ('Hundred times of Kalidasa') a statement by Ponna, tenth-century Kannada poet was reiterated repeatedly, underscoring the inescapable ties with Sanskrit.

However, what is intriguing is that 'Marga' did not manifest in the Sanskrit poetry of Kannada poets. Alongside Kalidasa and Banabhatta, Dandi's *Dashakumarcharita* stood as an influential work during Pampa's era. In the technical terms of Old Kannada poetry, it is categorized as a 'story of mischievous heroes'. Interestingly, for Jain poets, it was their Agamakavyas (spiritual literature) that truly conveyed the essence of 'Marga'. In the accurate sense, *Dashakumarcharita* is 'Desi', even though it is in Sanskrit. Kannada poets had to discern the nature of the relationship that Kannada needed to have with Sanskrit. A study of how Kannada poets have deployed Sanskrit is yet to be undertaken. In Pampa's statement in *Adipurana*, 'Vyasamuniendra Rundra Vachanamrita Vardhiyaneesuven' ('I will swim in the milky ocean of Vyasa's vast poetry'), the use of the word 'rundra' (vast), a term even Sanskrit poets hesitate to employ, aptly captures the unfamiliarity of that unexplored sea and the poet's daring adventure. Similarly, in 'Sulpadeyalappudu kana mahajirangadol' ('Your turn will come in the Great War'), the juxtaposition of the Kannada word 'Sul' and the Sanskrit word 'Mahajiranga' naturally conveys a meaning beyond the literal sense. This illustrates the purpose of Pampa in describing Draupadi's *swayamvara* (in Hindu Puranas, it is a ceremony for a woman to choose a man as her husband from a group of suitors) in the language of Kalidasa's depiction of Indumati's swayamvara—signifying a competition of sorts. Kannada had to be refined to generate new meanings, and similarly, Sanskrit had to be adapted to align with the nuances of Kannada mannerisms.

Similar to 'Vastuka–Varnaka', the terms 'Desi–Marga' also belong to the glossary of poetics. These terms, akin to spies, possess the ability to conceal their true nature and unexpectedly unveil the secrets of poetics. They serve as testimony to the trajectory of Kannada poets, forging a path that runs parallel to, yet distinct from, the Sanskrit poetic tradition. However, these terms no longer carry the same meaning they once did. Terminology starts with a fixed meaning but gradually undergoes transformations. Yet, one thing remains certain: in its early stages, Kannada poetry endeavoured to elevate the 'Desi' to the status of 'Marga', and conversely, 'Marga' was made 'Desi' for similar reasons.

The narrative is still unfolding.

Pratyabhijnana

This essay is taken from Sanskruti Spandana, *a collection of essays published by Kurtkoti in 1986. Here, he succinctly discusses a topic that is important in his overall view of Indian literary theories about which he has a book published posthumously. Pratyabhijnana, deeply rooted in ancient literature, is pivotal in dramas, leading to recognition and revelation. It leads to tragic outcomes in Greek plays like* Oedipus *and joyful ones in Shakespeare's* Pericles. *However, Kurtkoti's specific interest here is the specific nature of pratyabhijnana in Sanskrit dramas, where, as in* Abhijnana Shakuntala, *it resolves conflicts and brings harmony. It symbolizes the rediscovery of connections and the pursuit of truth, making it a timeless theme in literature.*

In the greatest dramas worldwide, pratyabhijnana has played a pivotal role. In Greek dramas, the tragedy of the play often unfolds through pratyabhijnana. In Sophocles' *Oedipus*, the curse of Oedipus manifests dramatically in a final pratyabhijnana. Oedipus, in an attempt to defy the dreadful prophecy that he will 'kill his father and marry his mother', flees from his adoptive parents. However, unbeknownst to him, his efforts to evade the future only bring him closer to it. As he inadvertently fulfils the prophecy by killing King Laius and marrying his queen, Jocasta, Oedipus remains ignorant of his actions. It is only later, when he discovers the truth—that Laius is his father and Jocasta is his mother—that the irreparable nature of his actions becomes clear. The irony of this situation is so cruel that it lends itself to the very definition of misfortune.

Aristotle considers anagnorisis or pratyabhijnana to be indispensable in drama. However, there is no rule that pratyabhijnana must always lead to tragedy. The effect of pratyabhijnana can be quite delightful. In Shakespeare's final plays, pratyabhijnana occurs almost miraculously. For instance, in the play *Pericles*, the king's daughter, whom Pericles believed to be dead, is discovered in the middle of the sea. The girl who was lost in childhood emerges alive as a young woman, making it difficult for Pericles to recognize her. When he finally does, it feels unreal to him. 'But are you flesh and blood? Do you have a beating heart?' He finds it a wonder that she is alive and human.

Eliot's Interpretation

T.S. Eliot's interpretation of this scene from Shakespeare's play *Pericles* is as follows: 'To my mind, the finest of all "recognition scenes" is Act V, Scene I of that very great play *Pericles*. It is a perfect example of the "ultra-dramatic," a dramatic action of beings who are more than human, or rather, seen in a light more than that of day.'[4] Eliot believes that pratyabhijnana adds a supernatural edge to the play, showcasing an amazing experience where the supernatural emerges within the realm of reality. The return to life of a daughter presumed dead signifies an experience beyond the ordinary. Eliot even wrote a beautiful poem about this experience titled 'Marina', depicting through the use of symbolism how supernatural truth manifests, and its impact on the human mind. Eliot describes how Pericles saw Marina's face when she opened her eyes in the middle of the sea, 'More distant than stars

---

[4] T.S. Eliot, 'The Development of Shakespeare's Verse. Two Lectures', in Jayme Stayer (ed.), *The Complete Prose of T.S. Eliot: The Critical Edition, Vol. V: Tradition and Orthodoxy, 1934–1939*, 2017, https://collected.jcu.edu/fac_bib_2017/15

and nearer than the eye.' This description merges two seemingly distant things into one, giving birth to truth in their fusion. The relationship between the eye and the star blurs the line between the knower and the known, eliminating their distinction.

Eliot's poem doesn't extend beyond this interpretation. Its purpose is to depict the manifestation of divine truth as it presents itself. What is important to Eliot is the unwavering loyalty to the idea of truth's self-manifestation. However, in Abhijat (classical) dramas, pratyabhijnana serves other purposes as well. It can reveal the cruel irony of fate, such as when Rustum recognizes Sohrab as his son before dying. It can also highlight the limits of human consciousness, as seen in Oedipus's story, where he loses his eye while praying for light from the sun god. Alternatively, it may infuse human life with a touch of grace from supernatural truth, as seen in Shakespeare's final plays.

Major Role

Even in Sanskrit dramas, pratyabhijnana plays a crucial role, albeit with different purposes. In Kalidasa's *Abhijnana Shakuntala*, as the title suggests, pratyabhijnana is the central theme. The pivotal moment when Dusyanta recognizes and accepts Shakuntala as his wife, despite forgetting her due to a curse after falling in love with her at the Kanvasrama, forms the essence of the play. While it is true that the lost ring, found accidentally at Shachitirtha, plays a role in this recognition, it is Dusyanta's journey through oblivion, loneliness and pain that refines his mindset. In the fifth act, when Shakuntala stands before him, the depiction of Dushyanta's state of mind is remarkable. The curse has disrupted the connection between his intellect and emotion, leading to disharmony. Although his instinct acknowledges Shakuntala as his wife, his intellect questions the situation. In the first act, the intuitive pull controlled his mind upon seeing Shakuntala for the first time, but now, the conflict between intellect, senses and intuition persists. Without resolving this conflict and reconciling mind and emotions, true peace remains elusive.

However, the opposite mentality can be observed in Dusyanta in the seventh act. When he witnesses Sarvadamana playing with lion cubs at Sage Kasyapa's hermitage, it stirs something within his heart. Despite Sarvadamana's antics causing headaches to the ashram maids, they captivate Dusyanta. Upon seeing Sarvadamana, his heart feels a surge of affection as when seeing one's own offspring. Even though there is a doubt about Sarvadamana being someone else's son, this doubt doesn't confuse his mind. When a maid presents Sarvadamana with a clay peacock saying, 'Shakunthalavanyam prekshasva' ('See the charm of the bird'), he inquires, 'Where is my mother?' Upon hearing Shakuntala's name, Dusyanta resists the impulse of his mind, considering that there might be others with the same name. He exercises restraint to gain a deeper understanding. Dusyanta's pratyabhijnana reaches completion with Sarvadamana displaying the qualities of an emperor evident in his palm, and Dusyanta's survival despite holding Aparajita that had fallen from Savadamana's hands. By this point, the effect of the curse has waned, leaving his senses intact.

Literary Symbolism

The loss of connection between experience and understanding represents one of the greatest tragedies of human sensibility. This issue has grown increasingly acute in the twentieth century. It is not uncommon to grasp what one is experiencing before the actual experience. However, this problem doesn't seem exclusive to the present; whenever there's a rift in communication, it impacts language, turning what should be alive into something lifeless. I consider Bhavabhuti's play *Uttararamacharita* an exceptional work that examines this problem. During Bhavabhuti's time, Sanskrit was losing its vitality, transitioning from a vibrant language to one primarily for scholars. Bhavabhuti recognized the value of his play but harboured doubts about whether the audience understood it fully. Throughout the play, he introduces literary symbols saying, 'This is Rama's karuna rasa' and 'this is the plot's dexterity'. Moreover, the entire play embodies this underlying issue.

There isn't space here for a thorough analysis of *Uttararamacharita*, but within the play there's a noteworthy scene of pratyabhijnana. Rama's Ashwamedha horse arrives at Valmiki's hermitage, where Valmiki's disciples, including Lava–Kusha, encounter a horse for the first time. One of the boys sees it and reports that an animal called a horse has arrived. Lava–Kusha, too, have never seen a horse, but know about it based on their theoretical knowledge gained from animal science and war science. Despite lacking direct experience, they possess comprehensive understanding. For instance, they know from the Vedas the importance of prostrating before elders like Kausalya, Vasishtha and Arundhati, even without knowing their identities. They are aware of the tradition of including meat in madhuparka, a hybrid preparation used as a holy offering during religious rites. When Rama himself appears before them, Lava and Kusha don't recognize him initially. However, through Valmiki's poetry, they deeply understand Rama and Sita's love. Chandraketu, Lakshmana's son, introduces Rama to them, and when Lava asks why Rama's face appears pale, Kusha promptly explains, linking it to Rama's sorrow over Sita's loss. He defends his viewpoint by quoting two beautiful verses from Valmiki, showcasing their profound understanding despite their limited direct experience.

When Rama embraces them, his filial affection surges, as he feels a connection flowing between them. However, having experienced an uncertain separation from Sita, Rama harbours no hope of reuniting with his children. Despite standing close, the father–son relationship is not yet fully formed, or if it exists, there is little awareness. Rama's understanding aligns with the notion that 'na cha bahirupadhin jai preetayah sansthayanthe' ('love does not depend on external causes'). This encapsulates Rama's state in the initial phase. He is unsure whether Sita's touch is a happy or sad experience; instead, Rama comprehends the value of lost experiences. Even as he embraces Lava–Kusha, he doesn't recognize them as his children. Losing Sita and enduring loneliness, Rama's connections are all severed. Kausalya adamantly refuses to return to Ayodhya without Sita, and Janaka doesn't accept Rama as his son-in-law for the same reason. The reversal of these relationships occurs through pratyabhijnana which binds the severed relationships, scattered beliefs of love and loyalties of the Raghuvamsa, forming a vital life force. The significant aspect of this play lies in the influence of Valmiki's poetry, shaping the pivotal act of pratyabhijnana.

Representation of Truth

One needn't search far to understand this phenomenon. The importance of pratyabhijnana encompasses both experience and understanding, which our ancient philosophers referred to as 'Bhava'. As expressed by Kalidasa's Dushyanta, 'Bhavastirani Janantara Suhridani', the bonds of friendship from past lives are embedded in the 'bhava' of people. It is through this innate feeling that what transcends comprehension becomes immediately evident to the mind. The essence of pratyabhijnana lies in this intuitive sense, not in mere intellectual understanding of truth. However, the intellect plays a crucial role in grasping the essence of truth. Only when the intellect aligns can truth's image endure. The significance of pratyabhijnana lies in the representation of such scenes.

Section 3

Literary Criticism

Courtesy of Criticism

This essay is taken from Sanskruti Spandana, *a collection of essays published by Kurtkoti in 1986. In this concise piece, Kurtkoti evaluates the shift in the approach to criticism between the past and present. He emphasizes the importance of criticism prioritizing the experience of literature rather than literature merely serving as a platform for criticism.*

I ventured into literary criticism in 1958 when the publishing house Manohar Grantha Male chose to publish the *Nadedu Banda Dari* volumes to commemorate its silver jubilee. Prior to that, I had reservations about venturing into criticism. My focus was primarily on writing poetry, plays and essays. Literary criticism was an occasional pursuit for me. Although I only donned this role for a specific occasion, the title of a literary critic has persistently clung to me.

My initial foray into criticism was a creative endeavour. The essay I wrote served as a medium to articulate the literary experiences that had been ingrained in me since childhood. At that time, beyond Bendre and V.K. Gokak (1909–92), I was not acquainted with any authors. Nevertheless, literary nourishment had continued unabated. In my uncle's house at our hometown, Kurtkoti, a collection of over 10,000 books awaited exploration. Amid the randomness, I read Dickens's novels alongside Bana's works, Kalidasa's *Raghuvamsa* and more. I made it a habit to finish reading books at G.B Joshi's bookshop, Jeevan Pustakalaya, before they hit the shelves for sale. My literary enrichment

extended beyond books—be it someone's speech, a folk song,
Siddharampappa of Handiganur's play during his financial
struggles, the annual programmes on Karnataka Day or the
readings of Bharata (Mahabharata/Kumaravyasa's *Bharata*)—
there was no respite from this continuous nurturing.

But I didn't concern myself much with questions such as,
'What is the use of literature? What is its responsibility? What
is the relationship between literature and life? What are the
obligations of literature?' Hundreds of such questions are posed
in contemporary literary criticism. Literature has had to withstand
these challenges and endure. There is also the debate on whether
literature should remain a pure art, amid the realms of science,
politics and sociology as it was before, or transform into a tool for
imparting knowledge like these other disciplines.

Essential Questions

It must be acknowledged that all these questions emerge in the
contact between literature and criticism. The responsibilities and
objectives of criticism are more crucial than those of literature,
especially in the context of our country's literary landscape. The
role of the critic is relatively new in our nation's literary discourse.
In the past, there were scholars of poetry who identified its
characteristics and classified literature into various forms but
refrained from engaging in evaluation. Their contributions were
limited to writing critical notes on renowned poems, pointing out
figures of speech and prosody, occasionally exploring connotative
meanings and discussing the appropriateness of rasa-bhava.
However, they did not pose theoretical objections about poetry.
Mallinatha, the commentator on Kalidasa's *Raghuvamsa*, expressed
a stance that encapsulates this approach:

Namoolam likhyate kinchit
Nanapekshitamuchyate

I would not write about what is not in the original,
or say what will not please the connoisseur.

In those days, the role of criticism was primarily to enhance the enjoyment of poetry. Questions like 'Is the poem good or not? Where does the dignity of poetry lie?' were the concerns of the connoisseur. However, today, these concerns have become the responsibility of the critic, which, from the perspective of our cultural heritage, is not a positive development. Poetry was once a vital aspect of life, and while we may not have concrete records of the benefits that the connoisseur derived from their appreciation of poetry, it was undoubtedly a cultural necessity. While a few words on the merits of poetry can be found in the texts of Lakshana Shastra (treatises on the characteristics of literature), the undeniable truth remains that poetry was an integral part of our cultural fabric at that time.

Such a situation no longer prevails. For many, literature serves as a form of entertainment—delightful stories, engaging essays and dramas capable of alleviating boredom, are what people desire. Works lacking this quality are only appreciated by literary scholars. Popular genres of writing are set apart from the 'standard' ones. A critic is expected to focus on the intricacies of 'standard' literature alone. There is no requirement to unravel words and their meanings like Mallinatha, no need to highlight obscure grammatical experiments, and it is unnecessary to classify, based on theories, whether the figures of speech used are similes or metaphors.

The concerns of the modern 'critic', a novel term, differ. The nature of literature is also evolving. New genres, like novels and short stories, have surfaced, while traditional ones such as poetry and drama have undergone transformation. New literary movements have emerged, and the rules of characterization have shifted. Literary criticism has to embark on a quest to explore the potential reasons behind these changes and evaluate works of art accordingly.

Birth of a Critic

All these transformations are inevitable, and it is within this context that the critic comes into existence. The role of the critic becomes increasingly significant as literature distances itself from people's lives. Their importance is further elevated by their awareness of certain subjects that creative writers may lack. Criticism evolves into an independent genre of writing. Problems arise when critical consciousness transforms into the arrogance of the critic. Criticism should depend on literature, not the other way around, otherwise, it ceases to be a civilized pursuit. Literary criticism should avoid becoming a mere game. This embodies the essence of courteous criticism.

The courteousness of criticism extends beyond these considerations. The examination of a culture's structure becomes a matter of critical interest. In an era of intermingling of ideas, the necessity for such interest is more pronounced than ever. Our modern ideas are not solely ours; they come from 'outside'. It is not a matter of self-respect to categorize them into 'ours' and 'outside'. Thoughts rooted in profound emotions can shape our vitality, similar to the circulation of blood in the body. However, there is a question regarding whether our current ideas possess that depth. Doubts persist that our creativity is confined to the extent of freedom granted by new ideas. The conflict between the repetitive nature of tradition and the progressive trajectory of history is increasingly apparent today. Old cultural structures must be reconstructed before they crumble. This task becomes imperative if the critic genuinely regards criticism seriously.

This embodies the courtesy of criticism.

Kumaravyasa

In this essay from Kannada Sahitya Sangati, *published in 1995, Kurtkoti conducts a comparative analysis of Kumaravyasa in relation to the Sanskrit Mahabharata, and the works of Bhasa, Bhavabhuti and Pampa, yielding two intriguing observations. First, Indian languages aspired to create their own renditions of Puranas like the Mahabharata, absorbing as much as they desired and needed; second, Kurtkoti highlights the concept of 'Kathantara' or retelling of stories. He further directs our attention to Kumaravyasa's method of distinguishing between story and poetry.*

The title of Kumaravyas's opus is *Karnata Bharata Kathamanjari*, often called *Gadugina Bharata*. The nomenclature itself unveils the essence of his creation. Primarily, this work stands as a Kannada translation of the Sanskrit Mahabharata. Second, it unfolds as a bunch of narratives. The dual nature of this undertaking is intrinsically intertwined. In our nation, the perpetual task of translating from Sanskrit to Kannada, mirroring similar translations to other languages, etc., has persisted. Embracing Sanskrit while challenging it, and recreating it while concealing its connection, both find expression in the art of translation.

The narrative concerning translations unfolds in a similar vein. The Mahabharata belongs to neither Sanskrit nor Kannada. The ancient saga of a royal family's strife in the north-western region of our land continues to stir us like an unforgettable wound. The narrative depicting an incident rooted in a specific time and place was first translated into Sanskrit. After completing the Samanta Panchaka Yatra, Suta, prompted by the memories of the past, relayed this tale to Shaunaka and other assembled sages at Naimisharanya. The urgency to narrate was palpable, met by an equally fervent desire from Shaunaka and the sages to listen. A shared longing to comprehend the unfolding events, an appetite for storytelling—when these converge, a narrative is conceived.

Yet, the narrative spun by Suta is merely a translation of another tale. Janamejaya, the Pandavas' grandson, had to listen to this narrative as a form of atonement for his involvement in the serpent sacrifice. This story was conveyed to him by Vyasa's disciple, Vaishampayana. The intriguing question is: Who recounted it to Vaishampayana? The answer is that Vyasa told this story to his eighteen disciples. Vaishampayana's rendition not only feels closer to the truth but also exudes certain freshness. However, uncertainties persist. Is Vaishampayana's account accurate? What compels us to overlook the others' versions of this tale? Another thread in the narrative suggests that Ganapati transcribed Vyasa's words. The plot thickens, mirroring the convoluted nature of the story itself. Grappling with this complexity is inevitable. The essence of the story must be gleaned within its own narrative. To achieve that, the tale must be retold. Through repetition, the story rejuvenates, taking on a new guise each time it is recounted.

The Mahabharata is composed of 'parvas', much like the 'kandas' in the Ramayana. While 'kanda' symbolizes the branch of a tree, 'parva' alludes to bamboo knots. The narrative's inherent nature is expansive, with each translation birthing a new 'kanda' or 'parva'. This propensity arises from a deep-seated desire to uncover the truth. However, adhering to the principles of plot often proves challenging when navigating the intricacies of truth. Maricha's words to Ravana in the Ramayana offer a pertinent insight into the predicament of truth within a narrative: 'Satyam bruyat priyam bruyat na bruyat satyamapriyam'—'Speak the truth, speak what is pleasing, but do not speak the unpleasant truth'. Seldom is truth found pleasant. Narration delineates two forms of speech: the true word and the dear word. Like Maricha, characters in a story are bound to convey the truth. Yudhishthira in the Mahabharata faces such a constraint, and the power of his truthful speech is exemplified by the devastating consequences of a single lie leading to Drona's death. However, within the narrative, only the narrator's words should be both true and dear, with elegance being a fundamental quality of their language. When the narrator speaks the truth, the listener must believe in its authenticity. In Bhavabhuti's play *Uttararamacharita*, Valmiki is referred to as 'Bhutarthavadee Prachetasa' (the son of Prachetas, who tells things as they truly are). Valmiki is the truth-teller of the Ramayana. The truth of that story resides exclusively within Valmiki. Although the truth he imparts may be mysterious and elusive, a linguistic transfer of the story—a translation—becomes essential.

Translation is more than mere linguistic migration; it can metamorphose into something entirely new. A striking example is Bhasa's six plays rooted in the Mahabharata. Each drama has a distinctive opening and end, adding structure to the otherwise boundless narrative flow. Take, for instance, *Pancharatra*, where the war between the Kauravas and Pandavas, a cornerstone of the Mahabharata, is conspicuously absent. Bhasa achieves the unthinkable in this translation. The Mahabharata's core theme deals with sibling rivalry. Bhasa addresses the intricacies of human relationships with seriousness. In *Duta Ghatotkacha*, it is Dhritarashtra who grieves the loss of Abhimanyu in battle. Arjuna's fury at his son's demise means that he will slay Jayadratha, and hence Dhritarashtra laments over the potential widowhood of his daughter. Abhimanyu, an adversary, also happens to be a grandson, and Bhasa deftly exploits this irony in his works. *Pancharatra* unfolds during the Ajnatavasa episode

of Virata Parva, illustrating the internal conflict of the Pandavas
when the Kauravas assail Virata's town during Gograhana.
The battle between Bhima and Abhimanyu is intense, marked
by unparalleled valour yet tinged with amusement due to their
familial ties. Abhimanyu, aligned with the Kauravas, unknowingly
confronts his great uncle Bhima. The crucial question arises:
which role holds greater significance? If Abhimanyu is deemed
an enemy, the Mahabharata battle is inevitable. Conversely, if
acknowledged as a son, it should and must be avoided. Bhasa
contemplates diverse alternatives in concluding his plays. In
Urubhanga, Ashwatthama crowns Duryodhana's son Durjaya with
his words, while Dhritarashtra, bereaved of a hundred children,
retreats to Tapovana, declaring, 'Dhigastu Rajyam' ('Kingdom be
scorned'). Ashwatthama embarks on Sauptikavadha, wielding his
weapons. Balarama's words, 'Guruputrena Udahritam Bhavishyati'
('this will happen as the son of the teacher stated so'), foretell the
tale's future. In real life, the conclusion eludes human control,
but within the narrative, someone imparts closure. Amid the
translation process from one work to another, discerning which
came first or last remains elusive.

Taking the example of Bhasa serves to illustrate the possibility
of translating a work within the same language. Following Bhasa's
lead, the Mahabharata has been translated into numerous other
languages, transcending linguistic boundaries to find new homes.
It has been translated into places too. To this day, remnants attest
to the Mahabharata's influence, such as the purported gymnasium
of Keechaka in Hanagalli or the stone chariots of the Pandavas
in Mahabalipura. Villages carry tales of Bhishma washing his
bloody arrows in a lake or Bhima lifting and rolling a colossal
stone. While these legends may not be deemed entirely credible,
such translations contribute to the pervasive awareness and
dissemination of the Mahabharata.

The initial Mahabharata in Kannada emerged through
Pampa's *Vikramarjunavijaya*. 'Vyasa   Munindra   Rundra

Vachanamrita Vardhiyaneesuven', reflects Pampa's buoyancy in the Mahabharata's vast sea rather than sinking into it. Perhaps Pampa's characters speaking on the brink of death stems from the pervasive wartime atmosphere. Pampa's verses skilfully measure what endures and how much persists beyond death. Crucially, Pampa's characters exude a distinctive sense of awareness. In Pampa's portrayal, Bhima poetically identifies Draupadi's abundant tresses as the 'root cause of Mahabharata', an insight derived from having knowledge of Vyasa's *Bharata*. Having immersed in Vyasa's 'Vachanamrita Waridhi', Bhima naturally expresses himself as portrayed by Pampa. When Pampa's Bhishma asserts, 'Bharatam Kalaham Idirchuvam Arigam' ('Arjuna will fight in the Bharata battle'), the Kauravas' defeat is inevitable. Yet, Bhishma also acknowledges Karna's military supremacy before their defeat, indicating a profound understanding of the Mahabharata's nuances. Pampa's characters resonate with vitality, emotion and exceptional action, embodying a dramatic consciousness that navigates dual existence. Duryodhana, in Pampa's rendition, rehearses his life from Vyasa's Mahabharata, enacting it on the Kannada stage. His performance goes beyond mere dialogue delivery; he comprehends what to say and how. Bhasa's *Urubhanga* features a dying Duryodhana, witnessing forefathers welcoming him, conversing with Abhimanyu—an element absent in the original Mahabharata but evident in Bhasa's experienced portrayal. Pampa's Duryodhana similarly displays this theatrical expertise. While our country believes in consciousness evolving across lifetimes, it is evident that the characters' depth develops distinctly from one literary work to another.

Bhasa and Pampa, in their retelling, distilled the vast narrative of the Mahabharata. However, reducing the scale isn't condensation. Pampa's *Bharata* is indeed more concise than the original Mahabharata, but its brevity arises from Pampa's artistic freedom to selectively include elements from the epic. Additionally, succinctness aligns with the inherent nature of Pampa's literary work, bound by its unique design. Despite a brief portrayal of Draupadi's Swayamvara, the chapter dedicated to the abduction of Subhadra is expansively covered. Arjuna holds a central role in Pampa's narrative, as he is compared to Arikesari. In this dynamic, when Arikesari assumes the role of Arjuna, Arjuna embodies the essence of Arikesari.

Regardless of Pampa's explicit intention, the Mahabharata seamlessly found its way into his literary creation. In Pampa's era, the Mahabharata had transitioned from being a historical account to a mythical narrative. This amalgamation of history and mythology is intrinsic to the Sanskrit Mahabharata itself. Pampa's time, marked by its distinctive history, is intricately woven into his work alongside the Puranas. Ranna eloquently encapsulates the spirit of that era in the verse, 'Gandar gunamane merevudu shastravranamam ninnante merevudiriva bedanga' ('Heroic men should display their valour by their use of weapons, O Bhima'). However, it is noteworthy that Draupadi imparts this wisdom to Bhima, illustrating their contrasting poetic spirits. Alternatively, one could argue that 'Iriva Bedanga' serves as the translation of Bhima, emphasizing how a translation transforms the original and interprets it in its own unique way.

Yet, this exchange holds a distinctive quality. While it is undeniable that the Mahabharata permeated the Kannada language, Kannada absorbed only as much as it desired and could accommodate. Language, like any other medium, enjoys both freedom and constraints. Pampa, influenced by the ethos of his era, infused the martial ethos of the Mahabharata—such as valour and chivalry—with a transcendental quality. According to Pampa, a hero transcends into greatness not by merely defeating foes but by embodying principles like 'Otti tarumbi ninda ripubhooja samajada bergalam nabhaketade' ('uprooting a cluster of enemy trees standing in the way'). He is like 'Ajandavemba attiya panol pulu' ('a worm in the fig fruit called universe'), destined to either die on the battlefield and ascend to heaven or emerge victorious and rule on Earth, echoing the sentiments expressed in the Bhagavad Gita, a part of the Sanskrit Mahabharata. These works share a unified vision. However, the Sanskrit Mahabharata holds an additional layer. It has the ability to unveil what is concealed and introduce elements not previously present. This dual function, of revealing hidden truths and introducing novel aspects, is the essence of narrative, suggesting that storytelling entails precisely these actions.

In the rewriting of the Mahabharata, history is transformed into something new. 'Jataham Dravide Deshe Karnatae Paramangata' ('Born in the noble Karnata region of the Dravida nation'). This encapsulates the narrative of the Bhakti Panth, where not only Shiva Bhakti but also Vaishnava Bhakti finds its roots in south India. Gajaraja Pandya takes centre stage in 'Gajendra Moksha', and Chandrahasa hails from the Kuntala region. References within the Bhagavata Purana from the sixth to seventh centuries validate these claims. The Krishna depicted in the Mahabharata intertwines with the Krishna of the Bhagavata and the Devakiputra Krishna of the Upanishads, evolving into the illustrious Krishna across centuries. Jain mythology doesn't draw a significant distinction between Krishna and Kama, eventually equating him with the Krishna of the Bhagavata. However, the Krishna portrayed in the Mahabharata stands out as the most profound personality. With this Krishna at its core, the Mahabharata eagerly awaited its entry into the Kannada realm.

A verse in the preface of Kumaravyasa's *Karnata Bharata Kathamanjari* captures this essence:

> *Padada proudhiya navarasangala*
> *Vuditavenuvabhidhana bhavava*
> *Bedakalagadu balla proudharumi kathantaradi*
> *Idu vicharise bariya tulasiya*

Udakadantireyilli nolpudu
Padumanabhana mahime dharmavichara matravanu

The scholars familiar with the tale should
refrain from delving into the elegance of words,
the allure of romance, or the narrative intricacies
within this retelling of the story. Rather than pondering over
how water trickling down from a tulsi leaf transforms into sacred
waters, one should solely contemplate the divine glory of Lord
Krishna and the teachings embedded in this poem.

—*Karnata Bharata Kathamanjari*,
Adiparva 1–14

'Kathantara' (retelling the story) is a remarkably astute choice
of words and a manifestation of the felicity of words. It can be
construed as between stories, amid two stories, transitioning
from one story to another and so forth. Kumaravyasa articulates
as if poetry stands distinct from the story, with felicity of words,
discussions on navarasas and the essence of the story all having
separate roles. In one sense, this assertion holds true. Kathantara
is perpetually open, a canvas which may be imbued with the values
of poetry to obtain significance. Alternatively, as Kumaravyasa
demonstrates, poetry may be imbued with the values of devotion.
Kumaravyasa conscientiously aims to delineate the distinction
between the two. The interplay of story and poetry can mutually
illuminate each other, as exemplified in Kumaravyasa's work.
However, the magnificence of Padumanabha, when viewed
through the lens of devotion, is distinct, endowed with the power
to bestow glory upon everything it touches.

D.R. Bendre and the
Nature of Kannada Poetry

This essay, written in 1961, is extracted from Kurtkoti's anthology of essays on D.R. Bendre, titled Bendre Hagu Kannada Kavyada Swarupa, *published in 1961. Kurtkoti aims to establish Bendre's significance for Kannada literature in this piece. According to him, Bendre holds importance not only due to his prolific and abundant poems, but also because he laid the groundwork for modern Kannada poetry. Kurtkoti highlights how Bendre fused elements of ancient Kannada poetry, elite poetry influenced by English traditions and the rich tradition of Kannada folk poetry. He asserts that Bendre's poetry embodies the essence of modern poetic tradition in Kannada, blending innovation, imagination, complexity, diversity, emotional depth, philosophical insights, playful expression, colloquial and formal language, and inspiration from Sanskrit, English and other poetic traditions. This essay serves as a compelling introduction to Bendre as a poet, exploring many of his major works while presenting a clear argument about his significance.*

Whenever I begin writing about Bendre's poetry, a certain inhibition creeps into my thoughts. This hesitation is a natural response when discussing any contemporary poet. Placing a contemporary poet within historical context is challenging; their poetry unfolds before our eyes, making it possible only to convey our immediate reactions. The worth of such criticism lies in the value of that response. It is not to disregard the depth of appreciation some enthusiasts may have for contemporary poetry, as such engagement is not without merit. However, the true measure of a poem's impact lies not merely in the admiration of a few but in its resonance with an entire nation. The cultivation of poetry is the cultivation of Rasanubhava (experience of rasa), requiring time, as do life experiences. Bendre is not only a contemporary poet but also as one of the most significant voices of this era. His poetry exhibits a poetic richness not found in the works of old Kannada poets from Pampa to Muddana. This doesn't mean that the former is greater than the latter; rather, it reminds us of the necessity of seasonal variation in natural creation. This diversity manifests through innovations in content, language, style and form. Such distinctions are readily apparent to a contemporary critic closely attuned to the nuances of poetry, who can comprehend these variations easily. Criticism is reflective of its time and encapsulates the prevailing tastes and poetic manners. Hence, concurrent engagement in contemporary criticism alongside poetry serves as a valuable guide for the succeeding generation of critics, fostering a deeper understanding of poetry.

Bendre belongs to the first generation of the inaugural phase of new Kannada poetry, known as the Navodaya period. Those who preceded him, such as B.M. Shri, Panje Mangeshrao, Hattiangadi Narayanarao, were all actively involved in forging a new poetic expression. Before Bendre's *Gari* ('Feather') was published, B.M. Shri's *English Gitegalu* had already been published in 1926, while Govinda Pai was also exploring the avenues of innovative poetry. However, these were harbingers of the new poetic form rather than its crystallization, with distinct contours, beauty and aspirations not yet clearly discernible. Many of the experiments undertaken by Bendre under the banner of 'Geleyara Gumpu' (The Society of Friends) contributed significantly to the establishment of a new poetic tradition. Bendre's resolve, encapsulated in the words 'Mine is but a flower's wish to leave some seeds behind', has borne fruit beyond his initial expectations.

Viewed from this perspective, Bendre's persona exhibits a dual aspect—he was not only a poet but also a pioneer in shaping a poetic tradition.

The second of these tasks demands a unique set of skills. A tradition-builder must harbour doubts about how far one can create great poetry by carefully observing both contemporary culture and the expressive ability of the language. Bendre's poems, in and of themselves, constitute a wealth of poetry and embody various experiments in modern poetic forms. Innovation is not merely a transient process of transforming a new idea into a novel technique; instead, it involves revitalizing primitive sentiments of the human heart with newfound significance across all facets of life. In his early years, Bendre recognized that it is insufficient for a poet to construct their poetic idiom just once. His poetry accommodates a diverse range of poetic expressions, not attributable solely to versatility but rather indicative of poetic abundance. Only such rich poetry has the capacity to establish a tradition.

Any study of Bendre's poetry grapples with certain complexities. The evolution of his poetry is not a linear progression. Apart from a few poems composed before the publication of *Gari* (such as 'Kogile' [Cuckoo] and 'Krishna Kumari'), it becomes challenging to discern the stages of development in the remaining poems. This doesn't imply that his artistic persona was firmly rooted in *Gari* and didn't evolve further. The intricacy and enchantment of his poetic form conceal this development. Regardless of the specific poem examined, each resonates perfectly with the contemporary milieu. While he had previously penned romantic songs more poignant than 'Kuniyonu Bara' ('Come, Let Us Dance'), when it was published, the emotional depth was unparalleled. The secret lies in the core of his poetry, where expression aligns seamlessly with its vital essence. Another complication arises from the poems' lack of immediate understanding due to the absence of context.

The same observation can be expanded and discussed further. As mentioned earlier, Bendre's poetic style assimilates influences from folk poetry, the songs of Anubhaava, the poetry of the ancients, Rabindranath Tagore, Aurobindo and numerous English poets, weaving them together in a surprising manner. It utilizes all these influences to approach the subject of the poem. Hence, categorizing his poetry becomes a challenging task. The poem 'Belagu' (Dawn) is not merely a description of the morning; the beauty of nature receives continuous enhancement in the poem with the creative process of the poem. Without it, the exclamation in one of the lines of the poem—'Idu bari belagallo, anna!' ('It is just dawn!') seems a mechanical stanza, included to fulfil metrical requirements. Attempting to categorize Bendre's poems thematically for critical assessment proves to be a complex task.

Consider two poems, 'Murthy' (from *Murthy Mattu Kamakasturi*) and 'Kalpavrikshavrindavanagali' (from *Hadu-Padu*). 'Murthy' (Statue) intricately explores the conditions and rhythms of human life through a stone statue. Initially, the poem details the natural form of the stone. Subsequently, a king aspires to fill the entire world with beauty. A sculptor, following the royal decree, chisels the stone. Upon successful completion, sacrificing his life, he erects an idol and breathes his last. The idol captivates the universe with its beauty, but over time, the order degrades. The idol's glory shifts from devotion (Bhakti) to material desires (Artha Kamas). The king's dream, the sculptor's art and a devotee's devotion lose their significance. Hearing the idol's praise, a man with a hammer shatters it. While the prose narrative might relay the story in a mundane manner, in poetry, like the stone itself, it acquires meaning. It is because the subject of the poem is not a statue but the history of human actions and destiny. Yet, the archetype within remains distinct. The characters in this tale are symbolic and not overshadowed by their personalities. The dreamt-of king hides behind the idol's glory, and the sculptor meets his demise upon completing his creation. The rhythmic cadence echoes the impassiveness of stone and this is why there is no room for personal lament anywhere. Even as the man with the hammer arrives to dismantle the idol, we hear the hammer's sounds, not the poet's sigh.

'Kalpavrikshavrindavanamgalali' ('In the Garden of the Kalpavriksha') is a distinct kind of poem. It describes the ecstatic joy at the height of lovemaking, yet the depiction is far from literal. The lines 'Alla eccharavu, alla niddeyoo, eno yogadinde' ('not waking, not sleeping, a certain favour of destiny') not only convey the singularity and uniqueness of the experience but also suggest that the enigma surrounding it will intensify. Amid this secrecy, however, physical details are not neglected:

Bala sutti hedeyetti toogutire
Bhogasuptakala
Ee tolinali holu mayiralu
Beesitindrajala

While the tail is coiled around, the hood is raised
in the state of blissful slumber, when in this arm twin bodies lie,
the magical net was spread.

The physicality of the experience, the allure of beauty and the intensity of the moment are conveyed through the serpent image, twin bodies and 'indrajala'. The subsequent experiences described are tangible yet ethereal. The starlight resembles a myriad of Indras opening their eyes; the light that arrives seeking the body is like the conjunction of Venus and the moon. Fragrance permeates the air, as if wind has flowered forth. Terms like 'Parijata', 'Mandara', 'Sumana' (names of flowers), and lines like 'Everyone has four hands there', 'Who knows if the hand that gives, gives on its own?' contribute to the dual nature of the poem. The line, 'Seen with the inner eye, somehow you became Radha', encapsulates the intricacy of the poem and signifies a moment of poetic accomplishment. The flute, heard by the inner ear, evokes the eternal sound of yogic experience. Radha, beyond being a symbol of sweetness, embodies the archetypal image of the beloved. The poem's expression is potent, capturing the essence of heavenly experience at one's fingertips. Its richness is deepened by revealing transcendental encounters through the senses. The mysterious and rhythmic cadence of the poem conjures vivid imagery in the mind.

However, not all of Bendre's poems exhibit this level of complexity, nor is it necessary. Complexity was required for the poems mentioned earlier, as they conveyed unique experiences. Poems like 'Krishna Kumari' and 'Padu' (Plight) are straightforward and uncomplicated. Bendre's simplicity shines through in works such as 'Kamakasthuri' (Sweet Basil), which explores folk romances, 'Karulina Vachanas' (Utterances of the Womb), certain stanzas and lead verses in 'Uyyale' (The Swing) as well as 'Putta Vidhave' (Little Widow), 'Manadanne' (Beloved), 'Nurse', 'Shravanada Vibhava' (The Glory of Monsoon), 'Maya Kinnari' (Magical Mirror), 'Hubballiyamwa' (The Guy from Hubli). Poems like 'Bisilugudure' (Mirage), 'Nanna Kaiya Hididake' (My Wife), 'Hudugalarada Dukha' (Irrepressible Sorrow) are profoundly touching. Rooted in the emotions of life around them, these poems reflect the poet's inspiration from his surroundings. To my knowledge, one of Bendre's objectives was to contribute to the cultural heritage of Kannada through his poetry. He sought to raise awareness of Kannada within the Kannada-speaking community and reconstruct the life of Kannada through poetry. Therefore, he employed colloquialism as a medium of poetry. The fusion of Desi and the Marga is one of the many facets of Kannada poetry's rich heritage. However, Bendre's use of the Desi has a unique quality. It was not merely aimed at invigorating the language of poetry through colloquial expressions, but as a poet engaged in writing social poems, he strived to avoid becoming a mere orator.

A further examination of Bendre's poems makes the above statement clearer. Three-quarters of his love poems are composed in a folk vein and style. Repeatedly, these lyrics unveil the social nature of love. Their merit lies not merely in their natural use of colloquialisms; their beauty is objectively distinct. The incorporation of the indigenous also establishes the poetics of the poem, as seen in poems depicting social injustices. Poems like 'Narabali' (Human Sacrifice), 'Puttavidhave' (Little Widow), 'Moovattamooru Koti' (Thirty-Three Crore), 'Henada Hinde' (Behind the Corpse), 'Annavatara' (The Avatar of Food), 'Manuvina Makkalu' (Manu's Sons) and 'Tuttina Cheela' (The Bag of Morsels) can be viewed from this perspective. The anger expressed in these poems perhaps finds resonance only in the poetry of our time. However, if the poet were to make this rage his own feeling and express it in his language he would succumb to the error of sentimentality and confront numerous contradictions. Personal feelings are not stagnant; the poet should embrace these feelings as elements of life and express them without displaying his reaction. Moreover, the poet has no language of his own; he should employ the language of the chosen situation. This quality is prominent in Bendre's poems cited above. The anger in those poems is intense and blinding. Lines like 'Deathless ghosts, overblown ghosts', 'Let the sleep of the God who lies on the sea of milk be disturbed', 'Even if the animal perishes, his bones are buried', 'They want to live eating the soil', 'The heart grumbles at the cowardice of the ten avatars', 'The burden of the head has fallen and the embers have grown' and 'In a gathering of songs, is it right to groan', exhibit gut-wrenching satire. However, since every poem is replete with drama, the poet's individuality does not disrupt the form of the poem, creating rasa-abhas. These poems

possess the earnestness of life without succumbing to the opinion
of newspapers. In the language of poetry, we hear not one but ten
voices; only one belongs to the poet, the rest belong to the world.

This quality is also evident in Bendre's highly personal poems.
'Sakhigeeta' (Song of the Companion) and 'Padu' (Plight) are two
significant autobiographical poems. 'Sakhigeeta' deals with the
delicate question of married life. However, since the poet is a
character rather than a person, individuality has no place there.
The rhythm of folk rhymes like Sangatya, (a ballad-like Kannada
metre), Desi bedagu (riddle-like compositional style), dialogues
and abundant folk tales, along with the description of seasons,
create a distinct atmosphere. The life portrayed in the poem
doesn't belong to the poet, but seems to be part of its own world.
It therefore absorbs the genuine essence of the poetry—rasa. The
individuals in this poem transcend the boundaries of personality,
becoming more than mere characters and though characters
are literary, there is a personality. It must be noted that 'Padu' is
not as successful. Despite considerable effort to transform the
experience of mourning, the loss of a son into a commonplace
occurrence without diminishing its intensity, the attempt falls
short. Lines like 'Dasharath, who is dead, mourned the living
Rama', 'I am not the first to have lost a child', 'We have no place
to sleep. How would the depth of death be known?' attempt to
convey the unbearable grief of the loss of a son, but fail to achieve
it. Even in Old Kannada, Raghavanka's 'Chandramatiya Pralapa'
('Chandramati's Lament') and Shadakshari's 'Tirukolavinachiya
Pralapa' ('Tirukolavinachi's Lament') seem elegiac like the
sharp note in singing rather than Karuna rasa. As far as I know,
Kumaravyasa's description of Subhadre's lament for the loss of
her son possesses natural objectivity and is complex. Subhadre's
lament oscillates between contempt for Yudhishthira, self-
reproach, and a narrative of Arjuna's misfortune that unfolds
a rich and multifaceted experience, particularly when recalling

Abhimanyu. Although Bendre's 'Padu' is acknowledged as the greatest lament in modern Kannada poetry, it is essential to make these observations.

This doesn't imply that all of Bendre's social and familial lyrics reached the same level of excellence, but his poetic style is masterful. Some of his earlier poems might exhibit a degree of failure. In poems like 'Nee Heenga Nodabyada Nanna' ('Don't Look at Me Thus') 'Ragarati', 'Nanna Kaiya Paddake' and 'Hubballiyamwa', the emotional tempo neither soars too high, nor sinks too low. The fresh images in 'Nee Heenga Nodabyada Nanna' stand on the emotional canvas and quiver. However, in some more recent poems, such an approach is not apparent, as seen in 'Muttaide' ('A Married Woman') 'Katheyadalu Hudugi' ('The Girl Has Become a Story') and 'Sanjiya Javige' ('At Evening'). The language used in 'Muttaide' (from *Jivalahari*) is straightforward yet accomplished. The poem eloquently but restrainedly expresses the dignified mercy of death. 'Katheyadalu Hudugi' (from *Jivalahari*) portrays the transience of life, presenting tragedy in the form of a sapling. Pun naturally permeates this poem, like a sprouted seed splitting into two. This prevents the poem from succumbing to sentimentality. The experience of this poetry is awe-inspiring, like a sliver of camphor being inflamed, turning into ash and fragrance. The flavour in poems like 'Sanjiya Javige' (from *Gangavatarana*) is of another type. It emerges as an impression of the imagination, producing a singular emotional consciousness in the senses:

> *Gulabakshi-mallige*
> *Kelyavo kallige*
> *Kalisode neerige*
> *Intha sukumarige*

> Rose and Jasmine ask the stone:
> Should such a beauty be sent for water?

These lines bring to mind the sentimentality of Shakuntala's fourth act.

A few reflections on the nature of Bendre's imagination may be presented here. Imagination, as the unique power of a poet, has the capability to perform all the functions of the senses, intellect and instincts in poetry. It can transform life experiences into poetic experiences. While the experience evoked in poetry retains its original form, it is through imagination that it attains distinctiveness. To say that this imagination is exceptional in Bendre's works would be an understatement. His imagination operates in multiple dimensions. Its impact extends beyond the creation of innovative metaphors. First, it reconstructs life experiences in the mould of poetry. This characteristic is often evident in Bendre's nature poems. The description of a butterfly with the words 'A piece of cloth made by churning the wind'; the description of winter with the words, 'Body is covered with the ends of a sari made of dew, as if a flowing stream of breath is weaved together'; the depiction of the wind as 'Sitting on the end of trees, tired of leaping forth and the wind quietens', are a few examples. The world depicted in these poems is as lively as the one around us but distinct. It becomes challenging to discern whether these are similes, hyperboles or metaphors, as all these elements are intricately woven into the poetic language. The emotions arising from this interplay are referred to as rasa.

Another role of imagination is to visualize abstract, intelligible concepts, imbuing them with colour, shape and rhythm. Poems like 'Hakki Harutide' (A Bird in Flight, from *Gari*), 'Balakaravala' (from *Gari*) and 'Nadalile' (The Joy of Music, from *Nadalile*) exemplify this function. When poets tackle abstract notions like time, they often resort to metaphors involving the seasons and historical idiosyncrasies. However, in these poems, a living metaphor, such as a bird, permeates the poem as a poetic object. As a result, the enchantment of the poem remains intact. The virtuosity of these poems is not the focal point; what matters is that the experiences articulated within them are tangible enough to be felt. The cacophony of 'Balakarawala' and the tender compassion of 'Nadalile' are as vivid as any other sensory encounter.

Creation of mythology is the next stage of imagination—challenging in this age of rationalism since belief in truth relies on coherent arguments. In earlier times, truth could be perceived through the eyes of imagination, and the emergence of profound ideas often occurred through mythology. Similarly, traces of mythic elements can be discerned in the works of great poets worldwide. Some of Bendre's poems illustrate how his imagination can give rise to novel myths. The essence of the poem 'Hoo' (Flower, from *Gari*) is imbued with such an idea. It narrates the tale of a righteous desire for beauty originating in Brahma's thoughts, seizing the verbal form of 'flower', blooming into a flower in the Earthly realm and ultimately manifesting itself in verbal expression. This narrative is not merely entertaining; it symbolizes a profound truth. Another new myth emerges against the backdrop of the old myth of 'Kamode' (from *Hadu-Padu*). This myth revolves around the lust that pervades the entire world in both animal and human forms. The story beautifully illustrates that this inclination has divine origins. When Vishnu beheld Mohini's reflection in the amritakalasa (a pot of ambrosia), it was as if the shadow gained substance through amritadrishti (divine eye) and amritasparsha (divine touch). This narrative suggests that the symbol is more potent than the original. Even after the enchantment of the figure of Mohini fades, the allure of these images and their reflections continues to captivate Earthly romances. Every detail in this theory is infused with rasas and bhavas eliminating abstractions. The depiction of lust in this poem is intricate and multifaceted. Another mythological composition that explores the three virtues of lust is 'Om Svagatamakke' (from *Hadu-Padu*). Originally a deity, Kamapravritti (lustfulness) assumes the guise of a degenerate

nymph akin to a sunbeam. Lust's enticement, fervour and anguish
find expression through various images. This portrayal surpasses
Keats's snake-nymph in the poem 'Lamia'. While Keats's details fail
to coalesce into a unified experience, Bendre's images are robust
and mutually reinforcing. Lines such as 'Tapagar hoydu/Tapatapa
Toydu/Nirilivudu Nee Muttidare' ('Falling fast, drenching drop
by drop, water begins to flow at the touch') along with 'Meenada
Kangulu Maitumba' ('fish eyes cover the whole body') envelop
our senses and delve into the depths of the soul. The description
'Minchina keladi/mannige ilidi/rekkegalavu ninagetakke/uri are
nande/hottisa bande' ('Lightning's friend, stepped down to Earth,
what are your wings for, I brought my spark to kindle a fire') in
particular, provides an intimate encounter with our hidden selves.
Poems like 'Chinte' (Worry) and 'Sittu–Santi' (Peace–Anger)
also fall within this category. In 'Chinte', an image of a nymph
emerges, while 'Sittu–Santi' (from *Nadalile*) narrates a story. In
these poems, the emotions created by the images take precedence
over mere description. Bendre has employed old mythological
stories in some other poems, but it is not a narrow application
of the mythic vision. He draws images from the mythological
works hidden in the depths of the unmanifest spirit, enriching the
poem's meaning. Mythology permeates the verses of poems such
as 'Dhruvmarga' and 'Govatsalile', providing a broad spectrum
to the narratives. Lines like 'Saptarushigalelettu hodeyutive haki
dhruvada gana/Merudandada ikshurasava hinduttalihudo jana'
('The seven sages as oxen orbit the mill of the star, listen, smart
fellow, they are extracting the juice of the cosmic spine') exemplify
this approach. The pinnacle of this technique is evident in the
poem 'Mahaprasthana' (Final Departure, from *Hrudayasamudra*),
where Bendre, using Shri Aurobindo's 'Mahaprasthana' as a ruse,
encapsulates all the visions witnessed by humanity from the dawn
of time till date.

Some of Bendre's recent poems warrant a separate discussion.
Every poet undergoes a period of growth in their life. If they are

a genius, every poem they create is innovative enough to surprise even themselves. The fundamental aspects of life, such as love, affection, patriotism and social ideals, constitute the poet's emotional landscape. As long as this emotional realm remains vibrant, the poet can continue to produce new poetry. However, societal transitions or personal changes may render these feelings devoid of meaning. Typically, the poet's values shift during this period, but they remain abstract, lacking the spontaneity of life. This phase poses a risk to the poet's poetic evolution. Successfully navigating this perilous phase requires profound self-examination. Poets who fail to overcome this challenge might succumb to creating mere mechanical verse. Nevertheless, there are poets who emerge from this crucible with a renewed identity, and Bendre is one such poet. Let us explore how he managed to achieve this transformation.

The inclination to navigate such perils is evident in his earlier works. Like all poets, Bendre crafted poems brimming with beauty, patriotism and idealism in his formative years. He vehemently protested and empathized against social injustices. Yet, even during this period, he composed emotionally charged and philosophical poems. Works such as 'Murthy', 'Sachchidananda', 'Nadalile', 'Aa Dina Nenedu' and 'Ba Kai Ta' bear witness to this. Romantic songs like 'Mareyuveyo', 'Elliruve Rajagambeera' and nature-inspired compositions like 'Ugadi' are introspective of Anubhaava. His talent was formidable right from the beginning, characterized by comprehensiveness. However, it would be inaccurate to claim that all poems written during this phase were uniformly successful. Some poems lacked impact when the philosophy appeared merely as an intelligible thought rather than a lived experience. The renowned poem 'Koneya Hadu' (The Last Song, from *Murthy*), for instance, can be examined from this perspective. Structured like a Bharatavakya, the poem deals with the essence of acquiescence. However, the genuine sentiment is not discernible in the poet's heartfelt language. This doesn't imply dishonesty on the poet's part; rather, it is like observing and describing that sentiment by holding it in the palm of his hand. The poem distils the pure experience of the 'untouched opportunity' from the complexities of the world. Notably, in lines like 'Rasave janana, Virasa marana, Samarasve jeevana' (rasa is birth, disharmony is death, harmony is life), the unique meaning and distinct experience of life are not vividly apparent. Works such as 'Chenna' and 'Yava devanidu?' carry a dreamlike experience, unfinished and evanescent, like moths fluttering in half-formed dreams. While both poems boast unusual imagery, the poet fails to establish a fitting context for them. 'Sachchidananda' (from *Nadalile*), however, stands out as a successful poem in this regard. Despite containing cryptic elements, its layer of meaning is robust, providing a solid foundation for the reader. The poem's core is accessible, distinguishing it from 'Chaturmukha Soundarya'. Among all the old philosophical lyrics, 'Elu Kannikeyaru' (from *Nadalile*) reigns supreme. This poem also unfolds within a dream. The poet awakens from slumber, entering a state of semi-awareness, and experiences a dream where seven maids materialize and rouse him. When he stands naked amid them like Gommata, they stand on his limbs like lamps on a lamp post. The poet's moral ego, resistant to allure, rises within him. However, as they touch his feet and lips, his soul begins to dissolve. At the moment of acknowledging his defeat, the ethereal lights vanish, leaving him resembling a beggar. He pleads for another chance to undergo the test. This poem captures the truth within the human psyche, gradually transforming into autobiography, narrative and tangible reality through metaphors in the poetic creation process. Lines like 'Like burnt butter, life dissolved within' and 'I fell down like a clay pillar' contribute to the enigmatic essence of the poem.

Hence, the foundation of Bendre's recent philosophical poems can be traced back to his earlier works. During that period, philosophy played a crucial role in his idealism, advocating through various avenues that devotion was the tenth rasa, and he composed devotional poems. Presently, many of his poems reflect a devotional tone, drawing inspiration from the rich

heritage of Indian devotional poetry. A distinctive aspect of
Bendre's devotional poetry warrants mention. Unlike traditional
Bhakti-kavya, where vatsalya-bhava (affection) was never static,
Bendre's devotional poems present an embodiment of affection.
In the Dasa tradition, the relationship between Krishna and
Yashode is portrayed with a glimmer of affection. Vatsalya-bhava
is evident in Sanskrit devistotras (hymns to Devi), particularly
in Sankaracharya's compositions. However, Bendre goes a step
further by constructing a world that embodies affection. Even in
his early works, such as the 'Karulina Vachanagalu' (from *Uyyale*),
a domestic form of affection is present. In poems like 'Alaukika',
the inaccessibility of the poem moves towards Anubhaava. He
recognized the seed of divinity in the affection of motherhood
early on, viewing the terrestrial nature of the Earth as a static
symbol of motherhood. In lines like 'Mai tumba Bai neenu/
tutimuddu nanna palu/edeyala moleyu neenu/maitumba nanage
halu' ('Bhoomitai', from *Namana*), a vision of profound affection
emerges. More examples:

> *Neladedeay arpanavu garbhagudiyali moodi*
> *Kalashamoleyaagi ado bayaligunisuttihudu*
> *Gali teluvina seraga maremadi*
> *O tore bantu tere bantu*
> *Haalaagi hakki salagi*

The offering of the Earth's breast emanating from the sanctum
sanctorum, the hills taking the form of breasts are feeding
the plains, draped in thin wind like saree-ends, oh, look it is
streaming, coming in waves, coming as milk, coming as a line of
birds in flight.

—'Harake', from *Sanchaya*

In this context, it is necessary to compare Bendre's poems with
Madhurachenna's poem 'Devata Prithivi'. Madhurachenna

traversed the landscape of a single emotion, and the beginning
and end of his poetry is in Anubhaava. His primary inquiry was,
'Hoovina makaranda/Hanneena madhurya/Halhinga innu mana
hyanga' ('If the milk is like the flower's nectar and the fruit's
sweetness, then how must the mind be?') He evolved into a
beholder of the unseen beauty beyond the scenic allure of nature.
Madhurachenna's philosophical quest is like the legendary quest
of the prince, who having accidentally obtained the blonde hair
of a nymph embarks on a search for the owner of that strand of
hair. The nature of Bendre's philosophical poems sets him apart.
Whether in romantic or devotional poetry, he has achieved an
understanding that transcends innocence. He can articulate not
only the beauty of the pristine but also its potential horrors. Every
experience in life has its own problems and nuances, and they find
expression through a great poet, and this diversity is evident in
Bendre's poems about affection. Poems like 'Navu Baratevinna',
'Ile', 'Chigirigangala Cheluvi', 'Nanu' and 'Ambikatnayadatta'
showcase a range of emotions.

Affection forms the foundation of all of Bendre's philosophical
poems. These poems extend beyond the ones on Earth, including
works such as 'Gangavataran' and 'Gayatrisukta'. Each poem
selects a specific deity as its focal point, and philosophical threads
are intricately woven around these deities. While the descriptions
within these poems carry doctrinal and symbolic nuances, the
experience they convey is vibrant. The vitality of these poems
can be attributed to the poet's profound emotions and expansive
vision. 'Gayatrisukta', for instance, holds its ground alongside
any romantic composition in terms of impact. Such eloquence is
achievable only because the poet is conscious of the poetic nature
of their expression.

It is intriguing how Bendre managed to infuse such diversity
into his philosophical poems. Perhaps this stems from the
distinction between a poet and a devotee. While a devotee directs
his focus towards the god at the centre, a poet stays on the

periphery of the circle, unable to detach from nature accessible to senses. Bendre's lines, 'Panchendriya Srishti beduva kavi ondu gavihokkantayite sahavasavu?' ('Has the life of togetherness become like a poet entering a cave in search of the creative powers of the five senses?'), or 'bari antarikshadi pakshi hariteshtu, beku tangalu mungaiyasareyu' ('How much can a bird fly in the sky? It also needs shelter to rest'), underscore this perspective. Unlike a devotee's, a poet's sentiment is not eternal; it evolves moment by moment, subject to constant transformation and perfection resulting in the experience of rasa. Additionally, the poet employs human language as a medium of expression, conveying both philosophical sentiments and emotions. As language is inherently symbolic, it embodies both the mundane and the transcendental. Poetry gains significance when the poet brings the philosophical experience to the level of common language and shared experience. Description, embellishment, clever expressions and erudition are tools employed by the poet for this purpose. The same holds for symbols and rasas and bhavas. While some may be conventional, others are crafted by the poet. But their use is predominantly social in nature and it is imperative that the poet attends to the demands of the sensitive reader.

Viewed from this perspective, the success of some of Bendre's philosophical poems is beyond doubt. The poem 'Jogi' (from *Gangavataran*) vividly portrays the terrors of the dark night in life. However, this experience is articulated through spatial imagery, transforming the horror into a visual spectacle. The entire poem is immersed in descriptions of the mysterious nature surrounding Dharwad—a hillock at the town's edge, a nearby graveyard, a moss-filled blackwater lake, a hill, a cluster of plants visible from the hill's summit, blossoming banyan trees, darkness, humming bats, a stray mango tree, a seven-headed snake and a cuckoo screeching with abandon on a mango tree. The procession of these animated statues jolts the body and stirs the soul, signifying not only a mystical experience but also

an emotional overflow. Lines like, 'What colour it has and what
its eyes should I go and see?', 'in the pulse somewhere within
the head has begun the song of harvest' and 'I hear the tune
in my dream and become the mango tree' not only convey the
urgency, passion and intensity of that experience but also hint
at something beyond it. The words, 'The sun is shining and has
brought the right conditions for rain' unmistakably suggest that
the present is a prelude to the forthcoming experience. Another
comparable poem is 'O Tai-Mai' (from *Hridayasamudra*), where
the divinely empowering response to Mumukshu's six questions is
delineated through a mother–child heart-to-heart conversation.
The structure, language and tone of this poem echo the essence
of folklore. The attachment of Maya, portrayed as the mother's
attachment, embodies the hunger for the verdant, rendering
life anguished. The mother reassures that once that hunger is
satisfied, liberation will follow. Throughout, lyrical elements
abound, showcasing how Bendre has distilled language to its
expressive core, as evident in the following lines:

> *Nadadi hakki nenello Magana hokyako bellakyaga?*
> *Nina tayi kan-hanimutta susatala manasa kolladaga*

The bird, crane, with its white feathers, your mother is raining
     pearls from her eyes in the lake of her heart.

The swan symbolizes the pure nature of the soul, creating an
atmosphere of affection along with the other symbols.

     In addition to these, there are many more poems of this type.
Valuable lessons can be gleaned from their study. Philosophical
experiences are not futile for poetry, but it is essential for the poet
to exercise caution in expression. Such profound experiences
must be brought to life within a unique context. The heavenly
visions seen by the poet must be manifested in an environment
that is intimately familiar to them. It is an adventure to transform

the ineffable into words—a duty of the poet. The poet must contradict the maxim 'yato wacho nivarthante arapya manasa saha' ('No writing, nor any mind can comprehend Him', *Taittirīya Upaniṣha* 2.9.1). Where else should the reconciliation between speech and experience occur if not in poetry? Bendre has devoted significant effort to this endeavour. Works by Aurobindo, Shankaracharya, Ramana Maharshi and Dnyaneshwar were translated as part of this effort. He did not lose his true poetic power. In Bendre's own words, this is an attempt at 're-blooming'. In the mature stage of life, every great poet reaches a point where they embark on a different kind of poetry. What is ambiguous needs clarification, and that experience must be felt through a poetic method. Therefore, a contemporary poet has no alternative but to assimilate the essence of all previous poets into their personality. The voice of a poetic tradition is more profound and influential than an individual poet's voice.

However, this process should not be misunderstood as mere imitation. No poet has ever become great through imitation. Yet, if a poet relies solely on personal talent, their poetry may lack a profound impact. The true significance of a work becomes fully apparent only within the context of a tradition. A poet born into a living tradition has an advantage; even in the context of heritage, the genius of the poet and the culture of that tradition stimulate each other. In the crucible of that stimulation, the poet transforms their life into a symbol and creates a work. Their task is to provide enduring expression to sentiments, ideas and principles that might otherwise fade in daily use. As there is no conflict between words and meanings, their poetry can directly touch the hearts of admirers. Through culture, a poet can alter the fundamental tendencies of life in a rasa without offending the taste of the people. Shakespeare, Kalidasa and Kumaravyasa enjoyed such advantages.

However, Bendre did not enjoy such convenience. Modern Kannada poetry was also taking shape when he commenced writing poetry. By the nineteenth century, the ancient poetic tradition, which had been fading in the eighteenth century, had vanished. A prose writer like Muddana had to remain its belated representative. All the efforts after that were aimed at saving the language. B.M. Srikantaiah brought the essence of English poetry into Kannada and inspired modern Kannada single-handedly. Thus, Bendre had to create tradition alongside poetry, a task not easily accomplished. On the one hand, there was the past glory; on the other, the myriad problems of the people. On yet another, the new culture of the well-educated—and these three did not align. Pandits who relied on past glory, well-educated individuals eager to reform society, common people who experienced only the emotions of joy and sorrow without any concern of these matters, all moved in their own directions. At the root of this disunity was the culture of the country, even if implicitly. However, that culture alone was not sufficient for rich poetry. The state of the language was more or less the same. There was a considerable gap between the language of poetry and the speech of the people. Similar circumstances were faced by the rest of the New Kannada poets alongside Bendre. Unlike Bendre, they did not construct an all-encompassing tradition. D.V. Gundappa, Govinda Pai and Sali Ramachandra Raya continued the ancient poetic tradition. Inspired by B.M. Srikantaiah, Kuvempu and Vinayaka, ventured on a new path and wrote well-educated poetry, taking English poetry as a model in terms of content, style and form. Madhura Chenna from one direction and K.S. Narasimaiah from the other upheld the tradition of folk poetry. (KSN's poetry has recently been evolving in a different way). It cannot be forgotten that all these three trends, though incomplete individually, have collectively contributed to building a legacy of modern poetry. Only Bendre has amalgamated these three in his poetry, constructing a representative and powerful tradition.

However, the harmony achieved by Bendre is not a mechanical equilibrium. He cannot be labelled a syncretist merely because he wrote numerous poems of these three types. He recognized early on that poetry can achieve completeness only when all layers of human emotions are laid bare. But such poetry needed to be unearthed from the roots of many evils, and for that, the entire structure of poetry had to be reconstructed. One had to contemplate the mode of expression. It was not feasible to express the fundamental tendencies and emotions of life in the manner of ancient poetry. For that, reliance on the instinct of folk poetry was necessary. Similarly, publishing new issues and high-brow ideas in a folk style was impractical. Whichever approach was chosen, elements had to be borrowed from the other. Only the unbroken genius of the poet could solve all these challenges. An example of Bendre's talent is evident in the new meaning he gave to the newly embraced lyric genre of Kannada poetry. In the poetry of the ancient tradition, language was entangled in a confusion of meaning. However, Bendre's genius discovered that just as a word can indicate a finite meaning, it can also convey an infinite feeling. Through this talent, he captured the emotion embedded in the language. Poems like 'Hoo', 'Ela Geete' and 'Bhav Geete' serve as examples of this notion. Similarly, his talent is evident in the management of poetic style and techniques. The variety of poetic form has emerged in proportion to the variety of life. Bendre's talent in formulating poetry is similar to Michelangelo's ability to discern the features that could be found in stone.

Thus, from all perspectives, Bendre stands as a leading poet of this era. A detailed discussion of the intrinsic values and beauty of his poetry can be left to other critics. For now, it can be asserted that his poetry is enriched by the nature of the Kannada language, the sensibilities of contemporary life, and the essence of Kannada culture. Bendre's poetry has, once again, laid the foundation for the true tradition of Kannada poetry. When Bendre began writing poetry, he faced a blank canvas. However, subsequent poets have the privilege of drawing inspiration from Bendre's poetry. This doesn't imply that future poets should emulate Bendre; it is not feasible. Yet, they must write within the context of the poetry created by Bendre. To deviate from this context would fail to establish a genuine tradition of Kannada poetry. This fact alone underscores the significance of Bendre's poetry.

The Novels of Kuvempu

This essay is taken from Kurtkoti's collection of essays titled Nooru
Mara Nooru Swara *(1998). Kurtkoti here elucidates the two major
prose works of Kuvempu, his two novels, offering several insights into
them, particularly regarding their distinct connections to nature and
characterization. He highlights how despite being set in similar social
contexts, the two novels diverge in their narrative techniques. While one
emphasizes a mind shaped by modern education as the type of consciousness
that can enhance the intellectual and emotional capacities of society, the
other novel presents a nuanced exploration of human experience.*

Kuvempu's novels *Kanooru Subbamma Heggadithi* (The House of
Kanooru[5]) and *Malegalalli Madumagalu* (Bride in the Hills) stand
out as masterpieces in Kannada literature. Critics have highlighted
their regionality, diverse characters, fantastical realism and vivid
descriptions of nature as strengths. In *The House of Kanooru*,
scholars have observed the character of Hoovayya as a symbol
representing the spirit of change during the Renaissance period.
If the world within the novel serves as the preamble, Hoovayya
emerges as the conclusion. Hoovayya dedicates himself tirelessly
to sanctify human relations. However, the vibrant life force within
the novel is so potent that it permeates Hoovayya's spirit. The
antiquity of tradition has not been the cause of making it appear

---

[5] Translated by B.C. Ramachandra Sharma and Padma Ramachandra
Sharma (New Delhi: Penguin India, 2000).

poor. As the world, comprising nature and people, collaborates in mutual cooperation and intense love, Hoovayya's consciousness distinguishes and merges with them in solemn contemplation.

In Kuvempu's novels, nature is portrayed as an independent force. The portrayal of nature in Kuvempu's lyrics is untouched by humans. With a few exceptions like 'Navilukallu' and 'Kavishaila' (both names of places), nature is depicted as an objective element rather than entities shaped by human perspectives. These novels underscore the idea that the companionship between nature and humans is not only desirable but also inevitable. Instances abound where nature actively engages with human actions. Baira constructs a waterhole for fishing, a vibrant tiger in the jungle lies in ambush for Jackey the Christian, and a stone plinth atop Hulikallu hill awaits the arrival of Chinnamma and Mukunda. These examples highlight the collaboration of nature in both positive and negative human endeavours. For instance, the forest serves as a home for hunters like Puttanna. However, when Puttanna witnesses Jackey the Christian being attacked by an even more ferocious tiger, a sense of detachment arises, offering a subtle commentary on the intricate relationship between nature and humans. This connection transcends simple notions of friendship or enmity, revealing a profound link between sustenance and survival. The novels also explore how this intricate relationship in nature mirrors the complexities found in human life. An illustrative example is the dynamic between the Gowda clan of Kanooru and the Anne Gowda clan of Lower Kanooru. The novels grapple with the question of whether this entwined fate is an inevitable aspect of human existence.

The novel employs a distinctive narrative technique to propose a solution to the complex issue it grapples with. This solution is embodied in the character of Hoovayya. An educated, cultured and sensitive individual, Hoovayya has a unique perspective that diverges from the general consensus. Despite actively participating in the hunting expedition on the full-moon night of Bhādrapada, he doesn't possess the temperament of a typical hunter. Even in matters of love, such as his affection for Sita, he transcends conventional viewpoints. The narrative strategically moulds the character of Hoovayya to serve as a divine arbiter of human nature. Characters within the story must adhere to its dictates, irrespective of their mental autonomy. The denouement of *The House of Kanooru* introduces a transformative shift in the way of life, symbolized by the declaration, 'the new sun is arising'. Hoovayya emerges as both an individual and an impersonal consciousness representative of the new age, embodying the novel's proposed solution.

Determining whether Hoovayya's personal consciousness can indeed reshape the world around him is a challenging question. The inherent forcefulness of the surrounding world complicates such an effort. In Kuvempu's subsequent novel, *Bride in the Hills*, a divergent narrative trajectory is adopted. Unlike Hoovayya, Mukundayya lacks willpower. His sole accomplishment is rescuing Deve Gowda from the clutches of the clergyman Jeevaratnayya. Hoovayya's experiences of joy, sorrow and friendship are distinctly his own, allowing him to observe the world from a detached perspective and articulate his reactions. In contrast, Mukundayya assumes a role among the multitude of characters in the novel, sharing experiences with them. While the variance between the two may seem subtle, it holds significance within the realm of narrative technique. Hoovayya embodies a character with a visionary and philosophical stance. On the other hand, Mukundayya lacks such a demeanour. Whether it is Mukundayya or the other common folk, like Puranic characters, they are created to serve a single purpose. The unpredictable nature of characters like the hunter Puttanna, Aita or Peenchalu adds an element of mystery. Nayigutti, who callously abandons his beloved dog in the river before departing for a distant land, exhibits a lack

of conscience—neither inherently good nor evil, unfriendly,
unsocial; he simply is Nayigutti.

The House of Kanooru is a narrative masterpiece that thrives on
its unique storytelling technique, exercising its literary freedom
to the fullest. Each character, from the prominent Chandrayya
Gowda to the cunning meat thief Soma, is meticulously crafted
with a specific purpose. Their mentalities not only shape their
personalities but also dictate their fates. For instance, when
Chandrayya Gowda suffers a stroke during the rainy season, it
aligns seamlessly with his established character, an unsurprising
turn of events. Similarly, the act of Ramayya cutting down the
flourishing champa plant, in response to Subbamma's moral
corruption, symbolizes the decline of family prosperity.

Despite their belief in fate, the characters of The House
of Kanooru hold a conventional understanding that borders
on disbelief. This belief is challenged and refuted by a more
profound consciousness. When after marriage, Sita refuses to
cooperate with her husband Ramayya, he, along with Chandrayya
Gowda, labels her as possessed by the devil, branding her arm.
Upon closer examination, it becomes evident that this act is not
a genuine belief in the supernatural but rather a manifestation
of violence—a twisted expression of love. It serves as a
deceptive ploy to punish the vulnerable by invoking an invisible
devil, mirroring the societal contrabands present in the minds
of individuals.

In the complex narrative of The House of Kanooru, Subbamma
Rangappa Setti's thieving enterprise thrives unchecked in the
arrogant household of Chandrayya Gowda, while the pure
friendship between Sita and Hoovayya takes an unexpected
turn. Confronted with this social quandary, a fair and cultured
mind must discern the true source of malevolence. The novel
emphasizes the limitations in the characters' sensibilities and
intelligence, highlighting a broader truth—the need for an

expanded consciousness, heightened sensitivity and intelligence. The underlying message is that the revival of the nation hinges on the widespread dissemination of modern education to enrich our intellectual and emotional capacities.

The world depicted in *Bride in the Hills* bears similarities to that of *The House of Kanooru*, with locales like Kanooru, Muttalli and Sitemane mirroring their counterparts in Konooru, Halemane and Simbavi. However, the novel's overall stance diverges, downplaying the importance of the narrative technique compared to its predecessor. Unlike *The House of Kanooru*, *Bride in the Hills* does not fully embrace the philosophy underlying narrative techniques. Significant events, such as Mukundayya's love affair, Devayya's conversion, Doddanna and Heggade's pilgrimage, Nayigutti and Thimmi's marriage, and Antakka's daughter Kaveri's tragic suicide, unfold concurrently rather than chronologically. Nature actively participates in shaping human affairs, exemplified by the romance between Chinnamma and Mukundayya, which might not have succeeded without the presence of the Hulikallu peak.

However, the narrative technique employed in this novel doesn't necessitate a character as self-aware and sensitive as Hoovayya. It is crucial to discern the distinction between the romance of Hoovayya and Sita and that of Mukundayya and Chinnamma. Mukundayya and Chinnamma's union is a youthful romance, unbeknownst to them. If they aspire to marry, it demands an adventurous approach, prompting both to embark on such an escapade. Mukundayya kidnaps Chinnamma on the eve of her wedding to another man and takes her to a hill. Nayigutti and Thimmy stand guard, with Nayigutti leaving Thimmy alone with his dog on duty. In the darkness of the night, Thimmy experiences a vision—a prince on a horse rescuing his lover and departing. This vision deeply affects Thimmy. While the novel partly explains this vision as a reflection of the romantic adventures associated with Hulikallu, a historical guard post, such an elucidation seems unnecessary. The novel ingeniously uses the technique of presenting visions experienced by lower-caste, uneducated individuals. Thimmy's lack of education becomes evident, and this serves as one of the novel's secret doors, revealing the unconscious mind's connection to truth. Perhaps, if Thimmy were better educated, she might have dismissed this event as a mere romantic trick. The romance of the well-educated often becomes mundane, but the novel's romance provides vivid scenes. Even if the observer recognizes the falseness, the relishing of rasa can be heightened. In this novel, however, the scene is not just a romantic notion; Thimmy witnesses it first-hand. Thimmy's ignorance is a secret passage unlocking the human unconscious in pursuit of truth.

The novel *Bride in the Hills* unabashedly employs various devices for entertainment. Consider the bustling activity at Antakka's coffee shop in Megravalli, situated on the highway. This coffee shop serves as a symbol of modernity, accompanied by the emergence of another modern institution—an upcoming school building. During the preparation for digging a well at the school site, a seemingly lifeless stick points to the precise location of water. The stick's inexplicable ability to locate water raises questions, yet water is discovered at the designated spot, weaving this well into the fabric of history. Antakka's daughter Kaveri, during disputes with her mother, often threatens to end her life by jumping into the school well. Tragically, Kaveri's fate takes a dark turn when she is raped and murdered, her lifeless body dumped into the same school well. This tragic incident is linked to a ring given to Kaveri by Mukundayya's brother-in-law, Devayya. The ring, originally belonging to a goldsmith couple, seems to bring misfortune to Kaveri, an innocent soul. Unlike the ring in *Shakuntala*, which serves as a symbol of recognition reuniting lovers, this ring in *Bride in the Hills* takes a grim turn. Kaveri's lifeless body is discovered floating in the uninaugurated school well, marking a stark contrast to the romantic reunions depicted in classical literature. The narrative introduces intriguing elements such as a policeman arrested by Gutti, meeting a mysterious demise in the forest during heavy rainfall. Gutti abandons his dog to drown in a stream and goes away. A stick seeking water, a horseman appearing from another temporality in the forest's darkness, a group of fireflies outshining a torch, and the ill-fated ring of a goldsmith couple—all function as unique ways of knowing, like scepticism and scales of understanding found in agamas. These elements are not mere symbols; rather, the novel unfolds its narrative using these scales of understanding. *Bride in the Hills* prompts readers to examine the cost and characteristics of truth, offering a complex exploration of the human experience.

Dramatic Structure:
Girish Karnad's *Tughlaq*

This essay is extracted from the anthology Vimarsheya Vinaya: Nataka, *published in 1985. It was originally penned for a seminar in 1969. Kurtkoti offers a thorough analysis of Karnad's* Tughlaq, *exploring its symbolism, character development and plot. He contends that these elements collectively enhance the play's dramatic structure, imbuing it with complexity. He suggests that it is this intricacy within the dramatic framework that renders the play 'modern'.*

Tughlaq is Girish Karnad's second play. All the expectations he generated in his first play, *Yayati*, have been fulfilled in this work. The significant quality of *Yayati* lies in the meaningful experiment, not in its success. The play's objective did not achieve clear expression through its material. A work is successful only when the writer's intention is turned into the purpose of the work. In the play *Yayati,* both the purpose of the work and the utilized mythological story are powerful, and the conflict between them obstructs the artistic development of the work. Puru's sense of character surpasses his personality and does not remain under his control dramatically. Similarly, in the last act of the play, it seems that the play has somehow fulfilled its purpose through the sentimentality of these two female characters, Chitralekhe and Swarnalate. Only in the play *Tughlaq* has Karnad not only successfully resolved this anxiety but also voiced the purpose of the work in the outlines of the work itself.

Tughlaq is a drama that narrates the historical story of fourteenth-century India. It is not crucial to emphasize that the author adheres faithfully to historical facts and meticulously constructs historical characters. While Karnad indeed exhibits painstaking realism in crafting the historical atmosphere, the play's significance transcends mere historical accuracy. The yugadharma manifests in the characters' behaviour, manners and ideologies, vividly portraying the splendours, virtues and filth of fourteenth-century India—from Delhi to Daulatabad. Had the play rested solely on historical fidelity, it would have been just one among many commendable Kannada dramas. However, its true technical significance lies in its dual nature, addressing a subject as ancient as human life yet profoundly modern. *Tughlaq* explores the timeless human inclination to dream of divinity, encapsulating a universal predicament. What elevates the strength of the play is that it avoids logical discourse on the matter, opting instead to embody the issue through characters and situations. Karnad skilfully transforms historical material into a new experiential realm to fulfil the play's purpose. Every character, from the outcast Aziz to King Muhammad, seamlessly integrates into this world. They are not only uniquely engrossed in the problem but also live it, vividly expressing it through their actions and words. The meaning of the work, therefore, may be understood through a study of characterization.

Given that the protagonist of this play is King Muhammad, universality naturally permeates his character. His reign is disrupted because of the complexities of his nature, evident in the very first scene where his rule is revealed to be flawed. A launderer named Aziz, adopting the guise of a Brahmin, arrives in Delhi and exploits Muhammad's new law of equal justice among Hindus and Muslims for personal gain—a seemingly inconsequential act that proves to be pivotal. Aziz, employing a cunning strategy, prevails until the play's conclusion, embodying one extreme of the dramatic consciousness in this drama, while Muhammad represents the other extreme. The tragic conflict lies in Aziz's sovereign spirit ultimately triumphing. In the intervening period, Muhammad's reign undergoes great turmoil: he orchestrates sending the cleric, Sheikh Imamuddin, in disguise and then kills him to emerge victorious in battle. Then, under the pretence of being liberal, he feigns granting freedom to enemies while subjecting them to constant torment. He adeptly evades an Amir's conspiracy to assassinate him and distorts the narrative of Shihabuddin's murder. For five years, prayers are suspended, the capital shifts from Delhi to Daulatabad, Ghiyasuddin, a descendant of the vizier and caliph, is killed, and Muhammad's stepmother prophesies his kingdom would be a 'closet of death'. These significant events are followed by public suffering, caused by drought, bloodshed and riots. The characterization in the play is intricate, warranting a more nuanced approach than theoretically stating that the root cause of the tragedy lies in the brutality in Muhammad's nature manifesting as the contradictions of life values. The dramatic potential in Muhammad's personality is paramount, impacting those who knew him, worshipped him and even those who criticized him. In the harsh environment of deception, proselytism, betrayal, intrigue, murder and counterfeit coins, Muhammad's personality triumphs. Aziz stands as the sole figure who transcends these limits and emerges victorious. Aziz's statement, 'No cleric has washed away so much dirt as a launderer,' is not merely sarcastic but a testament to his unique ability in exposing Muhammad's vulnerability. Though Aziz's innate disposition may be weaker than Muhammad's, it proves more potent. The tragedy of the play unfolds as Muhammad ultimately succumbs to Aziz.

The exploration of Muhammad's character development can be approached from another perspective, a technique rarely found in Kannada. Unlike typical dramas where the protagonist stands as the central figure, with other characters serving auxiliary roles, the sharing of experience in this play aligns with the story's unfolding. The hero's character encapsulates the core dramatic experience, with the hero's interaction with other characters constituting the essence of the story. The symbolism of experience resonates primarily through the protagonist, while the remaining characters contribute to the narrative's progression. In such instances, the authenticity of each character's personality becomes paramount, demanding an evaluation and review of individual qualities. In the realm of art, the tangible and abstract interplay dynamically, avoiding a rigid structure. A compelling narrative undoubtedly captures the transformation of life's experiences without losing its identity. As art adapts experiences to its own rules, it has been termed 'controlled anarchy'. The character formation in *Tughlaq* warrants examination from this perspective. While the story does connect the protagonist, Muhammad, with other characters, there are also other crucial relationships. The characters in the play are not only independent entities but also embodiments of Muhammad's persona and disposition—an artistic nuance that adds depth to the narrative. Muhammad's identity remains steadfast until the very end, his ostensible personality unaltered. His royal pride, swagger and wisdom persist consistently. Prayer, politics, violence, revenge—all are inherent facets of his nature from the play's inception to its conclusion. The shifts and fluctuations in his personality find expression in the predicaments faced by the other characters. The adversity brought by Muhammad upon the others in the story is, from the technical point of view, the error in Muhammad's character and symbolizes an all-encompassing misfortune within the work.

This point can be elucidated through some examples. Muhammad's stepmother, a relic from the past harbouring a secret voice, assumes the role of his conscience. Her behaviour resembles that of a ghost marked by restless longing and aimless wandering.

However, the original relationship between Muhammad and her reveals the nature of this conscience. It is not a legitimate or a natural, inclination; rather, it is an artificial bond they maintain to safeguard the secret of their sin—the murder of Muhammad's father and brothers. Shaikh Imamuddin, whose face bears a resemblance to Muhammad's, embodies a part of Muhammad's nature, symbolizing unfathomable religiosity. This becomes evident in their conversation within the mosque courtyard. Every word spoken by Sheikh Imamuddin serves as a counter-argument, contradicting the original statement even while justifying it. In a sense, their dialogue becomes a monologue, constructed as a conversation between them. Imamuddin hence easily succumbs to Muhammad's manipulations. The situation unfolds as if Muhammad is coaxing his own religiosity to serve his political ends. Najib, the vizier, symbolizes Muhammad's unyielding propensity for violence and statesmanship. Whenever violence is deemed necessary, Najib has the final say. He is the first to comprehend all of Muhammad's cunning tricks. Aziz emerges as the character most reflective of Muhammad's eccentricities. Having traversed multiple careers—from a launderer to subedar—Aziz serves as Muhammad's counterpart, not as a king but as a common man. Despite Muhammad's arrogance towards others and his disregard for all, he finds himself yielding to Aziz. In the concluding scene, Aziz transforms into the incarnation of Muhammad.

As previously noted, the secondary characters in the play serve as distinctive facets of Muhammad's personality, experiencing the shifts and failings in his character to bring them to a symbolic end. Through the killing of Sheikh Imamuddin, Muhammad irrevocably severs ties with his religious convictions. In a stark departure from his reliance on Hindu soldiers for protection against the Amirs, Muhammad, during prayer time, kills Shihabuddin and defiles the sacred act himself. He institutes a new law prohibiting prayer for five years, and with Najib's death, loses the power acquired through violence and politics. When his stepmother, his conscience, torments him by revealing the truth about Najib's murder, Muhammad kills her, thereby silencing his conscience. Muhammad experiences further loss when the historian Barani abandons him, leading to the demise of his cultivated self. In the play's culmination, as Muhammad, exhausted and disheartened, attempts to turn back to religion, to rekindle extinguished prayers and to seek God's mercy, he encounters Aziz in the guise of Ghiyasuddin. In the final scene, Barani helplessly listens as Aziz sarcastically recounts his autobiography which also happens to be the history of Muhammad, rendering history mute. By the end of the speech, Muhammad and Aziz merge into a singular persona. Aziz, liberated after losing Azam (who was a preacher of humaneness and an impediment from the point of view of conscience), emerges to challenge Muhammad. From the play's beginning, Aziz has been Muhammad's shadow, with Muhammad representing the culmination of his self. The irony unfolds in the scene where the shadow transforms into the body. When Barani suggests the punishment Aziz deserves, Muhammad rebukes him for entertaining violent thoughts. Barani, realizing that Aziz's punishment would implicate Muhammad as well, leaves in fear. Disheartened by Aziz's discovery, Muhammad, who had seen Aziz in various disguises, now finds himself in Aziz, and even though he accepts Aziz in principle, he is left desolate. Karnad masterfully employs dramatic irony in merging the two personalities with the profound resonance of the words 'Arasa' (king) and 'Agasa' (launderer). Aziz, in this intricate narrative, emerges as Muhammad's indispensable destiny.

The play's action takes on symbolic dimensions through the adept use of two or three crucial functional symbols by Karnad, thereby manifesting the essence of the play. These symbols seamlessly integrate into the play's actions, creating an unexpected yet compelling dramatic structure. The play's meaning is encapsulated through symbols such as Aziz's disguise and Muhammad's haunting vigil. Aziz, a Muslim, assuming the guise of Vishnu Prasad, a Brahmin, and misusing a law, is a sharp criticism of Muhammad's administration. This encounter marks Muhammad's initial confrontation with his veiled misfortune through Aziz. The act of disguise varies among characters, signifying both political manoeuvring and the strength of their relationships. When Sheikh Imamuddin, impersonating Muhammad, visits Ain-ul-Mulk, Muhammad's politics and their deep connection become evident. Muhammad's act of killing Sheikh Imamuddin symbolizes the demise of an aspect of his own personality. Muhammad's vigilance serves as a means of uniting his physical and spiritual tendencies and symbolizes his ever-conscious ego. Throughout the drama, Muhammad remains vigilant and cautious as a king, grappling with the pains of wakefulness as an individual, and distinguishing awareness from misconstrued self-awareness. From the news of Ain-ul-Mulk rebelling against Delhi, to sending Sheikh Imamuddin for negotiations, his political consciousness remains sharp. His lightning scheming to frustrate the plots of the Amirs against him further highlights his vigilance. Conversely, he roams restlessly over the fort of Daulatabad, deeply engaged in sincere contemplation. Seeing the young watchman standing in front of him as a poetic figure, he tries to feel alive in the memory of his boyhood. He feels jealous of Barani who, when sleep eludes him, turns to reading books. An even more frightful image is that of Muhammad walking amid a pile of coins in a garden: it is an image of a false persona dealing with its false karma. In the final scene, Muhammad finally falls asleep, a symbolic gesture of fatigue and defeat.

Foremost among the symbols is the chess motif. In the second scene, Muhammad discovers a strategic move to defeat Ain-ul-Mulk, his chess companion, within the realm of the chessboard. Chess, being a game of intellect, becomes a tool for

Muhammad to purge himself of sentiments. Later, he can't make himself feel any more. This scene develops into a metaphor that evolves throughout the play. Upon closer examination, the drama unfolds in two opposing rhythms, culminating in the last scene where the play's meaning is unveiled at the convergence of these two rhythmic forces. Similar to the king in a chess game, King Muhammad departs from the top row and moves towards the centre, forsaking Delhi for Daulatabad. With a calculated risk, he continues this trajectory, expending both his intellectual and subconscious energies. Conversely, Aziz ascends to the top like a pawn, manoeuvring to checkmate the king. Muhammad's cry of 'Shahamat Shahamat' in the final scene signifies Aziz's triumph. This dynamic contributes to the reason why Muhammad, despite the tragic nature of the drama, does not meet his demise. Even in the face of a deceased vizier and closed avenues, the king succumbs to a common man, mirroring the strategic nuances of a chess match.

Tughlaq's distinctive quality lies in its departure from the arithmetic of dramatic structure. The play prioritizes facilitating an experience of rasa through simple language and effective characterization. The meaning resides within the play's structure, making it a remarkable work, even if not readily accessible to common understanding.

U.R. Ananthamurthy

In this essay from Nooru Mara Nooru Swara, *published in 1998, Kurtkoti provides a comprehensive analysis of U.R. Ananthamurthy's principal fictional works. At the heart of Kurtkoti's investigation lies the inquiry into the connection between individual consciousness moulded by education and society. He examines the intricacies of historical development and social interaction within Ananthamurthy's novels and short stories. This perceptive essay serves as an excellent introduction to the themes and composition of Ananthamurthy's fictional oeuvre.*

Ananthamurthy was among the early authors associated with the 'Navya' (Kannada modernist) literature movement. Gopalkrishna Adiga and Ramachandra Sharma were Navya poets, and during that period, there was considerable debate about the sensibility guiding the Navya movement. Adiga contended that pre-Independence idealism inspired Navodaya literature, while post-Independence disillusionment and the assassination of Mahatma Gandhi gave rise to the Navya sensibility. While this view may be an oversimplification in one sense, it introduces a novel way of thinking about the relationship between literary creation and history. Bendre's poetry, though connected to contemporaneity, transcends its limitations and explores ideas beyond the immediate historical context. Unlike Bendre, Adiga's poetry responds directly to contemporary history, focusing on themes like 'broken bridge built by sages'. Adiga's portrayal of the contemporary world in his poetry reflects a corrupted society that has lost its ethical foundations. Consequently, two distinct poetic paths emerge in the latter half of his work, as evident in poems like 'Nehru Nivruttaraguvudilla' (Nehru Will Not Retire) and 'Kupamanduka'. These poems differ significantly. The latter has nothing to do with the history outside. In 'Kupamanduka' (A Frog in the Well) and 'Sri Ramanavamiya Divasa' (The Day of Ramanavami), individuals distance themselves from the community, engaging in internal reflections to nurture their personalities. This introspective endeavour poses different challenges, as depicted in lines like 'Gone bagi bale jeevanmukta halasutide/hindu hillugalalli pranavoori' ('The banana with overripe fruits is rotting/the tree rooting down in its own offspring'), illustrating a spiritual death devoid of life and fulfilment, portraying a genuinely 'modern' perspective distinct from Adiga's public poems.

Similar themes echo in Ananthamurthy's stories.[6] Characters like the hero in 'Kartika' grapple with the meaninglessness of their past way of life, while Keshav in 'Clip Joint' finds meaning in Subbanna Kakka's spiritual failure. He asks why the experience of cabaret makes him worm-like, but finds no answer. The protagonist Shankara in 'Prashne' (Question) searches for a bed that satisfies both body and soul simultaneously. These characters seek answers as to why education, voluntarily obtained, becomes a philosophical problem. Protagonists in Ananthamurthy's earlier stories share a subjective experience and knowledge, revealing a tension between experience and knowledge due to the imperative of change.

---

[6] U.R. Ananthamurthy, *Stallion of the Sun and Other Stories*, trans. Narayan Hegde (New Delhi: Penguin India, 1999); *Hunt Bangle Chameleon: Selected Short Stories of U.R. Ananthamurthy*, trans. Deepa Ganesh (Bangalore: Prism Books, 2014).

Ananthamurthy's work *Prajne Mattu Parisara* (Consciousness and Material Reality), deals with the relationship between consciousness and material reality. While consciousness is undeniably personal, it gains independence through education. Material reality, however, remains somewhat ambiguous. It encompasses a community's history, religion, cultural heritage, caste, sect and more. When individual consciousness detaches from this environment, it becomes alienated or orphaned. The individual consciousness critically evaluates the environment and its values. In stories like 'Ghatashraddha' and 'Prastha', where personal consciousness may be absent, it is the same consciousness that articulates the lifelessness and inactions of the environment through metaphors. Characters like Udupa and Yamunakka bear pain, yet there is no voice protesting against the source of that pain. This absence is deliberate, as all our stories and novels, regardless of literary form, are discourses crafted by the well-educated. The voice in these discourses is that of the well-educated consciousness, pointing to a separation between the individual and the community. However, the uneducated voice within these discourses lacks authoritative standing. The educated voice serves as a valuable voice of criticism, and if the educated perspective is liberal, it offers something precious in understanding the mentality of the uneducated.

The well-educated are aligned with history in the context of our country. This consciousness keenly recognizes the direction in which the face of history is turned to. Present-day literature is more or less a discourse of protest and discussing values of our heritage appears historical. Given that stories and novels, in a sense, embody contemporary history, the language of novels and short stories possesses a more historical nature compared to the language of traditional historical texts. Novels and short stories primarily aim to make society aware of the history it is living through. A novel, in essence, constitutes a contract between the author and society. However, a significant distinction between M.S. Puttanna's novels and modern novels lies in the unchanging form of history in Puttanna's works. His novels do not narrate the personal stories between individuals. Writers like Puttanna or Galaganatha present stories to readers that might be familiar without disrupting the formality of the narrative. The nature of these stories is distinctly historical, with the story's depth not necessarily mirroring the depth of the reader. In contrast, the language of modern novels is more intimate, often allowing readers to recognize their own stories within this intimacy—an intimacy sometimes described as universal relevance.

Whether in Ananthamurthy's stories or novels, there is a commentary on the present. Perhaps the structure of the story is crafted for the ease of such communication, yet the craftsmanship ensures that the stories' sculpting feels natural, devoid of artificiality. Unlike M.S. Puttanna's novels, Ananthamurthy's works lack the formality seen in traditional narratives. Ananthamurthy's imaginative prowess creates captivating metaphors and contributes to the enduring literary value of his works. However, the challenge lies in seamlessly blending the urge to convey significant messages with the imagination that creates beautiful metaphors. What needs to be communicated can be expressed successfully without the crutch of imagination, while the beauty created by imagination can independently convey its meaning. Ananthamurthy's works often demonstrate the coexistence of narrative and descriptive elements, with the intellectual insight of prose and the expressiveness of verse independently showing their effect within the same work. If writing maintains restraint, the work can effectively utilize both aspects. Numerous examples of such balance are evident in his writings. From this perspective, Ananthamurthy's poems, and the prose pieces in the collection Purvapara, seem similar. Whether in prose or verse, the images lack sociality, but the conveyed message is inherently social and easily understood in the current context. Notable stories like 'Prakriti', 'Kartika', 'Clip Joint', 'Bara' and 'Suryana Kudure' exemplify this characteristic, rooted in the contemporary social context.

It has been nearly thirty years since the publication of Ananthamurthy's novel *Samskara*.[7] At the time, it was recognized as a protest novel. It is now imperative to reflect on the technique and format of this novel. The social portrayal in novels like *Samskara* and *Bharathipura*[8] is undeniably purposeful and the precision of this purpose prompts one to consider if the social imagery was crafted for scholarly examination. The events in Durvaspur do not unfold in the nearby Parijatpur. While the Brahmins in Durvaspur grapple with the plague, Sahukara Manjaiah in Parijatpur contemplates calling a doctor from Shimogge for inoculation. Outside Bharatipur, creative activities are in progress, but life within Bharatipur has lost its creative spark. The novel's spatial and temporal constraints serve a purpose, constructing a world for its convenience. The geography and histories of Durvaspur in Samskara are independently created through these constraints. Durvaspur served as the bastion of Brahmanism, symbolizing a crucial social principle in the novel. Brahmanism, embodied in Praneshacharya, held both power and authority. Praneshacharya, committed to the grihastha dharma (a Brahmin's household duty), married not for personal pleasure but to fulfil the obligation of caring for his disabled wife. His daily routine revolved around worship, recitation, lessons and discourses, all aimed at preserving and upholding Brahmanism.

Other Brahmins in Durvaspur also embraced Brahmanism, expressing it through aspects such as food, clothing, conversation

---

[7] U.R. Ananthamurthy, *Samskara*, translated by A.K. Ramanujan (New York: Oxford University Press, 1978).

[8] U.R. Ananthamurthy, *Bharathipura*, translated by Susheela Punitha (New Delhi: Oxford University Press, 2010).

and notions of purity. Despite their shared Brahmanism, Praneshacharya and Naranappa represented two opposing poles. While Praneshacharya was deeply entrenched in Brahminical traditions, Naranappa, also a Brahmin, vehemently protested against Brahmanism. Praneshacharya, instead of expelling Naranappa, felt an intense desire to persuade and rescue him, viewing it as a service similar to caring for his wife. Despite facing insults during visits to Naranappa's house, Praneshacharya remained steadfast in this mission.

The dynamic between Naranappa and Praneshacharya introduces a novel element to the narrative. Praneshacharya sees Naranappa's rescue as his responsibility, viewing it as crucial for the future of Brahmanism. While the misdeeds of one Brahmin may not destroy Brahmanism, Praneshacharya fears that the defeat in dealing with Naranappa could erode the faith of other Brahmins in Brahmanism, at least within the confines of Durvaspur. The novel grapples with this historical dilemma and explores potential solutions. The complication intensifies with Naranappa's sudden death, which, despite its apparent naturalness, shapes the destiny within the novel's world. The implications of this one incident permeate the entire novel.

Naranappa succumbs to the plague, and his death rites pose a significant challenge to Brahmanism. Even though Naranappa had renounced Brahmanhood, Brahmanism did not desert him. Some Brahmins are willing to perform his death rites for the gold offered by Naranappa's concubine, Chandri, but they cannot openly admit to their greed. The term 'samskara' implies a public confirmation, yet Naranappa's rites are clandestinely conducted by a Muslim. The implications of this incident resonate throughout the novel, questioning the fate of both Brahmanism and Naranappa. Naranappa's death, entwined with the complexities of casteless Brahmin cremation, becomes a pivotal moment. Praneshacharya, seeking a sign from god on how to handle the situation, finds his destiny intertwined with Naranappa's demise. As Naranappa and his wife die, Praneshacharya, released from his bonds, experiences newfound freedom.

Although Praneshacharya left the village a free man, his predicament remained unresolved, compounded by a clandestine experience—the sexual union with Chandri. This pivotal experience holds significance from various perspectives, unveiling the core of Praneshacharya's ethics. Chandri, not being his wife and an untouchable, complicates Naranappa's cremation due to his association with her. Through a similar association with Chandri, Praneshacharya undergoes a moral rebirth, highlighting the unpredictability of such transformative opportunities. All others, except Praneshacharya, have encountered sexual union. However, this experience fails to instigate a rebirth in any of them. Even Naranappa, despite his association with Chandri, does not undergo a transformation like Praneshacharya due to his sexual experience. This sexual experience is neither moral nor immoral inherently. The issue of morality or immorality of sexual union only arises when its social and personal meanings diverge. Ethics is fundamentally concerned with interpersonal relationships. Chandri does not find her association with Praneshacharya to be immoral, not even perhaps Praneshacharya sees it that way. But the societal implications trouble his social persona. Fearing this, he leaves the village, only to be reintroduced to sociality by Malera Putta, who introduces him with Padmavati and makes him partake of the ritualistic offering of food in the temple. The defilement by death, like the plague, too is a contagion—giving rise to the social meaning. He forges a sense of sociality even within a small forest setting. Engaging in activities such as killing and cremating a snake, Putta deliberately introducing Padmavati, and participating in the temple offering of food—constitute social acts. The dynamics between this emerging sociality and Praneshacharya's personality become crucial elements, highlighting both relationships and conflicts.

In a parallel vein, Jagannath in *Bharathipura* navigates similar relationships and conflicts, albeit with a mission to uplift untouchable labourers, believing in the transformative power of touching the Saligram.

The novels *Samskara* and *Bharathipura* grapple with Brahminism and untouchability as social phenomena, exploring the intricate relationships between individuals and societies, consciousness and material reality. Ananthamurthy, positioning himself as a critical insider, reflects the novels' exploration of social relations. The increase in critical insiders since Raja Ram Mohan Roy signifies individuals who can love society while questioning its social fabric. This is exemplified in the sincere social concern evident in the writings of Ram Manohar Lohia.

However, challenges arise when honesty becomes a standard for literature. With history on one side and biographical or autobiographical narratives on the other, the novel as a form strives to remain literary. Even when histories and biographies are forms of writing, literariness is not a mandatory element. While novels narrate the world, society often expects a sense of otherworldliness from them. Works like *Samskara*, *Bharatipura* and *Avasthe*[9] present Ananthamurthy's stories that embody the honesty of characters like Praneshacharya and Jagannath. While literature can depict honesty, the question remains if honesty can be one of the standards for literature? Perhaps these are questions with no clear answers, as the creative process of literary works remains enigmatic, shrouded in a metaphorical dark room inaccessible to anyone.

As Praneshacharya departs from the village, the first person surfacing in his recollections is Mahabala, a former classmate from Kashi. Mahabala, more talented than Praneshacharya, mysteriously vanished one day, only to reappear later in the

---

[9] U.R. Ananthamurthy, *Avasthe*, trans. Narayan Hegde (New Delhi: Harper Collins, 2020).

house of a prostitute in Kashi. The narrative of Mahabala's life concludes here, and rightly so, as he discovers his own path to salvation. What stands out is Mahabala's departure from social conformity, a departure starkly contrasting Praneshacharya's unwavering commitment to society. Praneshacharya, devoted to societal service, engages with the people by reciting poetry and dramas such as Shakuntala, apart from delivering discourses on Puranas and tales of virtue. His insistence on rescuing Naranappa highlights the shared social personality between them. Both Praneshacharya and Naranappa aspire to shape society according to their ideals, navigating complexities like Chandri and her gold. Even in Praneshacharya's attempt to escape this society, Malera Putta persistently accompanies him. But Mahabala's connections seem limited to god or prostitutes, transcending the societal bonds dictated by the proverb 'uddharedatma natma na natmanamavasadayet' ('Raise yourself on your own, do not disparage yourself', from the Bhagavad Gita, ch. 6, verse 5). Such freedom from worldly attachments epitomizes liberation. Religion, politics, law, human relations and history all constitute moral realms. In such a world, the search for the best course of action is required at every moment. The ethical world represents an ongoing and unceasing pursuit of an ideal.

Although Praneshacharya is committed to the social, yet his relationship with society remains somewhat distant. While the local community acknowledges him and positions him as a guru, there is a lack of shared joys and sorrows. If Naranappa's funeral had not triggered concern, the existing rapport with Praneshacharya might have endured. However, this societal connection is confined to Durvaspur. The question of whether Praneshacharya's commitment to serve society might turn into an addiction like Naranappa's rebellion or Dasacharya's hunger remains uncertain. Nevertheless, Praneshacharya's existence is intertwined with society. Following his experiences with Chandri and the subsequent events, including his wife's demise and her last rites, he departs the village. Wandering alone in the forest for self-discovery, he encounters Malera Putta. From a certain perspective, Putta becomes Praneshacharya's destiny, adept at recreating him.

Praneshacharya's predicament arises from a lack of personal issues. Consequently, the unresolved matter of Naranappa's funeral becomes a crisis in his personality. The concern is not whether his intimate encounter with Chandri was morally right or wrong. Through their union, the world is reborn in the embrace of contentment. However, what preoccupies him more than the moral aspects of this experience is the reformation of his own identity and character.

Ananthamurthy's works seem to suggest that, alongside historical events, miraculous occurrences can emerge, transcending the bounds of history. In *Samskara*, Praneshacharya turns to his deity, Maruti, seeking a sign that might resolve the dilemma surrounding Naranappa's last rites. His reliance on this sign implies anticipation of a miracle. However, no divine sign appears, no miracle unfolds, and Praneshacharya must return disappointed. Instead, a miraculous event occurs: his union with Chandri. This unexpected incident defies the story's intended purpose, deviating from the logic of daily routine and common morality.

Similarly, in *Bharathipura*, Jagannath's demand that untouchables touch Saligrama, his household deity, mirrors a miraculous event. The redemption of untouchables is a facet of contemporary history. Gandhiji and Ambedkar strived to make history accept it. The present society has, even if half-heartedly, acknowledged it to some extent. Yet, Jagannath expects it to unfold as a miracle. The justice inherent in such miraculous events differs from the justice of historical progression. Ananthamurthy's works consistently endeavour to merge these two realms, illustrating that individuality arises from sociality and miracles emerge from history.

This perspective might shed light on Ananthamurthy's novel *Bhava*.[10] The work lacks the social principles typically found in novels narrating the history of three generations. The narrative unfolds in Vishwanatha Shastri's expansive forest home, Tripathi's residence in Haridwar, Uttar Pradesh, and Narayana Tantri's house in Mangalore. However, these settings lack interactions between society and individuals. Vishwanatha Shastri, known to society only for his Harikathe performances, engages in antisocial acts. Dinakar's story follows a similar trajectory. Prasad, the last of the three, seeks freedom. Despite their diverse backgrounds, all three are performers. The novel, oscillating between past and present, navigates the future. Here, everything seems accidental, or perhaps accidents represent the natural course of life. The taste of a dish made with flattened rice, given by Vishwanatha Shastri, triggers Dinakar's memories of his lost mother. Yet, he goes to Seetamma, his foster mother. The flattened rice dish, gold ornaments from the Vijayanagara era, dosa and idlis prepared by Seetamma serve as symbols narrating the story of life's nourishment.

Seetamma recognizes Dinakar standing before her as she draws a rangoli in the yard at dawn. Perhaps, unbeknownst to us, individuals can recognize their relatives through their unique scent. The novel abounds with symbols of recognition (anagnorisis). Despite his scepticism, Vishwanatha Shastri recognizes Dinakar as his son. Dinakar grapples with doubts about whether Prasad is his son, but Prasad is Gangu's son, as Dinakar is to his mother. Bhava unfolds amid these doubts and truths, where the characters encounter accidents and undergo repeated deaths. Vishwanatha Shastri and Dinakar grapple with overarching lust, while

---

[10] U.R. Ananthamurthy, *Bhava*, trans. Judith Kroll (New Delhi: Penguin India, 1998).

Seetamma's aged eyes radiate light. Her Kannada can converse with Dinakar's Hindi. Narayana Tantri recognizes Gangu as a woman. Tripathi's children only recognize the treasures of Vijayanagara gold. Each character follows their desired scent while developing connections in the living world. Dinakar forms relationships with numerous women but establishes a genuine connection only with Gangu. Social acceptance of this relationship is not a compulsion for either Dinakar or Gangu.

The history of human life unfolds through the network of social relations, a narrative explored extensively. Most stories and novels delineate this history, but Ananthamurthy's *Bhava* seeks the underlying philosophy of this history and the non-historical dimensions arising from within history itself. If one were to inquire about what lies beyond history, perhaps it can be aptly termed as 'bhava'. The traditional meaning of the word 'bhava' is culture or family, but when this connection becomes a constraint, life yearns for liberation. While our highest ideal is avoiding recurrence (mukti), in the context of this novel, the word 'bhava' assumes a distinct meaning.

Another notable aspect of the novel *Bhava* is Ananthamurthy's perspective on women. It doesn't refute the societal order of appropriating women as possessions, acknowledging the advantages men can derive. However, *Bhava* adeptly illustrates that a profound connection with a woman can be driven by means beyond mere lust. The relationship between Dinakar and Seetamma exemplifies this concept. The spontaneity of their bond is striking and despite Dinakar's prolonged absence, Seetamma treats him as someone from the village. This relationship not only holds significant cultural value but also serves as a momentous event revealing insights into life. This transcends the boundaries of history. Such situations were not present in Ananthamurthy's earlier works. While Praneshacharya might have undergone a moral rebirth through his association with Chandri in *Samskara*, the novel doesn't delve into Chandri's gains. In contrast, the relationship between Seetamma and Dinakar is characterized by a harmonious lack of disputes (*nirvyaja*), a quality shared only by Chandrappa and Prasad. These three characters, uniquely in the novel, surpass the confines of culture and history.

Ananthamurthy, like Gopalakrishna Adiga, played a pivotal role in the post-Navodaya era. However, they didn't enjoy the advantage of the early Navodaya writers, for whom heredity was less entwined in their immediate literary heritage. The literary creations predating them retained their contemporaneity when Adiga and Ananthamurthy entered the scene. Gopalakrishna Adiga focused on evolving a new poetic form, blending elements from the past into his poetry. In contrast, Ananthamurthy's consciousness operated differently. Inheriting the literary legacy of Shivarama Karantha, Kuvempu and Masti, he exposed himself to diverse influences and engaged freely with his contemporaries. Ananthamurthy deserves credit for introducing innovative methods in literary criticism, evident in his collection *Purvapara*. Above all, he harbours a sense of responsibility to guide literature's evolution in the right direction, navigating the boundaries of the new world shaped by freedom, education, politics, religion and culture.

The Plays of Chandrasekhar Kambara

This essay is taken from Kurtkoti's anthology of essays Nooru Mara Nooru Swara, *published in 1998. It offers a study of Kambara's five plays:* Rishyashringa, Jokumaraswamy, Jaisidanaika, Harakeya Kuri *and* Tukrana Kanasu. *It begins with a concise analysis of Kambara's narrative verse* Helatena Kela *to offer an insight into the rationale behind Kambara's use of folk material. He elaborates how the folk stories at the heart of Kambara's works reveal the 'profound loss embedded in the shifting sands of existence'. Kurtkoti elucidates the importance of Kambara's folk imagination and its relevance to the modern context in this essay.*

In Chandrasekhar Kambara's *Helatena Kela*, a narrative verse, we encounter a tale that paints a vivid tableau of a world, once unwavering, now unsettled by the myriad anxieties of the present. The demon responsible for Ramagonda's demise assumes his guise, infiltrating Shivapura and orchestrating a transformative shift in the village's way of life. Adding to the complexity, the demon impregnates the Gauda's (village head) wife, setting off a chain of bewildering events. After trying to appease the peculiar desires of the Gaudati, a disheartened Ramagonda, patiently awaits a saviour from the east. The narrative hinges on the belief that if the demon is anointed with the enchanted water wielded by the awaited saviour, its demise is inevitable. However, the poem's undertone suggests that even with the demon's demise, the bygone system of life remains irretrievable. The work, steeped in a sombre cadence, contemplates the profound loss embedded in the shifting sands of existence.

In the complex world of Kambara's poetic creation, *Helatena Kela* stands out for its unique quality. The mythological narrative woven into the poem reveals a set of concealed meanings and at its core lies the exploration of diverse forms of sexual encounters. Ramagonda, the legitimate son of his parents, undergoes a profound transformation as he endeavours to gratify his mother's forbidden desires, ultimately losing his true identity in the process. The narrative unfolds with Gaudati, the village head's wife, giving birth to a son after much labour pain. While the poem narrates this tale of Gaudati, the underlying story of the true self of Ramagonda and the birth of Balagonda in falsehood, remains constant. Remarkably, this narrative serves as the wellspring for Kambara's inaugural play, *Rishyashringa*, adding layers of complexity to the poetic design. The poem transcends its surface narrative, delving into the intricate dimensions of human experience and relationships.

The pursuit of truth does not readily transform into a narrative. The intricate relationship between Ramagonda and Balagonda, though rooted in brotherhood, is laden with complexity. The demon's act of assuming Gauda's form after slaying him adds an element of mystery, obscuring the true nature of this enigmatic entity, forever lost in the realm of sensuality. Balagonda, born of the union of the demon in Gauda's guise with Gaudati, prompts a quest for self-identity that finds its resolution in the dramatic realm. The play *Rishyasringa* unfolds as Gauda's son returns to the village after pursuing studies in Belgaum. Villagers anticipate rain with every five steps he takes, a belief central to the play. However, the anticipated rain fails to materialize even after he takes seven steps, leading Balagonda to question his lineage as Gauda's son. The virtuous lust of *Rishyasringa*, who brought rain during drought, stands in stark contrast to Balagonda's futile lust.

The revelation of his inadvertent mating with his mother, Gaudati, marks the climax, symbolizing the culmination of forgotten self-identity and guilt. The play goes beyond mere misunderstandings and delusions, exploring profound themes such as the blurring of the line between life and death as seen in Holera Bharamya's union with Yamani's lifeless body, and Doda Basya's poetic description of death when he describes the corpse found in the grave. It goes: 'New shirt, new pants, royal shawl, I want to speak to it.' Ramagonda and Balagonda emerge as potent symbols of this existential condition, embodying the profound complexity of human existence.

The predicament faced by Balagonda in *Rishyasringa* finds resonance in Ramagonda's plight in the play *Huliya Neralu*.[11] Both characters grapple with a profound uncertainty about their paternal lineage, sparking a relentless quest for the elusive truth. The complexity of human relationships and the pursuit of truth draw parallels to the struggles of iconic figures like Oedipus and Hamlet, who also sought to unravel the mysteries of their origins. In his fervent desire for truth, Oedipus implores Apollo to reveal the unbroken truth: 'Father, lord of the light beyond the sun, show this world the unbroken truth, Father . . . show the truth hidden in the shadows'. Hamlet, too, seeks to pierce through the shadows of his tragic reality. The notion of a 'shadow-less truth' is explored, where pure light lacks shadows, much as darkness devoid of shadows. Like Oedipus and Hamlet, Ramagonda is portrayed as a resolute individual yearning for a truth visible to his eyes and comprehensible to his intellect. In a poignant exchange with his mother, Ramagonda demands to know the truth, and she points to the barrier that the unborn foetus in her womb presents to the truth. Gaudati, a symbol of Earth's vitality, embodies the reluctance to face the truth, using the foetus as a metaphorical

---

[11] *The Shadow of a Tiger and Other Plays* (Calcutta: Seagull, 2000).

wall between Ramagonda and his quest. The drama unfolds with
Gaudati standing firm, concealing the truth within her womb,
while a demon and three Gaudas bow before her Maya, illustrating
the potent force of illusion in this captivating play.

Following the impactful play *Rishyasringa*, Chandrasekhar
Kambar explores the complex realm of human relationships
in his play *Jokumarswamy*,[12] originating from *Sangyabalya*. While
Sangyabalya's social and historical nature lays the foundation, its
primal essence resonates in the creation of numerous literary
works, each capturing its unique spirit. The ethereal quality of
Ganga's adultery in *Sangyabalya* is not merely embedded in the
language of its songs but intricately woven into their tone.
Likewise, Kambar's *Jokumarswamy* echoes this nuanced approach.
The play's language artfully portrays adultery in its social and
outcast manifestations. The union of Gaudati and Basanya
unfolds beyond societal norms, defying constraints. Despite
Gauda's impotence and evident malevolence, he adamantly
opposes the affair between Basanya and Gaudati. With immense
wealth and control over the town, Gauda's distorted sense of lust
and bravery becomes a dual manifestation of impotence and evil.
Gowda's gun serves as a symbol rich in multiple meanings. The
community's reactions mirror this complexity, oscillating between
fear, envy and a subtle sense of superiority over Gowda. Basanya
and Gaudati's romance takes a tragic turn, a destiny that, while
seemingly unjust, unfolds as an inevitable consequence of their
circumstances.

Kambara's *Jokumarswami* serves as a cornerstone in the rich
oeuvre of Kambara's literary works. The play unfolds in the
guise of a festival ritual, a cyclical event where Jokumars (a folk
deity) are born and meet their demise annually during the rainy
season. Kambara employs folklore as a distinctive language to

---

[12] Translation by Rajeev Taranath (Calcutta: Seagull, 1989).

unravel the intricacies of the contemporary world. The language of folk poetry and stories possesses an inherent self-sufficiency, encapsulating a world inhabited by eunuch Gowdas, lovers, harlots; gods and goddesses such as Parambi Karevva, Guddada Nirvani and Karimai; as well as talking wild animals, snakes in love with women, she-ghosts gifting mirrors, hinged horses and horns. This universal language becomes a conduit for understanding the complexities of the present era. However, complications arise as the meaning of folk language constructs its own distinct world. The profound advantage lies in the revelation of contemporary mysteries when translated into the folk. Yet, the key to unlocking the true beauty of this world is responding with sensitivity, much like appreciating the allure of a beautiful woman. Some may be captivated by the folk beauty witnessed in *Rishyashringa* and *Helateni Kela;* others venture further, ascribing meanings that have already dawned upon them.

Kambara's theatrical works, *Jaisidanayaka* and *Harakeya Kuri,* stand as poignant reflections of the contemporary world, both serving as political dramas. While the former unfolds in a village, the latter seeks to present the bustling cityscape such as that of Bangalore. In both plays, the intricate web of betrayals and deceit inherent in modern politics takes centre stage. A central theme woven into these narratives revolves around the erosion of individual integrity when one becomes entangled in the political arena. The betrayal depicted in *Jaisidanayaka* reaches its zenith in self-betrayal, emphasizing the impossibility of deceiving others without concurrently deceiving oneself. The underlying inquiry in these plays examines the absence of the steadfast honesty like that of an unchanging stone in human nature. In the feudal system, the qualities of goodness, genius, cruelty and wickedness were inherently honest. However, in the contemporary system, such unyielding honesty seems to have vanished, prompting the crucial question posed by the play: Why does man not exhibit the unswerving honesty embodied by a simple stone, regardless of whether it is placed, thrown or crushed?

Harakeya Kuri unfolds as an even more ambitious play, capturing the intricacies of new-age politics ensnaring the unsuspecting within a city like Bangalore. In Prakash and Saroj's absence from their house an elaborate and sinister drama unfolds. Prakasha Kavi, had he not been entangled in the web of politics or fallen prey to its trap, might have evolved as a poet. However, the touch of politics, like the Midas touch, manifests as an anti-life force, transforming what appears as a blessing into a curse. Siddhalingu, proud of being a political assassin for killing Srikanthji, eventually realizes that he is a mere instrument of Rudrappa. The act of making murder a sacrificial ritual becomes a highly political manoeuvre. In politics, values are not organically born; rather, they are adopted and manipulated, rendering even the lies unusable. This dynamic, perhaps, is the catalyst behind the dilution of meaning in religion, literature and culture, turning them into hollow shells within the political arena.

Kambara's *Tukrana Kanasu* stands out as a profound play, resembling his own work *Sambashivaprahasana* in its farcical nature. In farce, mockery prevails over the imitation of reality. The protagonist of this farce is an ordinary man among ordinary people, yet he harbours aspirations of etching his name in history. Driven by this dream, he endeavours to conquer the society surrounding him, a pursuit destined to fail, ultimately leading him to the gallows. In his final moments, he offers a prayer to god, seeking solace from Shivalingaswamy, the lord of all paths. Tukra's faith transcends conventional logic, extending beyond the realms of reason. His plea to god reflects a desire for divine illumination not only on the gallows but also on the path beyond. Tukra's unwavering faith makes conventional history irrelevant. Tukra's logic is uniquely his own. In the framework of human history, Tukra seeks a space to exist as himself, unburdened by the myriad distinctions and discriminations woven into the fabric of history. The play meticulously unfolds Tukra's quest for the power to shape history.

Kambara's dramatic songs, integral to his poetry, find resonance in both his theatrical and poetic expressions, with a shared source that underpins the essence of his creative endeavours.

Devanoora Mahadeva's *Kusumabale*

In this essay from Nooru Mara Nooru Swara, *published in 1998, Kurtkoti examines how Devanoora Mahadeva's 1984 novel,* Kusumabale, *challenges critical approaches to fiction and how through the use of diverse languages, authorial voice, narrative fragments and other diverse modes of communication weaves a multifaceted narrative making the text a complex work.*

Devanoora Mahadeva's *Kusumabale*[13] defies easy categorization, as the conventional terms fall short in capturing its essence. It can be labelled a short novel, yet this description inadequately encapsulates the multifaceted nature of the work. *Kusumabale* weaves a narrative, provides descriptions, sings and paints vivid pictures, utilizing diverse modes of communication that may initially befuddle the reader. The entire story of *Kusumabale* is succinctly presented on the opening page:

> Six years after Akkamahadevamma visited her hometown to commemorate her husband's death anniversary, she returned with her son, Yada, who is scorned for being born twelve months after his father's demise and labelled the son of a slave labourer. She boldly asserts her claim to a share of the family's land. In response, her brothers-in-law, Basappasomy and Siddura, react with anger and callously throw her into the cowshed.

---

[13] Translated by Susan Daniel (New Delhi: Oxford India, 2015).

Undeterred by the harsh treatment, Akkamahadevemma resiliently settles in the very spot where she was cast aside. With Yada by her side, she begins constructing a modest dwelling. As time passes, this humble abode transforms into a substantial house, eclipsing the residences of her once-contemptuous brothers-in-law, Basappasoami and Siddura, which now serve as its cattle shed.

Somappa, the son of Yadegowda, emerges as the village head. Kusumabale, the daughter of this influential figure, finds herself entangled in a clandestine relationship with Chenna of the Holeya caste. The revelation of Kusuma's pregnancy unravels the secret liaison, leading to Chenna's swift murder.

As the entire village prepares for the fire festival, Turamma grapples with destiny to safeguard her grandchild born to Kempi from Chenna's clan.

This is not merely a narrative but a condensed rendition that forms a miniature story within itself. Amid the various components, the birth of Yadegowda and the enigmatic murder of Chenna stand out, sparking intrigue. However, the subsequent extensive narrative fails to satiate curiosity. The crux of the tale lies in the tragic experiences of female characters like Akkamahadevamma, Tooramma, Eeri, Kempi and Kusumabale. The intricacies of Yada's youth, where he tended cattle, sheep and goats, sold them for a substantial sum in Nanjangud, and subsequently built a prosperous house in town, lack resonance with our contemporary consciousness. Details such as Yada purchasing the Maharaja's couch with the proceeds and Kittayya distributing sugar to celebrate the birth of a son appear disconnected. Amid this maze of disjointed anecdotes, the unstoppable current of life surges forward swiftly. Madhavacharya's daughter challenges traditional norms as her youth persists into her thirties without menstruation. Another eccentric episode involves the theft of sixteen tender coconuts by Garasidmava. Despite these peculiar tales, the fundamental life force flows unimpeded, and the rhythm of life remains undisturbed. Eeri and Tooramma persistently confront fate in their endeavour to safeguard Kempi's children.

The story's prelude lays a sturdy foundation for the reader, offering a stable vantage point to navigate through the narrative's complexities. Within this groundwork, a net of images intertwine, accompanied by a symphony of myriad sounds, requiring an adept ear to decipher the diverse languages spoken. Madhavacharya's discourse, while speaking about his daughter with Chenna at the bus stand, reflects not merely Brahmin Kannada but also a linguistic representation of cultural inadequacy, attempting to conceal flaws while flaunting refinement. Conversations that Amasa has with the Muslim traders, unveil not just Muslim Kannada but also a language tainted by the violence propagated by the mafia. It is through these languages that Chenna is resurrected in Mumbai, assuming a mystical aura as he rides a car on the tarred streets. Language transforms into news, an excuse, an exception and a narrative. Its intrinsic volatility echoes, serving as a mantra to subjugate gods and demons alike. The news of Chenna generated by the Muslim traders during a bout of abuse, metamorphoses into a superstitious lore told by an inebriated Garasidmava, eluding comprehension even by magicians from distant lands. Kusumabale anticipates Chenna's return, waiting with an ethereal patience like an angel. Her younger brother, Parsad, gazes at her with entranced eyes. Despite the attempts of sorcerers from Kollegala and Kerala, they fail to restore her to normalcy; even the whip with which the sorcerers beat her breaks.

At the end of this description comes a startling remark. The unschooled Kusumabale speaks in English and says, 'I want to be in my house.' Stripped of linguistic intricacies, her desire is clear: while others contemplate a journey to Mumbai in search of Chenna, Kusumabale wishes to remain homebound. An open door beckons with warmth, an anticipation that if Chenna returns, it would be to that familiar haven. Pursuing him seems futile; her home becomes the locus of expectation. Yet, the remarkable aspect lies in the mode of expression. How did Kusumabale, devoid of formal education, articulate this in English? The implausibility of an unlettered individual conversing in English poses a challenge. However, this anomaly demands scrutiny. Is it the language of mystical wizards? No, it is the language of Devanoora Mahadev. Does the author wield the authority to manipulate the language within his work? Much like a planchette channels the language of its holder, here, Devanoora Mahadev's influence guides Kusumabale's expression. It is a nuanced revelation: the educated author speaks through the uneducated protagonist, a symbiotic coalescence of varied linguistic deities invoked during the composition. Amid these diverse voices, the author's language seizes an opportune moment to subtly infiltrate the narrative.

The inclusion of an English sentence in *Kusumabale*'s discourse demands elucidation. This literary work traverses diverse linguistic realms, including Brahmin Kannada and Muslim Kannada. Amid the crowd gathered for the Dalit Sangha procession, Kuriyayya is impelled to expound on the genesis of the Holeya race, declaring, 'Blood inherits memories of generations'. This sentence transcends its immediate context, unravelling the enigmatic facets of human animosity. It offers an alternative perspective on the story's focal point, challenging the personal truths each character harbours. Similarly, Kusumabale's unlettered utterance mirrors this phenomenon. Oblivious to the underlying significance, her English sentence functions as a metaphorical blood-borne memory. The English language, permeating the narrative, assumes prominence within Kusumabale's receptive consciousness, despite her lack of awareness regarding its true nature.

'I want to be in my house.' This English sentence serves as a poignant focal point, possibly encapsulating the core metaphor of this narrative—the 'house'. The narrative's beginning sees

Akkamahadevamma losing her 'home' following her husband's demise. Six years later, when she returns seeking her share of the 'house', her brothers-in-law forcibly expel her. From the humble cowshed settlement, a shanty arises, gradually transforming into a big 'house', to which the house of her brothers-in-law becomes a cowshed. The evolutionary journey from farmhouse to hotel to house is laden with significance, governed by invasions and transitions. In this metamorphic process, men, likened to grazing cows (recall Yada's childhood and youth), contrast with women, the architects of 'houses'. Kusumabale, born into such a home, goes to Chenna's residence. Tooramma, Eeri and Kempi strive to reclaim the fleeing life back into their abodes. Just as the body provides identity to the life within, the house imparts individuality to its inhabitant. This, ostensibly, is Kusumabale's sentiment—a desire to remain within her abode. Much like Akkamahadevamma, Kusumabale yearns for a home that is unequivocally hers. She stoically awaits its realization, contemplating the possibility of Chenna's return. The answer echoes an assertion of Chenna's father: 'relationships matter'.

While 'I want to be in my house' is Kusumabale's statement within the narrative, as it is stated in English, it is spoken by Devanoora Mahadeva. We may say that here the meaning is that of Kusumabale and the language is that of Devanooru Mahadeva. But that is not a satisfactory interpretation as the sentence carries Devanooru Mahadeva's meaning too. The author strategically positions himself within the realm of this sentence, aspiring to harmonize the diverse worlds portrayed in the novel. Despite the disparate experiences of characters like Madhavacharya's daughter Bhagwati, Akkamahadevamma, Eiri, Kempi, Turamma and Kusumabale, a common thread of shared tragic destiny binds them. The recurrent theme of women being uprooted, expelled from their homes and rendered homeless is not just a contemporary phenomenon; Kuriyayya's 'vision' hints at its perpetual recurrence across generations. In the metaphorical landscape, if the female embodies the Earth, the male shapes its history.

This English statement serves as the nexus where Kusumabale's perspective collides with Devanoora Mahadeva's conceptualization. The narrative's thematic core unfolds within the conflict of these divergent meanings encapsulated in a single sentence.

Acknowledgements

This book is the result of a truly collective endeavour, and I am profoundly indebted to numerous individuals and institutions whose support and vision have been instrumental in bringing it to fruition.

I extend my deepest gratitude to the Ashoka Centre for Translation at Ashoka University and the Deshbandhu Trust for facilitating this work as part of their ambitious translation project. Special thanks to Rita Kothari for suggesting that I undertake this project; to Arunava Sinha and Sanchit Toor, for their friendship and encouragement.

I am especially grateful to Elizabeth Kuruvilla, Vineet Gill and Saloni Mital at Penguin Random House India for their editorial acumen, which enriched the manuscript immeasurably.

My heartfelt thanks also go to the Kirtinath Kurtkoti Trust in Dharwad and to Sameer Joshi, V.T. Naik, T.S. Satyanath and S.R. Vijayshankar, who graciously provided essential source texts and shared invaluable insights into Kurtkoti's life and legacy.

I am indebted to N.S. Gundur, S.R. Vijayshankar, T.S. Satyanath, M.G. Hegde, Rajendra Chenni, K.V. Akshara, T.P. Ashok and Siraj Ahmed; my stimulating conversations with them deepened my understanding of Kurtkoti's oeuvre. I am equally grateful to Shrirama Bhat, A.M. Shivaswami, O.L. Nagabhushan Swamy, Manu Devadevan and Govind Hegde; their expertise in Kannada and Sanskrit texts illuminated countless references within Kurtkoti's essays.

I owe a special debt to Dr Rajneesh Barnabas and BPHE Society's Ahmednagar College for their steadfast support throughout my academic career. I also thank my colleagues in the Department of English, past and present, for their ongoing cooperation.

To my family—my wife, Saji, and daughter, Disha, my brothers and sisters, and my in-laws—your boundless love and patience have been my anchor. To my cherished friends Sanjay, Sucharita, Harsh and Atul, thank you for lifting my spirits through life's vicissitudes.

Finally, I dedicate this work to Saji Bhat, the guardian of my spirit and sanity, whose sacrifices have been boundless. Her patience and unwavering support have made this journey possible in every sense.

Kamalakar Bhat

Scan QR code to access the
Penguin Random House India website